ANTI-LITERATURE

ILLUMINATIONS | Cultural Formations of the Americas Series

John Beverley and Sara Castro-Klarén, Editors

ANTI-
LITERATURE

IN MODERN BRAZIL AND ARGENTINA

THE POLITICS AND LIMITS OF REPRESENTATION

ADAM JOSEPH SHELLHORSE

UNIVERSITY OF PITTSBURGH PRESS

Published by the University of Pittsburgh Press, Pittsburgh, Pa., 15260
Copyright © 2017, University of Pittsburgh Press
All rights reserved
Manufactured in the United States of America
Printed on acid-free paper
10 9 8 7 6 5 4 3 2 1

Cataloging-in-Publication data is available from the Library of Congress

ISBN 13: 978-0-8229-6447-6
ISBN 10: 0-8229-6447-3

Cover art: "TUDO ESTÁ DITO," by Augusto de Campos. From *Viva vaia: Poesia 1949–1979*.
Courtesy of Augusto de Campos.
Cover design by Jordan Wannemacher

FOR DRU

I consider John Beverley's *Against Literature*, in all the richness of its self-conscious ambiguity, the inaugural text preparing and announcing the possibility for a new paradigm for Latin Americanist reflection in the humanities.

Alberto Moreiras, *The Exhaustion of Difference*

The limit of literature is its calling, its recall, meaning that the closure of literature cannot but be the demand for and opening to more literature.

Brett Levinson, *The Ends of Literature*

A historical account of literature unable to pose theoretical problems (in this instance, the question of Latin American literature as a theoretical problem) is one that will inadvertently inherit and reproduce the limitations already encapsulated within literature itself.

Horacio Legrás, *Literature and Subjection*

To face alterity is, above all, a necessary exercise in self-criticism, as well as a vertiginous experience of breaking the limits.

Haroldo de Campos, *"The Ex-Centric's Viewpoint"*

They are events at the edge of language.

Gilles Deleuze, *Essays Critical and Clinical*

CONTENTS

ACKNOWLEDGMENTS

THE CONCEPT and writing of this book are the result of indispensable support from numerous quarters. I wish to thank a host of colleagues, friends, and family members who have assisted me. I am likewise honored and wish to express my gratitude to the institutions that have nurtured this book's completion: Temple University, the University of California, Berkeley, and the University of Pittsburgh Press. The writing of this book took place over several years and in multiple contexts.

I wish to especially thank senior acquisitions editor Joshua Shanholtzer, Illuminations series editors John Beverley and Sara Castro-Klarén, and two anonymous readers, who had faith in this book and suggested improvements. I also wish to thank Peter W. Kracht, director of the University of Pittsburgh Press, as well as Alexander Wolfe and the editorial team for their good stewardship of the manuscript.

In large measure, this book is the product of my dialogue with a number of people. While it is impossible for me to name all, I wish to acknowledge Gareth Williams, Erin Graff Zivin, Earl E. Fitz, Charles A. Perrone, David E. Johnson, Brett Levinson, Alberto Moreiras, Jon Beasley-Murray, José Rabasa, Justin Read, Fernando J. Rosenberg, Kate Jenckes, Stephen M. Hart, Rachel Price, John Beverley, Sara Castro-Klarén, Horacio Legrás, Adriana Michéle Campos Johnson, Patrick Dove, Kenneth David Jackson, Francine Masiello, Gwen Kirkpatrick, and Julio Ramos. I wish to particularly recognize Gareth, Erin, Earl, Charles, David, Brett, José, Alberto, Jon, Justin, and Fernando for having left their mark on the conceptual development of this book and for their valued friendship and support.

At Temple University I have had the great fortune to work in an extremely supportive environment. I wish to thank my colleagues, past and present, in the Department of Spanish and Portuguese for their example and camaraderie: Hiram Aldarondo, José Manuel Pereiro-Otero, Luis González del Valle, Hortensia Morell, Montserrat Piera, Gerardo Augusto Lorenzino, Víctor Pueyo Zoco, Jonathan Holmquist, Paul David Toth, Sergio R. Franco, C. Christopher Soufas, Teresa Scott Soufas, Alira Ashvo-Muñoz, and Roger Santiváñez. In particular, I am grateful to Hiram, Luis, and José Manuel for their exceptional guidance. I also wish to thank the department's outstanding staff: Annette Vega and Michelle Pugliese. In addition, I count myself fortunate to have had many conversations and class sections with bright students who fast became interested in Brazilian and Spanish American literature and who helped me think through some of the book's ideas. While there are too many to list, special thanks go to Erica O'Brien Gerbino, Daniel Raso Llarás, William J. Ryan, Gabrielle Profock, Steven Costa, and Christopher Black. What is more, I have also benefited from exchanges, both formal and informal, with colleagues outside of my department, including those affiliated with Temple University's Brazilian Delegation, the Center for the Humanities, Global Studies, and the Feinstein Center for American Jewish History: Michele M. Masucci, Mark Pollack, Peter Logan, Priya Joshi, Heather Ann Thompson, Hai-Lung Dai, Brooke Walker, Rodrigo Andrade, Dominique Klinger, Martyn Miller, Erika Clemons, Lu Zhang, Kimberley Goyette, Robert Kaufman, Sherri Grasmuck, David Elesh, Rosario Espinal, Shanyang Zhao, David Ingram, Pablo Vila, Peter Marshall, Nicole González Van Cleve, Ann Shlay, Richard Immerman, Mohsen Fardmanesh, Rachel Blau Duplessis, Jena Osman, Elizabeth S. Bolman, Gerald Silk, Adele Nelson, Terry Rey, Jay Lockenour, Rebecca T. Alpert, Jeremy Schipper, Lila Corwin Berman, Ronald Webb, Kevin J. Delaney, Erin K. Palmer, Evy Feliciano-Lopez, and Nélia Viveiros. I wish to thank Rebecca Lloyd, Brian Boling, and David C. Murray for their skillful work as librarians for Latin American studies and Brazilian poetics. Several trips to archives in Brazil were generously supported by Temple University's Office of the Provost. Likewise, I wish to express my deep appreciation for a Faculty Fellowship Award from Temple's Center for the Humanities. I am also grateful for a Temple University sabbatical award that helped bring the manuscript to completion

In Argentina, I would like to thank Noé Jitrik for agreeing to meet with me on several occasions. Special thanks to Gabriela García Cedro for arranging meetings with David Viñas and for the conversations on the Argentine vanguards. I also wish to thank Emilio Bernini and Guillermo Korn for their assistance at the Instituto de Literatura Argentina "Ricardo Rojas." Likewise, I am very grateful to Rolando López, Nerina Ornella, Máximo Eseverri, C. Adrián Muoyo, and distinguished directors José Martínez Suárez, Héctor Olivera, and Javier Olivera. In Brazil, I benefited especially from research at the Casa das Rosas Espaço Haroldo de Campos de Poesia e Literatura. There, I attended a seminar by Frederico Barbosa on concrete poetry and had illuminating discussions with Barbosa, Augusto de Campos, Julio Mendonça, and Ivan Persio Arruda de Campos. In similar fashion, I learned a great deal from conversations with Ferreira Gullar, Armando Freitas Filho, Affonso Romano de Sant'Anna, Antonio Carlos Secchin, Dante

Pignatari, Jorge Schwartz, Maria Eugênia Boaventura, Paulo Franchetti, Daniel Bueno, Luciana Facchini, Sandra Nitrini, and Viviana Bosi. Special thanks to Sandra Nitrini for the informative dialogue on the works of Osman Lins at the University of São Paulo. I would like to thank Litânia and Letícia Lins for granting permission to photograph original typescripts, letter correspondences, and rare documents by Osman Lins at his archive sites located in Fundação Casa de Rui Barbosa in Rio de Janeiro, and at the Instituto de Estudos Brasileiros in São Paulo. I am also grateful to the Academia Brasileira de Letras, especially to chief librarian Luiz Antônio, for assistance in copying rare documents and for setting up the interview with Antonio Carlos Secchin. Additionally, I wish to thank Ermelinda Ferreira, Adria Frizzi, Leonardo Cunha, and Claudio Vitena for their assistance in my research on Osman Lins and Clarice Lispector. I am thankful for the generosity of Augusto de Campos, Dante Pignatari, Ivan Persio de Arruda Campos, Paulo Gurgel Valente, Litânia Lins, Manoela Purcell Daudt D'Oliveira, Lucia Riff, Tarsila do Amaral, Amanda França, the *Folha de São Paulo*, Sebastião Salgado, Ronald Pledge, Jeffrey Smith, José Martínez Suárez, Héctor Olivera, and Rolando López, who facilitated or granted permission to reproduce images.

At the University of California, Berkeley, impactful debates took place with too many colleagues and friends to name, but I wish to thank particularly Dru Dougherty, Ana Maria Mão-de-Ferro Martinho, Laura Elisa Pérez, José Rabasa, Richard Rosa, Ivonne del Valle, Jesús Rodríguez Velasco, Pheng Cheah, Ignacio Navarrete, Candace Slater, José Luiz Passos, Francine Masiello, Tony Cascardi, Michael Iarocci, Estelle Tarica, Natalia Brizuela, Harley Shaiken, Dionicia Ramos, as well as Aurélie Vialette, Nelson Ramírez, León Salvatierra, Seth Kimmel, Mónica González García, Maya Márquez, Mayra Bottaro, Alfredo César Melo, Brenna Kenji Keneyasu Maranhao, Allove Wiser, Jeremias Zunguze, Matthew Losada, Aurélie Vialette, Eduardo Ruiz, Dena Marie, Victor Goldgel Carballo, Sarah Ann Wells, Heather McMichael, Sarah Schoellkopf, Ana E. Hiller, Sarah Moody, Amelia Barili, Clélia Donovan, Javier Huerta, Orlanda de Azevedo, Rakhel Villamil-Acera, Chrissy Arce, Anna Deeny, Craig Santos Perez, Verónica López, Mari Mordecai, and Cathy Jones. Finally, I wish to express my deep appreciation to the Department of Spanish and Portuguese and the Center for Latin American Studies for providing travel grants to conduct research in Brazil and Argentina.

Many friends and colleagues from beyond these institutions have also been helpful: Christina Yingxian Chen, Severino J. Albuquerque, José Luis Gómez-Martínez, Carmen Chaves Tesser, Luis Correa Díaz, Stacey Casado, Hernán Díaz, Daniel Balderston, Cristina Moreiras, Julianne Fitz, Regina

Rheda, Pituca Dougherty, Debra Castillo, Betty Salum, Miao Han Wang, Patricia Henderson, Abraham Acosta, Sam Steinberg, Sergio Villalobos-Ruminott, Nelson Cerqueira, Sol Pelaez, Jaime Rodríguez Matos, Robert Wells, Julio Ariza, Claire Solomon, Santiago Colás, Tracey Devine Guzmán, Joseph Marques, Ivani Vassoler, Gerardo Muñoz, Nancy Roane, Nelson Cerqueira, Marília Librandi-Rocha, Roland Greene, Nicholas Jenkins, Armen Davoudian, Irana Gaia, Marcia Kina, Leonice Moreira Alves, Rahile Escaleira, Priscilla Martins, Diana Klinger, Andrew Rajca, Charles Hatfield, Odile Cisneros, Alessandra Santos, Claus Clüver, Vlad Popescu, Tomomi Koyama, Marco González, Andrea Julissa Gálvez Aguilera, Allison de Laveaga, Janet Sovin, Wendy Miller, Caroline Cohen, Ronnie Boynton, Marsha Sofia Polovets, and Bethany Chrisman. I am especially grateful to Christina for her unflagging support and care.

I feel fortunate to count on the unwavering strength of my family. I owe much to my late grandparents, Gerry and J. R. "Shelly" Shellhorse, and Mae and E. N. Hightower. In a similar fashion, I wish to express my heartfelt gratitude to my mother, Joan Karam, to my father, Andrew Jerald Shellhorse (1945–2008), to my sister, Laura, to my brothers Drew and David, and to my stepfather, Tom Karam, and to my entire extended family. I dedicate this book to Dru Dougherty, mentor, and friend.

An earlier version of chapter 1 appeared in *Política Común: A Journal of Thought* 6 (Fall 2014). http://hdl.handle.net/2027/spo.12322227.0006.012; it is reprinted with permission from Michigan Publishing, the University of Michigan Library. In similar fashion, a previous version of chapter 3 was published in *Revista Hispánica Moderna* 68.2 (December 2015): 165–90; it is reprinted with permission from the University of Pennsylvania Press. Finally, an earlier version of chapter 4 was published in *CR: The New Centennial Review* 14.3 (Winter 2014): 219–54; it is reprinted with permission from Michigan State University Press.

ANTI-LITERATURE

INTRODUCTION

Anti-Literature

MALIGNED, DIVISIVE, yet irrepressible, productive discussion on the literary in Latin American studies hinges on a critique of what is meant today by "literature." This book produces a counterframework for reassessing the politics of representation and margins in Latin American experimental writings from the 1920s to the present, and aspires to theorize the subversive dimensions of multimedial, minoritarian, and feminine writing procedures as a worthwhile, *anti-literary* task.

Anti-Literature articulates a rethinking of the fundamental concepts of what is meant by "literature" in contemporary posthegemonic times. Advancing an understanding of the legacies, power, materiality, and relevance of literature at a time when influential critics bemoan its divorce from questions of social justice, my conceptualization of anti-literature posits the feminine, subaltern, and multimedial undoing of what is meant by "literature." Through a multilayered theoretical analysis that engages the work of such writers as Clarice Lispector, Oswald de Andrade, the Brazilian concrete poets, Osman Lins, and David Viñas, the book addresses the problematic of experimental writing as a site for radical reflection under contemporary conditions. Always *in* theory, that is, questioning, at each step what constitutes "literature" and its relationship to other disciplines, this study's attention to Brazil provides an important case of comparison and expansion for the field. In particular, I explore the importance of Brazil to the ongoing discussion

3

about the "nature" of Latin American literature and the need for a globally minded, inter-American framework. My thesis is that modern Latin American literature is no longer characterized by the old ideas of "literature" as an exalted form of individual expression and "high" culture, but by new ideas (politically progressive in nature) about the importance of authors, groups, and media long marginalized and thought to be exemplars of "low" culture. By paying especial attention to Brazilian and Argentine anti-literature as crucial to the rise of a new kind of thinking about literature, this book endeavors to change the larger discussion about the historical projection and critical force of Latin American literature.

The rationale informing this volume turns on a fundamental problematic: the ongoing dominance of traditional approaches to the Latin American literary, and the absence in the field concerning a sustained interdisciplinary reflection on Brazilian and Spanish American experimental writings. In similar fashion, studies of what is known as "avant-garde" in the field often turn on long-standing identitarian narratives that seek to "found" the literary as an autonomous subject that is at last capable of "provincializing" the European. There is no universal "new narrative" in the 1960s, just as there is no such thing as a universalization of Latin American literary vanguardism. If Brazilian and minor Latin American writers have always known this, their radical contributions have long been ignored. Indeed, Brazil functions as an all too often internalized outside in Latin American studies. As a reassessment of the projection of literature in the field that underscores the need for a sharper, more comparative, and inter-American mode of thinking, my conceptualization of anti-literature is grounded through theoretical, historical, and, above all, close materialist readings of Brazilian and Argentine experimental texts from the 1920s to the present. What is more, this volume engages a unique, diversified corpus of texts that includes the visual arts, concrete poetics, film scripts, and literary works that defy genre, representation, and the word-center.

Anti-Literature is organized as a broad-based discussion of theoretically informed work on Latin American historical, cultural, political, and social processes. It seeks to contribute to a deeper understanding of the literary, and responds to recent scholarship on the legacies of the avant-garde.[1] The book is, therefore, not simply a "literary" account, but a thoroughgoing critique of the historical projection of what is meant by "literature" in the field, as it combines historically situated close readings of experimental texts and multilayered theoretical analysis that probe the limits and possibilities of the literary as a site for radical reflection and reaction to contemporary conditions.

Critical studies focusing on the nature of literature in the field remain marginal. Ángel Rama's *Transculturación narrativa en América Latina* (1982) was a watershed study that at once concerned itself with defining the nature of Latin American literature in terms of identity, and largely gave shape to the contemporary dissatisfaction with literature's institutionality, historical projection, and link to culture in the field. Let me briefly recast Rama's arguments in order to frame my arguments about anti-literature. As an activity inaugurated by Creole patricians at the dawn of the nineteenth century, Latin American literary writing is conceived by Rama as a decolonizing search for cultural representation, independence, and originality. While, to be sure, Latin American literature emerges as an elitist affair, for Rama, it evolves in the mid-twentieth century as a universal cultural ground—especially with the international success of the Latin American "Boom" novel—by rediscovering and translating its popular roots, or better put, by "transculturating" the diverse subaltern cultures of the interior.[2] One can liken Rama's evolutionary model for Latin American literature to the image of a developing nation-state advancing in time from the legacies of colonial backwardness to modernity. In sum, Latin American literature's historical project, for Rama, was to overcome its formal and cultural dependency on European ideas by modernizing its writing procedures, and culturally, by expressing the original life-worlds of its autochthonous peoples. Like the state, Latin American literature is seen as an apparatus that incorporates and represents the diverse voices of the nation.

I will return to Rama's culturalist account of Latin American literature in chapter 1 in my reassessment of Clarice Lispector as a renegade, anti-literary writer, but for now, let me briefly consider four of the most influential book-length studies that challenge Rama's evolutionary model. These are: John Beverley's *Against Literature* (1993), which, taking a cultural studies approach, concerns itself with "a way of thinking about literature that is extraliterary, or . . . 'against literature'" (2). Moreover, Beverley's landmark book, *Testimonio* (2004), interprets subaltern testimonial writings not as hierarchical forms of "literary" expression, but as real forms of truth and agency: "Testimonio appears where the adequacy of existing literary forms and styles . . . for the representation of the subaltern has entered into crisis" (*Testimonio* 49). On the other hand, influenced by Beverley's anti-paternalist critique against literature, as well as by Alberto Moreiras's deconstructive reading of the very notion of Latin American literary writing in *Tercer espacio* (1999), Brett Levinson's *The Ends of Literature* (2001) examines the part played by literature within contemporary Latin Americanist thought and seeks to show, in the context of the neoliberal demise of the sovereign state during the 1980s, that literature in Latin America now functions as a double sign whose privileged status as universal ground for Latin American culture is doomed to closure. Latin American literature operates as a double sign of closure for Levinson because, first, its "literariness" or figurative status takes one to the boundary of common sense through defamiliarization. Literary writing is not representational; it does not speak for the people, as was assumed in Rama, but disrupts common sense through its inherent procedures of translation and "analogy," that is, literature is "the bearer of the relation or likeness between (at least) two fields of concepts, one that neither concept can represent or disclose" (27). Second, literature not only frustrates common sense and fixed opinions, but significantly doubles as an institution tied to markets, conformity, and class-based idealism, because it claims prestige, authority, and transcendence: "[I]t always claims to transcend the common, the languages/forms in circulation and in public, indeed lending itself to the appropriations that support conservatism and existing class, as well as other hierarchies" (28). Finally, for Levinson, insofar as Latin American literature does not represent, in essentialist fashion, an original cultural identity, it constitutes an apposite figure for the translation of the ever-shifting, and relative, crisscrossing of worlds (pre-Hispanic, European, and modernity). Indeed, the pervasive "return to origins" narrative in Latin American literature, for Levinson, embodies not the expression of lost origins, as many have thought, but rather the inexorable trace of hybrid historical inheritance and "the incapacity to lose or translate origins" (17). However divergent the critique of Rama's theory of Latin American literature, the abovementioned cultural theorists have highlighted a larger historical phenomenon that has led to impasse in the field: the exhaustion and limits of the historical representational project of Latin American literature as a paternalist, state-centered, and limited project.[3] Inspired by this dissatisfaction and the corresponding appeal to interrogate the problematical nature of Latin American literature in hitherto unstudied ways, my goal in this book is to pose the problem of anti-literary modes of writing in modern Brazil and Argentina as part of a crucial, unexamined countertradition. Moreover, I argue that an assessment of anti-literature not only challenges classical, monological, and long-entrenched hierarchical notions of literature but changes the larger discussion about the "nature" of Latin American literature and allows us to reconceptualize the problem of writing the subaltern, the feminine, literary politics, and the literary debate in Latin American studies today from a distinctly comparative and original Brazilian context. As already indicated, reflection on Brazilian writers within the framework of Latin American studies remains rare. To the extent that the divorce persists, this volume endeavors to not only reenergize and redirect the critique of literature in the field, but to work unexamined connections between Brazilian and Spanish American literature.[4]

Methodologically, this book desires to move beyond static notions of literature through theoretically informed readings of Brazilian and Argentine anti-literary texts. My aim, however, is not only to unearth pariah traditions, but to argue for the necessity of a multidisciplinary approach that engages some of the most influential cultural theorists and ideas that have led to the crisis of the idea of Latin American literature in the first place. As I will show in my arguments, insofar as anti-literature subverts monological conceptions of literary writing (i.e., literature understood in terms of a strict form-content divide, in terms of the traditional culturalist paradigm, and in terms of rigid genre separation), we need to create a new typology of the text and methodology of reading that understand literary form as a verbal, vocal, and visual complex of perception that structurally dialogues with other media and marginalized social groups. Concerned with anti-literary writing's powers of perception and alliance with other regimes of signs, an important theoretical strand that I examine in this book is the notion of posthegemony, which Jon Beasley-Murray broadly defines as the questioning of the categories of the nation-state and hegemony as the organizing principles for an analysis of culture and politics (xvii). While I will explore Beasley-Murray's ideas more fully in their relationship to Haroldo de Campos's anti-literary prose poem *Galáxias*, in chapter 4, it is important to note that posthegemonic reflection on the Latin American literary today places emphasis on affect against representation, that is, on the dual power of bodies to affect and be affected.[5] In this book, I posit the idea of anti-literature as a multidisciplinary, minoritarian, and multimedial "body" of writing that produces affects and new modes of perception. This idea will, in effect, challenge current, fixed conceptions of literature in the field, and will contribute to the larger discussion/impasse about literary politics.

However, it should be clear that the prefix *post-* designates not so much a chronological dimension ("after" hegemony), but rather a *critical* and *differential* signifier. In this sense, a reading of anti-literature's subversive potential can be considered posthegemonic, but only if we are to read for the text's affective, feminine, multimedial, and subaltern threads. Literature behaves as anti-literature, I argue, precisely when it subverts not only social and cultural norms, but itself: literature is not literature, at least not the way we have been trained to read it as a culturalist regime of representation. My contention is that it is only by accounting for this relation of nonidentity—literature is not literature—that we can begin to read again, anew. This book's analysis of the different genres and media that Brazilian and Argentine anti-literary writers assemble—feminine writing, poetry, film, nonverbal anti-poetry, baroque ornamentation, and so on—deepens our understanding of what is meant by "Latin American" literature as well as what it means to read.

Moreover, in our move against the grain of traditional identitarian interpretative practices, we will see that anti-literature's subversive potential does not rest in a transparent identification with a particular political ideology, or social/cultural identity, as was the conventional wisdom in Latin American literary studies for several decades. As already indicated, the long-standing "originary" linkage between literature and culture in Latin America has been marked as questionable due to the fact that it presupposes a paternalistic representational regime or, in the words of Patrick Dove, "a monolithic, idealized view of literature" (23).[6] Such a teleological image of literature has fettered the field's critical horizons. *Anti-Literature* is concerned with creating a new perspective for literary studies. It does so by conceptualizing the critical force of anti-literary modes of writing while addressing urgent debates in Latin American studies and literary and filmic production: subalternity, feminine writing, posthegemony, concretism, affect, experimental poetics, marranismo, and the politics of aesthetics.

Let us now consider Jacques Rancière's conception of the sensible and its relationship to the mixed regimes of signs at play in anti-literary texts. By the sensible, Rancière refers to "the system of self-evident facts of sense perception that simultaneously discloses the existence of something in common [*l'existence d'un commun*] and the delimitations that define the respective parts and positions within it" (*Politics* 12; *Le partage* 12). The sensible denotes "a common habitat" (*la constitution d'un monde sensible commun, d'un habitat commun*) (*Politics* 42; *Le partage* 66). It describes the system of implicit rules for seeing, speaking, and making that unite and divide a community. Before official politics, the community is first a sensible realm, governed by rules and habits of perception. The distribution of the sensible is therefore not simply an ethos, or system of rules for social behavior, but rather a space of possibilities that is essentially polemical, plural, political, and perceptual. Rancière's basic argument is that art and literature constitute inventive "cuts," or ruptures within the order of the sensible, and thus intervene as "dissensual" forms of subversion (*Dissensus* 202).[7] Art intervenes as a struggle over experience. The politics of literature does not reside in the opinions of writers or in expressing messages, but rather turns on enabling words with the power of framing "a common polemical world": "what links the practice of art to the question of the common is the constitution, at once material and symbolic, of a specific space-time, of a suspension with respect to the ordinary forms of sensory experience" (*Dissensus* 153; *Politics* 23).

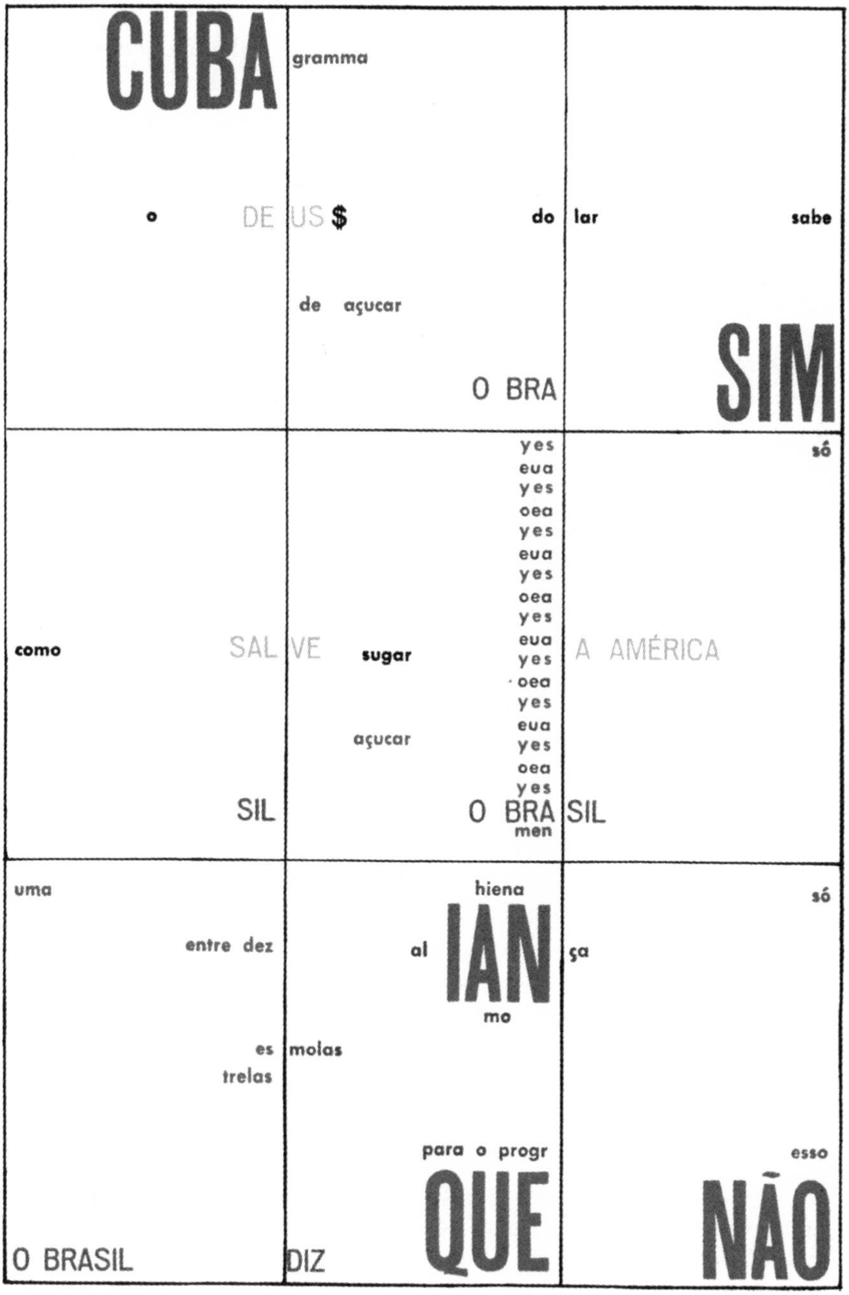

CUBA gramma

o   DE US $ do lar   sabe

de açucar

O BRA

SIM

                                    yes   só
                                    eua
                                    yes
                                    oea
                                    yes
                                    eua
                                    yes
                                    oea
                                    yes
como   SAL VE   sugar   eua   A AMÉRICA
                                    yes
                                    ·oea
                                    yes
                     açucar   eua
                                    yes
                                    oea
        SIL   O BRA SIL
                                    men

uma   hiena   só

        entre dez   al IAN ça
                            mo

        es molas
        trelas

                    para o progr   esso
O BRASIL   DIZ QUE   NÃO

Fig. I.1.   "cubagramma," by Augusto de Campos. From *Invenção: Revista
de Arte de Vanguarda*, no. 2 (1962). Courtesy of Augusto de
Campos.

The politics of anti-literature and its specific affair with the sensible comes into focus through reflection on the limits of the literary medium. Consider Augusto de Campos's "cubagramma" (1962). Concerned with articulating an inventive, transgressive, and polysemic mapping of the polemical status of Cuba in Latin American political debates during the 1960s, Campos's constellation poem problematizes official political representations, pointing to margins and multiple modalities of writing, reading, and mediating the impasse of intellectuals regarding politics.

This poetic field is organized in nine quadrants through six colors—a prominent red that points to Cuba and its revolution, a green that metonymically points to Brazil, and the colors marine, orange, yellow, and "Old Glory Blue."[8] Syntactically, words become fragmented, cross-sectioned, and intercepted by the quadrants and contrasting colors. There are no stanzas but semantic blocks that, like Deleuzian rhizomes, produce offshoots of sense and half-sense—abrupt lines of semantic flight that turn the poem into a laboratory of readings that encircle the prominently displayed, yet fragmented syntagma in bold red: CUBA/gramma SIM IAN QUE NÃO (CUBA/grammar YES YAN-KEE NO). The accentuated visual limits and divisions to the poem-design not only allow the reader to construct multiple readings vertically, horizontally, through color combinations, and across the quadrants, but call attention to the poem's "concrete grammar" and compositional coordinates.

It could be said that the poem's compositional character takes on protagonism over the poem's field of representation. Indeed, the word *gramma* constitutes a double entendre. *Grámma*, from the Greek, refers to letters, to that which is designed, and to the written register. In the second quadrant, it also clearly refers to grams as units of measure, constituting a poetic play with Cuban sugar and US neocolonial interests in the 1960s. In addition to graphing the poem's "grammar," the poem displays, in phonetic fragments and metonymies of color, the neocolonial political context that includes the nation-states of Cuba, Brazil, and the United States. Foregrounding the stakes of the poem as a radicalized medium that condenses multiple regimes of signs, it is significant that *gramma* also suggests the official newspaper of the Cuban Communist Party, the *Granma*.

No doubt "cubagramma" articulates a self-reflexive, anti-literary mediation of a prominent political problem in the 1960s. Far from presenting a poetic resolution to the poem's inquiry on the Cuban Revolution and its possible "alliance" with an increasingly revolutionary Brazil in 1962, where the masses were fast gaining agency, the poem first maps its structural and syntactic grammar—the building blocks, colors, and limits of composition—as an interpellation of the reader to critically mediate this political impasse from the standpoint of construction, as opposed to abstract schemata and official politics. Far from speaking for the nation-state and the people, as one is wont to say of identitarian accounts of Latin American literature, Campos's poem suspends ready-made solutions and the imposition of the ideological, inscribing across the poem's colored words and political field a modifiable present for the reader.

As we can see from Campos's insistence on the radicalized medium as a condition of possibility for recasting what is normatively meant by literature and politics, anti-literary works disturb the common sensible fabric, the customary regimes of perception, identification, and interpretation that establish what is understood by literature. In *Anti-Literature*, I show that the choice is never between literature and politics, or between literature and the other arts. Rather, at stake, I argue, is a subversive, anti-literary understanding of form, understood as a combination of creative forces or interplay between distinct media. All of this amounts to recasting the fundamental problem that pulses through this volume: that anti-literary works articulate an exodus from the regime of visibility of the Latin American literary regime and its cultural politics of mastery and cultural identity, resurgent during the 1960s in Latin America and still prevalent in the field, as many influential accounts of Latin American literature exemplify. Indeed, it might be said, following David Viñas, that for all its merit the Boom discursive formation has hindered the field's critical horizons and impeded the voices of minoritarian writers ("Pareceres" 28, 16). Irrespective of the position one takes regarding the superbly innovative novels of Gabriel García Márquez, Mario Vargas Llosa, Carlos Fuentes, and Julio Cortázar, a regime of interpretation has emerged in their wake that persists in positing the Boom as *the* exemplary Latin American literary subject and key to the canon. While it outstrips the purposes of this introduction to delve deeper into this prickly subject directly, suffice it to say that the Boom's well-documented exclusions—concerning women's writing, Brazil, and minoritarian works—remain an urgent gap in the field that this volume seeks to address.[9]

Against linear unity, accordingly, the structure of this book takes on the shape of the collage or constellation so as to register disparate yet interconnected events of writing. Behind historically grounded analyses that chart the polyvocal procedures of writing at stake in each work, one discerns what could be likened to an interstellar conversation among mutant stars. Opening onto all discourses and producing multiple regimes of signs, to invoke the galactic image of writing at stake in the volume's penultimate chapter dedicated to Haroldo de Campos, these are works that throw light over literature's limits and excess. The constellation, no doubt, denotes the interplay of levels, discourses, and intervals between literature, politics, and theory.

As a figure that crosses the limit and the clear-cut rules of representational logic, the constellation dismisses any unitary subject matter for literature.

OVERVIEW

In diverse ways, the historical case studies contained in this volume place in question the traditional image of literature. There is a traditional image of literature in Latin America. It is a regime of representation that endeavors to speak for the marginal, the feminine, and the regional other. Literature becomes a vehicle to translate and integrate an intractable field of difference. Implicit in this image is a method for locating and thinking difference through representations. Affirming the primacy of identity, this image is typically national and identitarian, but has taken on a variety of avatars since the nineteenth century whose analysis far outstrips the purposes of this introduction.[10]

In chapter 1, I provide a new investigation of the problem of writing the feminine and the subaltern in Latin American studies today through a reading of Clarice Lispector's hitherto unexamined, anti-literary legacy. If, according to Lispector, "literature is a detestable word" and the task of the writer consists in "speaking as little as possible," I engage the recent proliferation of bibliographic research to foreground the difficulty Lispector had in assuming the problematic of politics, literary vanguardism, and commitment during the 1960s and 1970s (*Outros* 165). My countergenealogical portrait highlights Lispector's personal crisis that led to the writing of *A hora da estrela* (1977), her final work and testimony, on which much of her international fame rides. Just as Lispector's final work articulates a critique of literature and a new vision of writing in regard to the subaltern and the feminine, I draw on the work of John Beverley, Gareth Williams, Alberto Moreiras, and Bruno Bosteels to situate the importance of a subalternist framework in rethinking literature and its crisis. Accordingly, I argue that the task of regrounding literature in its specific concern with the sensible calls on a new framework that rehistoricizes works such as Lispector's through their singular, heterodox enunciative procedures. I then turn to the problem of writing the feminine in Lispector by juxtaposing her radical compositional procedure with the writings of Hélène Cixous, Marta Peixoto, and Luce Irigaray. Through a reading of the metaliterary and the feminine in *A hora da estrela*, I argue that Lispector's writing articulates a "fluid" relation to language and politics that defies a unitary, representational, and hence colonizing subject of writing. As an interrogative call to a feminine, reflexive, affective, and creative mode of relationality and social dwelling, a new image of writing at stake in Lispector is ushered forward—one concerning not only the politics of literature, vanguardism, and subalternity in Brazil in the 1960s and 1970s but of subversive composition and the question of taking positions in the present.

Chapter 2 provides a new investigation of the problem of literary politics through a reassessment of David Viñas. Whether through his novels, film scripts, plays, or highly regarded critical essays that fused a sociological examination of the conditions of intellectual production with a heterodox writing style that defied the "myth of literature," Viñas introduced a new image of writing in Latin America and a polemical way of posing problems. And yet, because of Viñas's defiant character and adherence to a critical Marxian perspective, critics have overlooked the subversive character of his novels and film scripts. Conflating political viewpoint with experimental composition, these critics have interpreted Viñas's literary production through a representational optics and order of reasons that limit "literary commitment" to the production of messages. Accordingly, I show how the dis-encounter with Viñas's literary politics turns on a fundamental misreading of his relationship to Jean-Paul Sartre, Marxism, and cinema. On the other hand, I explore how Viñas's novels restore immanence to the mediation of the political and social field. By examining his adaptation of narrative montage technique and recourse to parody, I elucidate how Viñas's will to write the historical constitutes an always open process. My argument is that to "give body" to writing, following Viñas's materialist motto, means not the incarnation of a mechanical Marxist thesis but precisely this: to make of the literary work a milieu of mediation bearing on the minoritarian and violence in history (*Sarmiento* 134). At stake is a new image of "political" writing in Viñas—one that maps history, politics, and writing while undoing the power of their oft-unquestioned teleological effects. Accordingly, in an engagement with Jean-Luc Nancy's conception of literary finitude, I provide a theoretical examination, for the first time, of the subversive stakes and affective force of Viñas's montage narrative technique in the film script turned novel, *Dar la cara* (1962).

In chapter 3, I provide a new reading of Oswald de Andrade's cannibal that charts its subversive avatars in Brazilian concrete poetry from the 1950s to the present. Shifting the terms of discussion on the legacy of anthropophagia through a reading of Andrade's poetry, I argue that the critical force of his cannibalistic poetics lies not in identity but in its self-reflexive, multimedial defiance of representational logic. Second, I investigate how the Brazilian concrete poets resuscitate Andrade's poetics to take what they famously called the "participatory leap" into politics during the 1960s.

The Brazilian concrete poets constitute an understudied, subversive chapter in Latin American studies. Indeed, it could be said that no literary tendency exemplifies more powerfully the theoretical complexity of the historical Latin American avant-garde movements. As an anti-literary project, I show how Brazilian concrete poetry breaks down and blurs the lines separating traditional literary genres and constitutes a visual, verbal, and vocal poetic field of immanence in order to engage the reader with the problem of politics, revolution, subjectivity, subalternity, and vanguardism. Hence, drawing from a diverse array of multimedial poems, I illustrate how the largely misunderstood participatory leap hinges on the ways in which the Brazilian concrete poets "devour the nonpoetic" so as to renovate poetry in a public sphere in crisis. Such a poetics constitutes a new image of vanguard writing in Latin America—one that abandons the collective, representational, word-centered function to engage what the concrete poets deemed the postliterary, postverbal era of late capitalism. Marking the limits of literature even as it opens an outside space to consumption in late capitalism, I conclude by elucidating the continuity of the anthropophagic, properly political preoccupation in concrete poetry as an untimely matter of counterconstructing the present with a reading of Augusto de Campos's iconic poem "mercado" (2002).

Chapter 4 investigates the crisis of the Brazilian avant-garde during the years of the military dictatorship (1964–85) through an assessment of Haroldo de Campos's monumental prose poem *Galáxias* (1963–76). Challenging the prevailing view that posits the text's conflictive relation between "autonomy" and concrete intervention in history, I examine the text's intertextual dialogue with numerous literary, philosophical, and political sources (Dante, Japanese Buddhism, the Brazilian concrete poets, the military regime's propaganda) and how the work investigates the culture industry and the crisis of the impoverished subaltern. Through a comparative, close reading of the *Galáxias* with Ferreira Gullar's "street guitar" political poetry of the 1960s, I suggest the ways in which a thinking of materiality in the *Galáxias* (as affect, as self-reflexive intertextual galaxy, and as concretism) allows us to reconceputalize the literary debate in Latin American studies today from a distinctly Brazilian context.

Drawing on recent discussions of the Latin American Boom, chapter 5 deploys the paradoxical case of Brazilian writer Osman Lins to chart a new framework for interrogating the politics and impasse of the literary in Brazil during the 1960s and 1970s. If I begin with a discussion on the heretofore unpublished polemic between Lins and Haroldo de Campos concerning the "anti-vanguard" character of Lins's novel *Avalovara* (1973), it is to foreground what I conceptualize as the nonunitary, baroque, and subalternist antinomies of anti-literature. Upending all teleological models, I argue that this is the secret residing in Lins's baroque, anti-literary poetics: a new mapping of subalternity that wrests from transculturation's torpor a forceful thought of the political. In my examination of Lins's intensely experimental "Retábulo de Santa Joana Carolina" (1966), I throw light on the means by which Lins blends multiple regimes of signs such as medieval *cantiga* poetry, theater, and the visual arts to engage the structural violence of exploitation and subalternity in the Brazilian Northeast. Situating my argument within the debate on the legacy of the Boom, I engage Rancière, the Latin American Subaltern Studies Group, and the writings of José Rabasa to address Idelber Avelar's influential reading of the Boom as a discursive formation that prizes the figure of the demiurgic writer. For Avelar, the Boom is understood as the site in which Latin American writers seek to restore the literary's "aura," understood as Latin American literature's historical task of creating a lettered elite and representing the people, in a postliterary society marked by the crisis of the state (29). In contradistinction, I examine how Lins's baroque poetics intensely negotiates violence and authority through enunciative ensembles that are anti-representational and anti-literary. Just as with Viñas in Argentina in the context of the fiercely politicized years of the 1960s, I conclude by showing how subalternity in Brazil is imagined by the literary otherwise—not so much as an object of ideology but as a figure of tension for a new poetic and political word.

Anti-Literature concludes with an examination of Haroldo de Campos's poem "O anjo esquerdo da história" (1998), which Campos composed following the massacre of nineteen members of the Landless Workers Movement (MST) by the military police in the state of Pará. I examine how "O anjo"—as theoretical inquiry, denunciatory poem, and avant-garde experiment—is constructed through a montage accretion of images that incessantly call attention to the limits and force of literature. Accordingly, interested in wresting a sensorial language from the remains of the subaltern dead whose truth it knows it cannot name, Campos's poem will overthrow all literary ontology. More specifically, the poem will be concerned with creating a language that is adequate to the incalculable horror of the event, even as it attempts to reactivate subaltern affect and the MST's revolutionary forms of struggle. In an engagement with Walter Benjamin, John Beverley, Gareth Williams, Sebastião Salgado, Giorgio Agamben, Michael Hardt, and Antonio Negri, I elucidate how Campos's poem configures an investigation of the materiality of poetic discourse that opens the life-world pertaining to words in all their sensory, semantic, historical, and political dimensions. In other words, even as the poem posits its limits in its inquiry to redeem subaltern tragedy, I show how Campos makes of the poem an untimely configuration of sensation that resists history, from its margins, as a politics against "literature." Extending the threads of our research to the present impasse over the literary question in contemporary Latin American studies and to

Brazil's largest social movement of more than 5 million landless peasants, I argue that the achievement of Campos is to have produced a politically inspired limit-work that approximates a liberated image for reframing the crisis of the social bond. Going beyond the looking glass of literature and the state, it is a radical work, then, about justice, about literature's untimely role in reactivating subaltern affect, and a contemporary form of subalternist, anti-literary force that hooks up literature to revolutionary forms of insurgency and ways of reimagining the past in a perilous present.

FIGURATIONS OF

IMMANENCE

Writing the Subaltern &
the Feminine in Clarice Lispector

SIFTING THROUGH Clarice Lispector's numerous notes, fragments, chronicles, and interviews, one finds an entire archive of anti-literary statements. "Literature," Lispector states, "is a detestable word—it's outside the act of writing" (*é fora do ato de escrever*) (*Outros* 165).[1] Literature, for Lispector, becomes reactionary with its system of prizes, etiquettes, and, above all, reductive classificatory procedures. In a final, 1977 televised interview, Lispector is asked about the role of the Brazilian writer and whether literature "alters the order of things." She seemingly brushes aside this burning question that contextualizes Brazilian literary production in the 1960s and 1970s. Anchored as the question is to a repressive military dictatorship that would not falter until 1985, Lispector affirms that the writer's role consists in "speaking as little as possible" and that literature "alters nothing."[2] What are we to make of Lispector's anti-literary utterances? Are we to conclude, like many critics on the Left in the 1960s and 1970s, that Lispector's writing was ultimately alienated from the political and the epochal question of engagement? And what are we to make of her final novel, *A hora da estrela* (1977), in which the question of writing the feminine and subaltern configures a central problematic?

The crisis of the Brazilian state in the 1960s triggers a crisis of language. Politicized literary movements blossom throughout the country.[3] The military coup on 31 March 1964 pushes the social relevance of literature front and center, while the repressive crackdown on students, artists, and dissidents through Institutional Act V in December 1968 amplifies the problematic. In a revelatory text, "Literatura e Justiça" (1964), Lispector examines her much-critiqued incapacity to approach "a coisa social" (the social problematic) (149). The question of social justice to whose cause Lispector is committed seems for her overly obvious, while writing is only ever arduous "procura" (searching). For Lispector in the 1960s, to write is not to communicate political messages or to reflect the social in its totality. Literature as process, as intimate *procura*: writing becomes the name for a "linguagem de vida" (language of life) detached from any criteria or program (*Outros* 106).

With the hardening of censorship and the torture of students and dissidents, Lispector partakes in the March of 100,000 against the dictatorship. Indeed, she iconically walks at the front of the protest with a host of artists from Rio. And yet, in the late 1960s, Lispector undergoes a crisis. While producing chronicles, short stories, newspaper columns, and children's books, she complains to close friends of having lost the desire and ability to write. Upon completing the mature, experimental novels *Água viva* (1973) and *A hora da estrela* (1977), Lispector confesses her distaste for her "lighter" works and the chronicle form. Lispector will have rediscovered the necessity for writing.[4]

With trepidation, Lispector delays the publication of *Água viva* for three years for its lack of storyline. The central thread that runs through the novel's fragmentary mode of expression and its series of metaliterary sketches (*esboços*) is perhaps best summarized in an initial utterance: "Este não é um livro porque não é assim que se escreve" (This is not a book because in this way one does not write) (*Água* 13). The novel's defiance of genre, chronological ordering, and flight from "reason" articulate its resounding achievement. Its self-reflexive procedure of laying bare the device finds echo in *A hora da estrela*. More than this, the work ushers forward an impressive meditation on an anti-literary, constructivist mode of writing. Words only achieve their splendor, perceptive field, and intimate life by freeing themselves from the prison-house of language as a system of representations. And one way to attain this power of the word is by making writing a fragmentary system of questions without answers. Writing will only reach life, will only transfigure itself in vision and sensation, by thinking its own limits: "é como o verdadeiro pensamento se pensa a si mesmo, esse espécie de pensamento atinge seu objetivo no próprio ato de pensar . . . pensamento primário" (it is as though true thought thinks of thinking itself, this species of thought attains its objective in the proper act of thinking . . . primary thought) (*Água* 107–8). On examining Lispector's annotations or "roteiro" (itinerary) for the book's revisions, one finds an interesting, anti-literary project: "abolir a crítica que seca tudo" (abolish criticism which dries up everything) (Varin 186).

Lispector's resounding fame today, as Benjamin Moser relates, largely rides on *A hora da estrela*.[5] In revisiting such reach, one cannot ignore the fact that the book in 1985 was made into a movie by Suzana Amaral that won numerous international and national prizes. Yet if we were to speak of it as a unified, plot-driven story, as many critics inevitably do, we would run the risk of reducing a book with thirteen names and thirteen titles. Moreover, such a plot summary often falls within the trappings of a representational logic that interprets the impoverished protagonist, Macabéa, as a hapless victim. Lispector will maintain a far more ambitious project. In her televised interview, Lispector condenses her vision of the protagonist: "é uma história de uma moça, tão pobre que só comia cachorro-quente; mais a história não é só isso . . . é a história de uma innocência pisada, de uma miséria anónima" (it's the story of a girl, so poor that she only eats hotdogs, but the story is not only this . . . it's the story of a trampled innocence, of an anonymous misery). In a manuscript note, Macabéa is described as "hardly material . . . in its most primary form" (Varin 96). From the figure of the impoverished girl, to an impersonal, collective landscape of misery; from anonymous misery, to the primary form of a material that knows no reason (*A hora* [1998] 69). The great problem underwriting *A hora da estrela* is the problem of pushing literature to its limits. Let us consider the novel's design through its metaliterary focus.

A hora da estrela begins at the border of literature by inscribing the abyssal presence of Lispector as author. For example, Lispector's signature is one of the work's thirteen possible titles, and the opening dedicatory begins by framing her as the "(in truth author)" (*A hora* [1998] 9). The novel next delimits the story as a formidable writing project by protagonist-narrator Rodrigo S.M., who has decided to transgress, via experimentation, his former literary "limits" (13, 17). The plot begins, then, really at a second border, *in media res*, with heightened attention toward the work's medium (*meio*) (24, 35), and a philosophical justification of the text's heterogeneous style. Comparing himself to a carpenter, manual labor, shapechanger, soulcatcher, playwright, and a form of "knowledge" (82), such a style will evoke, Rodrigo assures, a multitude of media and questions: popular poetry (*literatura de Cordel*) (33), cinema (*em tecnicolor*) (10, 29), photography (17), discordant music (11, 22, 24, 30), abstract painting (17, 22), melodrama (82), tragic and absurdist theater (21, 23, 48–49, 71, 84–85), stuttering (23), stabbing tooth pain (24), as well as a simultaneous search for "primary life" (13, 16, 21), messianism (19), facts (16), metamorphosis (20), and personal ethics (13). Foregrounding the existentialist theme, Rodrigo affirms his commitment to tell a story of wide social implications (*é minha obrigação contar sobre essa moça entre milhares delas*) (10, 16). Rodrigo's experiment moreover mixes intertexts from Woolf, Dostoyevsky, Sartre, Bram Stoker, Shakespeare, Anita Malfatti, the Bible, Joyce, and Hollywood. Yet as an exodus from "literature" (70), his project will not simply concern questions of form, but rather aim at attaining a productive dimension of "nakedness" between writing and life (82). It is the limit, as boundary and passage between worlds, that has sparked Rodrigo's inquiry: his haphazard glimpse at an impoverished girl in Rio has damned him on a mission to cut all ties with literature and to create a hybrid text that hooks up writing to outside forces. Cultivating a writing style concerned with expressing "primary life" (13), Rodrigo's capacity to perceive the sensuous life of this anonymous indigent girl coincides with his newfound ability to capture "the spirit of language" (*o espírito da língua*) (18).

No longer interested in writing literature, Rodrigo's break, then, implies a gambit: a painfully objective writing technique that will propel him to create the impoverished Macabéa, and to lay bare the literary device in two fundamental ways as a "force" (16, 18). First, Rodrigo reminds us that, due to difference in education, class, gender, and language, he is struggling with all his might to bring to life the socially marginalized Macabéa. Second, he ceaselessly comments on the writing of the story. Such suspensions of the fictive order parallel Rodrigo's regime of privations, which includes abstaining from shaving, soccer, and sex. In sum, Rodrigo will endeavor to affirm the "truth" (*sentido secreto*) of writing subaltern experience (14), even if it means composing a story that "kills" all authority, including his own (86). Accordingly, beyond the prevailing view that perceives Macabéa as a hopeless victim, I argue that she embodies forces of life that shed light on the problem of writing the feminine, the subaltern, and the political in Lispector.[6] Macabéa as the woman without particularities and subjectivity, Rodrigo as the pariah of literature that cannot stop interrupting this impossible writing project—such are the contours of Lispector's monumental anti-literary work that goes a step further than *Água viva* in its exploration of writing subalternity and the feminine.

THE ANTI-LITERARY & THE LATIN AMERICAN LITERARY REGIME

Lispector once said, "[P]erhaps I understand the anti-story best because I am an anti-writer" (*porque sou antiescritora*) (qtd. in Borelli 71). When asked of her outsider yet consecrated position with respect to the Brazilian and Latin American literary traditions, she never hesitated to mark her distance. Against professionalization and etiquettes, straying from what she called "the superficial world of literary writers," Lispector's constructivist approach turns on problematizing the separation between writing and life (qtd. in Varin 195). The consummation of her vision, what she called "a linguagem de vida" (a language of life), implies an exodus from the Latin American literary regime of representation (*Outros* 106).

I am here invoking a larger debate within Latin American cultural studies and its subalternist orientations. To speak of the subaltern is to critique a stagnant concept of culture and the historical entwining of Latin American literature with politics since the nineteenth century. The impetus informing Latin American subaltern studies, in its various guises and camps, begins with a critique of state-centered conceptions of culture. Gareth Williams, Alberto Moreiras, and José Rabasa have written of the exhaustion of unitary models of analysis and of the subaltern as a relational term and epistemological limit. Like Macabéa, who is characterized by Rodrigo as a "porous material" (*A hora* [1998] 13), we can understand the subaltern not as mere downtrodden marginals but as a "constitutive outside," a limit term or fissure, where the fictions of state-centered, unitary discourses become suspended (Williams, *Other* 11).

Beginning in the 1990s, literature and literary criticism in Latin American studies become suspect due to a sequence of related yet divergent sources. In the wake of the debt crisis of the 1980s and the electoral defeat of the Nicaraguan Sandinistas, the first source of this contrarian vision concerns the emergence of Latin American subaltern studies as a response to the sedimentation of neoliberal models across the continent, as well as to the crisis of Marxism and revolution (Bosteels 147). To the extent that the Latin American Subaltern Studies Group's "Founding Statement" (1992) calls for reconceptualizing "the relation of nation, state, and 'people,'" it does so in order to question the then dominant conception of cultural production, most notably, the literary, understood as a representational, class-based apparatus of representation that endeavors to "speak for" the subaltern (137, 140).

Another source concerns the critique of Ángel Rama's cultural theory of Latin American literature as transculturation. As already indicated in the introduction, Rama likens Latin American literature to a unified culturalist project, a "sistema" or "campo de integración" (*Transculturación* 56) assigned the anthropological task of representing the continent's marginalized peoples as an act of difference and "descolonización espiritual" (20). Consider the example of Rama's analysis of João Guimarães Rosa's novel, *Grande Sertão: Veredas* (1956). Through the monologues of retired killer Riobaldo—which, akin to the narratives of William Faulkner, intertwine experimental writing with regional voices—Guimarães Rosa is able to achieve an organic conception of Brazilian culture. Faced with the homogenizing tendencies of a "corrosive" modernization (*Transculturación* 31), Guimarães Rosa's procedure of "neoculturación" restores an original, representative vision of a Latin American region through modern, literary criteria (39). This is why the task of literature, according to Rama, is to "coronate" culture (*las obras literarias no están fuera de las culturas sino las coronan*), to reestablish literature's mediational relevance and role as spokesman for the organic roots of Latin American popular and subaltern cultures (19). However debatable Rama's vision of literature, he places his finger on a larger historical phenomenon: the historical Latin American literary regime of representation. By the historical representational regime of Latin American literature, I refer to the interpretative, integrating, and representational functions that Latin American writers assigned to the literary beginning in the nineteenth century and that run all the way through the twentieth to Rama's monumental theory in 1982. In short, the literary becomes inexorably linked to the state. And literature is assigned the task of expressing the "spirit" of the nation—however hybrid, disenfranchised, or marginalized its peoples—as willed cultural difference. This brings us back to the problematic of anti-literature.

The move from "literature" to subversive invention entails making the historical distinction between the institutionalized field of literature as a *habitus* that conflates experimentation with identitarian description, and literary works that redistribute the encoding of social reality.[7] Against the redundancy of representations that subject and reduce the immanence of both work and social field, the experimental work is always inaugural, cutting through the established hierarchical sensory, gender, and class divides. The innovative composition reveals a new capacity of language, a new image of writing at stake in the present, immanent to its subversive design-structure (*linguagem*), refractive and open to its very finitude, to nonlanguage, to nonverbal systems of communication, and to other media. I refer to the problem of the anti-literary's perceptual and constitutive powers, its radicalized medium, and the ways in which it defies what is normatively meant by "literature."

Marking the distinction between the institutionalized field and the singularity of the inaugural work entails, consequently, going against the grain of the Latin American literary regime of representation.[8] The Latin American literary regime of representation encodes, territorializes, and represses the revolutionary potential of the experimental text. Constituted through a willed cultural difference and an irrevocable class divide that informs its mode of expression, under the literary regime, as we see clearly in the example of Rama, writing becomes subsumed through an instituting discourse of identity.

Against the regime's claims to national popular synthesis and its disavowal of composition, anti-literary works challenge and rearrange the sensible encoding of the real. Even so, indistinction, rife today, lies at the very
origin of the Latin American literary regime. Claims to purity have led likewise to a disavowal of the literary's power. For all of this, there is no question that the literature debate in Latin American studies today has reached
a state of impasse. Or is it that, at worst, weighed down by its critiques,
literature is simply disregarded altogether as passé by a new generation of
thinkers? Refusing to go this route, the regime's stagnation summons a new
horizon for reassessing the literary problematic in Latin America and its
culturalist avatars: the imperative of constructing a countergenealogy, an
anti-literary line, to use Décio Pignatari's lucid expression, an insurrectional
return to the past ("Marco" 149). For anti-literature, as experimentation,
constitutes a procedure of the sensible that investigates and redistributes,
through its form, the social-political. Form converges with critique such
that representations of the social become reflexive, affective, and polyvocal.
De-linking art from politics, as specific domains, allows for a regrounding of
literature in its specific concern with perception, affect, and the sensible. In
effect, anti-literature subverts the traditional idea of literature and the Latin
American literary state model: it does not encode texts or cultures in essentialist framings but breaks down structures in their ideological moorings
and, following Gilles Deleuze and Félix Guattari's thesis in *Anti-Oedipus*
(1972), articulates flows of desire, affect, and perception as a revolutionary
potentiality (32).

Now what Rancière and the philosophers of desire in *Anti-Oedipus*
could not have seen in their postulations on the political potentiality of literature is what I conceptualize as the problematic of anti-literature, which
is so key to the political force and redistributions of the sensible in Brazilian
and Latin American experimental works of the twentieth and twenty-first
centuries. Against the disavowal of innovative composition as narcissistic,
elitist, intransitive, or parodic in the narrow sense, the anti-literary reveals
a new capacity of language in the work, a new design for language that includes its feminine dimensions. This chapter theorizes the productive, feminine dimensions of Clarice Lispector's final novel, *A hora da estrela*. It does
so from within, through immanent critique, and by closely engaging the
novel's self-inscribed problematic centered in writing the feminine and the
subaltern. Importantly, it also does so from without, as a gesture of affirmation of the subversive, anti-literary character of Lispector's legacy in Latin
America.

WRITING THE FEMININE

What are we to make of the problem of the feminine in Lispector? It is Hélène Cixous's achievement to have pinpointed some of the most radical dimensions of Lispector's project. In her reading of *A hora da estrela*, Cixous claims that Lispector "accomplishes a form of writing that does not tell" in order "to write as closely as possible to the living" (162). For Cixous, Lispector's narrative art may therefore be seen as the antithesis of the classical novel, which "gives a survey" and always "comes back to events" so as to produce "a frightening mode of enclosure of the living in verbal form" (161–62). Drawing on the work of Jacques Derrida and Jean Genet, Cixous is concerned with the ways in which *A hora da estrela* splinters the distinction between an inside and an outside of the text, so as to suggest the stakes of a feminine libidinal economy. By feminine economy, Cixous does not refer to an identitarian representation and viewpoint of women and their affective states but to a principle of "general equivalence" and "capacity to not have" (156). The feminine for Cixous constitutes the antithesis of giving the proper name, and hinges on the ways in which *A hora da estrela* places in check the representational dimensions of writing, so as to take the reader to a barren landscape of signs, "a passage through zero," negotiating the wordless, and without social class (143).

Cixous's work does much to illuminate Lispector's project.[9] And yet she does not situate the notion of writing the feminine against the larger cultural context of Brazil in the 1960s and 1970s. Nor does she explore, in full, the problems of identity, immanence, subaltern desire, and figuration at the level of Lispector's radicalized medium that I hope to make clear. For that matter, Cixous rarely speaks of the political implications that follow from Lispector's syntax.

Marta Peixoto's influential article, "Rape and Textual Violence in Clarice Lispector" (1991), examines "the field of textual interactions charged with violence" in *A hora da estrela*.[10] Peixoto's fundamental concern hinges on the modes through which Lispector constructs "an acute gaze to the exercise of personal power, to the push and pull of the strong and the weak, particularly to the dynamics of victimization" (183). Victimization becomes the lens through which Peixoto tracks "the suspect alliances of narrative with forces of mastery and domination" (184). Peixoto reads Macabéa as "a bona fide social victim" (191). This is so, according to Peixoto, insofar as "Macabéa is victimized by everything and everyone . . . while patriarchy neutralizes her sensuality and foreign stereotypes of beauty encourage her and others to despise her body and its color" (191–92). Peixoto reads this process of "beating" and "raping" of the subaltern in a double key: through the story of Macabéa's exploitation and through "a meditation on writing the victim, a process that itself duplicates and inscribes the act of victimization" (192).

While Peixoto astutely registers the subalternization of Macabéa and the novel's metafictional character, her argument is organized through a dialectic that does not register the problem of immanence and the event of writing that follows from Lispector's compositional plane. To the extent that Peixoto's reading engages the question of power, gender, and the metatextual in Lispector, it marks an important contribution. Compromising her conclusions, however, is the fact that her reading does not track the consequences of the composed character of the work and the radical suspending mediation at play in Lispector's novel.

Problematic, too, is Peixoto's parabolic reading of Macabéa's story. For the extent to which she reads Macabéa through the key of a moral is the measure by which she determines the novel's ultimate lesson: "This hyperbolically naive, unprotected, bewildered young woman—'adrift in the unconquerable city' . . . —signifies the shared human helplessness of beings engulfed in the brutality of life" such that "Macabéa dies in utter abjection, learning nothing from her trials. The narrator finds no moral in his tale" ("Rape" 199–200). We are confronted with an image of writing centered in guilt whose endpoint is the victim: the "slaughter" of Macabéa as a "sacrificial rite" such that "Lispector questions, I believe, the very possibility of innocence: she enacts a guilt-ridden struggle with the mastering and violent powers of narrative" (201).

While it is clear that Lispector destroys any question of "innocence" by "implicat[ing] . . . all the subjects who engage in the narrative transaction" (Peixoto, "Rape" 194), what are we to make of the multiplying images of composition, of the constant parenthetical mirroring back of the text's limits? Indeed, must we conclude that there is a single, unifying subject of enunciation in *A hora da estrela*? How are we to decipher the fact that Rodrigo, as narrator, dons a mask in the guise of the "in truth" autobiographical Clarice Lispector? Or is it the other way around? Is this not a subversion of sense once again in *A hora da estrela*, of the *"specula(riza)tion that subtends the structure of the* [unified and metaphysical] *subject,"* and indeed, of the "necessities of the self-representation of phallic desire in discourse" (Irigaray, *This Sex* 116, 77)? What are we to do with this first inscription in parenthesis, this curving mirror that inaugurates the novel by upsetting the problem of authority and "truth," of literature and the social?

Of the potential stakes of a feminine writing (*"style," ou "écriture," de la femme*), Luce Irigaray has stated that one never begins from zero; one starts a fundamental work on language from the middle, beginning with having "a

DEDICATÓRIA DO AUTOR
(Na verdade Clarice Lispector)

Fig. 1.1. Author's dedication, *A hora da estrela*, 1977.

fling with the philosopher" (*Ce sexe* 76; *This Sex* 151). Against the language of the logos, against speaking at the level of greatest generality, at issue for Irigaray is the deployment of "other languages," even silence, so as to construct some other "mode of exchange" that might not say the same logic (*This Sex* 150, 79). This aporia of discourse relating to the feminine as a limit to rationality must be engaged through an inhabiting of philosophical practice—"to go back inside the philosopher's house"—centered in the logos as "that general repetition [that names the feminine as] *the otherness of sameness*" (151, 152). The "domination of the philosophic logos," Irigaray notes, "stems from its power *to reduce all others to the economy of the Same*" (74). This "general grammar of culture" organized through a masculine imaginary has excluded "a place for the feminine within sexual difference" (155, 159). Against the grain of the "proper," appropriating character of language and mimetic practice, Irigaray asks how one can achieve a *"non-hierarchical* articulation" (161, 162).

Inspired by Gilles Deleuze's concepts of desire, ontological difference and repetition, and the body without organs, Irigaray's problematic is organized around the critique of the metaphysics of presence, a nondialectical conception of desire as expression of multiplicities, and a trenchant affirmation of difference through the creation of a "dynamogenic," feminine economy of meaning (*This Sex* 114). Irigaray's aim is to debunk all dichotomizing dualities, all modes of thinking and representing that configure the field of the specularized subject, the metaphysical subject of culture. By specular economy, Irigaray invokes the staging of self-conscious representation set in motion through Jacques Lacan's mirror stage.[11] Through a Gestaltian projection of the *I* in the world as an ideality, the mirror stage, for Irigaray, "authorizes misapprehension" of the world and Being (117). This is so because the mirror stage fetters the phenomenal world in all its singular projections, intensities, and flows by turning them into "solids," into ideal projective forms that refer back to "the mirage" of the "mental permanence of the I . . . [and] its alienating destination" as the ground of order (113, 116, Lacan qtd.). The mirror stage, in sum, authorizes a dialectics of the subject that subjugates the world to its own image. In such a conception, there is no mutual resistance regarding *"what is in excess with respect to form,"* nor is there place for what Irigaray calls a "dynamogenic exchange or of reciprocal resistances between the one and the other" (110, 114). An excessive language of fluids would refer to that which persists in immanence outside the proper, the solid form, and the purview of the subject—to a conception of the feminine not circumscribed by the de-sexed, "castrated" image of woman in Freudian and Lacanian psychoanalysis.

Significantly, in an engagement with Karl Marx, the specular economy also refers to the ways in which, through capitalist production, women become objects of value on the marketplace, or commodities of masculine speculation.[12] Just as a commodity becomes "disinvested of its body and reclothed in a form that makes it more suitable for exchange among men" (*This Sex* 180), so too are women "transformed into value-invested idealities" (181). Accordingly, in such a standardized order, women's value does not flow from their bodies, their language, or their constitution as singular beings "but from the fact that they mirror man's need/desire for exchanges among men" (181). "By submitting women's bodies to a general equivalent, to a transcendent, super-natural value," Irigaray notes, "men have drawn the social structure into an ever greater process of abstraction, to the point where they themselves are produced in it as pure concepts" (190). In sum, the specular image of thought imposes a form that organizes and duplicates experience and Being in a distribution that is dialectical and identitarian, constituting a nondynamic language of abstract appropriation and speculation that cannot cope with fluids and the singular projectiles of Being. In her critique of psychoanalysis, Irigaray's concept of the specular comes to signify the distorting mirror that allows the masculine subject to conceive of himself as an ideal subject, and to understand and utilize all of matter and nature to his ends. In order to jam the circular character of this theoretical machinery that "standardize[s]" signs and things in the image of man, in order to defy the law of the father, one must put on a mask, perform a theoretical masquerade by inhabiting the philosopher's discourse, in such a way as to reflect and free up its figures of discourse (180). The feminine, in short, for Irigaray would constitute the affirmation of difference as a field of multiple singularities. These singularities would thereby be conceived not as parts of an identity to be integrated into a whole, but as a generative productivity or "flux" consisting of presubjective, presubstantive differential elements that are always more than one on a plane of consistency (*This Sex* 215; *Ce sexe* 214). Put differently, Irigaray's affirmation of the feminine as a multiple, nonunitary, and resistant mode of relating to masculine discourse can be productively compared to Deleuze and Guattari's anti-dialectical injunction to reconceive the material world as a field of immanence or "body without organs," which, defying the order of the metaphysical subject and idealism, allows one to rethink desire, discourse, sexuality, otherness, and the "real" in terms of dynamic flux, disparate multiplicities, and force (*Anti-Oedipus* 281; *Thousand* 255).

"We haven't been taught, nor allowed," Irigaray notes, "to express multiplicity. To do that is to speak improperly" (*This Sex* 210). This language of the "improper," the language of what Irigaray calls women's "self-affection"—"two lips kissing two" in Irigaray's poetic formulation of an affirmed difference that goes beyond identity and representation—concerns the invocation of an untimely flight from the grid of representations that cross-section, codify, and constitute the subject (132, 210). This is a radical appeal to movement, an opening of pleasure (*jouissance*) through a fracture in the lines of the representational (*Ce sexe* 210): "We have so many voices to invent in order to express all of us everywhere . . . we have so many dimensions . . . You are there like my skin" (*This Sex* 213, 216). When Irigaray speaks of such openness and inventiveness as an affirmed exteriority that defies the dialectical, she is referring to the creation of a new mode of expression and its plane of composition centered in connections, contiguity, and multiplicities so as to organize a new relation to language, sexuality, and the world that is not modeled on man or the state.[13] This language of composition and connection, grounded in an untimely mode of critique and creation that defies the order of things in terms of presence, thwarts any identitarian pretense. It allows one to rethink the terms that have structured, imprisoned, and deadened the categories of sexuality and language through a metaphysics of presence, for example.

Like Irigaray, in her writing the subaltern and the feminine Lispector was no doubt concerned with creating a new relation to language and politics that defied the dialectical.[14] The notion of curved, distorting mirrors, wearing the male mask, performing masquerades, or having "a fling with the philosopher" certainly resonates as one reassesses *A hora da estrela*'s series of parenthetical comments, multiple titles, and its always in question "in truth" authoritative voice. Beyond juxtaposition, Lispector's text articulates itself as a problem and imperative in Brazil, as an *emergent emergency* (*acontece em estado de emergência*), in a public sphere in crisis (*calamidade pública*) (*A hora* [1998] 9–10). If it is not a politics of identity, if it is not a matter of negating the contradiction through a representation of the victim, we are beckoned by the text to consider the "improper" matter of the literary.

"The reflection on discourse, on language, to which I was led through linguistics," Irigaray reflects, "enabled me to interpret the history of Western philosophy, to interrogate the particularities of its truth and its lacks. One of these is particularly evident: the small number of logical means the masculine subject has developed for communicating the present with another subject different from him, in particular with a subject of another gender" (*Conversations* 9). In so doing, Irigaray puts her finger on the conceptualization of a multiple, relational mode of discourse, centered in refractive mediation over representation. Such a feminine discourse powerfully connects with Lispector's radical compositional plane. Indeed, Irigaray's appeal to begin in the middle echoes the words of Rodrigo S.M. when he begins Macabéa's narrative: "Vou começar pelo meio dizendo que—" (I'll begin in the middle saying—) (24). From the pun in Portuguese, *meio*, referring to "the middle" but also to the "medium," Lispector constructs a whole series connected to forging self-reflexive mediations that create further connections as opposed to imposing representations and judgments on the subaltern Macabéa: void, meditation, means, middle, parenthesis—Lispector's textual membrane marks all forms and affects as media, means of building new relations with the undecidable, untimely figure of the subaltern. And this textual membrane, this interfacing mode of discourse, constitutes a matter of the literary that is no doubt historical and tied to the political stakes that informed the conjunction of vanguardism and underdevelopment in Brazil during the 1960s and 1970s. What of the vanguard and Lispector?

In her conference paper "Literatura de Vanguarda no Brasil" (1963), Lispector examines the legacies of the Brazilian avant-garde of the 1920s in order to articulate her own vision for the 1960s. For Lispector, the concept of the avant-garde concerns liberating writing from "stratified," overly abstract conceptions (*Outros* 97). It implies the construction of a new "language of life" and a modification of "the concept of things" (106, 105). Lispector invokes the countercultural elements at play in the 1960s on the eve of the military coup of 1964. Politics for Lispector is best understood in its immediate aspects, as Deleuze and Guattari said of Franz Kafka's minor literature: politics as an affair of the people, as a syntactic liberation forged through a minoritarian treatment of a majoritarian language (*Kafka* 17, 16):

> For in a general way—and now hardly speaking just about politicization—
> the general atmosphere is best characterized as avant-garde, and our inner
> intimate growth will burst asunder the useless forms of being and writing. I
> am calling our progressive self-knowledge avant-garde. I am calling avant-
> garde "thinking us" through our language. Our language has not been
> profoundly worked on by thought. "To think" the Portuguese language
> of Brazil means to think sociologically, psychologically, philosophically,
> linguistically about ourselves. The results are and will be what's called lit-
> erary language [*linguagem*], that is, a language-structure that reflects and

expresses with words that instantaneously allude to things that we live; in a language-design that is real, in a language-structure that is simultaneously content and form: the word is, in truth, an ideogram. It is marvelously difficult to write in a language that gushes, foams; a language that needs more from the present than even from a tradition, in a language that, always worked on, demands of the writer that she work on herself as a person. The creation of a new syntax always articulates a direct reflection of new relationships, of a more profound examination of ourselves, of a sharper consciousness of the world and of our country's world. The creation of new syntax thus opens new freedoms. . . . Language [*linguagem*] is discovering our thought, and our thought is forming our literary language, and what I call, to my delight, a language of life.[15]

This statement seems essential. The general vanguard atmosphere of which Lispector speaks informs Brazilian literary production in the 1960s and is contextualized by the politics of underdevelopment and decolonization that influenced a generation of artists and activists in Latin America. In Lispector, the question of politics did not concern representing the marginal, the subaltern, or even women through literature. And it certainly did not turn on transculturation, whereby literature is understood as a translation device of cultural alterity. Against the grain of cultural synthesis, or an aesthetics of "writing the victim," for Lispector the question of *vanguarda* concerned the creation of a new relation to syntax and the being of language.[16] This difficult language of the real was to be achieved through a hard labor on language and on the ways in which the writer could "think" her relation to the larger collective context of Brazil (106). In order to write the experimental text and so articulate a new relation to the real, a new image of writing was called for, one that embodied a nondominating, feminine, and subalternist mode of reading, relating, and creating.

LITERATURE BEFORE LITERATURE—WRITING LIFE

Yet suffice it to say that the experimental and committed dimensions of the literary, championed in the 1950s, 1960s, and 1970s, began to be overlooked in the 1980s with the critique of the Boom as state centered, with the Latin American debt crisis, and with the turn to cultural studies. In short, the literary was given a bad rap in the context of anti-institutional discussions centered on the hegemony and postmodernism debate in Latin American studies. With the focus on what John Beverley has termed "literature's connection with the formation of the modern state," the question of revolutionary form in literature becomes displaced (*Against* xiii). On the one hand, scholars begin to question the impact and relevance of literature through a mélange of anti-Eurocentrism and critical regionalism. Accordingly, the subversive elements of composition, such as self-referentiality, are challenged as elitist and narcissistic *tout court*.[17] On the other hand, discussions as impacting as Beverley's place focus on undermining the literary's institutional status and connection to the state and, in the process, turn to an examination of writings by subalterns such as *testimonio*. Experimentation in the literary domain, as a politics and specific procedure of the sensible, becomes in large measure an afterthought.

The critique was important, useful, and illuminating but hinged in its most basic core on the premise of a subject-object divide. Let me state clearly here so as to shift the terms of the discussion: subject and object of writing give a limited approximation to the literature and politics problematic. In contradistinction to the contemporary cultural studies impasse, we return to our central question: how an assessment of the feminine, affective, and subalternist dimensions of *A hora da estrela* allows us to challenge the prevailing conception of what is meant by Latin American literature today.[18]

Beginning with Olga da Sá, Benedito Nunes, and Hélène Cixous in the late 1970s, critics have commented at length on the text's self-reflexivity.[19] And yet, the implications of the gesture have been overlooked. For starters, Macabéa's name is palimpsestic with renegade valences, referring to the legendary Jewish rebel army, the Maccabees, that led a revolt against Greek rule from 174 to 134 BC.[20] Principle of minoritarian rebellion, Macabéa's characterization centers on her uneven relation to letters and society. In effect, as a migrant from the Brazilian Northeast, it could be said that she marks an important inflection in twentieth-century Brazilian literature and art. From Graciliano Ramos, João Cabral de Melo Neto, and Cinema Novo to the paintings of Candido Portinari, the migrant's flight to the city is framed as a paradigm of inequity: the long-standing divorce between the Brazilian lettered class and the subaltern.[21] No doubt *A hora da estrela* condenses Lispector's homage-response to this influential theme, as well as to the lifelong criticism she received for being "alienated" from social struggles (Borelli 53).[22]

The novel examines this divide in terms of an impossible, untimely love. Throughout, Rodrigo relates his great affection for Macabéa, as he admires her faith in life, however "miserable" its conditions: "A única coisa que queria era viver. Não sabia para quê, não se indagava" (The only thing she wanted was to live. She didn't know why, did not ask) (27). Rodrigo's love is structured through the fracture and margins of order that Macabéa's world illuminates. Macabéa's perception evinces a deviant quality in absorbing the signs emitted by the culture industry, and it presents us with a politics of the sensible as a first plane of visibility that the novel foregrounds. Images of commodities and Hollywood stars are placed at strategic junctures. During his theoretical preamble, Rodrigo alerts the reader that the text is written under the sponsorship of Coke and that reality is a matter of turning on a switch in a technocratic society (23, 29). I hasten to recall that, of the multiple narrative registers that Rodrigo deploys in layering Macabéa's story— such as popular Brazilian northeastern poetry, melodrama, music, painting, and theater—he states that the story is written in technicolor.[23] All of this sets up the problem of culture, media, and desire—the problem of what counts for reality and cultural visibility: if Macabéa desires to be Marilyn Monroe, drinks Coca-Cola, and adores advertisements, she also yearns to understand "que quer dizer cultura" (what culture means) and all the banal facts emitted by Radio Relógio (50). And yet this plane of mass culture and reified visibility that the novel invokes as "hoje" and "a realidade" is framed against a second plane of composition that Rodrigo sets in motion, an "exterior" reflexive history of the text (20, 34, 13). "Este livro é uma pergunta," notes Rodrigo, "a palavra tem que parecer com a palavra, instrumento meu" (This book is a question. . . . The word must appear as word, my instrument) (17, 23).[24]

While at first glance the "exterior story" describes Rodrigo's metafictional musings, the "exterior" incessantly blends into what is called "uma oculta linha fatal" (a secret fatal line) that unworks the text's figurative impulse (13, 20). "E só minto na hora exata de mentir," relates Rodrigo, "[m]as quando escrevo não minto" (I only lie in the exact moment of lying. But when I write I don't lie) (18). This paradoxical phrase brings the text's surface, like a refractive membrane, to the fore. Articulating a break, we are brought face to face with a *simultaneous mode of writing* that suspends the fictive at the exact moment of the fictive's inscription, at the exact moment of signification proper. The figure becomes line, surface, textual membrane, medium (*meio*) (24) and site of an exteriority related to sensation: "é verdade também que queria alcançar uma sensação fina e que esse finíssimo não se quebrasse em linha perpétua" (it's also true that I desired to attain a delicate sensation, and that this most delicate no would break in perpetual line) (20).[25]

Regarding the problem of sensation as an irruptive force of the text (*esse finíssimo não*), Rodrigo characterizes his project as a "writing with his body" (20, 16). From the beginning, he frames his relationship to Macabéa in terms of affect (16). Rodrigo's affective connection to Macabéa articulates the powerful feeling he undergoes while introducing her into the world as a singular and individuated creation. Affect thus takes place in a double movement. On the one hand, Rodrigo invokes his right to adopt a compositional attitude that is painfully "cold," "without piety," because his task is organized around transcending "narrative," "literature," habit, and routine: "Não se trata apenas de narrativa, é antes de tudo vida primária que respira, respira, respira" (At stake is not just narrative, it's above all primary life that breathes, breathes, breathes) (13). Objectivity in such a world is properly poetic and creational, the composition of an originating viewpoint connected to the forces of life.

But the facts and coldness to which Rodrigo's writing adheres, on the other hand, are dissolved in Rodrigo's flight into figuration and composed sensations, in his writing of the dramatized storyline that includes *the intensely felt drama of his writing project*. For Macabéa "sticks" to his skin and is depicted through an affective, conflicted register as "not wanting to get off my shoulders" (21–22). From "fatos" we are relayed the sensations of writing in the present. More than this, we are confronted with a sensation of responsibility to the undecidable figure, the "opaque material" that Macabéa's world forces Rodrigo to undergo (16). Charles Altieri explains that sensation can be productively read as "a material . . . that cannot be simply translated into the sign of representing some meaning" (239). In *A hora da estrela*, sensations consist in a nondetermined order of affects that draw the reader's attention to the medium and perceptual forces of writing. If the affect dissolves facts, it ignites an explosion of relations within the constituted order of things. The affect relates to the sensation of writing the impossible, the undecidable, and that which lacks writing. Obsessed with writing the life of Macabéa, Rodrigo invents a necessarily multimedial and reflexive writing style. It is a project, in short, that forces him to fly into objectivity in the construction of his visions, on a perpetually breaking line, to the very limits of words and self-reflection (*A hora* [1998] 20).

Just as Rodrigo's words must appear as words in their limits, it is important to note that Macabéa, subsisting in an "impersonal limbo" (23), resists facile encapsulation as a social type insofar as she is capable of perceiving and feeling what others fail to experience: "ela prestava atenção as coisas insignificantes como ela própria" (she paid attention to insignificant things like herself) (52). The impersonal in Lispector constitutes a power and an opening to the outside. It points to desiring productivity, to the multiplicities at play in any event of desire. Indeed, Macabéa is compared to a saint who has yet to experience ecstasy, a paradoxical bearer of "so much interiority," who "believes" (*acredita*) in life and prays "sem Deus" (without God) (34, 38). Without definitions, without ordering discourse, without knowing how to define the projects and rational contours that might constitute a self, Macabéa emits a system of signs that configure a pulsating world of subalternized desire. Macabéa's eyes wander, as though in a deep dream, across the fringes and disintegrated detritus of capital: the weeds in the cracks of

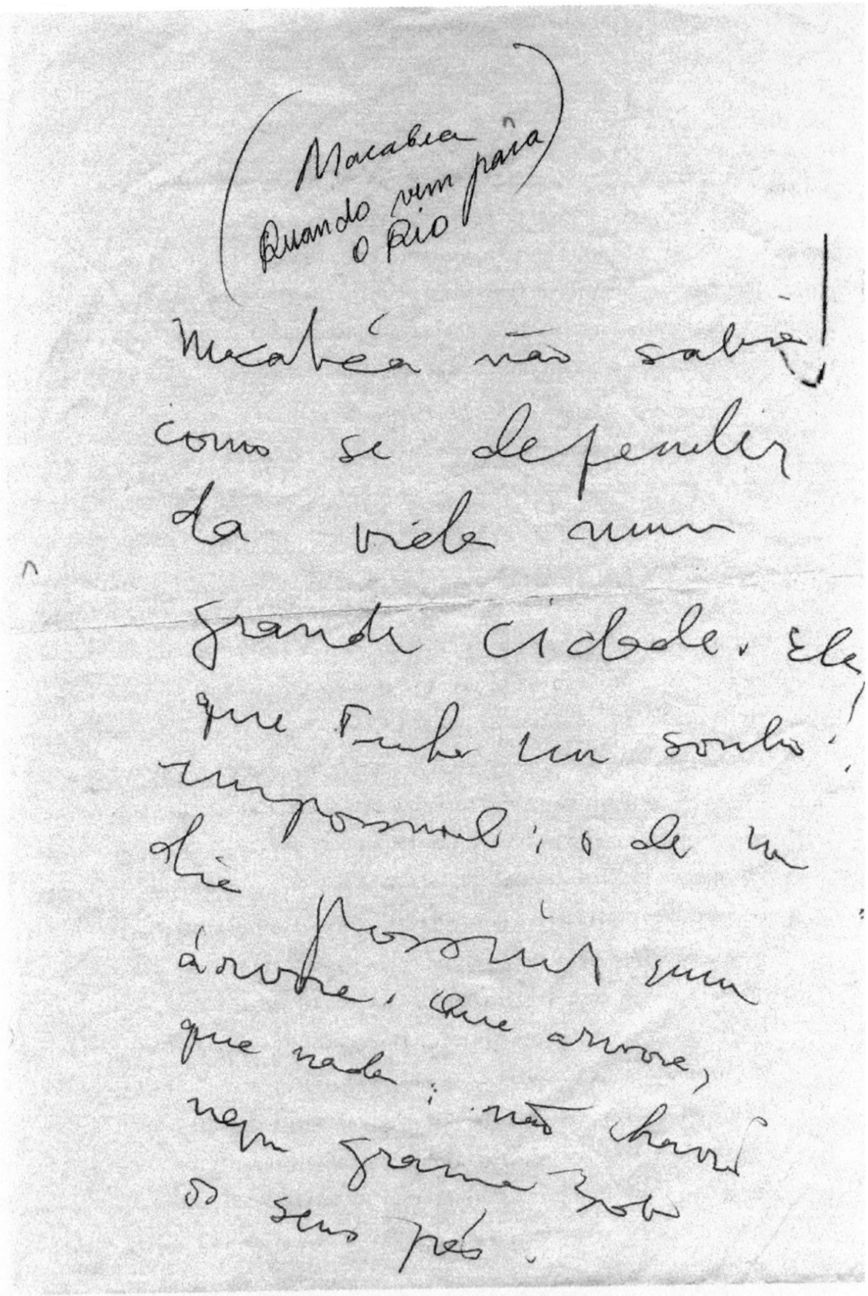

Macabea
Quando vem para
o Rio

Macabéa não sabe
como se defender
da vida numa
grande cidade. Ela
que tinha um sonho
impossível; o de ter
possuir uma
árvore. Que árvore,
que nada: não havia
nem grama sob
os seus pés.

Fig. 1.2. "Macabéa quando vem para o Rio" (Macabéa when she comes to Rio). Manuscript note by Clarice Lispector and Olga Borelli. Courtesy of the estate of Clarice Lispector.

the sidewalks, the faint cawing of a stray rooster in the quay, dilapidated doors, placards, and mannequins. Pregnant with an interior life that she cannot name, Maca also yearns for the "untouchable": the pretty man in the pub she so nervously craves or having a room of her own, as in Virginia Woolf (37, 41). And we should not overlook her pleasures: monthly trips to horror films, an advertisement album, hotdogs. On the other hand, at an affective level it might be said that Macabéa's turbulent interiority, her nameless sensations and excessive "sensuality," turn on the problem of mimesis (60–61). The site of the subaltern interior—the problem of desire as much as a problem of discourse—points to a zone of immanent singularities beyond representation as copy and capture: a rapture of the senses and a notion of mimetic play that could be described, following Irigaray, as an abyssal feminine alterity within the narrative structure.[26]

The fact that Macabéa's emotions are encapsulated through the medium of a parenthetic structuring sequence of (explosions) connects us to the refractive plane of composition to which Rodrigo incessantly draws our attention, to the tracing of the text's finitude, and to its openness and appropriation of other media. "Macabéa separated a stack of cards with a trembling hand: for the first time she was going to have a destiny. Madame Carlota (explosion) was a highpoint in her existence. . . . And so there you have it (explosion) of a sudden it happened: the face of Madame kindled all illuminated. . . . Madame was right: Jesus in the end paid attention to her. Her eyes were dressed by a sudden voracity for the future (explosion)."[27] Composed through free indirect discourse, as a passage of consciousness between the narrative voice and the mind of Macabéa, such a procedure is not innocent. The parenthetic sequencing of Macabéa's (explosive) affects, connected to her newfound "voracity for the future," inscribes a horizontality and multiplicity of textual flows that move against the grain of Rodrigo's self-proclaimed project of getting to the facts. In Lispector, this noncategorizable language of the affect inscribes the imperative of framing subalternized desire and its virtual field, which is articulated across the "portraits" (retratos) of the subaltern Macabéa (39). In other words, the parenthesis that encircles the (sensuality) of the subaltern disrupts a dialectics of desire structured through lack, demand, and identity. It ushers in, moreover, the problem of subaltern desire redoubled: as a field of (repressed) affective singularities that place in question the field of the representational. Far from imposing a form on the subaltern, and powerfully generating a rupture in the narrative flow, the explosion sequence interpellates the reader into a problematized present that had been structured hitherto in the narrative past. To the extent that the parenthesis performs a suspension of representation, it simultaneously triggers the untimely coming of critique and evaluation, the time of the present. Denoting the impossibility of speaking for the subaltern, I hasten to add that the parenthetic delimitation of Macabéa's affects simultaneously points to the opening up of Rodrigo's writing to new systems of signs and enunciative modes. In the above cited example, the narrative modality has shifted to melodramatic discourse, which Rodrigo disclaims at once: "Não me responsabilizo pelo que agora escrevo" (72).

To the extent that the limits of discourse are framed through a series of untimely parentheses that encircle Macabéa's affective states, we recall that Rodrigo repeatedly bemoans the difficulty he is experiencing in the act of writing. Like self-reflecting mirrors, these remarks surface throughout the work in a series of parentheses that read as aphorisms. The aphoristic remarks disrupt and evaluate the text in its course and configure the site through which Rodrigo "theorizes" and admits the impossibility of his writing project.

> She was quiet (for not having anything to say) but she liked noises. They were life.
>
> . . .
>
> (As for writing better a living dog)
>
> . . .
>
> (It is my passion to be the other. In this case, her. I shudder equally squalid like her.)
>
> . . .
>
> (With excessive boldness I'm using the written word and all this trembles inside me and I remain with the fear of distancing myself from Order and falling into the howling abyss: the Hell of freedom. But I shall continue.)
>
> . . .
>
> (I see that I attempted to give Maca one of my situations: I need each day a few hours of solitude, if not I die.)
>
> . . .
>
> (How boring to deal with facts, the day-to-day annihilates me, and I'm too lazy to write this story which is a relief, and hardly that. I see that I'm writing beneath and beyond myself. I take no responsibility for what I now write.)
>
> . . .
>
> (I see that it's useless to expand and deepen this story. Description tires me.)[28]

A mechanism of suspension and the untimely, the parentheses proliferate as much as they refract, and they draw our attention to the text's multiple titles. Consisting of thirteen alternating leitmotifs for understanding the story, the theme-titles are arranged through a system of *ors*, highlighting the text's constitutive power and alterity. The rotating thirteen titles express, then, a

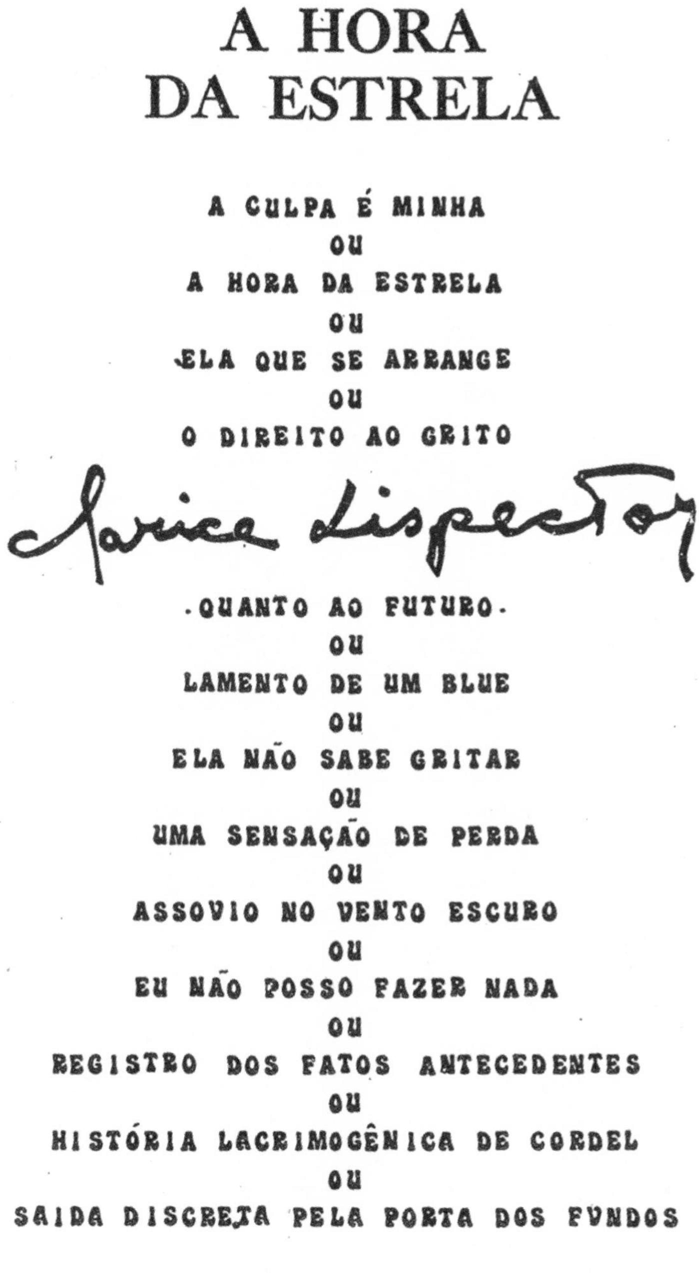

A HORA
DA ESTRELA

A CULPA É MINHA
ou
A HORA DA ESTRELA
ou
ELA QUE SE ARRANGE
ou
O DIREITO AO GRITO

Clarice Lispector

.QUANTO AO FUTURO.
ou
LAMENTO DE UM BLUE
ou
ELA NÃO SABE GRITAR
ou
UMA SENSAÇÃO DE PERDA
ou
ASSOVIO NO VENTO ESCURO
ou
EU NÃO POSSO FAZER NADA
ou
REGISTRO DOS FATOS ANTECEDENTES
ou
HISTÓRIA LACRIMOGÊNICA DE CORDEL
ou
SAIDA DISCRETA PELA PORTA DOS FUNDOS

Fig. 1.3. Title page, *A hora da estrela*. From the 6th ed., 1981. Courtesy of the estate of Clarice Lispector.

paradigmatic articulation of the becoming immanent of Lispector's syntax and authority, as her very signature constitutes an "or" title.

If, as Augusto de Campos states, the fundamental problem of the concrete poem is the anti-poetic combination of media and the communication of the text's verbal, vocal, and visual dimensions, it could be said that the novel is organized as a multimedial assemblage and that it images a constant problematization of the appropriative powers of mimesis. Like the concretes, as we will see in chapter 3, we recall that Lispector likened the experimental word to an ideogram, or a constellational structure of diverse dimensions: "A palavra na verdade é uma ideograma" (*Outros* 106). Accordingly, Lispector's text suspends the formal system of elements comprising Rodrigo's writing system in order to extract an alternative order of things from the margins of the polis. The migrant worker in the city is thus portrayed twice over: as a parenthetic, problematical fracture in civilized order (subalternized subject), and as a multiple, feminine, noncodifiable heterogeneous (medium) of fluid and feminine desires, perceptions, and affects. The gesture explains Rodrigo's self-reflexive yet powerfully creative enterprise: to write a language of (feminine, affective) life capable of responding to the political and representational problem of subalternity in Brazil.

For example, the first depiction of Macabéa is a distorted mirror image. When she goes to the bathroom and stares in the mirror in shame because her boss has berated her incapacity to spell correctly as a typist, we do not see her face but that of the narrator. "Vejo a nordestina se olhando ao espelho," Rodrigo notes, "e—um rufar do tambor—no espelho aparece o meu rosto cansado e barbudo" (I see the northeasterner gazing at herself in the mirror and—roll of the drum—in the mirror appears my gaze tired and bearded) (22). The image of the mirror is not innocent or Oedipal but constitutive, contiguous, and essentially connective. It is the gesture of incessant critique that accompanies the maneuver of radical creation that *A hora da estrela* articulates in every single turn of phrase, in every liberated syntactical detour that comprises its refractive textual status. In its mirror series, which articulates an allegory and "gradual vision" of writing as "emergência," in the double play of emergency and emergence (12, 10), *A hora da estrela*'s open compositional plane—which converts every sign, every word, and every reference into a constitutive power of writing—could be seen as a relational, incessant creation/critique with respect to identitarian, representational politics.

THE PROBLEM OF DEATH & THE LITERARY IN *A HORA DA ESTRELA*

In the preceding pages I have zeroed in on Lispector's self-purported strategy of constructing a radical image of writing, or *linguagem de vida* (a language of life), against the problematic of writing the subaltern and the feminine. And yet, what are we to make of the overriding theme of death that informs the novel's conclusion? How does death in *A hora da estrela* relate to the so-called "exhaustion of the literary" in the field (Moreiras, "Newness" 131), or to what John Beverley has called "the discursive orientalization that has operated, and still operates within the Latin American 'lettered city'" (*Latinamericanism* 21)? Moreover, can the stakes set out in Lispector's mediation of death in *A hora da estrela* productively provide us a new, improper, and untimely opening to alterity, subalternity, and the debate on the literary?

Predicated on an inversion of Madame Carlota's prophecy, Macabéa's death ends in melodrama. But, significantly, this is a far cry from the melodrama of narrative identity politics, whereby writing would endeavor to capture, map, or "transculturate" the subaltern and integrate her into its representational regime.[29] This is a melodrama that defies dialectics.[30] Far from encountering her fairy-tale prince, as she begins to cross the street— "moved by words"—Macabéa is run over by a yellow Mercedes (79). We next find Macabéa curled in a fetal position on the asphalt, like a question mark, but also struggling for life like a nascent embryo. Macabéa's death reads in slow motion with enigmatic undertones. "Vou fazer o possível," Rodrigo relates, "para que ela não morra" (I'm going to do everything possible so that she doesn't die) (81).

Rodrigo postpones Macabéa's death, deferring it across a sequence of self-reflections that concern his role as creator and critic of the text. Rodrigo becomes endlessly refracted across the broken body of writing's limits. For the extent to which Rodrigo reflects on the meaning of Macabéa's death is the constantly interrupting measure by which he questions his very own authority and limits as a writer. Indeed, death becomes the site of a fundamental transmutation of roles: Macabéa's hour of death constitutes her "cinematic" stardom, marking the end of the protagonism of the narrator's writing project (83). "Macabéa killed me," Rodrigo states (86).

Enigmatic promise of closure, but also the affirmation of a new beginning, the question of death for Rodrigo constitutes the promise of "self-encounter" (*A morte é um encontro consigo*) and of symbolic "resurrection" (86, 83). We are broaching the promise of the present at stake in Lispector's project, the hour of the subaltern figure's death, but also that of the narrator's authority. Ontological interruption of the narrative universe, the present of the text is configured as a "pulsating inflexible geometry," as a compositional plane of immanence that decomposes the representational flow of the storyline (82). *Death is a self-encounter, is an event of writing* in Lispector insofar as the compositional plane, painstakingly erected in her

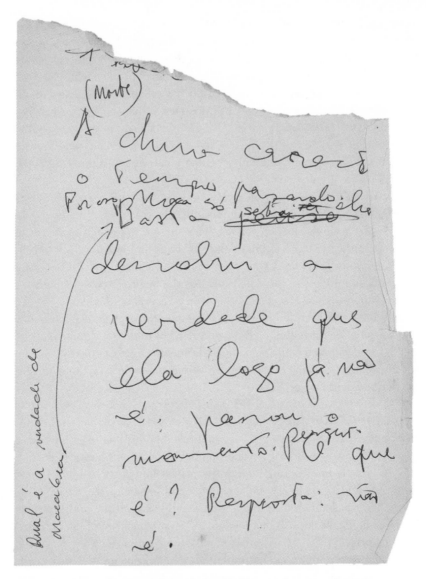

Figs. 1.4 "Morte de Maca" (Maca's death). Manuscript notes for para-
1.5 graphs 483, 484, and 488, *A hora da estrela*. Notes by
1.6 Clarice Lispector and Olga Borelli. Courtesy of the estate of
Clarice Lispector.

work, simultaneously decomposes and dissects its discursive elements—its protagonists, its narrator, its story, its system of symbols, figures, and narrative registers—marking them as constructs like mapped-out lines on the textual surface for the reader.[31]

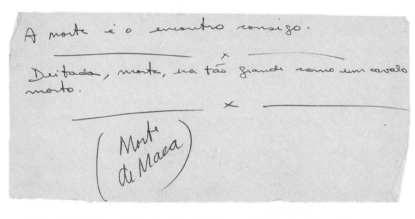

The problem of the reader, tied inexorably to the problem of a radical, de-ontologized present of the literary, is not simple, and it certainly does not hinge on merely making the reader active, as one is wont to say regarding modernist works. With respect to the much-commented "Author's Dedication," Rodrigo states, "Trata-se de livro inacabado porque lhe falta a resposta. Resposta esta que espero que alguém no mundo ma dê. Vós?" (This work is incomplete because it lacks a response. A response that I hope someone in the world will give me. You?) (10).

Previously in the "Author's Dedication" we learn of the narrator's passion for music, whose preferred composers such as Bach, Chopin, Beethoven, and Stravinsky he compares to "profetas do presente" (prophets of the present) (9). The immanence of affect as a becoming, as an ensemble of perceptions and sensations that one undergoes in the present, in Deleuze's lucid account of the percept in art, becomes a vehicle that sheds light here on Lispector's multiple, literary present.[32] But this present, duplicitously inscribed through the literary, is one of self-undoing, of self-refraction, of breaking down, interruption, and undergoing as opposed to dominating.[33] Defying the logic of mastery, it is properly abyssal, feminine, yet affirmative, a present that is constituted on a radical plane of composition that is always more than one. Simultaneous creation and flight into auto-critique, the self-reflexive dimensions of *A hora da estrela*, composed in the final year of Lispector's life, articulate a refractive "opening" to what Gayatri Spivak calls the "undecidable figure" (72).[34]

Not an open-ended exposure to the "other," or a neo-Arielist "orientalization," then, but a maintenance, multiple in stature, of a tension (Beverley, *Latinamericanism* 21). Alberto Moreiras has called the "exhaustion of the literary" the fundamental recognition of the "limitations of representation" and what led him and a host of critics in the field into theory, in an exodus from traditional "literary studies" in the 1980s ("Newness" 131). His overarching question for this generation is "how can recourse to cultural and civilizational elements" become nonidentitarian and "freely strategic" as practices of "non-domination" (Moreiras and Villacañas, "Introduction"). If there is an exhaustion of the literary, this would concern the literary's institutional, identitarian, and representational integrating pretensions, which have been critiqued at length (Moreiras, "Newness" 131).

While the literary may die in Clarice, and with Clarice, it is the condition of possibility for her "yes" to a radical mode of writing that she composes with force in *A hora da estrela*. This is where I am taking Moreiras's lucid appeal a step further regarding the literary regime of representation, and his critique of transcendental, identitarian, and teleological political ideologies that inform the study of literature and cultural systems. It involves a new image of writing at stake in Lispector, concerning not only the problem of the politics of literature, vanguardism, and subalternity in the Brazil of the 1960s and 1970s, but of composition, immanence, and the question of taking positions in the present. It is a legacy and a mark from within the text that begs our *resposta* today. Throughout I have conceptualized the problem of strategy in Lispector as the simultaneous affirmation of the immanent life and death of the text—a text composed and decomposed, affirmed and critiqued, on an incessantly refractive plane of composition so as to charge the reader to see the present as entirely fabricated and a site of struggle, and in consequence, worthy of incessant critique and reconfiguration.[35] This is Lispector's momentous *sim* (yes) to a new image of writing in Brazil of the 1960s and 1970s, one that inaugurates her final novel as a critical enterprise to write the subaltern (*A hora* [1998] 87). She ends it in immanence as an act of affirmation, on the very limits of the literary letter, with the simultaneous death of both writer and figure. Against the "death" of writing, or any rigid modality of identitarian fixity that would claim to speak for the subaltern as a final inflection of the literary regime of representation, the aesthetic dimensions of *A hora da estrela* articulate a *sim* to the exigency and irreducible joy of counterconstructing the present: an act of dis-identification and collective, immanent self-encounter.

Anti-Literature & Politics
in David Viñas

NO ARGENTINE novelist was more polemical, but neither was any nov-elist more maligned. To understand the reason for this, it suffices to un-derscore David Viñas's thesis on the politics of aesthetics: "la estética es, en última instancia, teoría política" (*De Sarmiento* 133). It is not sufficient, however, to show how Marxism and existentialism are combined in this the-sis which affirm the primacy of history even as they deny the idealist order of representation. We should rather begin with the sequence of anti-literary utterances that made Viñas's work an object of derision in 1962. Mere weeks after publishing his best-seller screenplay turned novel, *Dar la cara*, Viñas relates, "Te confieso que me da vergüenza tener que decir literariamente 'doy la cara.' . . . Hoy y aquí el compromiso literario no es más que la ilusión del compromiso. Ser revolucionario en literatura, y quedarse ahí, sólo en ese plano, es darse buena conciencia o hacer carrera literaria" (qtd. in Valverde 115).[1]

Viñas's anti-literary remarks find resonance in the problematic of en-gagement that will mark his generation. Indeed, the rise of Peronism in the 1940s becomes shorthand for massive political participation, a tidal-wave phenomenon that will throw all Argentines violently into history. "The very identity of the intellectual and artist in the relationship between culture and politics," notes Oscar Terán, "was undergoing a process of reformation" ("Culture" 271).[2] Just as with Lispector's Brazil during the 1960s, we readily perceive in Viñas's anti-literary utterance the harrowing context of a radical process of transition in Argentina. It is a time of populist, revolutionary fervor in which avant-garde proposals increasingly posit literature's limits and exhaustion. Moreover, much ink will be spilled calling for the dissolution of art into politics, even as the autonomy of intellectual labor is placed in question.

This chapter examines the force of Viñas's anti-literary legacy, the very problem of literature's dissolution into politics, cinema, and other media, through a reading of Viñas's polemical best-seller, *Dar la cara*. As a multi-medial text dedicated to the problem of "facing up" and intervening in the present, the novel constitutes, I argue, a radicalized medium that places in question customary accounts of what is meant by literature and literary politics. Accordingly, I begin by challenging prevailing interpretations that have shortchanged Viñas's literature as a vehicle of ideology. I then shed light, for the first time, on Viñas's narrative montage technique as a procedure of the sensible. My aim is to recover an anti-literary, intensive, and polyvocal reading of Viñas's project from the grasp of influential social realist accounts that have failed to reflect sufficiently on the role of affect, cinema, and the multiple regimes of signs at play in his work. Concerned with constructing an alternative way of "committing" literature to the world of politics and intermedia, I conclude by showing how Viñas's hybrid work produces a generative, self-reflexive, and multimedial "body" of language that demands a new poetics of reading the limits, porous borders, and politics of literature.

LEGACIES & THE LIMIT

There is a long-standing commonplace among Viñas's critics: his novels shun complexity in favor of the thesis. Emir Rodríguez Monegal asserts "la impericia de Viñas para la narración puramente novelesca" ("David Viñas" 325). For Rodríguez Monegal, Viñas's novels are full of "defectos" because they lack "el medio tono de la presentación objetiva de la realidad" (326). We will return, of necessity, to the problematic of the "real" and an impure, powerfully polyphonic "medio" in Viñas. But let us continue navigating the long line of literary criticisms. Another claim concerns Viñas's well-documented relationship to Jean-Paul Sartre. For Oscar Masotta, Viñas's novels ultimately fall short of the Sartrean "model" due to the author's affection for "general ideas and schematic proposals" (143). Masotta argues that Viñas's idea of a "committed literature" rotates around "lo irreflexivo"; that is, through passion, spontaneity, sincerity, and "fluid expression," Viñas aims to exercise "una relación de fascinación sobre el lector, a despertar su pasión" (124).[3] There is no question: Viñas's technique involves the matter of the affect. And his project is certainly indebted to Sartre.[4] But we must tread with due caution, as Viñas never relied on any master. There is no ideological motivation, only ever a doing with and against Sartre's writings. It is enough to pinpoint the problem of underdevelopment and cultural colonialism that pulse through the pages of Viñas's work. And yet what we here witness—even in Masotta, a colleague and friend—are the contours of a literary tribunal that buries Viñas's contributions for their impurity and *anti-literary* quality.[5]

The revolution taking place in Argentine criticism in the 1950s and 1960s is largely ignited by Viñas and his brother, Ismael, in the legendary journal *Contorno*. Brandishing the banner of "revista denuncialista," which should be read, in the spirit of Domingo Sarmiento's *Facundo*, as an irreverent translation of the French *existentialiste*, the Viñas brothers, notably alongside Rozitchner, Jitrik, Sebreli, Gigli, Alcalde, and Masotta, will construct an anti-genealogy of Argentine literature. *Contorno* significantly displaces the Argentine literary fathers with pariahs of the literary regime: Roberto Arlt and Ezequiel Martínez Estrada. Now to denounce one's "contorno" for Viñas means precisely this: to demystify all values that imprison Argentine reality through a stagnant set of representations.[6]

In Viñas's thought, Argentine literature has become a breeding ground for idealism. Literature not only ignores the primacy of the body but breeds narcissism and widespread passivity. To be sure, literature inscribes a way of being. It is a polyvocal way of relating with life, and very concretely, with politics. And it is only from the vantage of the rejection of literary idealism, literature as a concrete struggle over experience, that Viñas's approach is understood. As already indicated, in 1962 Viñas detonates a polemic on the impotence of "literary" intellectuals: "el intelectual argentino no sirve concretamente para nada. . . . Tendríamos que analizar lo que se conoce con el nombre de burocracia literaria" (qtd. in Valverde 114). Against the "dulce y respetada inoperancia del escritor" that assumes the book as model or "mirada" of the world, Viñas's writing unfurls as a heterogeneous working of matters ("Escribe" 15).[7] The body will serve as its model—the body in extension as opposed to the finalist illusion of a pure subject that controls its environment through representations. The notion of what is meant by "literature" in Viñas is nothing short of the image of the pure, the decorative, the spiritual, and the organic. For this reason, Viñas will associate "literature" with the saintly and the bureaucratic. Alienated from the body, from social experience, from the masses, "literature" violates experience. From his readings of the Argentine literary tradition, he will decipher a series of *sometimientos* (subjections).[8] Viñas never stops denouncing the fact that one is subjugated by dint of historical habit to a fixed "spiritualist" image of literature, even as one writes from the body to decode it: "hace

CONTORNO
REVISTA DENUNCIALISTA

Número 2 dedicado a ROBERTO ARLT

CeDInCI

Fig. 2.1. Flyer for *Contorno*, issue number 2, dedicated to Roberto Arlt (May 1954).

falta instalarse en otro lenguaje para ver la relatividad y límites del lenguaje burgués" (*De Sarmiento* 133).

If Viñas is always at the border of the literary, in what precise sense does his project dismantle "literature"? According to Viñas, Argentine literature's redundant, reified avatars—historically grounded in liberal idealism, "reason," and notions of progress—will not be dethroned through propaganda, the social realist insistence, or through the aping of Sartre. Rather, similar to Lispector, what is at stake is a necessary regeneration of language that purges it of the abrasions and ideological clichés of bourgeois calculative logic. Literature must turn against itself, in opposition to its historically sedimented image, and thereby become uncertain of itself in its most intricate texture. In effect, any consideration of the core problems of politics, literature, history, and realism in Viñas hinges on an understanding of how he manipulates multiple regimes of signs as a means of exploring official discourse's limits. Let us begin our reading, then, at the limit of Viñas's critical reception, with a consideration of the writer's underappreciated relationship to cinema.[9]

In collaboration with movie director José Martínez Suárez, Viñas completes the screenplay for *Dar la cara* in 1962.[10] Yet prior to the film's screening on November 29, he is already a rising star in the industry. *To overcome the writer's alienation in the age of mass communications*, in interviews, Viñas never ceases to affirm cinema's promise of diffusion and potential political impact. Indeed, Viñas will write the screenplays for Fernando Ayala's blockbuster, *El jefe* (1958), and the less acclaimed *El candidato* (1959), even as he actively incorporates montage technique in his early novels: "[f]íjate, tu ojo está en función de ver cine, es inherente a la literatura" ("El cine" 14).

Viñas's cinematic involvement is part and parcel of an unprecedented historical pact between literature and cinema in Argentina during the 1950s and 1960s. And this coming together of the arts arises no doubt from an opening for free expression unleashed by Perón's fall.[11] Tomás Eloy Martínez has clearly demonstrated that the various relations holding between Argentine cinema, commercial film, propaganda, and the state reach a crisis point following the military's ouster of Perón in 1955. To situate this shift, it is useful to recall that in the years leading up to the 1950s modern Argentine cinema turns largely on the mythic narration of Creole origins.[12] Underwriting this tendency is the militarized unity of the culture industry. We underscore here the military regime's creation of the Sub-Secretariat of Press and Information in 1943, whose task will be to ensure "the defense and exaltation of the historical tradition, culture, and moral and spiritual values of the Argentine nation" (Eloy Martínez 9). "Organizing the propaganda of the state," the Sub-Secretariat exhibits, by decree, national films every two months for the duration of a week, with the proviso that Argentine state-sanctioned cinema operate as an "instrument of education and illustration bearing on the historical, scientific, literary and artistic archive of the country" (10). Perón will no doubt ratify this measure, but under more stringent conditions that protect the state from any element of critique. Chained to patriotic realism and pedagogy, decadence ensues. In short, the Argentine industry will progressively lose its public and the Latin American markets. Writing in 1962, Eloy Martínez places his finger on an important phenomenon that was widespread during the first Peronist regime: with rare exception, cinema was being made by the same people and through the same schematic, commercial, and derivative formulae of early Argentine cinema of the 1930s. Stunting the spectator's imaginary through the might of an entertainment industry plugged into officialdom, dissonance and contradiction are banned.

As was tacit in his polemical interview statement of 1962, Viñas's early work emerges in response to the crisis in Argentine cultural production. For starters, Perón's overthrow in 1955 provokes disorientation in the industry. Film production wanes, becoming paralyzed in 1956 and for the greater part of 1957. To counter this paralysis, at the end of 1956 the new state designs a statute to promote Argentine film of high quality. Independent filmmaking blossoms, replacing the reign of the stereotype.[13] Consequently, in collaboration with Ayala and Héctor Olivera, Viñas enters the new fray by writing the above mentioned scripts for *El jefe* and *El candidato*. In both films, the allegorical specter of Perón looms large, while generational conflict functions as thematic pivot.[14] Toward a critical, parricidal realism that

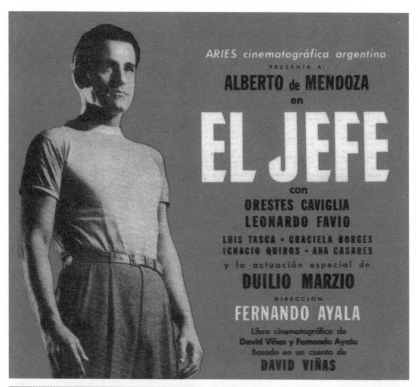

Fig. 2.2a, b, c. Movie posters for *El jefe*, *El candidato*, and *Dar la cara*. Courtesy of Héctor Olivera and José Martínez Suárez.

upends the stagnant values of the Argentine fathers and the transcendental myths of national destiny: the Viñas-Ayala-Olivera collaborations seek to testify to what was widely deemed a betrayed generation. "Debemos hacer de nuestro cine," Ayala affirms, "un testimonio de nuestra época, de nuestros problemas, de nuestros anhelos" (qtd. in Eloy Martínez 22).[15]

In diverse ways, Viñas's cinematic writings frame a generation marked by the irrepressible father figure's abdication (Perón, and later, Frondizi but also importantly the collapse of liberal, oligarchic, and Creole-centered values in the age of industrial society). Reminiscent of Fellini and the films of Italian neorealism, anguished characters traverse an urban, modernizing Buenos Aires. Escaping the confines of the Creole mansion, these youthful social mutants will seek, in whatever corner of the city, through whichever fraudulent act, the upending of all hierarchy. Or inversely, as in Faulkner's sagas of the Old South, a decrepit old guard rehearses the illusion of reviving the past through hopelessly exhausted values. In these anti-Peronist works, characters form no immutable essence or identity. Characters rather emerge as forgers and rejects in a series, as they endeavor to create their lives in a deeply politicized atmosphere. Consider the inaugural tracking shot in *El candidato*. Emerging from the darkness, a strident multitude bursts onto the screen calling for its candidate leader: "Bazan! Bazan!" Or consider the news delivery scene that opens *Dar la cara*: the headlines announce Fidel Castro's revolutionary struggle in the Sierra Maestra.[16] Politics has become an affair of the masses but also an unsettling affair of selfmaking and self-questioning. However much the old order seeks refuge in dilapidated mansions and delusions of past glory, Viñas will weave an unsettling, polyphonic image of time that testifies to the irrepressible heterogeneity of the social body. Individual intrigue is caught up in collective problems. Moreover, if all finalist values are dead, the true is what is made, even if it is fraudulent. Consider the profusion of conmen, commercials, billboards, popular songs, neon lights, modern jazz, radio announcements, and newspaper kiosks that Viñas deploys to attest to the mass syntax of the age. It is an age of the false, of the spectacle, of managed and fabricated affect, but also of urgent revolutionary, global interconnectedness. This brings us to the central problem of realism.

Regarding the stakes of the real in Viñas's heterogeneous corpus, Emilio Bernini has convincingly observed, "[H]ay un proceso indudable de búsqueda de una representación realista, que [Viñas] sin dudas ha impuesto más allá de las decisiones de los directores, puesto que en las películas de Ayala y Martínez Suárez, sin los textos de Viñas, ese realismo—no subjetivo, político, totalizador—no puede reconocerse" (Bernini). Yet would not realist "totalization" in Viñas imply, following Sartre, a rejection and flight from the "equivocal givens of experience" (Sartre, *Search* 24)? This much is certain: *Dar la cara* articulates an allegory of the Argentine "lost generation" of the 1950s and early 1960s.[17] Generational confrontation and existential anguish, after all, line the novel's pages: between youth and elders, sons and fathers, patriarchs and pariahs, free-spirited feminists and dutiful daughters. But it is the staging of experimentation as a radical relation to history and creation proper that the work will insist on telling us. Indeed, if this cinematic novel "tells" us anything, it suggests quite clearly that narrative is no longer successive, chronological, and organized through an organic time-image based on the true. Organized through four chapters and sixty-four episodic cuts, *Dar la cara* effectively utilizes cinematic montage technique to "proliferate perspective and character" (Bernini).

Far from a univocal "totalization" of the social, Viñas's adaptation of narrative montage technique testifies to the desire to write the historical as an always open process. More than this, the stakes of history at play in Viñas's novels might best be envisioned through Deleuze and Guattari's conception of seriality and the habitus. As such, history would designate the set of material conditions and habitual social practices from which one resists the present. For Deleuze and Guattari, politics precedes being, while history is only made by resisting it.[18] Regardless of his debt to Argentine novelist, Roberto Arlt, is there any other way to understand the proliferation of marginals, homosexuals, and *marranos* in Viñas? And can we not read their recurrent crises of consciousness as so many internal struggles to break free from entrenched habits of thought? The image of the vicious circle, the dog eating its tail, configures a matrix trope in *Dar la cara*. Now to "give body to writing," following Viñas's materialist motto, means precisely this: to make of the cinematic-literary work a milieu of sensation bearing on the minoritarian and violence in history. This takes us to the heart of the novel's multimedial project.

THE BORDER & BODY OF DISCOURSE

As a multimedial assemblage, *Dar la cara* defies narrative genre. First a film script, then refashioned as a novel "by addition" in the same year, it can be discussed whether such a work belongs to the very Argentine literary tradition that Viñas will spend a lifetime denouncing (Valverde 298).[19] Published in the same year that witnesses President Arturo Frondizi's ouster by the Argentine military, the work marks a turning point for Viñas that will lead him to renounce literature for four years.

Let us consider this exceptional work's compositional design, including its heterogeneous image of time, and the problem of what I will call the work's inscriptions of a resistant real. According to Bernini, *Dar la cara* inscribes itself at the forefront of a new line of Argentine cinema. Breaking with linear narrative, time in both the novel and film becomes an affair of the simultaneous. Director José Martínez Suárez relates, "El guión permitía abordar tres clases sociales y tres escenarios muy diferenciados entre sí: el grupo del universitario, el de la industria del cine y el del ciclista, que es de una clase social inferior. Había un gran horizonte para trabajar. Podía quedar muy poco fuera de esa 'pintura'" (Martínez Suárez, "Dar la cara").[20] Like a mixed-media collage, *Dar la cara* generates the portrait of a generational crisis within a precise historical framework: 1958.[21] Set in a sprawling Buenos Aires, the work has multiple interlocking plots and a large cast of characters who hail from the spectrum of Argentine society. There is no hero, only marginals in flight: Jewish marranos, subalterns, homosexuals, feminists, moviemakers, activists, cyclists, and writers. The generational theme anchors the work's polyphonic aspiration to chart *a resistant real*: the work focuses on a handful of youth who forcefully break with the establishment. From the initial scene set in the military barracks, a clear allusion to Perón's ouster, we follow the exodus of three youths from three social classes, Beto, Bernardo, and Mariano, who leave the military to enter the immanent flux of time and desire to create their own projects. The existentialist theme is tangible: anguished monologues riddle the work's pages. Yet even as the protagonists abandon status-quo assumptions encircling their class, ethnicity, or sexual orientation, they are far from subjective monads. Nor are they "liberated" individuals. It is significant that the original title for the work was "Salvar la cara."[22] To save face or face up: in *Dar la cara* characters flee majoritarian logics only to fail at forging new social alliances. Everything happens as though the contradictions inhering in the collective situation following Perón's ouster were too large, too big, too unwieldy.

Dar la cara could be likened to a bildungsroman in reverse or an antifoundational fiction: the story of the protagonists ends in non-integration with their social milieu.[23] Narrated in the present, the plot takes place across a fresco of mass situations: we witness firsthand the polemic on the social function of the university and its privatization (*Libre o laica*), the aforementioned independent turn in the film industry, the advent of the Cuban Revolution, and the qualifying cycling tournament for the 1960 Rome Olympic Games. Concerned with intervening in the present, the novel is crosssectioned by references to Argentine history, political figures, and writers and heavily inflected by dialogue and popular speech.

Highlighting the contours of this unfulfilled national allegory, critics have underscored the work's concern with social content. *Dar la cara* fails at totalization, so we read, and the work attests to something like an allegation against the system. In the seams of this failed narrativization, in the troubled, ambiguous stories that the work tells us, we find the allegorization of a stagnant, bourgeois order that has reached its limits. While this interpretation rings accurate, in part, concerning the novel's investigation of an Argentine public sphere in crisis, such a representational reading remains problematic. This is so because the prevailing interpretation hinges on a realist dialectic that pays little heed to the labor of Viñas's medium and the affect. Literature is posited as a vehicle of the state. Similar to Lispector, Viñas will maintain a far more radical project. There will be no purity of form, no neatness of discursive domains, no rote imposition of ideology in Viñas, but rather a redistribution of writing that scrambles all normative majoritarian codes.

As in Sartre's *Reprieve* (1945), which framed for the philosopher-novelist the "interior monologue" of France during World War II, in *Dar la cara* narrative unfurls through the discontinuous perspectivism of free indirect discourse (Sartre, *What Is* 189).[24] Warping in and out of the thoughts of characters, rupturing any chronological sequencing of events, elliptical shifts in perspective are a mainstay in the novel. Moreover, language is structured through kaleidoscopic yet cutting syntactic configurations that mimic mobile camerawork. We are immersed in a multiplicity of proliferating optical, mental, and aural situations that go a step further than the film in framing the intensive texture of this "interior monologue," if we may say so, of Buenos Aires in crisis at midcentury. I hasten to add that both film and novel are organized around the production of an independent film feature whose purpose is to "face up" to the Argentine present. While production of this film-within-the-film fails due to the exhaustion of funds and the directing crew's internal disagreement about the film's purpose, what we are left with at the work's denouement is a chaotic screening of shots taken from the city.[25] Indeed, at the novel's close—and over the course of three of Viñas's more experimental pages—the reader becomes explicit spectator of this failed silent film-within-the-film. Consisting of a mélange of silent shots of the city, and organized through aleatory montage sequences that resist linearity, this film-within-the-film, as Bernini has shown, anticipates the Third Cinema of Getino, Solanas, and Birri. What is more, the film-within-the-film throws light on what was always at work in Viñas: a multi-medial, self-reflexive becoming of his writing as condition for its "politics" of sensory intervention. I hasten to add that syntax, in *Dar la cara*, is always generative and polyphonic. Never settling for stagnant description, Viñas's protean montage prose emphasizes the cut, the prismatic, and the connective. Against what Viñas bemoaned as "the equilibrium" of bourgeois, self-contained writing, and against the redundant purity of Creole-centered cinema, Viñas's composition becomes ever more saturated and intensive. In order to thread this plural text in movement and its inexorable relation to subversion, a reading of parody, cinema, and affect becomes key.

Discourse in *Dar la cara* begins, accordingly, at the border of language and chronology with the prolonged image of a violated body: "Ya iban arrastrándolo hacia el fondo de la cuadra . . . eran tres, cinco, los que lo habían agarrado y lo llevaban en vilo, y en medio de la penumbra Bernardo vio ese cuerpo desnudo: un manchón reluciente en el pecho y algo oscuro en el vientre" (7). Graphic pantomime that will proceed in slow motion for the novel's first five pages: on the last night of his conscription service the wealthy white-skinned nephew of a movie producer, Mariano Carbó, is being sexually harassed—quasi-raped—by a throng of dark-complexioned fellow conscripts. The scene immediately conjures the founding fiction of the Argentine literary tradition: Esteban Echevarría's *El matadero* (1839). In the climax of *El matadero*—in whose story, it should be noted, is inscribed a piercing allegation against the infamous *caudillo* of Buenos Aires, Don Manuel de Rosas—we witness a young gentleman on horseback being ambushed by a gang of social marginals at a slaughterhouse. Tied up like a Christian effigy, the befallen hero experiences a mortal hemorrhage. Curious overture that inscribes a fold within syntax, what are we to make of Viñas's parodic introduction? What is at stake in this evident inversion of foundations, in a work whose title signals a "facing up" to the present?

In his critical writings, Viñas affords pride of place to Echevarría's fallen "poet." For Viñas, Echevarría's martyr delimits, above all, a fissured literary origin. If Argentine literature's origin lies in the specificity of this violence, Viñas reasons, it inscribes itself as such to register a fundamental dissonance in the early nineteenth century: the sacrifice and ouster of the Creole intellectual by his rude brothers, the Federalist masses. But the wider implication, Viñas will insist, is that Argentine literature is born out of an elliptical promise for vengeance. Echevarría's remarkable text marks a debt, a future settling of the score: Argentine literature will henceforward "civilize," represent, and inscribe this "other" as its fundamental matter and task. Literature becomes a civilizing device of national identity and the state.

At the border of literature, *Dar la cara* begins through an act of self-exposure. Interrupting inheritance, syntax unfurls as a passion for the limit. Yet the return to Echevarría's book marks no plenitude, no civilizing vengeance. Refusing to pose matter, the body, the "other," as a presence or frontier that is stable, sufficient, or fundamentally there, syntax enacts a montage sequence of scriptural events. The inaugural parody, thus far from innocent, constitutes a duplicating textual incision; it is a layered discursive space in which one witnesses Mariano Carbó's naked body emerge as multiple and punctured: "Los pies de Mariano aparecieron más blancos que nunca. El mago de la bayoneta, arrodillado entre las piernas, con ese jugo le marcaba unas cruces o las iniciales de alguien" (10). The synecdoche of the violated body as an *infraimage of writing* that defies domination: the movement of writing in Viñas begins through a performative incision that summons an act of reading beyond the boundary of the figure. *Infra*, from the Latin adverbial preposition, relates to that which passes "below, underneath, beneath," as well as to that which comes "later than" or "smaller."[26] Let us underwrite this gesture of self-exposure following Viñas, the saboteur of syntax: the multilayered, inaugural page ushers in an immanent design for writing. In effect, it is significant that this violated *scriptural body* emerges from the refrain, "en medio de la penumbra" (7). The expression will evoke a second border, a second parodic layering: the allegory of Plato's cave. While Plato's cave canonically stages the allegory of an enchained people blinded by false forms, the expression also summons the mainstream Argentine movie house, which in *Dar la cara* represents a cloistered, propagandistic space where false forms reign.

Just as the body of discourse becomes progressively prismatic, so expression in *Dar la cara* will encircle and multiply its referents. Expression precedes content. Form merges with critique. What is "real" becomes. And all becoming, the becoming-cinematic and parodic of prose, finds articulation in the combinational, multimedial character of syntactic design: an *infraimage of writing* that seeks an outside, an escape from all confines, an excess to representation. Outstripping closure from every angle, the procedure of syntactic montage in *Dar la cara* becomes increasingly saturated. Caught up in the problem of the "real," from the titular infinitive, "dar la cara," discourse begins, in other words, from the middle, through the radical self-exposure of the body that forcefully signals yet defies the violence of the literary state.

HISTORY & LITERATURE "A MEDIAS"

The question of subversion, the very problem of "literature" at stake in the novel's overture, results from Viñas's painstaking experimentation with his medium and not from the social realist hypothesis. But other than the parodic sabotage of literary foundations, what are we to make of the work's historical basis? After all, the novel zeroes in on the polemical year of 1958, the year of Arturo Frondizi's ascendance to power. Let us consider this fundamental historical component, what critics have called the novel's drive to realist totalization, and the constellation of events encircling the young Viñas.

Following Perón's ouster in 1955, the Argentine elites succeeded in forming a modernizing coalition. If the masses had been abandoned, so one reasoned, popular political desire needed to be rechanneled. What is more, the new Argentine state had to secure legitimacy in the context of a new world order. Like Brazil and the rest of Latin America during the postwar conjuncture, Argentina had been deemed a peripheral, semi-industrialized nation, a product of the third world. To counter years of uneven development, one had to restore democracy and, above all, industrialize. "La Nación Argentina inicia hoy un nuevo período constitucional," relates President Arturo Frondizi in his inaugural address on 1 May 1958, "que las circunstancias han convertido en comienzo de una nueva era . . . [e]n lo profundo este acto inicial está presidido por un ideal moral: la clara e inequívoca voluntad del reencuentro argentino y de reanudar el desarrollo nacional" (11). But such a reencounter never materializes. The internal scission brought about by Peronism in Argentine society will undermine the liberal dream of a reconsolidated national subject.

If it is true that Perón's fall placed Argentina at a crossroads, then the insistent permutations of the novel's thematic matrix, the dog eating its tail, becomes politically legible: the crossroads inscribes the broken pact, the failed state. Like most elements in Viñas's novels, such figures are not only grounded historically but frame the historically incisive. At the crossroads of figuration and history, in Viñas, the reader is interpellated to consider history critically from the standpoint of representational crisis. For starters, Frondizi's government was the product of multiple broken pacts. If Peronism was outlawed in 1955 by an apprehensive military regime, it is significant that Frondizi rides into power in 1958 only by pacting with Perón and legalizing the powerful Peronist syndicate, the CGT. Frondizi will break this arrangement through multiple crackdowns on the workers' movement in 1959. Even so, hailing from the Unión Cívica Radical, Frondizi represented for many progressives a promising synthesis: a liberal, anti-imperialist who promised to integrate the masses and protect the nation's oil reserves from foreign interests. Disenchanting progressive sectors, including Viñas's brother, who had worked as Frondizi's secretary of culture in 1958, Frondizi allows for the controversial privatization of the university and the nation's oil reserves.[27] While Frondizi's betrayals are legendary, and indeed thematized throughout the novel, it is important to highlight the significance of the Cuban Revolution in 1959. During this age of internal fragmentation brought about by underdevelopment, the Cuban reorganization process—strategically focalized during the newspaper delivery sequence that opens the film and closes the novel—was emblematic of a desired, decolonized nation-state. The inverse of the dog eating its tail, Cuba was visible proof that a Left-driven collective transformation was possible.

Where does this historical crossroads, dramatized certainly in *Dar la cara*, lead the young Viñas? Beginning in the 1950s, following his days of anti-Peronist militancy as president of the University of Buenos Aires, the activity of writing for Viñas unfolds across two core problems: as a response to underdevelopment and as a means of creating a new anti-literature. In effect, due to literature's seeming irrelevance in a rapidly modernizing public sphere, for Viñas, one had to create a discourse capable of engaging the ambiguous character of the Argentine present.

Against the literary establishment in the 1950s, embodied in the figures of Borges, Ocampo, and Mallea, Viñas's discourse moves in three directions: to Sartre, to Latin America, and to cinema. Viñas will establish his break by inverting what he deemed conformist, idealist, and Eurocentric: an entrenched, state-centered cultural apparatus that failed to perceive its internal limits. Inverting what he considered the master paradigm of the Argentine intellectual's love affair and "sanctification of Europe," Viñas turns his gaze turns to the south, certainly. But more important, more concrete, more material and incisive is the radicalization to which Viñas subjects his creative medium. Viñas will find a way to break through the historical limits of official literature. To traverse the limit, Viñas counterposes an alternative discursive body, namely, a multimedial, historically inflected literature "a medias" and its powers of finitude against the idealist impositions of the Creole literary state: "Escribir aquí es como preparar una revolución de humillados: opaca, empecinada, casi dura y casi cotidiana. Como vivo en un país semicolonial soy un semihombre y un casi escritor que escribe una literatura a medias" (*Las malas costumbres*).[28]

Underscoring the limit and the suggestive image of this literature "a medias," we recall that the central film-within-the-film sequence turns on a parody of Fernando Birri's photodocumentary *Tire dié* (1958) and Roberto Arlt's novel, *El juguete rabioso* (1926).[29] Like the inaugural parody of Echevarría's *El matadero* examined above, the recourse to such marginal works is fundamental, albeit corrosive. Indeed, the parodic gesture sheds light on a new relationship to literature and life: against the canon, Viñas forges a palimpsestic perspective that explores history at its crossroads and steepest gradients. Yet against Birri's populism and the then in fashion social realist reduction of Arlt's novels, we would be mistaken to imagine this space as the site from which the "subaltern speaks."[30] And such a space certainly does not ride on an identitarian ground: the center-periphery model from which underdevelopment and Third Cinema theory issue.[31] No, the task of mediating history and politics through parody and cinematic cannibalization concerns an anti-literary gesture that refracts literature's limits.

LITERATURE & SUBALTERNITY

Against the social realist thesis that buries the force of Viñas's legacy, our critical task consists in tracking the ways in which Viñas's montage prose testifies to a new power of relating. Julio Ramos has lucidly shown that beginning with Sarmiento's *Facundo* (1845), Argentine literature assumes a subaltern place vis-à-vis European models. For Ramos, "[i]n Sarmiento a radical mimetic ideology coexists with a critique of the unmediated importation of European knowledge" ("Other's" 9). Literature assumes the capacity to hear "the other's knowledge." Writing from the margin, the peripheral writer "claims a knowledge (*saber*) distinct and at times opposed to the European concept of discipline" (9). In the *Facundo*, the fall of Argentina's lettered class hinges on the exclusion and *misreading* of the gaucho, now incarnated in Rosas and his regime of regional *caudillismo*. Doubtless, during Rosas's reign of tyranny, one had to modernize and reconfigure a public sphere in crisis. And that meant subjecting the new American reality to the discipline of writing. Accordingly, one needed to integrate the world of the other by precisely *hearing* the other's knowledge, and by incorporating its living speech and ways of life into the nation-state. Sarmiento will consequently assign to "literature" an uneven, mediational role. The famed "indiscipline" of Sarmiento's literature authorizes access to barbarian life. Part ethnography and part poetry, "literary" writing could reconcile two divergent modernities—that of the lettered and that of the popular subject.

Different from Sarmiento, literature for Viñas in the 1960s had become the site of a profound autonomization of the intellectual disciplines. Literature becomes the name of a specialized, well-regulated discursive domain, the site of a corpus of knowledge and division of well-defined genres that presupposed a certain mode of perceiving and ordering things. Yet like the underlying hybrid project at stake in Sarmiento's *Facundo*, reflection on Argentine literature in the 1950s and 1960s establishes the problematicity of national reality and the Creole class's "other": namely, the waves of Peronist and immigrant masses. As already indicated, debates on Argentine identity, the role of intellectuals, and what to do with the masses proliferate. Art often dissolves into politics. And as we will see in the case of Brazil in the next chapter, mass media, such as film, had come to dominate the public's imaginary.

Like Sarmiento, Viñas will assign literature a subalternist function to mediate between the Argentine lettered class and its margins. But there is a key difference. Through explicit, rationalizing commentary, Sarmiento subjects his unwieldy narratives of the gaucho to the discipline of representation and to an overarching conception of history as progress (Ramos,

Fig. 2.3. Film still from *Dar la cara*: filming the outskirts of Buenos Aires. Courtesy of José Martínez Suárez.

"Other's" 16–17). However hybrid, literature becomes a model for the state. If the radical alterity inhering in the other's orality represented a danger for Sarmiento's discourse, in Viñas, Sarmiento's foundational operation had to be reversed. *To write literature in reverse so as to barbarize writing*: against the image of literature as projection of the rationalized state, Viñas's work forges a "barbarous," intensive mediation of the "real" by condensing multiple regimes of signs. The story of the film-within-the-film is the "savage" focal point through which the questions of aesthetics, subalternity, politics, and writing most poignantly converge.

Working in collaboration with the leftist scriptwriter León Vera and an experimental cameraman, Meyer, we learn early on that Mariano Carbó's independent film feature promises a break with the entrenched national cinema of Creole identity. We recall that Mariano was "violated" by conscripts at the novel's opening. Through parody, Mariano took the place of Echevarría's poet—he is hence the violated "civilized man" of cinema by popular subjects following the collapse of Peronism. Indeed, his father figure, Basilio Carbó, represents the entrenched authority that controls the Argentine cinema scene and whose films no doubt embody the Creole-centered old guard previously discussed. Accordingly, Mariano's break with the father can be read along three parodic, anti-literary lines: (1) Mariano's break will parallel

Fig. 2.4. Film still from *Dar la cara*: the film script and Arlt's novel. Courtesy of José Martínez Suárez.

Viñas's project to invert the historical projection of Argentine literature as *civilized vengeance against the barbarian masses* (first scene of the novel and parody of Echevarría's *El matadero*); (2) Mariano's filming of the city's *villas miserias* will inscribe Viñas's implicit homage and problematization of Fernando Birri's project to film "raw reality" in the photodocumentary, *Tire dié* (1956–60), which was a short "survey" film that chronicled slum life in Santa Fe, Argentina; and (3) taking us to the border of literature and official history, Mariano's film is based on what Viñas deemed a marginal work in its own right, Roberto Arlt's *El juguete rabioso* (1926). Let us briefly focus on the last.

At first glance, it would seem that Arlt's novel constitutes the film's principal topic. We should here underscore that the reference to Arlt in the 1960s conjures the notion of an anti-canonical writer, "un escritor de kiosko," blacklisted from Argentine literature for, among other things, "writing poorly."[32] For Viñas, Arlt summons, moreover, a subalternist discursive space, a site where homosexuals and "los de abajo entran a la literatura" (Viñas, "Roberto Arlt: Periodista" 10).[33] Yet curiously the team never arrives at adapting Arlt's novel. While the film version makes Arlt a focal point—in a remarkable plaza scene, León tosses Mariano a copy of *El juguete rabioso*—in the novel there are only oblique allusions. Arlt is never named. What is

Fig. 2.5. Film still from Fernando Birri's *Tire dié*. Courtesy of the Instituto Superior de Cine y Artes Audiovisuales de Santa Fe Fernando Birri.

more, in the movie as in the book, we recall that the film-within-the-film results in failure: a patchwork of proofs that are never ordered and distributed as a film. The idea of the failed and/or false translation is significant, and takes us back once again to Argentina's literary origins, to the enigmatic epigraphic sequence that inaugurates the *Facundo*. Indeed, like Sarmiento's famous false translation of Diderot, "On ne tue point les idées," to the nationally inflected, "a los ombres se degüella las ideas no," at a structural level, the nonadaptation and, so to speak, false translation of Arlt in the movie summons the notion of an absent center and an irreverent reading and writing space. Something always escapes in *Dar la cara*. And this escape from narrativization is a primary stake of Viñas's anti-literature. Managing to produce a mere patchwork of proofs before Mariano runs out of money, the film-within-the-film will nonetheless endeavor to capture the "real" Buenos Aires. And it will do so strategically by filming the city's slums. I hasten to add that the reference to Sarmiento's *Facundo* plays itself out at the precise moment when the reader becomes spectator of the three-page film-within-the-film sequence. Even if the film is never distributed, even if it is never organized, Viñas makes sure we become reader-spectators of his anti-film. Subverting "literature," then, as it traverses the limit, Viñas's novel interweaves montage and parody to corrosive effect: "Esas imágenes se sucedían en la pantalla de la moviola . . . muchos chicos con banderitas, un reloj, banderitas argentinas, maestras argentinas hablando, Sarmiento, Sarmiento ceñudo, Sarmiento enseñando a leer a niños argentinos, los botones de Sarmiento, medallas, Sarmiento general, un ejemplar del *Facundo*, otra vez los niños con banderitas argentinas, el sol, el sol más cerca, Sarmiento en la cama muerto" (529).[34]

THE LETTER'S LIMIT

If the "world of representation" is marked by the "primacy of identity" according to Deleuze, then the world of *Dar la cara*—rotating around the axis of the failed film-within-the-film—will have made apparent the advent of a mutation within the core of literary representation, a groundless ground that registers a subalternist, anti-literary politics (*Difference* xix). Insofar as Viñas raises the problematicity of forging a relationless relation with the subaltern through literature, could we not envision his protean project as articulating something akin to Jean-Luc Nancy's concept of literature's "death-work" (*Inoperative* 80)?

It is through the transgressive gaze of scriptwriter León Vera that one best focalizes *Dar la cara*'s concern with a certain culture of the book and its undoing. With his last name connoting the true (*veritas*), León is the protagonist through whose eyes is imaged the possibility of an anti-literary practice. There is a force in common to Viñas and León: opposed to conformist generalities, insisting on being in the exception to transcendental laws, each makes of the political a threshold of writing. Even so, León is not without his own internal contradictions. It will be Pelusa, his former lover, who is capable of seeing through his blind spots.

At the center of the book, but omitted from the film, Pelusa accompanies León to an intellectual roundtable discussion on Argentine culture and politics. As the important intellectuals of the day debate the burning topics of dependency theory, cultural imperialism, and independence, she will suggestively liken the scene to Christ's Last Supper:

> "Parece la última cena," calculó Pelusa en su butaca. Una última cena amarillenta, con el manchón verde del tapete que cubría la mesa y esos cinco hombres que se interrumpían, miraba hacia la platea y querían ganar— *Lo único que hacemos es no estar conformes*, le había dicho León—. *Buscamos, eso es lo que hacemos.* Ella no se lo admitía *¡Qué van a buscar!* . . . *Lo que hace cada uno es querer imponer lo que piensa.* —*Eso no es cierto*, protestaba León. —*Sí que es cierto: cada uno tiene su verdad bajo el sobaco y quiere encajársela a todo el mundo . . . Ustedes no quieren enseñar, León, quieren violar a la gente.*
>
> —*Y, será la única manera: si enseñar es violar . . .*
>
> —*¿No ves, no ves?* —lo acusaba ella. Y en ese teatro ya no se aguantaba más[.] (314–15)

Casting corrosive light over León and Mariano Carbó's project to film the "real" Buenos Aires, the flashback riddles the scene of representation. But through its jagged, italicized seams we read the idea clearly enough: *enseñar es violar*. At the roundtable, Argentine intellectuals are staged as self-absorbed saints who robotically "talk like books" (357). Pelusa's insight should be taken quite literally: how to interrupt the "violating," vertical apparatus of the intellectual's gaze? How to arrive at nonpresentable, nonscriptural difference? How to invert the master trope of civilization versus barbarism in Argentina as a vicious cultural circle and state-centered project of representation?

Viñas will take us to the border, to a fundamental mutation within the order of discourse. To capture the truth of the city, as in Birri's documentary, one will dwell in discourse's exception: "[n]ecesitamos una villa miseria," León relates (404).[35] It is only through exodus and exception to conformist powers that one arrives at "facing" the real. Toward the frontier then: the outside is the site of encounters and alliances. But the outside does not articulate a discursive site of redemption concerning the socially downtrodden.

This is not a space of cultural othering, nor does it aim to incorporate the popular subject through recourse to mythic foundations. Rather, marginals issue forward as the site of the nonpresentable.

Herein lies the secret to Viñas's anti-literary poetics: against the dissymmetrical gaze of the intellectual who violates experience and fails to reflect on his hierarchical locus of speech, the work becomes a milieu of mediation through which the boundaries of filming, seeing, writing, and reading converge. After all, the theme of *reading the film* parallels the film's fragmentary mode of enunciation. To be sure, the film's always in question *readability* constitutes the tenuous thread through which the script moves. Mariano never ceases to question León concerning the work's status as cinema—is this really cinema? really?—as well as the public's capacity to understand it.

Certainly, many of Viñas's novels begin with images of a vertical gaze and seem to tell the story of a fundamental violence: *Los dueños de la tierra*'s founding scene, for instance, where we witness, from a hillock, the massacre of indigenous subjects—the historical "conquista da la Patagonia"—at the hands of entrepreneurs at the turn of the nineteenth century. *Un dios cotidiano* begins with an ironic image of Catholic discipline through the eyes of the onlooking priest: children marching in circles as a form of punishment. Even *Cosas concretas* begins by choreographing a gaze over a militant's bruised body. *Dar la cara* is no exception. The work's two film shootings begin by taking us to the city's outskirts. The two scenes configure mirror images, where we witness León in a mentor role to Mariano. Everything happens as though we were watching Sartre's dialogical theater of anguish and choice, not in Paris but in the open space of the Americas, from a bird's-eye perch. One could easily imagine such aerial scenes being taken directly from Pablo Neruda's *Canto General*. Predictably, dialogue revolves around ontological questions, the matter of Mariano becoming "a man" and the film's objectives. In each scene, a subaltern population is sighted: the *villa miseria* and an imaginary Quechua village.[36] In the latter, the image of the infinitesimal Quechua village gives way to an apposite analogy: León will liken the film to "an implacable eye" that is gazing over the city "from up high" and that seizes "people from behind" (394–95).

Meanwhile, in the former, the team descends into the slums. At a loss for words, they will translate their experience to "landing on the moon," to arriving at the final frontier of Spanish conquest, and to discovering the legendary cities of gold (407). Invariably, all referents are inflected by the subject of discourse's colonizing gaze, as the image of Mariano becoming-man gives way to a nonknown entity, an entity that is death-in-life, the subaltern. "Están muertos," relates León, as he descends into the valley (406). Playing

Fig. 2.6. Film still from *Dar la cara*: Pelusa and Beto. Courtesy of José Martínez Suárez.

the role of conqueror, apostle, translator, and vanguard artist, León will call this otherworldly place the real Buenos Aires: "Esto es Buenos Aires . . . [e]sto" (408). Everything which began as an existential question of taking control of one's circumstances, a conversation with Mariano about manning up to life, now unfolds as León's total loss of control as he endeavors to capture the real through the camera. Filming the subaltern at civilization's border: the camera breaks down as a heavy downpour submerges the valley. The univocal gaze of the seeing subject slowly dissolves under the pelting rain and the wads of mud the subaltern is now hurling back at the film crew. For the subaltern will have said "no" and "vayánse" at a crucial juncture: when León attempts to translate or "dumb down" the film project's objectives to the villagers as something like a newspaper story he's in charge of, they will have resisted with all their might the violence of representation and commodification (410). The writing subject loses its power in favor of a resistant real, even as a multilayered syntax is ushered in to expose representation's limits. *There* is a political secret to Viñas's montage poetics: *enseñar es violar*. Mediating between civilization and barbarism, but this time writing Sarmiento in reverse: such is the formula that courses through Viñas's anti-literary work.

Against the prevailing view that declares Viñas's forfeiture of form in the name of the thesis, I have shown that the problem of expression, in Viñas, hinges on the destruction of the myth of the literary subject. Why is the literary subject so inimical to the nonscriptural body, continuously violated in Viñas's works? What is the relationship between the literary subject, the order of representation, and the body in Viñas?

According to Deleuze, the idea of the subject is inexorably linked to the order of representation. Representation erects a dualist subject-object conception of the world. Accordingly, representation cannot register the force of affects, the presubjective and subrepresentational world of affirmed difference: "Representation has only a single center, a unique and receding perspective, and in consequence a false depth. It mediates everything but moves nothing. Movement, for its part, implies a plurality of centers, a superposition of perspectives, a tangle of points of view, a coexistence of moments which distort representation: paintings or sculptures are already such 'distorters,' forcing us to create movement" (*Difference* 55–56). Taking consciousness as its starting point in opposition to all that lies outside it, representation, as propositional consciousness, cannot comprehend the concrete compositional order of causes. "What characterizes [the order of representation]," write Deleuze and Guattari, "is that all matter is assigned to content, while all form passes into expression" (*Thousand* 369). It is instructive to recall that Viñas never stops denouncing literature's betrayal of the body. Literature betrays the body—a nightmare trope in Viñas's novels and nodal inflection in his criticism. But what is actually meant by the body in Viñas? While certainly invoking social marginals, the class struggle, and the subaltern, there is another body in Viñas that surpasses representation and knowledge. Of course, for Viñas, the "bourgeois" body politic not only establishes the order of private property but defends the spiritualist representation of its class as subject of history. Irrevocably sutured to the state, the Argentine literary regime nonreflexively translates, speaks for, and violates its "other" as an identity politics: "Clave central del *libro burgués* que al operar seductora o distanciadamente con los símbolos, 'espiritualiza' la materia organizándose como un mecanismo no de reconocimiento sino de defensa ante los otros" (*De Sarmiento* 124).

In *Dar la cara*, Jewish law student Bernardo comments on how he often forgets and fears his body. At the novel's close, he will not only remember it but forcefully affirm its primacy. When his room is sacked by a group of student fascists who have written on the wall "*Get out Jew*," Bernardo reflects, "Rebelarse, era ser judío para ésos . . . [y] los que no invocaban a los paraísos, sino que *apostaban a su cuerpo y sobre todo a sus manos*: ¡Judíos esos, nada más que judíos!" (586, emphasis added). This affirmation of difference in defiance, as a certain minoritarian becoming-Jewish by Bernardo, does not inscribe a nonreflexive, identitarian conception of the subject. After all, until this final scene of violation that parallels Mariano's at the book's beginning, the question of Bernardo's Jewishness is relegated to an afterthought. Forgetting his body, indeed, Bernardo is more internally torn between returning to Santa Fe as a lawyer or remaining in Buenos Aires, where the struggle over the university continues. But here in resistant response and flight from fascist domination, in the ambiguity of the novel's closure that brings the trope of violation full circle, the becoming-Jewish of Bernardo concerns the affirmation of a body that is, above all, "hands" and exodus.[37] Bernardo as the Jewish marrano, the converted yet impure Argentine Jew, the provincial student in Buenos Aires: as rebel border-hopper, Bernardo comes to know his body in flight, in reaction to fascist inscription, against the perilous writing on the wall: "Los que no se conformaban con lo que les habían enseñado los viejos o en la escuela, y los que tampoco se quedaban tranquilos con lo que habían descubierto, eran judíos, judíos de alma" (586).

Just as with Bernardo's minoritarian-marrano realization, what representation as (fascist) domination really cannot fathom is the compositional character of bodies that trigger resistant writing and thinking in the first place. Such is the primacy that Spinoza affords the flow of affects that one undergoes as a body. "The order of causes," Deleuze writes of Spinoza's immanent conception of causality, "is therefore an order of composition and decomposition of relations" (*Spinoza* 19). Inscribing itself as a fixed, transcendent power over the body, representation will only endeavor to dominate bodies. But the body, according to Spinoza, is best described not as an organic form with parts that are controlled by a center of command (the brain or spirit); rather, the body is incessantly composed and decomposed on an affective, presubjective plane of immanence. In short, the body constitutes a compositional milieu of relations in movement and intensity, as well as a capacity to enter into new combinations, new alliances, and new compositions. Like Viñas's anti-literary medium.

Throughout, we have investigated the conditions of emergence that inscribe the fusion of literature, history, politics, and cinema in Viñas. We have, moreover, mapped a resistant image of writing that places what is meant by Argentine "literature" in crisis. For to effectively read the body, on the one hand, as Spinoza, as Deleuze, and as Viñas, is to arrive at the nonscriptural. It requires dissolving all finalist illusions: "the process of composition must be apprehended for itself, through that which it gives, in that which it gives" (Deleuze, *Spinoza* 128).

One only enters by way of the middle. And for Viñas this means constructing a new language design, an anti-literature that is not based on the myth of a spiritual subject. In a remarkable passage that introduces us to the mainstream cinema scene in Buenos Aires, Bernardo observes a movie poster advertising Viñas and Ayala's very own blockbuster, *El jefe*. Gazing at Viñas's name written in large letters, Bernardo reflects on Viñas's half-Jewish heritage:

> *Próximo estreno en esta sala: El Jefe. Dirección de Fernando Ayala y libro de David Viñas*, leía Bernardo con aire aburrido. "David Viñas." Él lo había conocido: los bigotes excesivos, un poco ridículos. Alguna vez había pensado que se las tiraba de mazorquero para disimular su origen judío. "Medio judío." Judío a medias, mazorquero a medias y ese reportaje al tío de Mariano que parecía un minuet entre dos elefantes pulcros y malignos. "Nos hacen esperar a todos" y golpeteó la espalda contra la pared. *El Jefe. Próximo estreno en esta sala. Dirección de* ... [. . .] Viñas, sí, siguió Bernardo, uno de esos veteranos que siempre daban la lata con lo del 45 esto y lo del 45 aquello. Bueno, hicieron lo suyo. Es decir, se habían hecho romper la cabeza para no comprender nada durante diez años, 1945–1955: diez años repitiendo lo mismo. . . . "Pobres." Próximo estreno en esta sala. David Viñas; y los héroes del 45. ¿Pero quién había entendido algo en ese año? (99–100)

Viñas once said that a text without its context becomes a myth. One could very well add to this materialist formulation: a text becomes myth if it fails to reflect on its limits. Interrupting foundations, this is not simply a question of writing a history inflected literature. It would be a mistake to read the primacy of social content in Viñas as the betrayal of the so-called "autonomy" of the literary or to read his commitment to Marxism as foundational for his conception of literary politics. And it certainly is not a question of merely shocking the reader by laying bare the device. "[O]nly the limit is common," writes Jean-Luc Nancy, "and the limit is not a place, but the sharing of places, their spacing" (73). The collective task of literature, according to Nancy, hinges on the mediation of a shared sensible realm. If capital imposes divisions and representations denying "a preexisting generality," that is, the immanence of the social body, then literature's task is to reconfigure this sensible, living material realm as "a whole of articulated singularities" (75, 76). "[S]ingular beings are never founding, originary figures," Nancy relates (79). There is, accordingly, a "death-work" involved in Nancy's concept of literary communism that maps well onto Viñas: expressive singularities are exposed in common (80). By interrupting the myth of representational fixity and the mythic figure of literature proper, one resists the seductions of spiritualist domination.

Far from foundational, Viñas takes us to the body, to the nonscriptural. Charting writing's encounters with the nonscriptural body—in literature, in film, in filming the subaltern—Viñas suspends what he writes and tells us all along that he is suspending it. Suspending the illusion of representation, in the contours of Viñas's metacritical gesture, an immanent, minoritarian, marrano community is summoned.[38] "Escribir aquí," Viñas writes, "es como preparar una revolución de humillados: opaca, casi empecinada, casi dura y casi cotidiana. Como vivo en un país semicolonial soy un semihombre y un casi escritor que escribe una literatura a medias" (*Las malas costumbres*).[39] Such are the stakes of Viñas's self-proclaimed literature "a medias." Composed by a marrano, that is, by this Jew "a medias." As a duplicitous pun suggesting the notion of the medium and underdevelopment, the expression "a medias" also inscribes the notion of the figureless border that restores immanence to a common field of relating. The border never exists in and of itself: a literature that is halfway literature, a literature that parodies and profanizes the Argentine tradition, and a literature that cannibalizes film. Even as it inscribes history, in proliferating syntactic arrangements, that undo linearity and blur discursive distinctions. Why should we insist on the force of such borders in Viñas? Because the border pulses through his work, because the border unfounds even as it bounds, and because it is only through the border that a marrano identity-skirting register emerges as a power and politics against "literature."

The Poetics of Antropofagia
in Brazilian Concrete Poetry

OSWALD DE ANDRADE'S legacy has been fettered by a long-standing ambiguity: was his poetry itself really poetry or was it a violently "primitive" anti-poetry? A response to this question begins with Andrade's conception of language. In his famed manifestos, Andrade never stops framing the crisis of poetry. He tells us that lettered Brazilian society codifies everything through Eurocentric erudition. "Eruditamos tudo," Andrade relates with no shortage of sarcasm (*Utopia* 60). Such a lettered class fails to perceive poetry, hidden, *barbarian*, and Brazilian, in the *fatos* (facts) of national existence (*Utopia* 59). Poetry becomes an anti-codifying mechanism, and a creative mode of relating to the Brazilian world. In other words, at the core of Andrade's manifestos is a forceful contestation of a certain way of doing poetry. Poetry here concerns a way of relating not only to form, but to Brazilian society, history, and politics. Andrade suggests that the poet has lost touch with the body of language. And this body of language is the language of Brazilian society in the diversity of its rich material composition, from its *favelas* to its locomotives. Claude Lévi-Strauss's notion of the *bricoleur* maps well onto Andrade's procedure: Andrade's poem-collages are constructed from the residue of ready-made structures, including canonical texts, clichés, and poems, and from the icons of popular culture.[1] The poem's central problem will concern its contact or lack thereof with the "actual sensibility of modern man" (Andrade, "Diario" 50). Through brevity, visual layout, and semantic condensation, the poem operates as a multimedia text so as to participate in the language and sensibility of its time.

Just as with the cases of Clarice Lispector and David Viñas, whether we delimit Andrade's project as poetry or anti-poetry today remains a pressing problem. This is so given the fact that scholars rarely frame anthropophagia through poetic or anti-poetic criteria. And when they do consider Andrade's poetry, it is more often framed as an afterthought that privileges an identitarian, consumptive reading of the term. According to Augusto de Campos, Andrade's concept of anthropophagia has been diluted and banalized through a sociological school of interpretation ("Pós-Walds"). According to this view, Andrade's cannibal allegorizes a larger national, identitarian project of consumption, whose task is to critically assimilate European ideas in national coordinates. In reducing anthropophagia through an identitarian framework based on consumption, critics have not raised the question of what I call anthropophagia's subversions of the sensible, that is, precisely how and to what extent anthropophagia intervenes as a multimedial anti-poetry with respect to the sensible distribution of social reality. Such a vision concerns a new understanding of Andrade's legacy that has nothing to do with the representational order. Through a reading of Andrade's poetry, I argue that the critical force of his cannibalistic poetics lies not in identity but in its self-reflexive, multimedial defiance of representational logic. Consequently, my reading shows how Andrade's poetry not only blurs the boundaries between poetry and pop culture but performs a powerful syntactic and sensory sabotage of the discursive codes of official culture. This reading will allow me, in turn, to investigate how the Brazilian concrete poets resuscitate Andrade's anthropophagic poetics to take what they famously called the "participatory leap" into politics during the 1960s.[2] In the spirit of Andrade's anti-poetry, which concerns its violent "disidentificação" with the literary regime through "versos pondo em crise o verso" (verses placing in crisis verse), I illustrate how the largely misunderstood participatory leap hinges on the ways in which the concrete poets "devour the non-poetic" so as to renovate poetry in a public sphere in crisis (Pignatari, "Marco" 46, 52).[3]

With respect to this anti-literary reflection that unites Andrade with the concrete poets, for almost a century critics have bemoaned the fact that Andrade's prized concept of anthropophagia lacks philosophical rigor.[4] Working against this view, my argument is that a keener understanding of Andrade's poetics is crucial. This is so for two interrelated purposes: first, for reassessing Andrade's unquestionable impact on Brazilian experimental poetry and the arts in the twentieth and twenty-first centuries, and second, for reexamining the subversive force of anthropophagia as a multifaceted poetic procedure.[5] More precisely, by conceiving of the text as an intersemiotic assemblage that brings into play a multitude of nonpoetic regimes of signs, I show how the poetics of anthropophagia disrupts the spontaneous logic of the consensus and articulates a disruption of the sensory order of things. Such a poetics constitutes a new image of vanguard writing in Latin America—one that abandons the representational, word-centered function to engage what the concrete poets deemed the postliterary, postverbal era of late capitalism. The gesture is revolutionary, as the poets take the "participatory leap" through the cannibalization of popular media, advertisements, industrial design, and the spectacle of capitalist ideology. The poem interpellates the reader but through an inverse operation relative to Louis Althusser's state apparatus—one that is far from imaginary. As a sabotage of the sensible as ready-made, I show how the poem constitutes itself as an auto-regulative, constellational structure so as to extract from social representations what I theorize as mutant forms within form: new assemblages of enunciation that dismantle and redistribute the codified field of the social. Marking the limits of literature even as it opens an outside space to consumption in late capitalism, I conclude by elucidating the continuity of the anthropophagic, properly political preoccupation in concrete poetry as an untimely matter of counterconstructing the present with a reading of Augusto de Campos's iconic poem, "mercado" (2002).

THE VIOLENCE OF THE NEW

The Brazilian concrete poets offer literary critics a new model: the *paideuma*. Originally a concept created by the German ethnologist Leo Frobenius, for the concretes, the term comes from Ezra Pound's rendition of it in *Make It New* (1935) and *Guide to Kulchur* (1938).[6] Understood as a cast (*elenco*) of poet-inventors whose work displaces the discursive linearity of traditional verse, the concrete poets construct a new framework for examining literary history.[7] Like Borges said of Kafka, the Brazilians "create" their precursors. And they will create such precursors with the idea that experimental, nonlinear poetry possesses the capacity to establish a relationship with the "syntax" of the contemporary world.[8] Through an interdisciplinary approach to language, the poem will intervene in the sensible distribution of reality.

Beginning in 1964, Oswald de Andrade's incorporation will become "the strongest reference of the group, on an equal plane with Mallarmé and Pound: as center of ideas, positions, creations and thoughts" (Aguilar, *Poesía* 67). While references to Andrade prove sporadic in the 1950s, it should be mentioned that as early as 1956 Décio Pignatari will cite Andrade's iconic verse sequence, "américa do sul" (drawn from the 1928 satirical poem "Hip! Hip! Hoover!") in his manifesto "nova poesia: concreta":

América do sul
América do sol
América do sal

Following the reference to Andrade, Pignatari will suggestively call for an interdisciplinary, nonlinear, "pop" poetics: "uma arte geral da linguagem. propaganda, imprensa, rádio, televisão, cinema. uma arte popular" (a general art of language. propaganda, journalism, radio, television, cinema. a popular art) ("nova poesia" 67). Invoking the same poem in 1965, as a "verdadeira tomada pre-concreta" (true, preconcrete position), Haroldo de Campos elucidates Andrade's cut-up technique ("Uma poética" 51). Like a cybernetic machine, Andrade's fragment operates through a procedure of serialization. Foregrounding the idea of Latin America in the initial verse, the fragment morphs into a prism where "América do sol" and "América do sal" constellate. The poem turns on the repetition of the expression "América do" (America of) and vowel permutations that take place in the word *sul* (south). *Sul* becomes *sol* (sun) and *sal* (salt), producing, for Campos, the effect of an ideogram, the sensation of a serialized industrial product, that articulates the idea of Latin American underdevelopment ("Uma poética" 51).

As an art of signs that displaces a literature of representation, Pignatari's rediscovery of Andrade comes about through a consideration of the "anti-literary" ("Marco" 42–43).[9] Andrade's project is anti-literary, Pignatari relates, insofar as it constructs a new language-design (*linguagem*) that breaks the barrier of the verbal by cannibalizing the "nonverbal" (*Errâncias* 46). Echoing Andrade's pun-layered dictum, "a massa ainda comerá do biscoito fino que eu fabrico" (the masses will yet consume the fine cookie I fabricate) (H. de Campos, "Uma poética" 65), Andrade's "ready-made" poetry communicates with the masses insofar as it breaks with official "literature" through its parodic incorporation of mass media.

To grasp Andrade's break with official literature, it is fruitful to consider the genesis of his poetic project and its relationship to language. In Brazil during the 1920s, literary language is contextualized by the tired myths of proper speech. The year 1922 will signal the centenary of Brazilian independence from Portugal, and a second proclamation of independence by a group of deviant artists. "[U]ma sintaxe para a liberdade criadora de nossa gente" (A syntax of creative liberty for our people), Andrade writes, emerges out of the wreckage of the explosively anti-academic Week of Modern Art in São Paulo (*Estética* 54). Jorge Schwartz has convincingly shown that one of the fundamental utopian dimensions of the historical Latin American avant-gardes is "the possibility of conceiving a new language" (*Vanguardia*

55). Andrade will be up to the challenge. In effect, the "cannibalist" turn in the first decades of the twentieth century will inform Andrade's "pesquisa alta" (high research) (O. de Andrade, *Os dentes* 355).[10]

To write, for Andrade, meant to assimilate the lessons of the European avant-gardes from an irreverent, playful, and parodic position.[11] By inhabiting popular speech and media, Andrade's poetry articulates "primitive" Brazilian new man insofar as it places "tudo em questão em matéria de poesia" (everything in question in the material terms of poetry) (H. de Campos, "Uma poética" 9). Such a gesture involves de-sacralizing poetry and ridding the poetic object of what Walter Benjamin called its traditional "aura" in the age of mechanical reproduction. Following Augusto de Campos, one "devours" the nonpoetic to renovate poetry (*Poesia, antipoesia* 7–8). Andrade and the Brazilian concrete poets converge in complex ways over this seminal strategy. In the common search for relevance, the idea of devouring the nonpoetic will not only inspire the "participatory leap" of the concrete project in the 1960s but will continue to inspire the experiments of the Noigandres poets long after. Indeed, akin to Andrade's concern with renovating poetry in an increasingly industrialized society, we do well to situate the Brazilian concrete project as a search to secure poetry's relevance in a public sphere in crisis, where popular tabloids, movies, and music dominated the public's imaginary.

LESSONS, LEGACIES, & LIMITS

As an exodus from the literary regime, one may liken Andrade's anti-literary lesson—that of devouring the non-poetic—to what Nietzsche said concerning the great thinker. For Nietzsche, a great thinker shoots an arrow into the heavens as an untimely yet necessary gesture. In his or her wake, a new thinker picks up this arrow and reconfigures it, shooting it once more into the distance. Untimely yet urgent, the writer's present inscription marks this debt, this lesson, to an interruptive genealogy of radical thought and invention. Indeed, on numerous occasions, Andrade will suggest that Brazilian poets "hear" the lesson of Nietzsche, because for Nietzsche modern poetry's task consists in restoring the kingdom of the primitive, the child, and the madman (*Estética* 117).

Augusto de Campos's "porous prose" poem "América latina: contra-boom da poesia" (Latin America: counter boom of poetry) (1986) forges a vision of poetry from such an arrow (*O anticrítico* 9). Part of the Nietzsche-inspired volume entitled *O anticrítico* (The anti-critic), the hybrid poem levels a critique at the institutionalization of the Spanish American Boom for having forgotten "poesia": "no mercado comun das letras latinoamericanas / (onde só os brasileiros não vendem nada)" (poetry in the common market of Latin

américa latina: contra-boom da poesia

Fig. 3.1. "América Latina: Contra-boom da poesia" (1986), by Augusto de Campos. From *O anticrítico*. Courtesy of Augusto de Campos.

American letters / [where only Brazilians sell nothing]) (161). The poem counterposes an experimental line of Brazilian poetry against the Boom *qua* institution: "de oswald à poesia concreta . . . criou-se uma linha experimental / antropófago-construtivista (from oswald to concrete poetry . . . emerges an experimental / anthropophagic-constructivist line) (162). Campos's line of differentiation between the two Latin American traditions turns on a conception of anthropophagic-constructivist discourse that will incessantly question language-as-structure (*linguagem*), even as it constitutes itself as "um qorpo estranho" (strange body) that defies conventional poetic language (*poesia de linguagem / e não de língua*) (163).

Even as Andrade constitutes the arrowhead of this subversive genealogy, scholars of Brazilian concrete poetry have primarily underscored the centrality of European and international influences such as Pound, Mallarmé, Cummings, and Joyce. When on rare occasions scholars do speak of Andrade's relationship to concrete poetry, the tendency has been to bracket off poetry so as to speak of anthropophagia as a consumptive or identitarian device. What one overlooks is not only the emphasis the poets place on Andrade as the principle for a new poetry, as we can clearly see in Campos's poem above, but the power and intervening force that the concrete poets ascribe to Andrade's poetry as a "strange body" that questions language. To speak of anthropophagia's seminal importance to concrete poetry remains a historical, political, and properly poetic problem. Accordingly, a consideration of the 1960s and its imperative of engagement will help us bring about a truer reckoning with Andrade's legacy.[12]

As we saw previously in the case of Lispector, Brazil in the 1960s witnesses a crisis of the state. The military coup of 31 March 1964 punches a hole in an "ideological atmosphere" that is charged with anti-capitalist sentiment (Schwarz, "Culture" 145). Prior to the coup and immediately after, a Left-oriented populism permeates the cultural field. Public genres such as theater, popular music, cinema, and journalism gain in importance, while literature is increasingly marginalized. "On an ideological level," writes Roberto Schwarz, "we were introduced to an apologetic and sentimentalizable notion of 'the people,' which embraced (and without distinction) the working masses, the lumpenproletariat, the intelligentsia, the financial barons and the army" (131). However diffuse such a social program might have been, Schwarz underscores a central problem: "intellectual production was beginning to reorient its relationship with the masses" (135). In effect, after the coup, the search for the revolutionary intensifies. However, it will not be until Institutional Act V in December 1968 that the military renounces its compromise: closing the national Congress, it will institute censorship, suspend habeas corpus, and begin a harsh crackdown on intellectuals.

Responding to the crisis of verse, at a conference in 1961 Décio Pignatari calls for Brazilian concrete poetry to take the "participatory leap." In his essay "Situação atual da poesia no Brasil" (Contemporary situation of poetry in Brazil) (1962), Pignatari will chart the achievement of concrete poetry as having "desloc[ada] a linha divisória entre poesia e prosa" (dislocated the divisive line between poetry and prose) (65). By dissolving the normative genres and restoring to poetry a self-reflexive, intersemiotic communicational capacity, concrete poetry participates in the "syntax" and "physiognomy" of the times. The word becomes an isomorphic word-thing (*palavra-coisa*) that micro-aesthetically communicates its verbal, vocal, and visual structure. No longer entrapped by sense or the limits of lyrical subjectivity, the concrete word becomes a sensory synthetic ensemble that explores its dynamic structure as a being of language. It is no coincidence that the question of participation, then, turns on the notion of the poem's mobility: it will "leap" into political "participation" but only through a structure that is dynamic and self-reflexive of its limits. "A poesia concreta," writes Pignatari, "vai dar, só tem de dar, o pulo conteudístico-semântico participante. Quando — e quem — não se sabe. Nem se será percebido, numa sociedade onde a poesia, sôbre ser gratuita, é clandestina" (Concrete poetry is going to produce, it only needs to produce the meaningful-semantic-participatory leap. When—and who—one does not know. It won't even be perceived in a society where poetry, being gratuitous, is clandestine) (66).

One neglected "secret" behind the participatory leap, I would like to suggest, is the lesson of Andrade's cannibal, as well as a careful reading of the ways in which the concrete poets endeavor to create multimedial poems that sabotage the sensible. Pignatari intimates as much in his "rediscovery" article of 1964: "A poesia concreta cortou as amarras em 1958, retomou Oswald e deu uns passos adiante, rumo a um novo salto radical. Suas mais recentes realizações — a serem dadas a público ainda este ano — envolvem a criação de novos alfabetos, novos léxicos, nova sintaxe e novos conteúdos" (Concrete poetry broke free from its chains in 1958, resuscitated Oswald, and took steps forward, on the way toward a new radical leap. Its most recent creations—to be made public this year—encompass the invention of new alphabets, new vocabularies, new syntax and new contents) ("Marco" 54). Akin to Andrade's *Pau Brasil* revolution in the 1920s, the participatory leap will consist in the radicalization of poetic language through the cannibalization of multiple regimes of signs. These include the invention of wordless semiotic poems, collage-posters, and murals that "devour" the icons of popular culture with a critical function that is far from representational. Abandoning a word-centered understanding of poetry, we broach what Pignatari calls Andrade's "roteiro" or anti-literary, internationalist itinerary that the concrete poets will actualize in the 1960s and beyond.

Even so, failing to perceive the problem of the sensible at stake in the participatory poems, critics have not judged the experiments kindly. Nor have they unearthed the critical force and specific ways in which Andrade's legacy lies at the core of the concrete project. Indeed, in his influential book-length study on the movement, Gonzalo Aguilar has problematized the reach of the participatory leap and its hybrid semiotic experiments. He does so by arguing that the poets fail to question their own "modernist principles" of composition. Let us read in detail his argument:

> The first number of *Invenção* . . . announced the beginning of a new phase of the [concrete] movement, that [the poets] called "the participatory leap." But *the modernist criteria were so engrained [persistentes]* that it is much more adequate to invoke the figure of the *turn [viraje]*—as opposed to the "leap"—to describe this change, since the members of the group did not question their presuppositions but rather became concerned with integrating—from their poetics—the changes of their surroundings [*entorno*]. . . . The participatory leap was, more than a contribution to a revolution that ultimately never took place, the experience of *a collision between two*

paradigms of modernism and political experience. . . . The lack of resolution for this tension between the specific situation of field and extra-artistic reception made it such that the "participatory" stage ended up lacking the necessary continuity and persistence in the concrete works. Already in the third volume of the [*Invenção*] review, *the question of engaged poetry seemed a thing of the past*, and in the fourth, the presence of Oswald de Andrade eclipses the previous positions and redefines them.[13]

Aguilar's conclusions are compromised by a concern with what he calls the fixed persistence of the modernist criteria of "homogeneidad, autonomía y evolución" (homogeneity, autonomy and evolution) (150). Anchored to these criteria, Aguilar's approach cannot register precisely how the concrete poem "participates" as an interdisciplinary ensemble of expression and perception. That is, the modernist criteria do not allow Aguilar to read the political implications that follow from these explosively experimental, antiliterary texts. Pignatari will relate: "A coisa, não a idéia da coisa" (the thing itself, not the idea) ("Marco" 53).

While Aguilar's reading is evidently important insofar as it provides a precious mapping of Brazilian concrete poetry's genesis and trajectory, he does not fully investigate the inner life, sensory force, and legacy of Andrade's poetic procedures in the participatory concrete poems of the 1960s.[14] To the contrary, Aguilar's reading sets up a counteraesthetic order to an implied real order of politics as positivity. Such a framework does not account for concrete poetry's intervening capacity at the level of the sensible distribution of social reality. If there is "participation" in this poetry, it would not be either of the extremes: propagandistic or a matter of creating a poetic language of "subtraction" and "contradiction" with respect to real political experience.[15] Participation would concern, as I illustrate in the pages that follow, the poem's intervention as an interdisciplinary ensemble of expression.

Returning to Andrade's legacy and lesson, we could say, following Deleuze, that experimental writings constitute an event on the edge of language (*Essays* v).[16] Traversing the boundary between poetry and nonpoetry, such limit-works do not impose a counterform and representation to the political order, a subtraction that is autonomous and purely aesthetic, but rather unfurl as a living, forceful intervention at the level of the formation of symbols, perceptions, affects, and repressive habits. And so the question remains: what is the revolutionary force that one can extract from an anthropophagic poem? Whither the poetic force of anthropophagia, and precisely how does it unfold in Brazilian concrete poetry?

A CANNIBALIST POETICS

Prior to the 1960s, Andrade's poetic works remained relegated to their initial print runs. This was due largely to a narrow understanding of Andrade's poetry. For example, in an influential publication, *Apresentação da poesia brasileira* (1945), acclaimed poet Manuel Bandeira concluded that Andrade's poetry was the verse of a novelist "em férias" (on vacation) (139).

Beyond Bandeira's ungenerous judgment, what do we mean when we speak of Andrade's cannibalist poetics? In his essay "A crise da filosofia messiânica" (1950), Andrade argued that when man ceases to devour man, he turns the other into a slave (143). This image of Andrade's thought refers to the anthropophagic rite of devouring one's enemy so as to transform and absorb the adversary's powers. The procedure articulates the permanent transformation of the taboo into a totem, meaning precisely: the transvaluation of what had hitherto served as a limit and adversarial power into a weapon. This new image of Brazilian "primitive" thought defies representation and identitarian logic because the anthropophagic poet devours any higher value that transcends its concrete, material, and ludic compositional coordinates. Thought becomes a reading machine that *devours representation to its bones*: the anthropophagic aphorism and poem seize for thought new values from the digested, de-sacralized structures of old. Indeed, Pignatari suggests that Andrade's compositional procedure configures the contours of the first anti-poetry of the Americas.

Is it an image of the New World or its cannibalistic re-mapping? An element of decoding runs through Andrade's poem "crônica" (1927), published in *Primeiro caderno do aluno da poesia Oswald de Andrade* (fig. 3.2). This poetic field rotates around the axis of the iconic globe sketching, with Latin America as its centerpiece. Like in the works of his Uruguayan contemporary, Joaquín Torres-García, Andrade's "crônica" operates through an epistemological redistribution of hierarchy, no doubt concerning the global North/South divide. More than an anti-Eurocentric sentiment and iconoclastic, decolonizing gesture, the poem's text, written in the register of a micro-fairy tale—"Era uma vez / O mundo" (Once upon a time there was / a world) (70)—serves to connect the image-design of the globe to the title and multiple texts of "crônica."

Of course, the titular "chronicle" denotes the series of foundational, European letters of "discovery" to the Portuguese Crown. Beginning with the "Carta" of Pêro Vaz de Caminha in 1500, these epistles mapped Brazil as a tropical Eden, as an outpost of raw materials, and as a site of "savage" future subjects of the Crown in the sixteenth and seventeenth centuries.[17] Defying grandiloquence and the classical verse form, the poem's minimalist

A René Thiollier

crônica

Era uma vez
O mundo

Fig. 3.2. "crônica" (1927), by Oswald de Andrade. From *Primeiro caderno do aluno da poesia Oswald de Andrade*. Courtesy of the estate of Oswald de Andrade.

text—written in the ready-made register of the fairy tale—performs an act of sabotage on official history and the mythical founding narratives of Brazil. Like all the visual poems in Andrade's *Primeiro caderno*, "crônica" unleashes a set of intersemiotic processes. Through its procedure of calling attention to its constructed, metapoetic quality, in its visual and multiple textual registers, "crônica" exposes this foundational form as a fabricated, intersemiotic assemblage.

PERO VAZ CAMINHA

A descoberta

Seguimos nosso caminho por este mar de longo
Até a oitava da Paschoa
Topamos aves
E houvemos vista de terra

Os selvagens

Mostraram-lhes uma gallinha
Quasi haviam medo della
E não queriam pôr a mão
E depois a tomaram como espantados

Primeiro chà

Depois de dansarem
Diogo Dias
Fez o salto real

Fig. 3.3a, b, c. *Upper left,* "História do Brasil," text by Oswald de Andrade and design by Tarsila do Amaral. *Upper right,* "Pau Brasil," by Tarsila do Amaral. *Bottom,* "Pêro Vaz Caminha," by Oswald de Andrade. Courtesy of the estates of Oswald de Andrade and Tarsila do Amaral.

Fig. 3.4. "A Carta" (1500) (The letter) by Pêro Vaz de Caminha. Reprinted from Caminha, "Carta do achamento do Brasil," in *Os sete únicos documentos de 1500 conservados em Lisboa referentes à viagem de Pedro Alvares Cabral*, edited by Abel Fontoura da Costa and Antônio Baião.

The transgressive mapping of national origins in "crônica" coincides with Andrade's project of *Pau Brasil* poetry.[18] Published in 1925 in Paris with illustrations by his then-lover and future spouse, Tarsila do Amaral, the title, *Pau Brasil*, refers to the iconic brazilwood tree, the first product of commercial interest to the Portuguese in the sixteenth century. It is significant that *pau*, in Brazilian Portuguese, conjures the irreverent image of a phallus through paronomasia. Andrade's vanguard *Pau Brasil* poetry is no doubt a play on the notion of disseminating Brazilian poetry as a product of export, as opposed to the formulaic lyric of an entrenched, Parnassian lettered class.[19] The book's cover design by Amaral mirrors Andrade's antifoundational project: it is a ready-made flag, like the encaustic paintings produced by Jasper Johns some thirty years later, which disrupts the modernizing slogan, "Ordem e Progresso."

Divided into nine sections, the first sequence of poems is entitled "História do Brasil" (figs. 3.3a, 3.3c). This sequence of poems constitutes a collage of ready-made citations from the founding chronicles of Brazil by European scribes, monks, missionaries, pioneers, and the prince of Portugal, Dom Pedro. As in "crônica," the montage-poems disclose the hands of the saboteur poet, the mixer of discourse.

As a counterfoundational gesture, Andrade's ready-made constitutes a radical metapoetics. Interpellating the reader as critic, the "poem" devours representations and sabotages the hallowed sites of national enunciation. To create the new, Andrade had to traverse the heresies of language, undermining the sacred cows of official history and literature. Andrade's *Pau Brasil* poetry constitutes a countergenealogy of the present. To see the present as fabricated, to invoke Alain Badiou's writings on the legacies of twentieth-century vanguard arts, is to displace the falsely conceived unity of a vanguard national subject, even as it presupposes the crucial insight that poetic writing has a vital stake in the present ("Avant-Gardes" 140).[20] Such a poetry announces a war on the present's manipulations and the untimely coming of an event bearing the directive of radical sensible procedures. This takes us to the core question: what is the critical force of Andrade's legacy in Brazilian concrete poetry?

A NEW LITERATURE

In 1964, the concrete poets begin an active campaign to revive Andrade. The campaign will consist in writing critical essays and introductory pieces to accompany the reissue of Andrade's work. It will also signal the advent of a new phase of concrete poetry: one that is cannibalistic. The studies will uniformly signal Andrade's relevance as precursor and poet-inventor and will serve to legitimize this new poetry as deeply political. In an editorial statement, the new review for Brazilian concrete poetry, *Invenção: Revista de Arte de Vanguarda*, will call Andrade "o principal criador de nossa nova literatura" and dedicate its fourth issue (December 1964) to the tenth anniversary of his passing: "This issue of INVENÇÃO—the fourth—arises deliberately under the invocation of Oswald de Andrade. To Oswald—the greatest figure of our literary modernism and the principal creator of our new literature—we dedicate, in this year that commemorates the tenth anniversary of his death, a special section" (Foreword, *Invenção* 3).[21] In the context of the military coup of March 1964, what are we to make of the heroic invocation of Andrade in the 1960s? Before answering this, we do well to interrogate a set of central problems that contextualize the concrete project in its initial "geometric phase" and its underexamined connection to Andrade during the 1950s. Décio Pignatari relates that Brazilian concrete poetry, consolidated in 1956, establishes a new semantic field of objectivity for poetry ("Situação" 65).[22] By semantic field of objectivity, Pignatari refers, on the one hand, to the concrete poets' conviction that their poetry was up to date with the most radical aesthetic experiments in a world context. On the other, semantic objectivity for poetry relates to the concrete poem's self-reflexive communicative structure. The procedure entails the "concretion" of its verbal, vocal, and visual elements and the displacement of verse, which was identified with convention, subjective expressivity, and lack of rigor. In brief, the achievement of this internationalist vision, which finds suggestive echo in Andrade's aphorism, "Apenas brasileiros de nossa época" (Brazilians only in our time), hinges on establishing a dynamic design for poetry, interdisciplinary in character, that is up to date with the international experiments of its time, including the abstract geometric experiments of Piet Mondrian, Max Bill, and Waldemar Cordeiro (*A utopia* 66).

As we have shown, Andrade already figures prominently in this internationalist constellation of inventor-precursors. In an interview with the newspaper *Diário Popular*, dated 22 December 1956, the poets underscore Andrade as the initiator of a "linha criativa" in Brazilian poetry: "A violenta compressão a que Oswald submete o poema, atingindo sínteses diretas, propõe um problema de funcionalidade orgânica que causa espécie em confronto com o vício retórico nacional" (The violent compression to which Oswald subjects the poem as a means to attain direct syntheses; the poem proposes the problem of organic functionality, which causes a direct confrontation with the vices of national rhetoric) (A. de Campos and H. de Campos).[23] Against an identitarian rhetoric of nationality, the poets highlight the dynamic, nonlinear structure of Andrade's poetry. More specifically, through Andrade's anti-representational montage technique, the reader is forced to participate in the creative process (H. de Campos, "Uma poetica" 21–22).

Fig. 3.5. Photo-montage, "Estela ao Pensamento Bruto de Oswald de Andrade" (Stele for the savage thought of Oswald de Andrade) (1964), by Décio Pignatari and José Nania. Courtesy of the estate of Décio Pignatari.

```
                se
                nasce
                morre  nasce
                morre  nasce  morre
                            renasce  remorre  renasce
                                     remorre  renasce
                                              remorre
                                                   re


                re
                desnasce
           desmorre  desnasce
      desmorre  desnasce  desmorre
                      nascemorrenasce
                      morrenasce
                      morre
                      se
```

Fig. 3.6. "nascemorre" (1958), by Haroldo de Campos. From *Noigandres* 4 (1958). Courtesy of the estate of Haroldo de Campos.

Andrade's synthetic technique violates the traditional structure of the poem: like the concrete poem, Andrade's poetry foregrounds its structure as an operative field of intersemiotic relations. Indeed, in his manifesto for the National Exhibit of Concrete Art in December 1956, Haroldo de Campos underscores the crucial question of *perception of structure* as a central axis on which the concrete project turns: "uma arte — não q presente — mas que presentifique o OBJETO" (an art—that doesn't present—but makes present the OBJECT) ("olho" 73).[24]

Haroldo de Campos's iconic "nascemorre" (is born/dies) (1958) is exemplary of the "heroic" phase of Brazilian concrete poetry and recalls, if not radicalizes, Andrade's synthetic experiments. The poem constitutes a machinelike semantic field that suspends representation even as it sets in motion, dynamically so, a procedure of visual, verbal, and semantic self-echoing and self-mirroring. Four poetic columns comprising sixteen lines relay, like a dice throw, the combination and countercombinations of six distinct signs: "se / nasce / morre / re / desnasce / desmorre" (if / is born / dies / re / is unborn / un-dies) (103).

The poem configures an ideogram where word and textual design operate through analogies and cross-correspondence, as in the Chinese character. The text's visual image and phonetic echoing constitute a reading space that defies a left-to-right reading sequence and replaces, in consequence,

beba coca cola
babe   cola
beba coca
babe cola caco
caco
cola
        c l o a c a

Fig. 3.7. "beba coca cola," by Décio Pignatari. Courtesy of the estate of Décio Pignatari.

the inscription of a unidirectional poetic logic. Verb and thing, in the web of the ideogram, become inseparable. The problem of movement and the problem of representation are key. The poem ushers forward, across the white spaces that frame it, the communication of its self-referential, dynamic structure as a verbal, vocal, and visual assemblage.

Beginning in 1962, the poets begin to explore explicit political "objects" in their poems. These include, but are not limited to, the problem of subaltern hunger, agrarian reform, capitalist propaganda, the bombing of Hiroshima, and the Cuban Revolution. Even so, we recall that Pignatari's participatory leap insists on maintaining the lesson of formal poetics. A vital tension is summoned. The question remains: how do the concrete poets participate in practical terms? *By revolutionizing language.* To make the poem, as Augusto de Campos states, is to take a risk with language (*Poesia é risco*). In other words, like Andrade's poetry in the 1920s, innovation requires a venture into the desert spaces of nonpoetry.

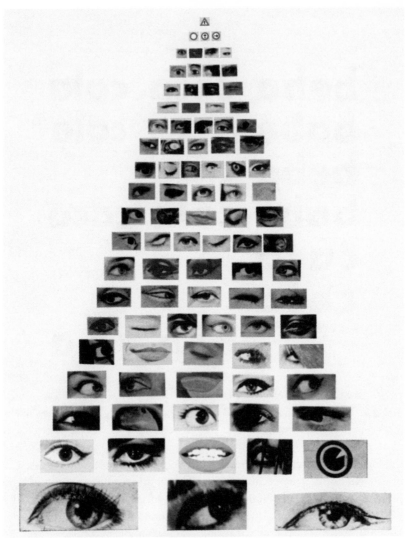

Fig. 3.8. "OLHO POR OLHO," by Augusto de Campos. From *Invenção: Revista de Arte de Vanguarda*, no. 4 (1964). Courtesy of Augusto de Campos.

And yet, already in the heroic phase of the concrete project in the 1950s, Pignatari's iconic poem "beba coca cola" (1957) takes the leap, through the semiotic, into the political field.

Like "nascemorre," this poetic field refracts its structure as a system of ideogrammatic relations. Inhabiting the industrial design of the commercial "Drink Coca-Cola," the poem generates a system of permutations from the series "beba," "babe," "coca," "caco," and "cola" (drink, drool, coca, shard, glue). Reading the first column from top to bottom, one notes that the vowels in "beba" rotationally shift to "baba," producing an emphatic, playful semantic effect: from drink to drool. The same procedure takes place with "coca" and "caco," as though the poem were an auto-corrective, auto-generating cybernetic machine. Every element of the composition interconnects and self-refracts. The word "caco," the broken glass shard, metonymically connects to the term "cola" or glue and the poem's overarching form, as though the self-generating poem articulated its own structure as a constellation of self-reflecting shards from a broken commercial simulacrum. At the poem's base, a mutant, erratic form, "cloaca," issues from the words "coca," "cola," and "caco." Referring at once to a sewage pit and intestinal outlet, the term "cloaca" articulates a pictographic transformation and semantic transvaluation of the Coke advertisement.

From the ad, to its de-coding; from consumption unquestioned, to a countergenerative code that opens the ad to rearrangement. From the heights of utopia promised in the beverage as ideology and commodity fetish, a system of basic, inner material components mutates and moves in a downward spiral to an erratic, outside sewer underbelly. The outside/inside relation inscribes the poem's dissonant, dissensual task: interrupting and inhabiting the ad's image and ideology from within the basic elements of composition, the poetic field works to decode, expose, and generate a mutant form-in-form that opens the field of relations as a field of immanence.

Inspired by Andrade's recourse to the ready-made, Augusto de Campos's poster poem, "OLHO POR OLHO" (EYE FOR EYE) (1964), functions in terms of a singular problem nexus: how to see clearly in the postverbal era of pop culture, the society of images and commodity fetishism? How to create a new syntax for the poem, semiotic in character, that defies the reification of the sensible as ready-made? How to elicit the creativity of the spectator through the collage-poster poem?

Our reading flows from following the poem's structure and expressive dimensions. This poetic field is derived from magazine clippings. Cut-out eyeballs—of politicians, poets, stars, starlets, statues, and animals, accompanied by traffic signs, mouths, fingernails, and machine parts, including the eyeballs of Fidel Castro, JFK, Sean Connery, Pelé, and the poet himself —form a pyramid structure. A heterogeneous set of patterns emerges. At the poem's apex, four tiny traffic signals configure a visual ideogram that bears on a local and epochal political problematic: the traffic signals point to the Brazilian military coup of March 1964, which stifled the Left's ascent, and to the Cuban Revolution. The top tier exclamation hence allegorically marks the head of the pyramid as a site of danger, while the second column indicates that going left is prohibited and that the right is free to pass. The

Fig. 3.9. The Great Seal of the United States.

middle "go ahead" sign, the arrow pointing up, inscribes a metacode for reading the nonverbal syntax of the poem; it also relates to the poem's direct path to the political field as a site of danger.

Following the design further, the poem foregrounds the syntactic centrality of the eye for both poet and reader, as the pyramid forms a veritable eye chart. Indeed, twenty clippings, the majority of which are eyes, configure the pyramid's left and right columns. The poem also cannibalizes the pyramid in the Great Seal of the United States, located most notably on the US dollar, whose singular eye refers to the Eye of Providence that watches over the new world order led by the United States.

If in the age of the society of the spectacle and late capitalism, according to Guy Debord, social relations are replaced by ready-made images, the ready-made image, for the Brazilian concrete poets, had to be cannibalized. The dollar icon itself no doubt functioned as a political sign of

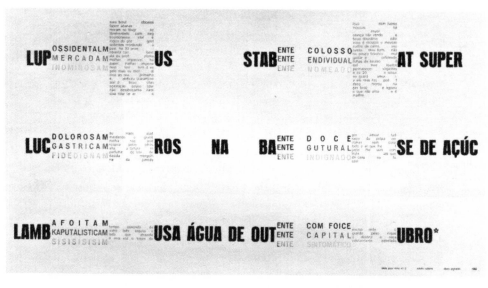

Fig. 3.10. "stèle pour vivre n°3 estela cubana," by Décio Pignatari. From *Invenção: Revista de Arte de Vanguarda*, no. 2 (1964). Courtesy of the estate of Décio Pignatari.

neocolonialism in Latin America. What is at stake, in other words, in Campos's semiotic pop poem is another view of committed literature: an interpellation of the reader as creator-critic from the cannibalized "bones" of popular culture and mass media. By bones, inspired by Oswald de Andrade, I refer to the way in which the poem lays bare its limits even as it devours and redistributes the images of pop culture as so many fragments made relational, parodic, and critical. That is, against the blind celebration of images as imaginary representations that suture the social, we are relayed—across the spaces of the poem—a collage syntax that devours the icons of culture as materials of construction. Hence, the poem throws light on the political, through a politics of the sensible, as a constructivist task for the present.

Pignatari's "estela cubana" (Cuban stele) (1962) constitutes a powerful mapping of a revolutionary crisis in Latin America: the Cuban Missile Crisis. A mural poem, first published in December 1962 in *Invenção* following the Cuban Missile Crisis of October of the same year, "estela cubana," according to Donaldo Schüler, "obliges us to relearn how to read."

As a montage of the Cuban Revolution, "estela cubana" is structured around the typography and semiotic design of a newspaper, and organized through three horizontal headline series and abundant wordplay. For example, the boldface headline caption, "LUP," refers in Latin to a wolf that aims to devour a lamb, presumably Cuba, but also refers to the English word *loop*. Through the pun, the loop iconically denotes aerial projectiles, as in planes, missiles, or spacecraft, but also points to the mutating, expressive dimensions of the poem: iconic readings of words issue, like stars, from the design of words themselves. I hasten to add that LUP suggests the French *loup*, for mask, and also the Spanish *lupa*, for magnifying glass. In effect, the text moves from large font to small, implying the need to read closely and between the lines. The three headline sections evoke the image of the Cuban flag with its three blue stripes; indeed, an asterisk star is positioned in the poem's southeastern corner to corroborate this possible pictograph.

"Estela cubana" utilizes a sequence of intertexts such as Mallarmé's *Un coup de dés*, Aesop's fables, and the biblical book of Genesis. While a detailed analysis of the intertextual complexity of the poem outstrips the purposes of this chapter, I wish to briefly focus on an allegory that the poem develops.

Discerning a logic of connections from the montage of fragments, one reads a vertically descending allegorical system of relationships. In the first subtitle block, the figure of Adam eating fruit emerges. As we see in the upper left corner (OSSIDENTALM / MERCADAM / INOMINOSAM), this allegorical Adam is connected to the Market, to Adam Smith's theory of capital, and to an ominous Uncle Sam. *The poem becomes a geopolitical map that devours all ideologies*: it is important to note that the series of capitalist terms is located in the poem's northern hemisphere, while Cuba and its star are to the south.

The allegory of the forbidden fruit proceeds from the Babelic, pun-driven syntax in the upper level to a clearer syntax in the lower. In this lower plane, where Cuba is located, the fruit is spit out. This spewed-out fruit morphs into an imagistic, asterisk star—the metaform within form—that recalls, from the Portuguese *esputa*, the Soviet Sputnik satellite, the star of the Cuban flag, the exponent sign in mathematics, and the figure of capital as prostitute (*es-puta*). The star-asterisk revolves around the word UBRO, from October, for the Cuban Missile Crisis of 1962, but also suggests the word *urro*, for noise, referring to the poem itself as *counternoise* to the news in the headlines of the commercial media.

The fruit is spit out in what the poem describes as "tempo concreto." The time of the concrete, as in Andrade, is the time of mapping the limits of words as anti-representational elements of composition. If the concrete for the revolution entailed spitting out the fruits of capital, for the concrete poem, politics concerns the radicalization of poetic language. Far from speaking for the revolution, allegory in the poem unfolds as a site of semiotic multiplicities and becoming. In this way, "estela cubana" powerfully maps the poem's limits, not as a passive spectator to politics and history, but so as to create from them a plane of consistency that affirms semantic multiplicity, becoming, and immanence as principles of countercomposing the present.

FABRICATIONS OF A VIOLENT PRESENT

"Só se atinge as massas," writes Pignatari, "sendo-se humanamente radical. Só a anti-arte levará a arte às massas" (One only reaches the masses by being humanely radical. Only anti-art will bring art to the masses) (*Contracomunicação* 125). We have seen how Brazilian concrete poetry in the 1960s claimed Oswald de Andrade's cannibalist poetics and savage thought as its own. The question of the political in concrete poetry, the matter underlying the famed "participatory leap," concerns abandoning not only a word-centered understanding of the poetic but also cannibalizing the sensible as ready-made. Against the grain of a national-identity center, metaphysical in character, we are broaching the matter of an anti-literary image of the Brazilian vanguard tradition.

In *What Is Literature?* (1947), Jean-Paul Sartre famously banned poetry from his model of committed literature. For Sartre, poetry fails to utilize language so as to communicate with the reader. On the side of painting, architecture, and sculpture, the poem is conceived as a word-thing that projects a rarefied, alternative reality, while prose, an art of communicational signs, discloses directly the political situation of alienation so as to provoke the reader's anguish and enthusiasm to change it (21–47).[25]

Against the rigid divide implied in Sartre's curse on poetic commitment, the concrete poets detach the poetic from the literary regime. More specifically, they take the participatory leap, and poetry becomes the site of a risk with and through the languages of intermedia. In so doing, the concrete poets explore, devour, and redistribute, through their poetic experiments, the conditions of the social's intelligibility so as to elicit the reader's creativity. The poet becomes designer of language, a cannibal of intermedia, in the postverbal, postliterary era. This passion for the real within the element of the cannibalization of all formal systems constitutes a critique of a representational understanding of the literary and the political.

As the literary once again finds itself at a crossroads in our global present, what are we to make of Brazilian concrete poetry today and the irrepressible question and legacy of commitment?

Augusto de Campos's poem "mercado" (market) (2002) traces the poem's limits, even as it inscribes the absence of the poetic in the time of the spectacle of late capitalism. Concerned with the present, with our global present, the poem configures a risk: a sabotage of the sensible as ready-made. Throughout, I have highlighted the problem of extracting from the

tudo à venda

cdtvcinema

o gênio da raça

a mortalidade infantil

a má distribuição de renda

a comunicação de massa

a injustiça do sistema

o risco brasil

nenhum poema

Fig. 3.11. "mercado," by Augusto de Campos. From *Não: Poemas* (2008). Courtesy of Augusto de Campos.

concrete text the communication of the auto-regulative structure and its savage mutations as a force and power of the literary. Against seeking equilibrium in representation or confining their texts to a failure to communicate, we are concerned with what is alive and vibrant in these texts that comes about through the interruption of communication as ready-made.

Recalling Andrade's "crônica," the poem cannibalizes the globe as a market where "everything is for sale." At the poem's center, the word "distribution" spins around the three-dimensional globe. The spherical, symmetrical shape of the poem, including the white text against the black background, inscribes a mirroring reading procedure of visual and semantic correspondences, where the first line can be read against the last, "nenhum poema." The metapoetic reference, the form within the form, is key. Articulating an outside space of consumption, a material base with respect to the superstructural engine of ideas issuing from the market's absolute all-for-sale principle, the no-poem mirrors back and inhabits the ill effects and intermedia that produce the global distribution of the sensible. *Nenhum poema*—poetry's limits and absence: poetry becomes the anti-literary form, inhabiting poetry's limits at the limit of an ever-unfolding spectacle of late capitalism. Communicating its structure in spinning circles like news flashes, opening the verbal to the nonverbal, Campos's poem opens us to a re-conceptualization of the poetic that is entirely continuous with the radical, anti-literary Brazilian avant-gardes of the twentieth century. Such a poetry is far from linear and does not impose meaning on the reader. To the contrary, such a poetry articulates a new time for the poetic, a time of the poem's absence and limits, even as it maps as its imperative an untimely counterfabrication of the present.

THE UNTIMELY MATTER OF ANTI-LITERATURE

The Politics of Representation in Haroldo de Campos's *Galáxias* (1963–1976)

DUE TO the crisis of the Brazilian state in the 1960s, the idea of writing becomes opposed to the traditional image of literature. Detached from its representational function, no longer encumbered by an illusion of autonomous purity, what nonconformist, *anti-literary* image of writing is at stake in Haroldo de Campos's monumental *Galáxias*?[1] This chapter provides a reassessment of the legacy of Campos's radical image of writing in its relation to the crisis of the avant-garde and the classical political function ascribed to the Latin American literary, and aspires to chart a new vision, through an immanent reading of *Galáxias*, of the untimely matter of Latin American literary politics today.

Just as with the lesson of Oswald de Andrade's cannibalist poetics in the previous chapter, which entailed the subversion of the sensible as ready-made through sensory synthetic ensembles, the matter of the untimely in *Galáxias* concerns its modes of resistance to the present. Indeed, as articulated throughout this book concerning anti-literature's task for the present, whatever critical force to be extracted from the literary question in Latin American studies begins with a critique of what is meant today by "literature." We will return, accordingly, to the problematic nexus that intertwines literature, theory, the affect, and an untimely "ground" in Campos. But for now it is enough to establish the following thesis: through its formal investigation of what constitutes literary and political materiality, *Galáxias* effectuates a powerful mediation of the social bond that will chart literature's limits and the crisis of intellectuals. A limit-text, accordingly, without linear sequence, but rather operating from a syntactic "flux of signs" without punctuation, Campos's project effaces the distinction between poetry and prose and endeavors to lay bare "language in its materiality" (*linguagem na sua materialidade*) (H. de Campos, "Dois" 112). Revolutionary, engaged with the problem of the representative function of writers, it is an experimental text that approximates a liberated image of theory for reframing the crisis of the social bond.

Critics have commented at length on *Galáxias*'s inscription within the contingent space of the social through the text's system of references and incorporation of popular discourse.[2] And yet in lieu of analyzing *Galáxias*'s intense, permutating redistribution of the social as a politics of the text, they have ultimately softened the hybrid prose-poem's social stakes. For example, Gonzalo Aguilar's *Poesía concreta brasileña* (2003) examines in pioneering fashion the question of politics in *Galáxias* and Brazilian concrete poetry in general. Indeed, Aguilar reads *Galáxias*'s "opening of writing to history" (*abrir la escritura a la historia*) in terms of two vying tendencies—one aesthetic, one political (*Poesía* 359, 358). Yet what prevails, for Aguilar, is not the articulation of the historical but aesthetic "acción restringida" (restricted action) (*Poesía* 359). In other words, Aguilar posits an autonomous literary subject centered in nonfulfillment (*Poesía* 359; "Some" 185). Against the grain of this view that limits politics to a model of representation (*la búsqueda de un fuera-de-texto*) and textual autonomy (*la resistencia de la forma . . . el repliegue hacia sus potencialidades inmanentes*) (*Poesía* 358), in this chapter I investigate the question of *undoing the present* in *Galáxias* as an untimely matter of the literary. In an engagement with contemporary theories of the avant-garde, posthegemony, and subaltern studies, including the writings of Deleuze, Derrida, Gareth Williams, Jon Beasley-Murray, Theodor Adorno, and Max Horkheimer, I provide reflection on the task of subversion in *Galáxias*, as well as the subalternist function of Campos's constellatory writing procedures as nonhierarchical, radical "formas de fome" (forms of hunger).

Throughout my reading, my aim is to tease out the complex ways in which Campos's protean prose poem resists, through a painstaking work on its materials, the order of the present. Such a contestation evidently concerns traditional modalities of doing literature. This *anti-literary* reflection, which concerns the nodal tension between the poetic, the prosaic, and the political in the *Galáxias*, will allow me, in turn, to re-examine Campos's well-documented yet misunderstood "participatory leap." To do so, I provide a comparison of the diverse poetic writing procedures at stake in the *Galáxias* to Ferreira Gullar's "street guitar" poems of the early 1960s. Through a reading of the *Galáxias's* most celebrated "political" text, I conclude by suggesting the ways in which a thinking of materiality in the *Galáxias* allows us to reconceptualize the problem of writing the subaltern and the literary debate in Latin American studies today from a distinctly Brazilian context.

THE DOUBLE DANCE OF WRITING

Composed during the Brazilian military coup of 1964 that would endure through the text's completion in 1976, *Galáxias* problematizes the very notion of literature and the stakes of writing in a socially exigent present. While scholars such as K. David Jackson, Marjorie Perloff, and Gonzalo Aguilar have provided keen analysis of some of the text's salient compositional procedures, we lack a theoretical articulation of *Galáxias* in light of history and the political dimensions that flow from its self-reflexive and affective syntax.

It is difficult to speak of the text in the singular, as the *Galáxias* were episodically composed over the span of thirteen years. Published in book form in 1984 and re-edited in their current, definitive version in 2004, the *Galáxias* consist of fifty nonsequential cantos or mini-stories. Each canto is configured thematically as a microcosm of the entire "bookvoyage" or "voyage of the book" (H. de Campos, "Dois" 112); hence any pretension on the part of the poetic voice to tell a story always folds back to the story or "double dance" (*doppia danza*) of the writing itself (*Galáxias*, "fecho encerro").[3] Embodying the idea of an endless recounting, it is no coincidence that the first "galaxy" parodies the *1,001 Nights*, just as the figure of Scheherazade will reappear, like a specter and feminine generative principle, in multiple instances. The same can be said of the project's parodic close/opening, whose final words invoke the unsurpassable vision, the "doppia danza" of the "true constellation" of the Holy Trinity in Dante's *Paradiso* (*avrà quasi l'ombra della vera costellazione e della doppia danza*). Like a collage that works with the idea of a galaxy of signifiers swarming in self-genesis, the work combines fragments of poems, novels, translations, and personal experiences of the author while traveling. At a linguistic register, the *Galáxias* pulse with a Babel of parodic citations, neologisms, portmanteaus, puns, and foreign words—from Japanese, Italian, Russian, Hindi, German, Spanish, English, and French, not to mention the polyphonic Portuguese of Campos.

The shape of each canto is the run-on constellation. Each constellation expands through word play, repetition, alliteration, and rhyme, which, as Marjorie Perloff has elucidated well, is both visual and acoustic ("Concrete Prose"). Words freely relate to others through the absence of grammar and punctuation. Backwards, forwards, or from the middle—one can begin reading just about anywhere. I hasten to add that the *Galáxias* were originally designed to introduce chance. Structure is thus configured to free the reader; syntax becomes a virtual field of possibilities. For this reason, the first and last texts, entitled "formantes," constitute the project's limits as interchangeable exit and entry points. When Campos published the first twelve *Galáxias* in 1964 in the avant-garde journal *Invenção*, he anticipated completing the multiple "book-object" as a "kinetic sculpture" of loose leaves (H. de Campos, "Do epos" 273). Concerned with weaving a textual fabric that was faithful to the sequence of desire as one reads, the introduction of chance fulfills at least two purposes: (1) such a structure renovates poetry with respect to the other avant-garde arts, such as Pierre Boulez's serialized music, at a time when Campos perceived the literary institution to be collapsing; and (2) chance opens poetry to its "other," as a continual passage to newness and the unforeseen.

As we can see, the problem of language, for Campos, is a complex one. The poet is conceived as *designer of language*. Campos began to brandish this term in the sixties and would never relinquish it. By claiming the role of designer, Campos breaks with the literary regime. To invoke a self-styled metaphor, the poet wages an anti-literary critique against normative forms so as to become a "cannibal" of intermedia. Therefore, when we contextualize the genesis of the *Galáxias* in their sociopolitical context, we do well to highlight the overlooked, yet urgent, political problem of poetic materiality and anti-literature for Campos. After all, in the 1960s, Campos and the Brazilian concrete poets were overwhelmingly critiqued as reactionary for their attack on verse by philologists and militants alike.

Before situating the matter of anti-literature in Campos, it might prove instructive to recall the effective state-popular nexus that breaks down with the military coup on 31 March 1964. Roberto Schwarz has convincingly shown that a Left-oriented populism constitutes something like a tidal wave before and after the coup. Working through numerous channels, such as popular music, football, cinema, theater, journalism, and architecture, the Brazilian populist wave is inherently anti-imperialist and anti-capitalist. Just as the case of populist, anti-imperial, and anti-establishment fervor in Argentina that contextualizes the work of David Viñas in the 1960s, literature and art increasingly dissolve into politics.[4] Schwarz underscores the fact that intellectual production was redirecting its relationship to the masses in an atmosphere of reaction ("Culture" 135). And as illustrated in the previous chapter, it will not be until Institutional Act V in December 1968 that censorship and violence against dissent becomes normative. For Schwarz,

> the coup appears as the massive return of everything that modernization had left behind: it was the revenge of the provinces, of small proprietors, of

sexual and religious prudery, of small-time lawyers. To grasp the extent of this regression, remember that in Goulart's time, public debate had been focused on agrarian reform, imperialism, the minimum wage or votes for illiterates, and so more or less corresponded, not to the experience of the average citizen, but to the *organized* experience of the unions, industrial and rural, of bosses' and students associations, of the mobilized petty bourgeoisie, etc. (136–37)

When Campos writes in his 1964 preface that the *Galáxias* should be read as a free "monólogo exterior. sem psicologia" of "coisas. gentes. visões. contextos. conexos" (exterior monologue. without psychology. things. peoples. contexts. visions. co-nexuses), he is announcing a struggle against literature's relative irrelevance in such a cultural milieu ("Dois" 112). Campos is also highlighting his project's relationship to the "exterior," that is, to the world of politics.

What is at stake when Campos lays claim to such a "real"? No doubt, the crisis of the state unfolds as a crisis of language for the engaged vanguard writer. One of the great historical problems underwriting *Galáxias* concerns the crisis of vanguardism—the loss of the representative function from the standpoint of a collective or group. To be sure, we do well to recall that *Galáxias* is contextualized by the "participatory leap" that the concrete poets announced in 1961 (Pignatari, "Situação"). As illustrated in chapter 3, the "leap" serves as the site through which we witness the founding members of the concrete project diverge in their individual projects as they endeavor to engage the political. Why this divergence? Beyond the raw historical pressure of the 1960s and the numerous critiques leveled at the poets for being alienated, the problem could perhaps best be framed through what Alain Badiou has termed the avant-garde passion for the real as war against semblance. To the extent that, for Badiou, "it's always a matter of going further in the eradication of semblance, representation, narrative or the natural," this is so "because the avant-gardes only think of art in the present and want to force the recognition of this present" ("Avant-Gardes" 132, 134). To break with the order of representation so as to leap into the "real," the preface effectively calls for a prose "without fabulation" (*sem fabulação*) or "hierarchy" (*todos os materias. não hierarquizados*) such that a "present" as "language in its materiality" emerges ("Dois" 112). Retaining this eventual image, we are now prepared to more fully address the current discussion on literary politics in the *Galáxias*.

As already indicated, it is Gonzalo Aguilar's achievement to have examined some of the more radical features of Campos's writing project.

According to Aguilar, "Hay que leer el comienzo de las *Galáxias* . . . en correspondencia con una linealidad evolutiva, esperanza épica en el horizonte potencialmente revolucionario de 1963" (it is necessary to read the beginning of *Galáxias* . . . in correspondence with an evolutionary linearity, with an epic hope in the potentially revolutionary [national] horizon of 1963) (*Poesía* 112). The notion of the text's opening to history, for Aguilar, is the central problematic that underwrites the genesis of *Galáxias*. But what enters into crisis throughout *Galáxias*, for Aguilar, is the very belief in the evolutionary line that underwrites the Brazilian concrete project and its relation to history. One should recall that the Brazilian concrete project, in its "Plano-piloto para poesia concreta" (1958), speaks of an evolution of forms and the exhaustion of verse. Insightful historical reading that correctly attributes to *Galáxias* its inscription as a space of crisis regarding the question of vanguardism in the 1960s, Aguilar's reading is organized through a dialectic that compromises his conclusions regarding the problematic of literary politics.

Aguilar's historical monograph ultimately softens the social stakes at play in the text by reading them through what he perceives as the literary subject's vacillation between the historical and the epiphanic. For Aguilar, to the extent that *Galáxias* "opens writing to history," it does so as a practice that "pone la autonomía de la escritura poética en los límites" (places the autonomy of poetic writing at its limits) whereby the search for the "epiphanic" comes to predominate.[5] To wit,

> [t]here exists, from the beginning of the project, an oscillation between history (epic) and restricted action (albeit epiphanic) that resolves itself in favor of the latter. . . . The evolutionary gesture combines here with a procedure that places autonomous poetic writing at its limits, even though, in the end, a movement in search of the epiphanic in poetic writing comes to predominate. This retreat toward the epiphanic (in the autonomous light that a text emits) is the other face of the frustrated political outlet. Between 1963 and 1976, the years in which these poems in prose were created, the defeat of the progressive movements and the hardening of the military dictatorship in Brazil frustrate these "epic" or utopian "insinuations."[6]

Aguilar's reading is organized through an image of writing centered in an *autonomous textual subject* that is divided at the core of its projection. As deferred action and aesthetic compensation, the poem's political vocation ends in "frustration." According to this view, the line of flight and decoding proper to creation ends in an aesthetic imaginary, self-reflexive of its limits, that does not intervene in the sensible:

In this linguistic constellation of thought, poetry provides all the resources of its materiality and even acquires a certain paradoxical value, on de-sacralizing canonical texts, at the same time that *it sacralizes the poetic act.* It is for this reason that the Haroldian *paradise* is nurtured by the poetry of Dante as a configuring presence of paradisiacal and epiphanic sense. Nevertheless, this paradise is not a transcendental reality but rather an immanent illumination that arises at the moment in which language and thought become galaxy, constellation. . . . The poetic act groups together its materials (discourses, books, mind) and relates them, opening in its imma-nence *the paradise of the poem.*[7]

Beyond this prevailing perspective that limits literary politics to a system of references that slowly loses ground to a self-reflexive interpretation, in what follows, I propose a "materialist" reading of the *Galáxias* through the lens of the sensible, the subaltern, and the untimely.

THE ENUNCIATIVE MODES

Galáxias tells no story, no moral, no sacralization of the text, but rather *un-furls* in its determinate negativity. Configured as a mass of words that are related asyntactically in terms of contiguity and juxtaposition, the text per-forms a generative mode of writing centered in the affective dimensions that flow from signs in their constellatory play. It is a limit-text that approx-imates theory. Defying literary genre, the achievement of Campos's project could be likened to what Badiou calls an "evental mutation" or the "raising up of an inexistent" (*Second* 84, 87). In effect, near the conclusion, the po-etic *I* describes the text as "matéria eventica" (eventic material) ("nudez"). For Badiou, in the wake of an event, there arises a "primordial statement" concerning the appearance of a new "subjectivizable body" (84–85), where "that which had been without any formal value suddenly find[s] itself trans-figured by an unforeseeable shift of the boundary demarcating what is rec-ognized as form" (83). How to perceive such boundaries? Why, where, and how does mutation unfold?

Campos likened the *Galáxias* to ripples on the water over whose refrac-tive surface the entire book could be glimpsed:

> *e começo aqui e meço aqui este começo e recomeço e remeço e arremesso*
> *e aqui me meço quando se vive sob a espécie da viagem o que importa*
> *não é a viagem mas o começo da por isso meço por isso começo escrever*
> *mil páginas escrever milumapáginas para acabar com a escritura para*
> *começar com a escritura para acabarcomeçar com a escritura por isso*

recomeço por isso arremeço por isso teço escrever sobre escrever é
o futuro do escrever sobrescrevo sobrescravo em milumanoites miluma-
-páginas ou uma página em uma noite que é o mesmo noites e páginas
mesmam ensimesmam onde o fim é o começo onde escrever sobre o escrever
é[.]" (*Galáxias*, "e começo aqui")

and I commence here and measure here this commencement and recom-
mence and remeasure and disseminate / and here I measure myself when
one lives under the species of voyage what matters / is not the voyage but
the commencement unfurls for this I measure for this I commence to write
/ a thousand pages to write thousandandone pages in order to end with
writing in order to begin with writing in order to endbegin with writing
for / this I recommence for this I disseminate for this I weave writing on
writing it's / the future of writing I aboutwrite and aboutslave in a thou-
sandonenights thousandone- / -pages or one page in one night which is the
same nights and pages / samingself initselfsamingself where the end is the
commencement where to write about writing / is [.]

The poetic *I* begins his project at the limit: "to endbegin with writing." Living under the species of voyage, he will go on to traverse the border: to
"weave writing on writing." The border, as scriptural threshold, inscribes
discourse at the limits of literary genre: let us consider how space emerges
in media res with the Portuguese conjunction *e* (and). But this initial, impersonal, seemingly insignificant "and" is also a wordplay on the copulative
"is" (*é*): syntax begins by becoming continuous and duplicitous. To write on
the limit: to end/begin with writing is only ever to "measure," "re-measure,"
and "recommence." The proliferation of the vowel *o* establishes not only an
alliterative, rhythmic circuit but is itself an immanent visual design. This
iconization of the letter *o* points to a beginning point, a zero, but also to the
Zen symbol, *enso*. A subject of Japanese calligraphy that Campos will study
throughout his life, the circular *enso* relates to emptiness and void, but also
to enlightenment (*satori*), to the moment when the mind can move past the
realm of illusions to freely create. Connecting to the reverse blank page, the
absence of pagination, as well as to the performative interruption of representation, the *o* connotes what Campos will call, following Roland Barthes,
Galáxias's zero degree of writing. In short, all signs point to the internal
workings of the writing itself. The repetition of the sound "o" moreover
suggests the incantation of the mystical Sanskrit sound, "Om," which is to be
repeated before prayer or the reading of the sacred Vedas.[8]

But we would be mistaken to subsume such gestures as Campos's way of sacralizing his materials. There will be no sacredness of literature, no spiritualization of Campos's materials. The text, after all, insists, persists on its very limits: *in media res*. To be sure, the poem's repetition of the morpheme *meço* parodies Dante's inaugural verse in *Inferno*: "nel mezzo del cammin di nostra vita." *Meço* means "I measure," "I mediate," or "I think" and refers to a precise syntactic operation: the suspension of the storyline in the moment of its inscription. *Meço* also denotes musicality and the score. In an insightful article, K. David Jackson highlights Campos's inspiration in Arnold Schönberg's permutating, dodecaphonic tone row ("Music").

To endbegin writing: in Campos's anti-book of "essays," the idea of the text *as an eventual milieu of sensation* is at stake in each fragment. Coming full circle to a misunderstood critical commonplace: the enunciative modes in *Galáxias* express epiphanic visions over narration. The epiphanic refers not to transcendence, but to the text's materiality, to a logic of limits and sensation. In effect, there is a vision of sensible ecstasy at issue—in a key passage, Campos likens the experience of the text to a psychedelic trip. But such ecstasy turns on a *procedure of expansive concretion*, whereby the sensible dimensions of words unfurl like the interplay of radicals in the Chinese ideogram.[9] Through the suspension of story, representation, punctuation, and pagination, the reader is interpellated to perceive things happen rapidly in the middle, as well as to engage in Campos's query concerning the limits of literature. For "this text that subsumes contexts and produces them as figures of writing" configures "a reproachable ex-permanent-memento of anti-literature . . . a proclivity for anti-art" (*este texto que subsume os contextos / e os produz como figuras de escrita . . . um reprovável experme-mento de aliteratura . . . procliva dessarte*) (*Galáxias*, "mais uma vez," "vista dall'interno"). Indeed, the question of anti-literature takes us to the core of Campos's literary politics.

POLITICS IN *GALÁXIAS*

Inspired by Gilles Deleuze, Pierre Bourdieu, and Baruch Spinoza, Jon Beasley-Murray affirms that social order is secured through immanent procedures, that is, through the affect and habit. Against the prevailing, binary view of a state-centered model of hegemony that attains power through the consent of those it governs, Beasley-Murray declares that hegemony has never existed as a presence. Concomitantly, no ideology can ensure the social status quo or the consent to be dominated. By turning our attention to the social habitus and affects, Beasley-Murray is concerned with explaining immanent material processes common to all, "from the ground up," that is, the modes through which "power works directly on bodies" (xiii). By habitus, Beasley-Murray understands "a collective embodied feeling for the rules of the social game that is activated and reproduced beneath consciousness" (x). At a presubjective, unconscious level, habits, routines, and repetitions structure daily life. Affect, on the other hand, following Spinoza, concerns "the power of a body (individual or collective) to affect or be affected by other bodies" (xi). Against the grain of redundant acts and debilitating habits, one can organize one's encounters, one can combine with other bodies and increase one's powers of affection and action.

The achievement of Beasley-Murray's theory resides in its radical break with the populist framework that informs Latin American cultural studies. It is a vision, in sum, that restores immanence to resistance and critique through an examination of the constitutive power of bodies, and a vision that thoroughly short-circuits shallow, representational understandings of the political. It throws light, moreover, on immanent procedures, on the composition of things in movement at presubjective, intensive levels, as a "logic from below that requires neither representation nor direction from above," for affect and habitus "undo the spatial metaphor of 'above' and 'below'" (xi).

The consequences of Beasley-Murray's posthegemonic vision are, therefore, important for reconceptualizing the legacies of Latin American experimental writings, especially with regard to anti-literary writers, such as Haroldo de Campos, who decisively break the pact with the populist paradigm that informs the Latin American regime of representation. Let us consider Campos's mediation of such a pact in the *Galáxias*.

Composed from January to July 1964, "no jornalário" constitutes a powerful mediation of the collapse of the Brazilian state. The text articulates the desire, as Theodor Adorno said of artworks, for the concrete. And yet the concrete, for Adorno, is what has not yet been (*Aesthetic* 134). Through the painstaking articulation of its materials, through a procedure of negativity that shows no compromise, for Adorno artworks form constellations with "the total nexus of abstraction" that informs the reified, administered society (135). In *Dialectic of Enlightenment* (1944), composed with Max Horkheimer, the authors diagnose the problem of "the weakness of the modern theoretical faculty" and what they call the "self-destruction of the Enlightenment" (xiii–xiv). In their critique, Adorno and Horkheimer are concerned with disclosing the ways in which the "Enlightenment has put aside the classic requirement of thinking about thought" (25), and with unveiling a social order dominated by computation, administration, efficiency, calculation, fungibility, and equivalence where representation as the capacity to dominate reigns. "Bourgeois society," they write, "is ruled by equivalence," such that "that which does not reduce to numbers, and ultimately to the one, becomes illusion" (7). On the other hand, "dialectic," write the authors, "interprets every image as writing," whereby "the task of cognition [no longer] consists in mere apprehension, classification and calculation, but in the determinate negation of each im-mediacy" (24, 27).

In "no jornalário," language is forcefully uprooted from representation. Like Adorno's conception of a negative dialectics, it makes of every habit, every immediacy, an image of writing. Without domination, free from grammar, Campos's text inscribes the constituent power of words and the affective flows that follow from arranged, yet anarchical constellations. Campos's task will consist in de-automating words and affects, in placing words in combinations that gather affective force. Syntax becomes a system of bifurcating traces. Each word echoes the other through juxtapositions, puns, portmanteaus, alliteration, and antithesis. The galactic syntactic procedure unveils the sensory and semantic valences of words as they combine, gather force, and articulate flows of desire. In so doing, as a politics of the sensible, *Galáxias* preserves the intermediate space and the rights of self-reflection—a procedure that is antithetical to sensory deadened habits, and to any project of domination or representation.

"[N]o jornalário" stages the crisis of a society enthralled by the spectacle of the commercial media. And it frames this crisis in terms of a peculiar dialectic: the very composition that one is reading is imaged as a propagandistic, porous book. To be sure, the titular word constellation "no jornalário" refers to the daily news journal as a "river" (*rio*) of signs, but also announces, crucially, the condensation of a social "alarm": "no jornalário no horáriodiáriosemanáriomensárioanuário jornalário / moscas pousam moscas iguais e foscas feito moscas iguais e foscas feito / foscas iguais e moscas no jornalário o tododia entope como um esgoto" (in the journalriveralarmy in the time-tabledailyscheduleweeklyplanmonthlyagendayearbook journalriveralarmy / flies rest flies equivalent and disguised made flies equivalent and disguised made / disguised equivalent and flies in the journalriveralarmy the allday obstructs like a corrupt subterranean conduit). Even as Campos's text simulates the nightmare of a calculated, positivistic world that is likened to an "inferno" (*infernalário*)—where everything is "equivalent" and where "disguised flies" issue from the "journal-river-alarm"—the text transforms its system of objects from the ground up, through wordplay, internal and visual rhyme, and juxtaposition. Form converges with critique. We are broaching the ways in which *Galáxias* articulates a revolutionary approach to politics and culture from immanent, commonly shared materials: from the examination and redistribution of the collective systems of signs, such as the newspaper and news channel, that inform the structuring of culture as a habitus.

From the text's middle, in the flux of rhymes and reversals, Campos interweaves references to the "participatory" poetic experiments of the

```
môsca ouro?            beba coca cola
môsca fôsca.           babe      cola
                       beba coca
môsca prata?           babe cola caco
môsca preta.           caco
                       cola
môsca iris?
môsca reles.                  c l o a c a

môsca anil?
môsca vil.

môsca azul?
môsca môsca.


môsca branca?
poesia pouca.
```

```
atrocaducapacaustiduplieiastifeliferofugahistoriloqualubrimendimultipliorganiperiodiplastipubliraparecriprorustisagasimplitenaveloveravivaunivoracidade
                                                                                                                                            city
                                                                                                                                            cité
```

augusto de campos (1963)

Fig. 4.1. *Upper left,* from "Servidão de passagem," by Haroldo de Campos. *Upper right,* "beba coca cola," by Décio Pignatari. *Bottom,* "cidade," by Augusto de Campos. Courtesy of Augusto de Campos and the estates of Haroldo de Campos and Décio Pignatari.

Brazilian concrete poets. Figures 4.1 and 4.2 show the parodic participatory series in *Galáxias*.

In the 1960s, the Brazilian concrete poetry project takes the "participatory leap" by cannibalizing the new media. That is, by foregrounding, inhabiting, and critically redistributing the systems of signs that issue from the modern city, such as commercial advertisements and industrial design, the concrete poets sought to de-automate language and summon a critical reader to read against the grain of a society ruled by the spectacle. Augusto de Campos's para-syntactic experiment, "cidade" (1963), constitutes perhaps the longest run-on anti-verse in Brazilian literature. By eliminating the suffix "cidade" from a set of words such as "atrocidade" and "caducidade," and by stringing together this long line of word fragments without punctuation, the reader is interpellated to perceive compositional procedure and its becoming from the middle, and to link the word "city" to a chaosmos of desiring productivity, where the blitz of communications and advertisements

sem um numero
um numero
numero
zero
um
o
nu
mero
numero
um numero
um sem numero

Fig. 4.2. "sem um numero," by Augusto de Campos. Courtesy of Augusto de Campos.

never cease. Justin Read has convincingly shown that the poem "cidade" is not only anti-representational but conveys a unique reading practice that places in question civilization's "order." The initial illegibility of the poem "produces a kind of hyperliteracy" ("Obverse" 293). As "an imaginary vir-tualization of the city of São Paulo," the poem ushers in "the time of an 'illiterate literature' that de-composes the *letrado*'s Baroque order of signs of regular stanzas and rational geometric urban plans in harmony with the universe" (295). In similar fashion, "no jornalário" simulates an interface with commercial mass communications so as to subvert their redundant, sensory deadening order as propaganda.

Beyond juxtaposition, the parodic brings to the fore the problematic of the subaltern and its mediation by Campos's experimental text. By the sub-altern, as we have seen in the cases of Clarice Lispector and David Viñas, I refer to not only the socially downtrodden, in terms of individuals or groups, but to the "points of excess" and fissures within state-conceived notions of history, politics, and literature. As an "epistemological limit" and relational term, the subaltern, for Gareth Williams, "obliges us to commit to a thought of relationality and potential finitude" (*Other* 11). During the 1960s, the Brazilian concrete poets mediate the question of the political, and this ques-tion no doubt concerned Brazil's large number of disenfranchised subal-tern populations.[10] Indeed, the problematic of agrarian reform constituted a burning issue for Brazilian poets and intellectuals. Far from speaking for the subaltern, the Brazilian concrete poets construct the self-reflexive, problematical poem. That is, in lieu of seeking to disclose, as spokesmen, a revolutionary present and thereby integrate the subaltern into class warfare, the concrete poets foreground in their poems the limits of the letter and writing's untimely, material force as a politics of the sensible.

For example, consider de Campos's reference to his brother's poem "sem um numero": "e assim reitero zero com zero o mero mero / mênstruo mensário do jornalario" (and so I reiterate zero with zero the mere mere / menstruate menmessager of the journal-river-alarm). Originally published in 1957 as a poem of social protest about the Brazilian peasant, "sem um numero" images the blades of a rotating fan. The first verse, "sem um numero," mirrors the last, "um sem numero," in terms of an antithesis: "without a number" becomes "a numberless number." The central "o" inscribes a reading rotational axis: one can read the poem just as well from top to bottom, or through mirroring, nonlinear rotations. The "o" also constitutes a visual ideogram of the subaltern, the number zero. However, the "o" also configures an incisive pun, denoting the Portuguese conjunction "or." Representation becomes suspended in its tracks. "[S]em um numero" refuses to name or speak for the part that has no part in society, the naked mere number zero, even as it inscribes as the poem's task the exposure of the poem's limits.

Taking stock of this self-exposing gesture as a means of engaging a political crisis, we do well to consider the counterexample of Ferreira Gullar's political poems, "Que Fazer?" (What to do?) and "A Bomba Suja" (The dirty bomb), which he published for the second volume of the collaborative *Violão da Rua* project in 1962. Organized by the Center for Popular Culture of the National Student Union, whose members would read their "street guitar" poems in factories and favelas, according to the poet and contributor Moacyr Félix, the purpose of *Violão da Rua* was to stimulate "the rebirth of a literature that responds to its time" by means of poems that "seek a language that is not distant from popular rhythms" (Félix 10). Through basic rhyme scheme and loose octosyllable, Gullar's poems cannibalize the language and style of the popular northeastern minstrels. To be sure, Gullar's poems issue an image of the poet as the political subject of truth: "Por isso meu companheiro, / que trabalha o dia enteiro / pra enriquecer o patrão, / te aponto um novo caminho / para tua salvação . . . te aponto o caminho nôvo de nossa revolução" (For this reason my companion, / who works all day / to enrich the patrão, / I point out the new path / for your salvation . . . I point out the new path / of our revolution) ("Que Fazer" 41). Published in the same volume, Gullar's "A Bomba Suja" provides, on the other hand, a political meditation on the poetic word becoming "real": "Introduzo na poesia / a palavra diarréia. / Não pela palavra fría / mas pelo que ela semeia. / Quem fala em flor não diz tudo, / quem fala em dor diz demais. / O poeta se torna mudo, / sem as palavras reais. . . . Mas precisamos agora / trabalhar com segurança / pra, dentro de cada homem, / trocar a arma da fome / pela arma de esparança [*sic*]" (I introduce in poetry / the word diarrhea. / It's not by the word's coldness, but by what it can plant. / Who speaks of flowers doesn't say all / who speaks of pain says too much. / The poet becomes mute, / without the real words. . . . But what we now need / is to work with confidence / within each man, / to trade the weapon of hunger / for the weapon of hope) ("A Bomba" 43–45). Meanwhile, in the first volume of the street guitar project, Gullar will publish his cordel-inspired poem, "João Boa Morte" (1962). While a formal analysis of the complex trajectory of Gullar's political poetry far outstrips the purposes of this chapter, suffice it to say that his street-guitar poetry of the early 1960s foregrounds the voice of the poet as the voice of the people that is capable of disclosing the path to revolution. Thus "João Boa Morte" concludes with the poet narrator's lesson: "E assim se acaba / uma parte da história de João. / A outra parte da história vai tendo continuação / não neste palco de rua / mas no palco do sertão . . . Já vão todos compreendendo, / como compreendeu João, / que o camponés vencerá / pela força da união. / Que entrando para as Ligas / que ele derrota o patrão, / que o caminho da vitória / está na Revolução" (And so ends / a part of João's story. / The other part continues / not on this stage in the street / but on the stage of the backlands . . . Now everyone is getting it, / just as João got it, / the peasant will triumph / by the force of the union. / That entering the Union alliance / he will defeat the patrão, / that the path to victory / is in the Revolution) (34–35). The divergence in approach to the political field through poetry, however common the stakes of the crisis, could not be more apparent.[11] Against Gullar's position, the concrete poets will call for a "lucid" mode of participation that carries the investigation of poetic language "to its ultimate consequences" (*leveram às últimas consequências a perquirição da linguagem poética*) (A. de Campos, "Da Antiode" 63).

Moreover, by calling attention to the limits of his project—to the limits of the letter with respect to the subaltern as a constitutive outside to institutional discourse—and through the procedure of calling attention to the now of his writing, Campos's text breaks its pact with the popular and the state. Composition becomes anti-instrumental. And the signifiers of culture are worked on, critiqued, made multiple and intensive, decomposed from their material grounds. The achievement of Campos's *Galáxias* is to have made the solid, wholesome image of Culture stutter and speak in a foreign tongue. I refer, of course, to the image of Culture issuing from the galactic jornalário, "onde nada é vário" and "onde o igual é talqual" (where nothing is varied and the same is always same-such), that is, to the image of Culture issuing from the news and from an unceasing administrative calculus.

WRITING THE SUBALTERN

According to Roland Greene, "circuladô de fulô" constitutes "the program piece of *Galáxias*" ("Inter-American"). As a text that evokes the great line of twentieth-century Brazilian writers who confront the problematic of writing the impoverished subaltern of the Brazilian Northeast, Greene's observation might very well ring true.[12] Yet if there is any "program" for Campos, such a program should be situated historically against the backdrop of his "participatory leap" in the 1960s. Like João Cabral de Melo Neto's *Morte e Vida Severina* (1955), "circuladô," Greene observes, "adapts language of long duration in the Brazilian and Portuguese lyric traditions, [and] directly evokes the minstrelsy of northeastern Brazil." While the meaning of the title, "circuladô de fulô," remains indeterminate, the text stages a powerful encounter between the poetic voice and a subaltern minstrel from the Brazilian Northeast.[13] But against the absolution of difference by claiming that the text "speaks" for the subaltern or simply stands for a textual homage, I want to reclaim the place of a sensory, investigative, anti-literary legibility in "circuladô de fulô" that bears on the crisis of representation and intellectuals that culturally grounds it.

No doubt the encounter between writer and subaltern minstrel configures an ambiguous procedure of identification. The term "circuladô" constitutes a series that connotes circularity, circles, circulation, but also the Portuguese verb *circundar*, which refers to framing, encompassing, surrounding, and limiting. Diction is derived through two principal series. On the one hand, words in *Galáxias* are deployed as a "written body" (*corpo escrito*) concerning the poetic voice's voyage in memory and the unconscious as he writes ("esta mulher-livro"). Far from nostalgic, this singular "corpo escrito" is imaged as always in process, staged through a patchwork of encounters with sundry objects, people, countries, and foreign languages that arise as he composes. The second series concerns, then, the poetic voice's thought and scriptural act in the now.

The task of the poet will be to summon the absolute other: an affective explosion issuing from the margins of the letter and state. He will reach this limit, dwell there in pain, in ecstasy, in delirium, in his experiment, by confessing to us the secret of the subaltern's music through the verbs *guiar* and *faltar*. Taking on a political connotation, the verb-theme "guiar" refers to the act of leading, guiding. But such is the intensity of the music—that sounds like the Japanese three-stringed *shamisen*, yet which issues from a makeshift *berimbau*, made from broomstick, old tin can, and wire—the poetic voice seems to renounce its capacity to guide the reader: "porque eu não posso guiá veja este livro material de consumo . . . / . . . não / sei mas ouça" (because I can't guide look at this material book of consumption . . . / . . . I don't / know but listen). As a pun, "guiar" constitutes a play on the "guitarra" instrument that the minstrel is playing. The pun also suggests a deliberate critique of the social realist *Violão da Rua* project examined above. For here, such a literary politics of the "real" is parodied, suspended, and brought to bear on its limit term, the other side of the popular, the subaltern (Williams, *Other* 15). Words of lack, negativity, absence, hunger, thinness, and poverty form a prismatic and musical series: "onde a boa forma é / magreza fina da matéria mofina forma de fome o barro malcozido" (where good form is / fine emaciation of miserable material form of hunger the badlybaked clay).

Theme-words such as these draw from and expand the problematic of restitution at the text's core: the memory of the marginal's music that has no representation by the state or "patronos do povo" (patrons of the people). The parodic surfaces at a key juncture: "forma de fome." "Forma de fome" references Campos's first "participatory" poetic experiment, "Servidão de passagem" (1962). A form of hunger would refer to desire, to lack, to the hunger for form, for a new poetry, for a new music. But the expression also condenses, through paronomasia, the idea of a form of lessness, a form that is destitute, a form lacking form, like the subaltern as the constitutive fissure in the state. The expression throws light on the political subtext informing the role and crisis of writing in the 1960s in Brazil that here comes to legibility.

The hunger for form constitutes a fracture in the conception of what the poetic voice describes as "the popular" as conceived by "the owners of the people." For just as the subaltern minstrel remains invisible to the "owners of the people," he also remains on the outside of what is considered a majoritarian, national popular culture: "para / outros não existia aquela música não podia porque não podia popular" (for / others he didn't exist that music couldn't because it couldn't be popular). The binary inhering in the popular dissolves into an anonymous, inventive, self-constituting people: "aquela música não podia porque não podia popular / . . . mas o povo cria mas o povo engenha mas o povo cavila o povo é o inventalínguas . . . / . . . mas ouça como canta louve como conta prove como dança e não peça / que eu te guie" (that music couldn't because it couldn't popular . . . but the people create but the people invent but the people object the people are the languageinventor . . . / but listen how he sings praise how he tells experience how he dances and don't ask / that I guide you).

The suggestive, corrosive, self-positing expression *forma de fome*, moreover, articulates an interpellation of the reader that disavows the authority of the writer's status as "guide" for the subaltern. This is not an act of renunciation. And certainly it should not be read as a gesture of simple humility. Deleuze once said that a great writer writes in the place of those who do not or cannot write, even in the place of animals; writes on that which has no-writing; writes so as to become anything, with anything, so long as her writing does not operate under the transcendental premise to end in becoming "the Writer."[14] Accordingly, against the grain of speaking for the subaltern, the self-reflexive dimensions of Campos's *Galáxias* articulate a suspension, a gesture of zero, a naming that names the name from the middle. Such a gesture no doubt preserves the intermediate space. That is, by guarding the very space of mediation, it guards a legibility of the present as suspension and exception—across its central, inexhaustible inscription of the limits and finitude of the letter, the site where naming converges with critique. What is antithetical to instrumental reason, Adorno relates, is theoretical capacity. Defying literature as institution, genre, instrumentation, *Galáxias becomes, in regard to the subaltern, a theoretical dice throw, a performative essay that creates a present.*[15] As an event of writing, it articulates a relationless relation with the subaltern, a rupture in the general laws of appearing and habits that structure the sensible: "mas more no meu momento desmande meu mandamento e não fie desafie / e não confie desfie que pelo sim pelo não para mim prefiro o não / no senão do sim ponha no im de mim ponha o não será tua demão" (but dwell in my moment uncommand my command and don't spin defy / and don't confide unwind that for the yes for the no for me I prefer the no / in the if-no of yes place in the im- of me pose the no will be your tomorrow). It asks us to dwell in the lucid moment of a resistant, reflective thinking and writing of the present that takes as its object the experience of the historical as unique, subversive, affective, from the bottom up, through the space and materials common to all, index of a new legibility. Against "literature," as *forma de fome*: it asks, if anything, for responsive legibility at the limit of all legibility. A thinking of *Galáxias* is a thinking that engages its compositional plane and its coefficient of expansive concretion as the site of redemption with that which remains, in fissures, anonymous, without representation, *formas de fome*, that ask for a new time of legibility today.

THE UNTIMELY MATTER OF THE LITERARY

In the preceding pages, I have attended to the problem of a resistant, untimely materiality at stake in the *Galáxias* that violently overturns the concept of what is meant by "literature." It goes without saying that anti-literary, fissured texts such as these ought never to be subsumed through hermeneutical models. For the *material force* at play in the interior of this work, that double-dancing procedure of writing whose contours I have sought to delimit, is always worked upon by an external system, a galaxy of textual referrals that undo any fundamental basis that would lead one to reinvest said materiality with a logocentric value that exceeds the conditions of its emergence. There will be no complicity with literary idealism in Campos, no falling back onto a transcendental signified. And yet even as I underscore the problematic of materiality in Campos, we must tread with due vigilance.

Readers familiar with *Specters of Marx* will recall Derrida's provocative elaboration of a "materialism without substance" (168). Yet already in 1971, in an interview with two Marxists, Derrida suggestively speaks of deconstruction's relation to matter as a form of "radical alterity": "It follows that if, and in the extent to which, *matter* in this general economy designates, as you said, radical alterity . . . then what I write can be considered 'materialist'" (*Positions* 64). For Derrida, "realism" is a modification of logocentrism. "Matter" becomes problematical, Derrida argues, at the moment when it comes to stand for a "fundamental principle which, by means of a theoretical regression, would be reconstituted into a 'transcendental signified'": "[Matter] can always come to reassure a metaphysical materialism. It then becomes an ultimate referent, according the classical logic implied by the value of the referent, or it becomes an 'objective reality' absolutely 'anterior' to any work of the mark, the semantic content of a form of presence which guarantees the movement of the text in general from the outside" (65). What are we to make of the relationship of "matter" to Brazilian or Latin American literature, and how avoid theoretical regression? Is there such a thing as a properly "Brazilian" or "Latin American" literature? Onward to our day, what is certain is that scholars have long designated "Latin American" literature's principal stake on "matter"—more specifically as a relation of masters and matter, matter understood here as a fundamental, legitimizing principle and fountainhead of the "real." Such an essence, the other posited as the same of the writing subject, is not only weighed down by a transcendental signified, but has long foreclosed discussion on the force of materiality at stake in experimental texts such as Campos's *Galáxias*. After all, we are here leaving the hegemonic grounds of the Boom discursive formation and its literary masters and entering the dangers, the wild, uncharted, absolute heterodoxy of an intervening Brazilian anti-literature concerned with the untimely inscription of its im-proper materiality. It could be argued, to be sure, that Campos's galactic project parallels, if not anticipates, in suggestive fashion, Derrida's critique of a metaphysics of material presence. Let us read Campos's delimitation of a certain understanding of literature as fundamentally underwritten by an ontology of matter and life:

Brazilian literature . . . was "born" under the sign of the baroque. . . . It cannot be understood from an ontological, substantialist, metaphysical point of view. It should not be understood in the sense of an idealistic quest for "identity" or "national" character. As a quest for "national spirit" or "soul" envisaged as a total presence, *terminus ad quem* to be reached after an evolutionary linear process of a biological type based on an "immanent teleology," according to the model proposed by the last century's "patriarchs," of romantic, "organicist" historiography. Baroque, paradoxically, means non-infancy. The concept of "origin" here will only fit if it does not imply the idea of "genesis," of a generative process with a beginning, middle-phase and maturity (or "climax"). . . . Baroque is, therefore, a non-origin. A non-infancy. Our literature, springing up from the baroque vortex, was never aphasic; it has never developed from a speechless, aphasic-infantile limbo into the fullness of discourse. ("Ex-centric" 3–4)

Loosening the limit that has closed "writing," Derrida and Campos suggest that matter be reexamined through the figure of the text. Matter is text, is "woven," is "textile" insofar as one frames it through "the problem of time" (Cheah, "Nondialectical" 146). An interrogation of matter cannot be guided by a fundamental principle of presence, because the order of presence is structured by the persistence, the living-on of forms in time (Cheah, "Obscure" 42). Even as a form repeats and persists in time, it is structurally marked by the giving of time, an incalculable gift of time, which announces the coming of an absolute other. A form, a being, a word is hence always marked and remarked, structurally exposed to the coming of an other that exceeds all oppositions and defies the order of presence. A presence is never fully present but interwoven, divided, and exposed in its repetitions to contamination, to the coming of the other. This is not to say that a presence is structured by a future program, as something scheduled, programmed, and foreseen. No, this coming of the other, for Derrida, is of the order of an event that cannot be anticipated, understood, or delimited in advance. If one could predict this event of alterity, it would never be an event. By the same token, if one could reciprocate this gift of time in a circuit of exchange, it would no longer be a gift. Accordingly, even as time constitutes no presence and withdraws from all visibility, Derrida affirms that "nothing *appears* that does not require and take time" (*Given* 6). Yet because we are finite, time is what we do not possess and what we cannot give (Cheah, "Nondialectical" 146). We cannot contain its overflowing. Time overflows all form. As such, time announces an im-possible gift that is the condition of all that is possible, a non-identifiable, absolute other that one will necessarily experience as nonappropriable. We are broaching the thinking of matter through the frame of the text as event—through a thinking of the absolute other that time gives as affect and arrival of the undecidable. Insofar as Derrida suggests we frame the force of materiality through the figure of the text and through the gift of time, he warns us not to fall into idealism.[16] We would fall into idealism if we limited our conception of the text to an illusory self-present, "pure" textual autonomy. Such has been the prevailing reading of the *Galáxias*. While insightful from the perspective of textual construction, this reading invariably insists on the play of auto-referentiality to the detriment of Campos's project of sensory intervention. Indeed, one idealizes the "autonomous" nature of the text such that its free-play becomes a foundational principle, the inverse of the "real" of metaphysical realism that still haunts the Latin American literary regime.

Against such a "literature," how are we to respond to the problem of matter in the *Galáxias*? Throughout, I have underscored the question of materiality as a certain eventness of the text. For if one posits matter as a presence, we lose all movement and all resistance. There will be no intervention, no operative concentration, no placing in question of rightful beginnings and endings, if we fail to perceive how this extraordinarily mobile text emphasizes a new experience of reading, writing, and relating. At issue is what I would call a certain *inframateriality* that bears on the experience of the text. This experience is nothing other than the text's resistance to domination, calculation, and representation. For Derrida, the freeing of any form comes about through its constitutive exposure to an unforeseen other as an "im-possible" event:

> The im-possible is not privative . . . it announces itself; it precedes me, swoops down and seizes me *here and now* in a nonvirtualizable way in actuality and not potentiality. It comes upon me from on high, in the form of an injunction that does not simply wait on the horizon, that I do not see coming. . . . Such an urgency cannot be *idealized* any more than the other as other can. This im-possible is not a (regulative) *idea* or *ideal*. It is what is what is most undeniably *real*. And sensible. Like the other. Like the irreducible and nonappropriable différance of the other. (*Rogues* 84)

Like all great texts, the *Galáxias* require a new experience of reading. Confounding the order of presence as a "porous" "multibook," such an experience demands the construction of another language. Let us frame/reopen this question of *reading materiality* and *another language* in the *Galáxias* with a consideration of its final experiment.

In the final galactic "formante," otherwise entitled "fecho encerro" (I close I finish), the reader is issued an aporetic injunction: to experience the closure of this "multibook" of sensory constellations as a "multiopening" to an undecidable other. The closure of the book as imitation and model of the world: could the question of writing materiality in Campos be posed otherwise? Under the pun-driven first verse, *"fecho encerro reverbero aqui me fino aqui me zero não canto não conto"* (I close I finish I reverberate here I finish myself here I zero not singing not telling), Campos first tells us that closure is not textual escape or the mere marking of the limit. In the suspension of all telling and singing, in the zero space of representational suspension, closure rather unfurls aporetically as an opening to an irrepressible joy: "I reverberate." But coming back from this singular pleasure in echo, the poetic voice returns and remarks the idea of the book, encircling the book unceasingly, finding its bearings so as to recount its trace and disappearance. Repetition marks a self-dividing mechanism, an iterative structure that exposes the book's insistence on origins and conclusions as a passion. But passion for another beginning and ending is precisely what must be experienced as an escape from the control and mastery of a sovereign voice: *"reverbero não conto não canto não quero descadernei meu caderno / livro meu meu livrespelho dizei do livro que escrevo no fim do / livro primeiro e se no fim deste um um outro é já mensageiro do / novo no derradeiro"* (I reverberate not telling not singing not wanting I unnotebooked my notebook / book mine mine bookmirror I said of the book that I write at the end of / the first book and if in the end another another other is already messenger of / the new in the last). Once the book resurfaces through this grammarless sequence, through the radical circuitry of proliferating synesthetic ensembles, its self-identification becomes elliptical, passionate secret that is incalculable: *"tua alma se lava nesse livro que se alva como a estrela mais d'alva / e enquanto somes ele te consomme enquanto o fechas a chave ele se / multiabre"* (your soul bathes itself in this book that dawns as a dawning star / and as you calculate it consumes you as you close the key / it multiopens).

The return to the book's closure here inscribes an incalculable other. Repeating the book's persistent desire for paradise lost and regained, the repetitive, rhythmical, and ruleless syntax constitutes writing's "multiopening" inasmuch as it provides passage beyond the book's boundary: play becomes operative so as to delimit an escape.

Rendering closure im-possible, this "eventic material" then "proposes the reader as a point of flight" (*Galáxias*, "nudez"). Over the surface of the work's synesthetic plane comes the repetition of the "bottomless dream" of writing, an image of writing as zero and abyss: "um texto se faz do vazio / do texto sua figura designa sua ausência sua teoria" (a text makes of the void / of the text its figure designs its absence its theory) ("vista dall'interno"). If repetition marks an overflowing of the book, then the book has never been present. Its matter, in Campos, was never linear, never a matter of naming, but of multiplicity in texture, weave, becoming through and by means of repetition: a time of writing that is multiple and incalculable. Such a time is an invitation that opens us to "theory," not beyond the boundary of the book, but to a space within it, joyfully, subversively circulating within its folds, undoing its circuitry and drive to self-sufficiency. Trace of the book's undoing, such a space also articulates a movement of freeing from the sovereign subject, to the undoing of the writing subject as master over matter: "deste livro inacabado . . . / . . . onde o vazio / inscreve sua insígnia todos os possíveis permutam-se nesse espaço de / antimatéria que rodeia a matéria de talvez" (from this incomplete book . . . / . . . where the void / inscribes its insignia all the possibles permutate in this space of / antimaterial that surrounds the material perhaps) ("principiava a encadear-se um epos"). The thought of writing at stake in the *Galáxias* implies the closure of the book. Forsaking rules, grammar, and punctuation, yet inscribing syntax as a proliferating sequence of sensory ensembles that affirm play, the aleatory, and endless permutation, the reader must undergo the ordeal of the affect, always undecidable.

Polivozbárbaro. Continuum of mutation and vertiginous experience of breaking the limits, the *Galáxias* mark a freeing of what is meant by literature. And yet the closure of the book does not announce the coming of another language that is fundamentally passive. Far from it. Even as the *Galáxias* de-substantiate the writing subject and its matter of mastery, the coming of the other forces one to act. To pose the problem in terms of force is already to overflow all passivity. Violence carrying literature and politics to the limit, the *Galáxias* intervene by forcing us to read, perceive, and act according to writing's finitude. Forcing language to stutter and speak in a foreign tongue, the *Galáxias* propose a reading of matter not as foundational principle or object of domination but as the singularity and inframaterial principle for another language to come. Marked by the irrepressible scar of dictatorial oppression and censorship, the achievement of Campos's *Galáxias* is to have made this coming language of connections pivot over the problem of matter as seen through the lens of the text. Concerned with the technomediated manipulation of reality, the problem of the subaltern, and the closure of the book, it is to have articulated this text not only through the randomness of chance but as an untimely collective assemblage for resistance: an affair delivered up to the other, in radical self-exposure, so that a present as event incessantly emerges from its politically charged folds.

THE ANTINOMIES OF ANTI-LITERATURE

The Politics of the Baroque in Haroldo de Campos & Osman Lins

The *Galáxias* conclude, in a certain way, the trajectory of Brazilian concrete poetry, which began with the foundation of *Noigandres* [in 1956]. The frondious, furious baroque—junglelike—decanted into a legible geometry, stripped to an almost transparency, like the Mineirian façades of Aleijadinho. . . .

Voice: mobile text in constant progress, Haroldo de Campos achieves a choral and declamatory organization: proliferation of timbres and diverse "colors," polyphony and elocution of textures and gammas at once wrinkled, soft, grave, deep, intimate, neighbor of murmuring—the voice of Maria Bethânia—that modulate and mark the Portuguese of the Americas.

Haroldo de Campos's oeuvre should be seen as the exaltation and unfolding of a *region* of diction, of a space of vast baroque speech like the map of his country: breath of air and articulation, breath and pronunciation: the birth of discourse.

The poem as syllable-germ that bursts, expands in the volume of the page and advances in the direction of concretion. (Sarduy, "Rumo" 125)

THESE LINES appear at the conclusion of Haroldo de Campos's second volume of poetry, *Signantia: Quasi Coelum* (1979). As a reflection advancing the stakes of sensation in Campos's project, we read Cuban writer Severo Sarduy's response with a certain pleasure. For in these remarks Sarduy will

119

make apparent, through his own performative reading, the unfolding of "baroque effects" beyond what is strictly "literary" in Campos. The baroque effect in Campos begins not in ornamentation but through a quickening of language: "concretion would be a particular state of *condensation* of verbal material, of saturation or intensity, of presence of the signifier to itself: *desire of the text* in its corporality that can find itself or coincide with the baroque effect" (Sarduy, "Rumo" 120). Doubtless, we would add to Sarduy's luminous reflection Campos's anti-literary relationship to the outside: syntax unfurls as an untimely procedure of sensation that redistributes the common perceptual coordinates of the community. Defying the idea of a master matter of literature, intent on sabotaging the sensible as ready-made, what is at stake is not representation but the unleashing of new affects. In Campos, the affect registers a change of perceptual scale: syntax passes into sensation as a virtual field of possibilities. Continuum of mutation that breaks all limits, the achievement of Campos's "baroque effect" concerns the concretization of a posthegemonic literary politics that frees up writing from the state-form that has guided normative, transculturating accounts of Brazilian literature.

Sarduy's baroque rendering of Campos maps well onto Deleuze, who conceives of the baroque not as an essence or period term, but as an operative concept, a folding procedure related to our time and our world. Like Sarduy's privileging of the *Galáxias*, Deleuze's favorite examples range from Japanese origami to Mallarmé's poetry and Jackson Pollock's paintings. Infinitely varied, baroque matter "reveals its texture" as a force (*Fold* 36). Deleuze likens the baroque fold to a system of complex interactions. "Every part," Deleuze writes, "is operative, a machine" (124). And like Brazilian concrete poetry, the baroque approximates the image of a *total art*, where the diverse arts crosses their limits, each prolonged one into the other (121). In a fundamental book, *Toward Total Poetry* (1979), Adriano Spatola will define Brazilian concrete poetry as a "visual baroque," where the "multidimensional ordering of signs" allows the word to go beyond its traditional limits (94–95).

A visual baroque in symbiosis with the times and whose subject matter is never stable, but distributive, fold upon fold: in the passage from verse to the ideogram, we recall Campos's early 1950s experiments as unveiling the project of a public poetry that would put an end to verse. That is, as a generative syntactic configuration, the concrete poem posits itself as endlessly open to new aesthetic information, new systems of signs: the multimedial poem that cannibalizes advertisements, as well as cinema, cybernetics, and radio. We further recall the folded, permutating image of writing at issue in the *Galáxias*: "o mar como um livro rigoroso e gratuito como esse livro onde / ele é absoluto de azul esse livro que se folha e refolha que se dobra / e desdobra

nele pele sobe pele pli selon pli o mar poliestentóreo" (the sea like a rig-
orous and aleatory book like this book where / it is absolute blueness this
book that texts and retexts and folds itself / and unfolds in skin on skin fold
upon fold the polistentorian sea) (*Galáxias*, "multitudinous seas"). Campos's
conception of the baroque, concretized in the aleatory play of the *Galáxias*,
summons a continuum of performative constellations that are never linear
and fixed but rather generative and dispersive. In effect, as early as 1955,
Campos will conceive of the avant-garde "open work" as paradigmatic of a
"modern baroque" that corresponds to the cultural syntax of the times ("a
obra" 53). This formulation becomes a veritable credo for Campos, even
as the signifier "baroque" takes on deconstructive, anthropophagic, and
political hues in his later writings. Campos's deconstructive delimitation of
Antonio Candido's monumental literary history in two tomes, *Formação da
literatura brasiliera* (1959), is a case in point. Campos will argue that the exclusion of the baroque from Candido's national literary history is not simply
historicist, but turns on Candido's ontotheological conception of literature.
Against Candido's "mission-centered" literary regime that "emphasizes the
'communicational' and 'integrative' aspect of literary activity," Campos argues that Candido's system cannot account for the play of sensation, autoref-
erentiality, and nonclosure (*paradigma aberto*) that is proper to the baroque
(*O sequestro* 34, 41, 76).

And yet, marked at its initial stage by the aspiration to attain to the total
medium, Campos's framework is not without road bumps.[1] Clearly, Campos's vision for a Brazilian baroque anti-tradition will come into conflict
with other propositions. Accordingly, a careful consideration of his original vanguard framework is important insofar as it condenses an enduring,
still-heated controversy regarding the legacy of Brazilian concrete poetry.
Regardless that the poets expand their selective paradigm of precursors
(*paideuma*) in the 1970s to champion a far-ranging poetry of the present
that went beyond concrete poetics, it goes without saying that their founding modernist vision created many adversaries, especially in the politically
charged years of the 1960s and 1970s. With a gesture of self-reflection, then,
this chapter begins by addressing the concretes' inaugural *paideuma* vision
for conceiving of literary history. We do so, what is more, because the theory of anti-literature at stake in this volume concerns not the affirmation of
universally valid vanguard works but the nodal tension that holds between
the politics of sensation, what is customarily meant by "literature" in the
region, and the stakes of a radicalized medium that abandons representation so as to intervene not only in "literary" but also social, historical, and
political processes. There were other pariah visions and other modalities of
subverting the sensible, doubtless, as we have seen in the cases of Oswald

de Andrade, Clarice Lispector, and David Viñas. At a more profound level, the affair of anti-literature does not concern imposing form on the question of lived experience. As exodus from identity, whether feminine, subalternist, or multimedial, it rather concerns reconfiguring what is meant by literary writing as a mode of intervening in the present.

Accordingly, the purpose of this chapter concerns reevaluating Campos's vanguard image of writing while preserving its anti-literary force. It does so in heterodox fashion through an assessment of the baroque poetics and literary politics of his rival, Osman Lins who—it must be said at the out-set—was a combative writer akin to David Viñas. Yet curiously critics have hardly touched upon the burning question of politics in Lins's or in Campos's writings, nor have they compared these writers within the framework of the baroque. In fact, similar to the reception of the concretes, critics have overwhelmingly cast Lins's project in the guise of a "pure" literary autonomy with idealist projections, namely, as a sort of a cosmogonic Platonism that returns the reader to the "spiritual" and the "mythological."[2] Simply put, such an image evacuates the historically grounded stakes of subversion in Lins's project. To the extent that Lins's writing abandons central perspective, blurs the boundaries between genres, and charts the crisis of the social bond, I argue against this prevailing idealist vision. More precisely, I examine how Lins's poetics cannibalizes diverse regimes of signs such as theater, painting, medieval *cantiga* poetry, and the Brazilian popular *romanceiro* to defy representational logic and chart the crisis of subaltern margins.[3]

This chapter therefore registers a displacement in the prevailing perception of what literature signifies in Brazil, and moves along three anti-literary folds into the thorny field of politics. First, I trace the historical limits of Campos's initial critical model through his polemical exchange with Lins. Second, I chart from the seams of this polemic two divergent images of baroque writing and their political and social resonance in the Latin American cultural milieu of the 1960s and 1970s. Finally, in an engagement with the writings of José Rabasa, Jacques Rancière, and Alberto Moreiras, I argue against the prevailing idealist reading of Lins's poetics in order to examine the ways in which his masterpiece, "Retábulo de Santa Joana Carolina" (Retable of Saint Joana Carolina) (1966) powerfully frames the problem of *writing violence*—symbolic, political, and everyday—from an aesthetic of ornaments.[4]

THE ANTINOMIES OF ANTI-LITERATURE

Let us begin this discussion on writing violence, the baroque, and literary politics in Lins with a polemical, heretofore unpublished letter, dated 4 October 1974 in São Paulo:

Professor Haroldo de Campos,

I saw the reference, I won't say unfavorable, but harsh, you made concerning my *Avalovara*, in an interview with *Textura*. . . .

[A]llow me to remind you that each writer makes their own literature and can copy no one. I, for example, cannot—and would not desire to—replicate yours. I have my own biography, formation, concerns, coming from another part of Brazil. . . . We're different. Is there any wrong in this? The variety of the search, here is where resides one of the forces, perhaps the greatest, of literature. To think otherwise, to become fixed to an exclusive path seems inadequate to the writer. . . .

Unfortunately, there are people nowadays in the field of the arts, whose deliberate pioneering position ends up limited and, what is worse, intolerant. They see no other path than the one they forge or imagine that they forge. . . .

But if I write you, it is not at all for this. Literary disputes, my God, are so ridiculous! . . . If I engage you here, it is due to another assertion—serious, in my view—, according to which (how would you have discovered such?) I had effectuated, in my novel, "a structural scheme à la mode." Here we are no longer broaching, in my opinion, an accusation, but something more serious which is the matter of my honesty as a writer.[5]

Lins's rebuttal foregrounds his aversion to concrete poetry, as well as his distrust in the avant-garde as an authoritarian phenomenon. Yet Lins's censure seems innocent enough. He was not the first to level blows against the concrete poets, nor would he be Campos's only adversary. Irrespective of personal opinion, in the seams of Lins's discourse a more pressing problematic emerges.

Let us consider Campos's interview statement as counterpoint: "With [João Guimarães] Rosa prose ended. Only *texts* are interesting now. For this reason I don't take into account any pretensions resulting in 'halfway avant-garde works,' which inspire and satisfy some. A very recent example: *Avalovara*, by Osman Lins. Here we have in essence academic writing with a traditional novel's scheme, to which was imposed, *from the outside (de fora)*, mechanically, and without any criteria of intrinsic structural necessity, a redistribution (*remanejamento*) 'à la mode.'"[6]

After Guimarães Rosa "prose ends." Lins's experimental prose, then, will be that of an imitator, a vanguardist "à la mode." In the postliterary space opened by Guimarães Rosa, in short, Campos does not take into account Lins's novel because it lacks, among other things, an internally necessary and novel generative syntactic structure. We should briefly consider it.

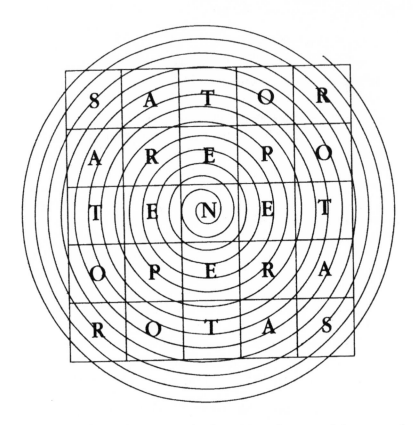

Fig. 5.1. *Avalovara's* frontispiece, by Osman Lins. Courtesy of the estate of Osman Lins.

Avalovara has been compared to Julio Cortázar's *Rayuela* (1962) because it allows the reader to read in an open sequence according to the Latin palindrome SATOR AREPO TENET OPERA ROTAS, whose translation reads, "The laborer carefully operates the plow over the furrows." The palindrome configures the book's frontispiece, where each letter represents a thematic storyline.

Accordingly, the reader may begin from the letter *N*, at the center of the square and where the spiral "ends." Or, alternatively, reading begins when the spiral coil, moving clockwise, first lands on the letter *R* in the upper right quadrant, and then on to *S* in the lower right, and so on in sequence as the spiral winds its way to the center, *N*.

Consider *Avalovara's* opening narrative related to the letter *S*, in the lower right quadrant, entitled "The Spiral and the Square." As a limit-text, Lins's mise-en-scène will return us to a founding freedom: protagonist Abel and his lover emerge not as simulacra but as forces of the text. Never linear or imposed, the staging of narrative will no longer *represent* since it will not function as the presentification of things. Rather, narrative will unfold as a baroque *spacing* of the text that cannot be contained: "Surgem onde, realmente — vindos, como todos e tudo, do princípio das curvas — esses dois personagens ainda larvares e contudo já trazendo, não se sabe se na voz, se no silêncio ou nos rostos apenas adivinhados, o sinal do que são e do que lhes incumbe?" (They arise, where really—having come, as everyone and all, from the beginning of curves—these two characters still larval and even so already bringing, one doesn't know if in voice, if in silence or in faces still to be divined, the signal that they exist and the charge they are encumbered with?) (13). As closure of representation, tone, time, and theme surface from the paused punctuation sequence. That is, littered by commas, this founding sentence evokes, from the curvature of the letter *S*, and the spiral reading pattern that announces its arrival—visually, rhythmically, and symbolically—the simultaneous creation and emergence of character from the idea of curves and alliterative cadence. Fold upon fold, script blends with theme and the reading process. Curious mise-en-scène, character portrayal calls forth forces of the text that have nothing to do with identity, but rather concern the power of the affect. We will return, of necessity, to the powers unleashed by Lins's baroque poetics and their inextricable relation to politics and violence. For now, though, we continue our query concerning Campos's initial critical model and its bearing for our theory of anti-literature as posthegemonic practice.

This latter notion is significant. For if dialectics brings closure and antagonism—to the extent that any subject-centered telos programs what finishes—the theory of anti-literature at stake in this volume concerns thinking writing's *opening* to its other as resistance to the sovereign subject. On the other side of this limit, precisely against state-centered thought, such a theoretical reflection will no doubt include writing's relation to the subaltern, as well as a reading of the literary letter torn from its traditional area.

If "literature" always already presupposes the monument as classic, the modular, and the canon, one will seek to transgress the absolute source. An anti-verse, then, that seeks to abolish conventional "poetry." Yet sifting through the numerous manifesto statements that the Brazilian concrete poets published in the 1950s and 1960s, one finds a totalizing impulse. As already indicated in chapter 3, in the "Pilot-Plan for Concrete Poetry" (A. Campos et al., "plano-piloto" [1958]), concrete poetry is conceived as the product of an evolution of avant-garde forms from across the arts, including poetry, painting, cinema, architecture, and atonal music. Framing this totalization of the modernist paradigm through Deleuze and Guattari, it could be said that a knot of "arborescence," a transcendental formation becomes interwoven in the acentered, anti-literary project of Brazilian concrete poetry (*Thousand* 15–25). The history of avant-garde literature unfolds at once as a sequence of discrete, highly revolutionary syntactic processes (Mallarmé, Joyce, Pound, Cummings, Andrade) that resist a representational, reified present, and as a genealogical agent of authority (dialectic of universally valid vanguard works).[7]

Yet that is not all. And concrete poetry was certainly not derivative or Eurocentric. The project entailed the cannibalization of literary fathers, as we saw in the importance the poets bestowed on Oswald de Andrade. Like Borges would say for the Argentine writer in regard to the tradition, one's patrimony was the universe through a willed irreverence. Significantly, for the concrete poets, one had to assume the crisis of language in modernity. Namely, the advent of a new configuration of the sensible that was no longer representational, discursive, and linear, but multimedial, virtual, and simultaneous. Humankind had entered the age of mass communications, of the nonverbal, of propaganda, cinema, and cybernetics. The futurist search for an ecumenical, common public language was taking place in Brazil during the dramas of underdevelopment and rapid industrialization. In effect, the 1950s and 1960s in Brazil were an age of promise and vanguardism. Campos relates that

> [i]n the 1950s, concrete poetry could envision this project for an ecumenical language: the new barbarians in a peripheral country, rethinking the legacy of universal poetry and overcoming it under the "decentered" banner (because ex-centric) of anthropophagic reason. . . . The circumstances were favorable: in Brazil, the futuristic baroque and constructivist capital, Brasilia[,] was erected. . . . [President] Juscelino Kubitschek skillfully achieved with his "Objectives Plan" . . . one of the rare interregnums of full democracy that our generation experienced. . . . [I]t was impossible for concrete poetry to not reflect this generous moment of optimism and project for the future. ("Poesía" 44–45)

> Without this "principal-hope," not as a vague abstraction, but rather as an expectation effectively nourished by a prospective practice, there can be no avant-garde understood as a movement. . . . In its totalizing impulse, the avant-garde provisionally shirks difference, in search of utopian identity. It transfers or alienates the *singularity* of each poet to the *sameness* of a sought-after common poetics, in order, at a final stage[,] to become dis-alienated, in an optimal moment in history that the future reserves for it, as the culmination or rescue of its progressive and de-differentiating struggle. The avant-garde, as movement, is the search for a new common

language, of a new *koiné*, of a reconciled language, therefore, from the perspective of a transformed world. ("Poesía" 44)

Brazilian concrete poetry will arrive at a revolutionary process of the sensible that dissolves all models. Yet it will also construct in its initial phase a modular history of the avant-garde that becomes, as we see in the case of Lins, an agent of "ecumenical" authority in its own right. But even if these extraordinarily creative pariahs of anti-literature had their hopes pegged on the leftist, futurist state (Brasilia), Brazilian concrete poetry was never populist.

The curious thing is this: the poets' self-critical exodus from the failed state *qua* military regime, in the 1960s, never precluded them from fusing sovereignty with discourse. Is this not what "literature" ultimately does as lure and institution of authors, of the classical, the canonical, and the readerly, as Roland Barthes attests (4)? All of this amounts to saying the following for our concept of anti-literature: there will be no renewal, no new stirring of desire regarding the social, political, and cultural assessment of literature in the field without calling into question established structures. According to Deleuze, "Desire is revolutionary because it always wants more connections and assemblages" (Deleuze and Parnet, *Dialogues II* 58). Yet due to its radical reframing of poetic language in the 1960s, Brazilian concrete poetry ends up overlooking other, incisive modes of revolutionary writing.

This is nowhere more apparent than in the case of Lins, another leftist experimental writer whose affinity with baroque poetics is unquestionable. But let us likewise not defend Lins from closer scrutiny, who himself deemed minimalist, experimental writing a bane to literary practice. Whichever way one frames the question, judgment, claims to truth, and classical values cast their shroud on the writerly, the anti-literary. In this regard, John Beverley's key insight in *Against Literature* remains operative: "[t]he problem is that Latin American left cultural politics is still founded on a model of cultural authority and pedagogy" (5). In spite of Lins and the concretes' revolutionary texts, would not their recourse to utopian judgment and sovereignty be best explained by the dilemmas and dramas of dependency theory in Brazil during the 1960s? In retrospect, such has been Haroldo de Campos's explanation. Let us be clear here: the concrete poets eventually abandon their evolutionary, ecumenical model in the 1970s.[8] And however closely tied to the aporias of the vanguard developing state, it should be emphasized that their initial model for literary history never diminished in the least the revolutionary force, singularity, and achievement of their anti-literary, multimedial texts that we have considered at length. Indeed, for their radical reconception of poetic writing, the concretes were bitterly critiqued by the Brazilian literary establishment. Hence, it is important to historically contextualize their inaugural, utopian, and polemical positions against a backdrop of literary reaction and revolutionary fervor.

Toward a politics of the text then, and its multiple entrance points. And so we return to our thesis: the matter of literary politics in this chapter will have nothing to do with "literary autonomy" and idealism. Rather, our question concerns the matter of writing violence and subalternity from the perspective of the affect.

Accordingly, to the extent that the polemical antinomies of anti-literature have allowed us to focalize our problematic, we now shift back to the curious case of Lins. In contradistinction to the *paulista* poets in Brazil's industrial epicenter, Lins hailed from Brazil's hinterlands in the Northeast, was interested in medieval art, and wrote his dissertation on a minoritarian Afro-Brazilian writer, Lima Barreto. And as we saw in his letter to Campos, Lins never hesitated to emphasize his "primitive" formation, his initial foray into popular theater in the 1960s, and his interest in regional and politically inflected themes.[9] Opposed to Campos's encyclopedic mastery of theory and world literature, Lins's "academic" writings were tinged with journalistic flair. And unlike Lispector, Lins never hesitated to call himself a "homem do povo" (man of the people), as he actively took positions on the social function of intellectuals. What is more, in his book on the social function of writers, *Guerra sem testemunhas* (1969), Lins explicitly denounces minimalist anti-art as alienated—a clear jab at the concrete poets, who had become household names in the field of Brazilian cultural production. Even so, let us make our thesis even more explicit: a line of anti-literary comparison should nevertheless be drawn. To the extent that Lins's baroque poetics configure an unfixed, anti-representational, and anti-subjective typology of the text, his work, like that of the Brazilian concrete poets, offers a new conception of what it means to write and intervene through literature.[10] Representation is replaced by affect and the permutating series. Such a vision concerns preserving, as Jon Beasley-Murray keenly observes, the intermediate space: a poetics of the sensible that does not dominate but rather frees writing from that which imprisons it: namely, from the sovereign subject, identity, and representation (6). Lins once said, "Quando eu procuro deixar claro que não sou um vanguardista pragmático, quando saliento a importância da tradição, na verdade estou procurando ir além do que ora se apresenta como vanguarda" (When I emphasize that I am not a pragmatic vanguard writer, when I highlight the importance of the tradition, in effect I am attempting to go beyond what is now considered avant-garde) (*Evangelho* 242). This reflection takes us to the problem of literary politics in Lins with respect to the larger cultural context of the 1960s in Latin America. For not unlike the concrete poets' utopian desire for a total poetry, such a milieu, according to influential critics, would envision the possibility of a "baroque" totalizing synthesis of the regional (traditional) with the universal (avant-garde) through the superregionalist "Boom" novel.[11] Yet as I hope to make clear, Lins will find a way to break through this consecrated image of writing.

TELEOLOGIES OF THE BOOM AND THE CRISIS OF WRITING

Due to the international market success of Latin American literary production in the 1960s, it has been argued that the literary reached a pinnacle of sorts and brought with it an age of intellectual rigor and political self-consciousness. While the so-called Latin American "Boom" did launch a handful of Latin American writers into the international arena, its critics and proponents alike argued that *at last* Latin American intellectuals from across the continent had succeeded in articulating a general consensus: a *we* that consolidated its authority through the signs of literary renewal and a subset of common conceptual and political adversaries; namely, the United States' recent cultural, military, and political hegemony in the international landscape, as well as the Latin American elites' entrenched Eurocentrism that betrayed the ethos of national popular revolution and agrarian reform.[12]

A discourse of a new type of Latin American novel and intellectual thus emerged, and coalesced around the cultural, economic, and political problematic affecting Latin American nation-states in the post–World War II conjuncture. Its more outspoken proponents, such as Carlos Fuentes and Alejo Carpentier, pushed forward arguments and positions claiming that the new Latin American novel had to surpass description, à la the *novela de la tierra*, in its depictions of Latin American cultural life.[13] This meant that the new Latin American narrative was assigned the task of extending its gaze beyond national borders and had to found its discursive authority under the rubric of the common continental problematic highlighted above: underdevelopment, modernization theory, and neocolonialism. "Dependency" infected, in short, all walks of Latin American cultural life.[14] Latin America, not unlike the nineteenth century's founding pronouncements, was therefore once again imagined as united: a consolidated historical subject that was advancing in time through its cultural expression and historical, political, and economic will to develop. Its literary production, posited as the "crowning" instrument of its cultures by a leading theorist of the time, became the privileged discursive site in which to authorize this vision (Rama, *Transculturación* 19).[15]

No doubt, the notion of the literary as a vehicle of consciousness and linguistic authenticity is representative of the post–World War II discursive formation that hinged on the "becoming global" of Latin American culture, and highlighted the novelist as capable of breaking through the "insularity" of the region (Fuentes 97–98). The Boom novelist, in this perspective, imagined himself as the harbinger of an alternative language, and as the rightful international representative of the continent. From continental philosophical trends that were impacting in Latin America, we could say, following Michel Foucault, that the new primacy of language explains, in part, the drive to becoming parodic, playfully textual, and semantically "universal" of the Boom novel (Foucault 383).[16] The other perspective, of course, would have to take into consideration the national popular horizon of underdevelopment and the ethos of decolonization that contextualize the 1960s.

This latter notion is significant. This is so because the North was seen as an *invader* and Eurocentrism became a problematic site of literary and political struggle for the Left in the 1960s. Accordingly, the violence of invasion, infiltration, and exploitation proper to neocolonialism had, for many of the region's thinkers, significantly morphed into the locus of culture: one forceful way that historical Eurocentrism could be challenged was through the so-called identitarian vision that Boom novels erected. As we have seen in the cases of Lispector, Viñas, and Brazilian concrete poetry, a discourse on the responsibility of the writer was therefore propagated through literary reviews, journals, and cultural supplements. Not unlike Sartre's widely distributed *What Is Literature?* (1947), intellectuals began to speak of the writer's vocation in society in terms of politics and class, and articulated sociological theories of the literary in its historical relationship to the public sphere.[17]

To the extent that one overarching objective inhering in this epochal vision of literary ethics was to decolonize knowledge, the Boom's will to universalization was not unproblematic in an epistemological sense. Paradoxically for many writers and critics of the Boom, the method to critique North American cultural hegemony and Eurocentrism's legacy was to recast the region as universal.[18] Imagined as universally common by virtue of neocolonialism and underdevelopment, it was commonplace to argue that the Latin American nation needed to develop, on all levels, into a form of international parity with the forces of the market. Consequently, the literary became the vehicle authorized and charged to unite the voice of the *we* and thus lay bare a vision of the entire continent's political and historical "coming to consciousness."

For Osman Lins—a Brazilian writer often ignored by narratives of the Boom—the invasion of the North American culture industry was one of the principal reasons for constructing his own baroque narrative poetics, whose technical procedures could, at first glance, very well be compared to narrative transculturation and magical realism.[19] In a fundamental letter to his

French translator Maryvonne Lapouge, dated 11 August 1969, Lins recalls the dilemma of imagining the national in the wake of the full-blown onset of cultural neocolonialism: "A falta do sentimento nacional é alarmante. Não se deve ser xenófobo. Mas também não se pode ser tão negligente como somos em relação aos nossos valores próprios, a nossa individualidade. Assim, não pode haver terreno mais propicio a invasão cultural. E o que é mais grave, a invasão cultural da pátria de Nixon e de *Mad*" (The lack of national sentiment is alarming. One shouldn't be xenophobic. But also one cannot be as negligent as we are in relation to our own values, our individuality. Thus, there cannot be a more proper terrain [to speak of this] than that of the cultural invasion. And what is worse, the cultural invasion by the country of Nixon and *Mad* [magazine]).[20]

Faced with historically imposed cultural models and the problem of defending the national, Lins's discourse turns in two divergent directions. The intellectual legitimizes his social vision and authority from the construction of a unique style that lays claim to an integrating function that includes the subaltern: "Nesta época de grandes fracionamentos, pelo menos o escritor, praticante de um ofício unificador por excelência, recuse ser também um agente de fragmentação" (In this age of great fractures and alienation, at least the writer, practitioner of a unifying vocation par excellence, refuses to be an agent of fragmentation) (*Guerra* 213). To integrate the fractured national subject from the locus of literature was to construct texts that negotiated political realities and representation proper. Images of scales, clocks, measuring sticks, writing utensils, and tableaux of cosmological order line the pages of *Nove, novena* (1966) and *Avalovara* (1973). It could be said that these symbols of order and measurement, when read across the ornamental structure of Lins's experimental narratives, configure on the one hand an apposite allegory of his writing style.

According to Sandra Nitrini, Lins's ornamental poetics ultimately reflect his idealism, and should be read philosophically as an engrained Platonism that inscribed a "nostalgia for [humankind's] lost unity" against the reifying forces of capital (*Poéticas* 268–69).[21] While Nitrini's reading remains illuminating on many levels, it is my contention that far from simply affirming Lins's idealistic penchant for constructing aesthetic harmony as a desire to recover humankind's "lost unity," as Lins himself liked to claim, Lins's chains of signification also articulate what I will call a halting, heterotopic mapping of the subaltern against the discursive formation of neocolonialism and underdevelopment in the 1960s.[22] At a deeper level, like the work of Lispector and Viñas, Lins's writing project had to become not more modern and craft-like but more reflexive, polyvocal, and intensive.[23]

And yet, to legitimize his discourse in the Brazil of the 1960s, Lins had to theorize and promote his own work from a national perspective. His tirades against publishing houses and corrupt editors, the absence of state support for writers, and his avid statistical reports on the number of books bought and distributed in the country, documented in *Guerra sem testemunhas*, clearly demonstrate that the intellectual, for Lins, had to make the national an important horizon of viability even as he championed, like many representative writers of the Spanish American Boom, the international and universal dimensions of literary culture.[24]

For Lins, in sum, the writer was imagined as an engaged public intellectual capable of weaving through multiple perspectives simultaneously the "plenitude" of the emergent subaltern nation (*nossa cultura em plena formação*) and exposing its fissures: "O escritor, na sociedade, representa essa voz, esse rumor; é uma força spiritual, a consciência de um momento, a secreta lucidez de um povo" (The writer, in society, represents this voice, this rumor: his is a spiritual force, the consciousness of the moment, the secret lucidity of the people) (*Guerra* 111, 216). The rich fissures and frontiers of representation, the epistemological "secret" casting of the ornamental subaltern signifier, as I will show, are one of the principal reasons a reassessment of Lins is in order today.

With respect to recent critiques of the Boom's alleged appropriation of the "regional other" or even its Eurocentric stance on culture, does Lins's project ultimately point to a new form of subaltern orientalism? What do the discourses of transculturation do for us in our remapping of Lins's historical self-positioning? How are we to negotiate the Boom's so-called triumphant assertions of the literary against the problematic of subalternity, affect, and representation that Brazilian and Argentine writers negotiated in their experimental texts?

According to Idelber Avelar's influential account of the Latin American Boom as a discursive formation, in the 1960s we witness a curious phenomenon that riddles the institution of literature across the continent: "literature had lost its functionality" in a public sphere that no longer needed it (31). In short, modernization does not liquidate the literary but places it in crisis. Avelar's argument is that the Boom represents the loss of Latin American literature's "aura"—its historical task of forming a "lettered" elite and representing the people—at the very moment it becomes "autonomous" (30–31). Put differently, the loss of the aura refers to the Boom's autonomization from the Latin American literary regime of representation. We thereby witness the emergence of a "compensatory mode" that is evinced through the *thematization of writing* in Boom novels: "The insistent thematization of writing by boom novels performed the task of carrying out the rhetorico-political vocation. A writer-demiurge postulated a realm that could both account (precede) and overcome (succeed) Latin America's unbearable cycle of politics and social repetitions" (32). To the extent that the writer no longer had a definite function in society regarding the representation of the people, the Boom "responded with an aestheticization of the political, or, more to the point, a substitution of aesthetics for politics" (30).

While evidently important and theoretically nuanced, Avelar's compensatory reading of the Boom's "autonomization" is problematic for several reasons. First, the image of writing that guides his formulation remains fettered to the Latin American literary regime of representation. Doubtless, the Boom discursive formation produced an ideology of the literary with its countless statements of triumph and transculturation. And as illustrated above with the case of Haroldo de Campos's ecumenical, evolutionary literary model, there is no such thing as a universally valid vanguard subject, much less an autonomous "new narrative" advancing teleologically in time. While this point is obvious, critics persist in claiming the Boom as the golden age and arrival of Latin American literature as though it were an autonomous *subject* as opposed to singular works that share a historical, political, and regional context in common. Second, Avelar's central account of the tendency toward the thematization of writing in Boom novels does not register the self-reflexive, parodic, feminine, subalternist, and multimedial dimensions of writing at stake in many of the so-called Boom narratives. In this book we have registered minoritarian counterimages of writing that upend any pretense of representation. One that especially comes to mind is the subaltern problematic and its anti-literary mapping as we have witnessed with force in Lispector, Brazilian concrete poetry, and Viñas. These anti-literary projects presented powerful cases of intervention and experimentation, while simultaneously tracing the limits of speaking for the subaltern as an insuperable problematic that explodes our commonsensical understanding of the "other."

The point is not to critique Avelar, for he has offered us a precious mapping of the Boom's discursive formation, and he himself qualifies his arguments as sketchily "outlined" (34). The point is rather to understand and problematize this ambitious articulation so as to produce a counterfocalization of Latin American subalternity through the historically grounded lens of anti-literature in Brazil and Argentina. Following John Beverley, the subaltern problematic lies at the heart of contemporary debates on the historical struggle over the literary and the "displacement of the authority of the lettered" in Latin America in the wake of the nation-state's weakening under global capital (*Subalternity* 19). If the subaltern has proven us wrong time and again in an epistemological sense, it is because the problem of "speaking for" is a colonial discourse of power. Following the founding problematic of the Latin American Subaltern Studies Group and its injunction to forge new modalities of thinking the political and the cultural by paying heed to the "structural dichotomies" that underwrite the historical relationship between intellectuals and subalterns ("Founding" 142), I understand the subaltern as a mediational term, fundamentally refractive, of the limits of the letter and theoretical discourse. The subaltern, in this view, not only calls "the nation into question" but functions as a powerful constitutive fissure for reflection (143).[25]

In its "Founding Statement" in 1992, the Latin American Subaltern Studies Group issued a field-altering injunction: to rethink the *problem of writing* against elitist, nationalist, and literary "translation" of subalternity (144). As I hope will become clear in my reading of Lins, the baroque poetics of sensation at stake in his work functions as a multimediational frame bearing on the problematic of writing subalternity.[26] In redirecting our attention to sensation, I agree with Alberto Moreiras's call to "turn literature against itself" by thinking through "the subaltern function of literary studies" (*Exhaustion* 182, 13). In doing so, I am also foregrounding one of the core problems at stake in this volume: that it is time to move beyond the examination of Latin American literature from the standpoint of the *Boom subject* and its authorial proclamations by returning to mediation, affect, self-reflexivity, the minoritarian legacies of the avant-garde, and the problematic of anti-literature.

A POLITICS OF ORNAMENTS

We lack a theoretical reading of Osman Lins's narrative aesthetics or what he called a poetics of the ornament (*ornamento*) beginning with the landmark publication of *Nove, novena* (1966). We lack, in other words, an interpretation of Lins's subversion of realist form. Never speaking for the subaltern, in what follows, our intention will be to show how Lins finds a way to narrate the violence of subalternity through an anti-realist, baroque procedure of ornamentation.

To grasp Lins's reworking of the realist aesthetic, we do well to frame the unfolding of textual space in Lins's acclaimed "Retábulo de Santa Joana Carolina," for it is here that setting, multiple narrators, and sentence pass through a polyvocal process of ornamentation. Consider the cast of rotating narrators who speak in the first person. These rotating narrators possess names, such as Totônia, but are first framed by a visual symbol that has poetic and cosmological connotations. In the final narrative, for instance, the infinity sign, ∞, designates a multitude of subaltern narrators that polyphonically chant the burial procession of the protagonist, "Saint" Joana Carolina.[27] The infinity sign also points to the medieval *retábulo*, or framed altarpiece, that serves as the work's structural matrix: Joana Carolina's death will correspond to the iconic representation of the Assumption of the Holy Virgin in August. From the tableau panel of infinite grace, subaltern ∞ narration will unfurl in choral song and point directly to the medieval *cantiga de loor* that Lins's narrative inhabits. Creative appropriation of traditional forms and blurring the boundaries between painting, sculpture, and song, the infinity narrative indicator, ∞, signals new correspondences, new semiotic offshoots, fold after fold. For the problem of overcoming realism through the baroque, in Lins, was never about closing the text in idealism, as his critics suggest, but about continuing the textual weave: geometry in errancy, shooting stars against fixed, heterodox rewritings of canonical texts. Would not infinity also point to what Candace Slater has rightfully observed as Lins's ideal form of *textual* theater, that is, as a *performative textual demonstration of writing and reading* against subjective dramatization?

What counts is the proliferation of series. In Lins's winding, comma-riven sentences, the object is elevated to a verbal, vocal, and visual state of language. Like the infinity signifier that suspends closure in the final narrative, "Retábulo" begins with the voice of a young black midwife, symbolized by the sun cross, ⊕. Denoting the earth, with its equator and meridian, the four seasons, four cardinal directions, and four elements, this narrative indicator immediately frames the classical feminine image of Libra, Greek goddess of justice, ♎, holding scales. It is, moreover, significant that narrative begins *in media res*, with a subaltern midwife seeing herself in the retable painting and holding Joana in her arms: "Lá estou, negra e moça, sopesando-a (tão leve!), sob o olhar grande de Totônia, que me pergunta: 'É gente ou é homem?'" (There I am, black and young weighing her (so light!), beneath the gaze of Totônia, who asks me: "Is it like us or human at all?") (72). With her speech rhyming like that of a popular northeastern bard, or *repentista*, we note how syntax begins by blending with visual symbol: the midwife focalizes her story through the retable painting: "There I am." But the accompanying parenthetical clause, "(tão leve!)" (so light!) also constitutes a performative inscription: Joana Carolina, the saint figure, the cross, is cradled in the midwife's arms, ⊕. To traverse the limit: the visual pun constitutes the idea of a primary focus, a target. The gaze over the saint, the eye that refracts the cross: syntax passes immediately into sensation. But begun in the middle, by a midwife who reads her story from the retable, syntax also shifts back to the technical, metaliterary plane of composition, to the notion of the medium. As a figure of infinite justice, would not this opening scene staged through the voice of the peasant, this Afro-Brazilian midwife, point to a larger political problematic in the 1960s in Brazil? Especially given the fact that as late as 1950, 74 percent of the rural northeastern

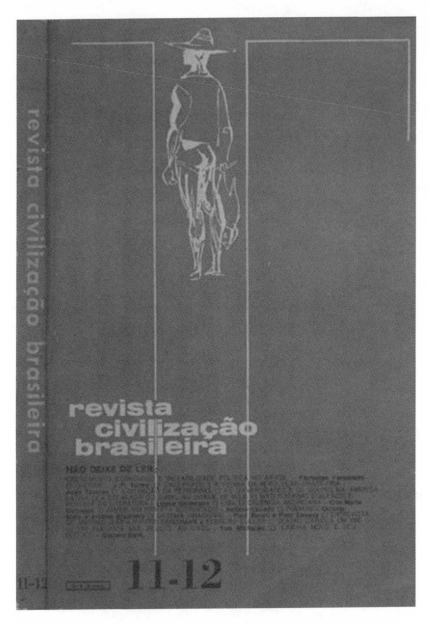

Fig. 5.2. Afro-Brazilian fisherman illustration for the leftist review *Revista Civilização Brasileira*, no. 11–12 (1967).

population was illiterate and could not vote—many of whom lived in no-madic, semifeudal conditions—at a contentious time in which the Left was promising revolution and land reform.[28] Synecdochal of future revolution, but also symbolic wound in the neocolonial state, we recall the iconic image of the Afro-Brazilian fisherman adorning the cover of the influential anti-dictatorial journal, *Revista Civilização Brasileira*, whose first issue surfaces in 1965.[29]

We will return shortly to the problem of mediating the subaltern. For now, let us continue our reflection on the baroque design of "Retábulo." As with poetic discourse, chronological time is burst asunder in the overflow of voices, visual symbols, and rotating narrators that comment on the past in present time. Syntax unfolds in large block formations, ranging from two to five pages in length, without paragraph breaks. If "Retábulo" critically appropriates the medieval *cantiga* form, we do well to trace an immediate parallel with the classical *Cantigas de Santa Maria*.[30] Written in Galician Portuguese in the thirteenth century and depicting the Virgin Mary in humanized fashion, these illustrated poems of praise to the Virgin parallel Joana Carolina's earthly, secular "miracles." Indeed, composed in syllabic square notation, Lins's justified script replicates the block patterns of medieval manuscripts. Via the retable painting that structures narrative, Lins also draws inspiration from medieval illuminations. In effect, the riddle texts that precede narrative function like vignettes in the *Cantigas de Santa Maria*: they are short poems that caption the illuminations. The ornament denotes syntactic method as much as textual performance.

From image to narration and song, setting takes place across a sequence of twelve tableau paintings that correspond to the twelve narrative "mysteries" of "Retábulo." Montage scenes that approximate cubism with their lack of central perspective, the paintings often appear at the beginning of narration, but sometimes surface in the middle or end.[31] Introducing the paintings, eleven of the twelve narratives begin with a riddle-poem that concerns one of Joana Carolina's "miracles." Or better put, the experience of miracles in "Retábulo" really registers *epiphanic changes in perspective* on the part of the narrators. To alter perspective: Joana Carolina is framed not so much as a subaltern "saint" but as a work of art and figure of defiance. In conveying and narrating her acts as depicted on the retable painting, narrators undergo a change in viewpoint. And like the Virgin Mary, Joana represents a change in scale, an affective register. This proves significant in a political sense, inasmuch as the narrators live and struggle in a world of violence. Or are they ghosts? Raised to the status of monument, reminiscent of the work of Juan Rulfo, a subaltern community's voice issues forth to tell us of their misery, their sun-beaten barren earth, their sparse laughter and song, their stories of exploitation. Similar to Macabéa in Lispector's *A hora da estrela*, the mysteries of Joana Carolina represent not liturgical hope for the downtrodden, but a fracture in the habitual modes of perception of the Northeast

Fig. 5.3. Cántigas of Alfonso the Learned, thirteenth century, folio 120v: "Praises of the Virgin and of the Archangel Gabriel," Biblioteca Nazionale, Florence. Reprinted from El Sabio, "Praises of the Virgin," in vol. 1 of *Spanish Illumination*, edited by Jesús Domínguez Bordona.

community—a break from the habitual, collective, day-to-day enduring in spite of miserable conditions.

The trope and leitmotif of the *change in scale* take us back to the inaugural symbol that opens "Retábulo": "o espaço desdobrado, as amplidões refletidas nos Espelhos do Tempo, o Sol e os planetas, nossa Lua e suas quatro fases, *tudo medido pela invisível balança*, com o pólen num prato, no outro as constelações" (space unfolded, its amplitude reflected in the Mirrors of Time, the Sun and the planets, our Moon and its four phases, *everything weighed by the invisible scale*, with pollen in one dish, the constellations in the other) (72, emphasis added). Even the devil himself, incarnate in the figure of the plantation owner, undergoes a change in perspective: "Joana Carolina foi minha transcendência, meu quinhão de espanto numa vida tão pobre de mistério" (Joana Carolina was my transcendence, my share of awe in this life so lacking in mystery) (88). Entranced in habit, victims of deep-seated structural violence—perhaps this explains Leila Perrone-Moisés's observation that narrative voice in "Retábulo" is almost neutral, deadpan, spectral. In "Final Mystery," for example, the subaltern chorus carrying Joana to her grave will speak of a life of exploitation endured by dint of habit: "nós, os ninguéns da cidade, que sempre a ignoravam os outros, gente de dinheiro e do poder . . . O mundo que foi seu e para o qual voltamos, de onde dentre nós alguns jamais saíram, terra onde . . . suamos, somos destruídos, pensando em ir embora e sempre não indo, quem sabe lá por quê" (we, the nobodies of this city, because the others always ignored her, the people of money and power . . . The world that was hers and to which we have returned, and which some of us never left, the land where . . . we sweat, are destroyed, thinking of leaving and never going, who knows why) (113).

It is not sufficient, however, to simply multiply perspective. Lins's baroque text develops a permutating series that registers movement and sensory experience on a multimedial path that abandons representation. For example, recalling the cannibalized *cantiga* form, Lins's riddle vignettes read as public songs of praise, summoning local muses, flora and fauna, the signs of the zodiac, and the four seasons. Like concrete poems, the structure of the mystery text is that of the associative assemblage. Syntax communicates its structure and unfurls as an intensification of language in verbal, vocal, and visual coordinates. As though poems emitted in public performance, the riddle texts are playful and emphasize not only the cosmos and religion but the aleatory and struggle for life. As captions for the retable painting, the ceremonial riddles welcome the reader to participate in the textual performance. What is more, the riddles serve as partitions separating the twelve tableau scenes. Pointing to Joana Carolina's ultimate apotheosis, they correspond to the twelve astrological signs and to twelve distinct phases

Fig. 5.4. Cántigas of Alfonso the Learned, thirteenth century, folio 1: "Alfonso the Learned reading his canticles," The Escorial, Library of the Royal Monastery, T. j. I. Reprinted from El Sabio, "Alfonso the Learned Reading His Canticles," in vol. 1 of *Spanish Illumination*, edited by Jesús Domínguez Bordona.

in Joana Carolina's life.[32] The twelve narratives also point to the Stations of the Cross insofar as the story of Joana Carolina's life is told in the key of violence.[33] That is, although Joana suffers acts of exploitation at the hands of corrupt landowners, all of her actions are contextualized by an enduring defiance and subtheme of martyrdom.[34] I underscore the fact that the reference to the *novena* in the book's title, *Nove, novena*, points to the nine days of prayer that commemorate the Christian Pentecost, or descent of the Holy Spirit, and the speaking in tongues.

According to the Portuguese dictionary *Novo Aurélio*, the *novena*, from Latin, refers to: "1) o espaço de nove dias [the space of nine days]. 2) Rezas feitas durante nove dias [A nine-day period of prayer]. 3) Grupo de nove coisas ou pessoas [A group of nine things or people]. 4) *Bras*. Castigo de açoites durante nove dias seguidos, que se inflige nos escravos [*Brazil*. Punishment for slaves by whip for nine consecutive days]" (1419). It is important to underscore that the *novena* in Brazil also refers to the institution of slavery. The *novena* thereby inscribes not only Christian religiosity and revolution in the title but also suggests an overlapping theme of subalternity and exploitation. Allegorically speaking, we could say that Lins's recourse to ornamentation mirrors this plural speaking in tongues. As we will show in our analysis of "Final Mystery," Joana Carolina is compared to Christ and her canonization is likened to a messianic second coming by the subaltern multitude.

As we move from form to the aporias of content, we could say, with Jacques Rancière, that we lack a closer reading of how Lins's texts articulate a politics of the sensible. Such a reading would clearly take us beyond Lins's frequent denunciations of the Brazilian public sphere. Indeed, the author's opinions have oft confined critics to a circular argument regarding his claim that narrative equates to cosmogony. In the limit-case of "Retábulo de Santa Joana Carolina," often perceived as Lins's masterpiece, the work was never spiritualist. However much Lins spoke of writing as a cosmologically inflected endeavor, everything turns on the material problem of the sensible: that of creating the collective monument for the downtrodden. Let me say this even more clearly: to make the monument for the subaltern will not be to project a representation. There will be no master translation of alterity, no ventriloquist speaking for the poor, no sanctification of the popular. Rather, we will witness the construction, in Lins, of a writing technique that deterritorializes all standards and measures—a threshold of illiteracy, in the apt expression of Abraham Acosta.[35] The problem of anti-literature will concern, then, the creation of new powers of texture, new modes of relating to the subaltern.

To the extent that the aesthetic of the ornament, in its most basic sense,

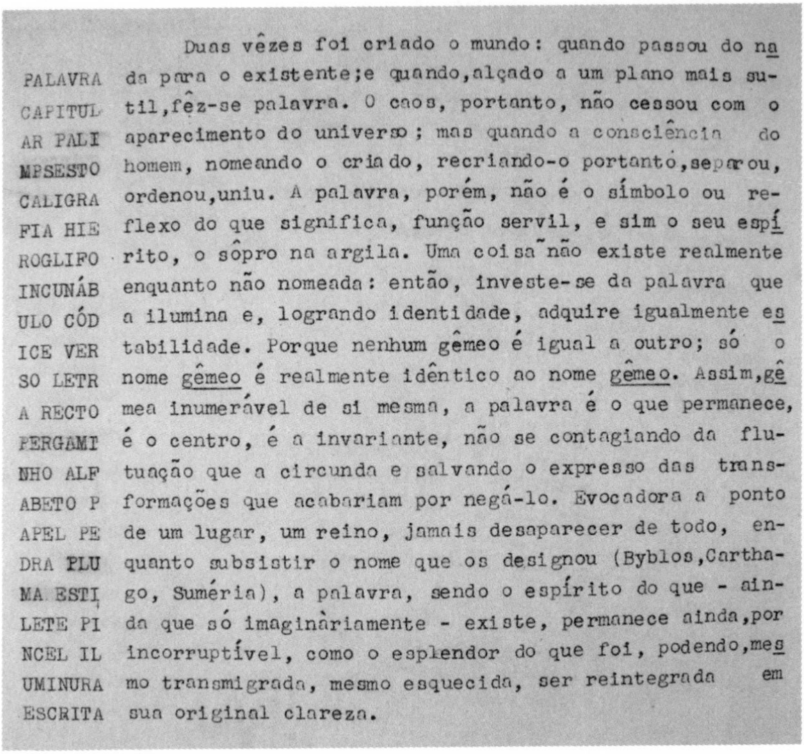
Duas vêzes foi criado o mundo: quando passou do na
PALAVRA da para o existente;e quando,alçado a um plano mais su-
CAPITUL til,fêz-se palavra. O caos, portanto, não cessou com o
AR PALI aparecimento do universo; mas quando a consciência do
MPSESTO homem, nomeando o criado, recriando-o portanto,separou,
CALIGRA ordenou,uniu. A palavra, porém, não é o símbolo ou re-
FIA HIE flexo do que significa, função servil, e sim o seu espí
ROGLIFO rito, o sôpro na argila. Uma coisa não existe realmente
INCUNÁB enquanto não nomeada: então, investe-se da palavra que
ULO CÓD a ilumina e, logrando identidade, adquire igualmente es
ICE VER tabilidade. Porque nenhum gêmeo é igual a outro; só o
SO LETR nome gêmeo é realmente idêntico ao nome gêmeo. Assim,gê
A RECTO mea inumerável de si mesma, a palavra é o que permanece,
PERGAMI é o centro, é a invariante, não se contagiando da flu-
NHO ALF tuação que a circunda e salvando o expresso das trans-
ABETO P formações que acabariam por negá-lo. Evocadora a ponto
APEL PE de um lugar, um reino, jamais desaparecer de todo, en-
DRA PLU quanto subsistir o nome que os designou (Byblos,Cartha-
MA ESTI go, Suméria), a palavra, sendo o espírito do que - ain-
LETE PI da que só imaginàriamente - existe, permanece ainda,por
NCEL IL incorruptível, como o esplendor do que foi, podendo,mes
UMINURA mo transmigrada, mesmo esquecida, ser reintegrada em
ESCRITA sua original clareza.

Fig. 5.5. Typescript of "Nono Mistério" (Ninth Mystery) in "Retábulo de Santa Joana Carolina," by Osman Lins. Photograph by author. Courtesy of the estate of Osman Lins.

is best understood as a layering procedure that calls attention to the *act of ornamenting*, we could say that Lins's text calls attention to itself in an original sense. Lins saw the ornament as a technique of sensory amplification.[36] The ornament not only decorates the story, but points to a continuous mapping of composition.

And yet Lins's ornament, like Deleuze's fold, does not refer to an essential characteristic. It is, rather, qualified by its operative function. The story line, in this sense, is always cavernous, generative, and active: the story becomes an *event of reading through multiple ornamental folds*.[37] To maintain a tense interface between narrative and the permutating ornament: the ornament jars, defers, and suspends the reader's judgment. The two planes of narration and decoration merge into a third field of metaperformativity that prompts a halting, contemplative frame.

I have made the point that we need to go beyond the author's explicit denouncements to understand the political vocation underwriting his baroque narratives, and the same must be said in advance regarding the issue of "representing" or giving articulation to the subaltern. Lins, like many intellectuals of his generation, such as Viñas, Campos, and Lispector, was aware of the seemingly insuperable divide between the intellectual and the institutionless "other." With this said, what are we to make of Lins's "beatification" of the subaltern Joana Carolina, as a saint figure for the downtrodden "nobodies" of the impoverished Northeast?

A first step in responding to this question is to go beyond biography, however interesting: the story deals with much more than an articulate homage to Lins's paternal grandmother, Joana Carolina, who raised Osman in the Brazilian Northeast. To the extent that the story's narrative structure constitutes a field of ornaments calling attention to its compositional procedures, a starting point in bridging the gulf—between the literary and the subaltern—is found in the notion of the secret or "mystery" structure that frames each of the twelve retable texts in "Retábulo."

THRESHOLDS: THE ORNAMENT AND WRITING VIOLENCE

I begin my analysis of "Eleventh Mystery" with the Latin citation, "Populus, qui ambulabat in tenebris, videt lucem magnam," which may be viewed as the terms by which the priest-narrator christens Joana Carolina as a saint ("Retábulo" 161). Further still, as a biblical intertext, the quote refers to Jesus Christ's migration from his home in Nazareth, after having been tempted in the desert for forty days and nights by Satan's variegated guises, false promises, and illusions. The quote literally inaugurates the Christian Messiah's nomadic preaching: "The people which sat in great darkness saw great light; and to them which sat in the region and shadow of death light is sprung up" (Matthew 4:16). It also refers back to Isaiah's messianic prophecy, which foretold of a Messiah who would serve as a "light of the Gentiles; To open the blind eyes, to bring out the prisoners from the prison, *and* them that sit in darkness out of the prison house" (Isaiah 42:6–7). The quote's representational valences also suggest a set of symbolic equations, and a generalized cartography of the narrative's plot sequence: Joana Carolina as Christ figure; the desert as the Brazilian *sertão*; the devil's temptations as those employed by the landowner, a primary agent and representation of structural violence, to seduce and break Joana's resolve in Mysteries Six and Seven, which result in her mother's death, her children's illnesses, and her having physiologically aged twenty years in a span of seven. The reference to a "people in darkness" (*populus, qui ambulabat in tenebris*), and by inference to Gentiles and Jews alike, may be seen allegorically as referring to the subalternized peoples of the Brazilian Northeast.

The Christ–Joana Carolina comparison reframes Joana's pedagogic nomadism as a teacher on a sugar plantation, and the mediation of her twelve miracles by a set of subaltern narrators. More specifically, in the case of the mystery of this eleventh "Retábulo," the quote at once becomes symbolic of the priest-narrator's epiphany regarding Joana's "secret beauty" (*aquela beleza secreta*) on her deathbed ("Retábulo" 112) and Joana's status as saint figure: it is precisely here, in the priest-narrator's eyes, and via a canonical articulation in the Catholic Church's official language, Latin, that Joana Carolina becomes canonized, as her face, her representation on the retable, multiplies and proliferates into a series of figures, phenomena, and conjectures that suggest the overcoming of poverty, duress, and exploitation that have been constant in her life (*daquela ressurreição fugaz*) (112).

But the question remains: how does one negotiate the priest-narrator's epiphany, relayed in Latin and through a gamut of symbolic ornaments, and the problem of subalternity? How is subalternity imagined, inverted, and displaced?

Joana Carolina's beatification by the Catholic priest is ambiguous, semantically cryptic, for the conclusion of the narrative ends in a sequence of ornamentations that blur the narrative's chronological closure: the Latin citation from Matthew is relayed to us with the priest walking away and the image of Joana Carolina in flames. In addition to the beatification theme, the text begins by imposing a duplicitous ontological query: "What is it, what is it?" (*O que é, o que é?*), which points to a second (iterative) plane of interpretation that concerns, I suggest from the epistemic crisis that the text stages, the problem of writing and interpreting the subaltern as a site of redemption (Frizzi, "Retable" 156; "Retábulo" 109).[38]

Looking closer at the duplicity of the question, what weaves together this ambiguous dispersal of ornaments are the self-referencing strategies that map the canonization of Joana Carolina as an object that "must be for an artist" (*como deve ser para um artista a forma anunciada*) (Frizzi, "Retable" 161; "Retábulo" 113). This key trope—as we connect it to the multiple references to art and writing that the text inscribes repeatedly over its objects—clearly articulates the way that Lins's ornament, as a modality of semiotic supplementation, stages an allegory of its own representational procedures and poetics of writing.

Does this ornamental encoding of Joana Carolina, and in consequence, of subalternity, reduce the problem to a discussion among artists and the lettered? Is Lins's canonization of the subaltern Joana Carolina another instance of literary transculturation of the regional "other" into a universal subject? Are we faced with the appropriation of difference through a teleological logic of modernity? Is this not a literary restoration of the auratic?

The problem of epistemic limits, in Lins, hinges on the ways in which his

Fig. 5.6. *Retable of the Virgin with Infant*, by Maestro della Maddalena. Tempura on wood, Florence (1275–80). Reprinted from *Les Arts Decoratifs*, digital image, 6 December 2014.

texts trace the limits of literary art with respect to subalternity as *violence*, and begins in "Eleventh Mystery" with the double inquiry of the opening riddle text: "What is it, what is it? Lion of invisible teeth, of tooth he is made and bites with his mane, with his tail, with his entire body . . . he is begotten, at times, by two flints. Even though he devours everything, denying nothing to his molars, canines and incisors, he symbolizes life" (Frizzi, "Retable" 156).[39] The astrological sign of Leo and the element of fire become the first terms in a sequence of ornaments that will layer and complicate the ensuing narrative sequence, which is more interpretative than descriptive, more imagistic than chronological—the priest-narrator's *reading* of the eleventh panel, his *reading* of Joana's life in the moment of her last confession, and his *reading* of his own institutional status: "Vendo-a (ou deveria dizer *vendo-as*, de tal modo eu tinha ante meus olhos dois seres diferentes, ambos reais e unificados só em meu espanto?)" (Seeing her [or should I say *seeing them*, for inasmuch as I held before my eyes two different beings, both real and unified, but was this so through my fear?]) ("Retábulo" 112; my English translation).

First reading: from the inaugural riddle, we move with the priest's eyes into the symbolic space of the panel scene. Angels hover over Joana as her hands hold feathers and a dry branch. The syntax is paused, meditative, littered with commas, while the objects in the tableau are distributed with very few verbs. Narrative time all of a sudden interrupts the still space of descriptive discourse, as the characters on the tableau leap out of the painting: "Vendo-me, segurou o meu braço. 'Estou lembrando quando o senhor veio aqui pela última vez'" (When she saw me she grabbed my arm. "I remember when you came here last") ("Retábulo" 110; Frizzi, "Retable" 157). Effectuating an inversion of power relations, we could say that narrative begins with the represented casting a countergaze to the enunciator of discourse, whereby the confessor forces the priest to confess his "sins" or weakness. In other words, the priest-narrator does not reply to Joana's evocation in the present, as her words become, like the panel scene, objects of contemplation through which he self-reflects: "Cultivo o hábito de esquecer. A um padre compete proteger-se da impregnação das coisas" (I cultivate the habit of forgetting. A priest must protect himself from the infiltration of things) ("Retábulo" 110; Frizzi, "Retable" 157).

Second reading: we are therein implicated into a space of contemplation, the priest's self-reflection in denial, a mental scene that likewise unfolds in the narrative now and divides the narrative once again. The priest's narration of this supposed confession, beginning with his description of the tableau, becomes *a multiple and fragmented reading space* (vendo-as, de tal modo eu tinha ante meus olhos dois seres diferentes) ("Retábulo" 112). This space delineates a clear tension separating Joana Carolina (subaltern) from the priest. If at first sight she is an object of contemplation on the tableau, when she surprisingly gazes back at the priest and speaks, bursting the frame and entering the time of narrative, her words become *textual* objects that *distance* her from the priest, who avoids "the infiltration of things" and "cultivates the habit of forgetting" (Frizzi, "Retable" 157). Like an ethnographic object, Joana Carolina becomes a frontier subject of the priest's discourse, as opposed to a disciplined subject who confesses to the Church: "Mas dentro desse rosto, que adquiriu de súbito uma transparência inexplicável, como se na verdade, não existisse, fosse uma encrosta de engano sobre a realidade não franqueada à contemplação ordinária" (But within [her] face, which acquired all of a sudden an inexplicable transparency, as if in truth it did not exist, as though it were a crust of deceit covering a reality that could not be penetrated by ordinary contemplation) ("Retábulo" 111–12; my English translation).

Third reading: the priest's object of contemplation, Joana Carolina on her deathbed, but also Joana Carolina as a representation on the tableau,

becomes a signifier of thresholds. The duplicitous depiction of Joana Carolina displaces the narrative unities of place, time, and action. Consequently,
in its dispersion and multiplicity, her representation becomes no longer a
simple object of discourse, but a counterfocal narrative point of view that
shifts the gaze of the reader back to the priest. "Eleventh Mystery," in this
way, is as much a narration of Joana Carolina's confession and death scene as
it is a mapping of the priest-narrator's rigid, institutionalized mental habits,
which eventually are dissolved by the aesthetic experience of recalling the
tableau and Joana Carolina's death. As the two narrative points of view shift,
multiply, disperse, and overlap, they configure a supplementary system of
signification that calls attention to the text's constructedness. In doing so,
narrative perspective in "Eleventh Mystery"—written in the speed of the
present tense but haltingly reflective—graphs a dizzying exchange of gazes
that ultimately *read as text*.

To read the confessing "other," in Mystery Eleven, is to narrate the ways
in which confession is suspended and launched back at the disciplining "rational" subject. And to narrate this final confession, this final taking inven-
tory of sins so that the subaltern may be "purified" by the institution of the
Church at the threshold of life and death, is to displace the solemn, passive,
docile object of contemplation. It is to resemanticize the confessor, subaltern
object, who progressively becomes a subject of discourse that is accruing
sense, multiplying perspective, and displacing the formulaic and repetitive.
Or perhaps better, the object of discipline and cognition displaces the gaze
of the interpreter who cannot "penetrate" it. If the encounter, rhetoric, and
logic of disciplinary confession is riveted by displacements and semantic
accumulation, and mimesis is betrayed by the fact that paintings jump to
life, the gel that allows these temporal and spatial ruptures to adhere together are the references to the text itself as artwork and as text: "Her voice,
fading, was like an old corroded instrument, a clarinet full of lichens and
spiderwebs. It was difficult for her to put together those last few words, as if
she were writing them out. . . . Something shone in the heart of these phenomena, a sentence, a word, a semblance, something complete, and at the
same time veiled, as the form announced, surmised, still unrevealed, still
unconquered must be for the artist" (Frizzi, "Retable" 158, 161).[40]

Fourth reading: but we would be mistaken to judge the priest's readings
of Joana as institutionally integrating, redemptive, and appropriative. Far
from articulating fulfillment, though evoking the biblical story of Adam, the
giving of names to the subaltern ends symbolically in flames, recasting the
initial tension of noncommunication and riddle-riveted sense: "Dentro de
mim, enquanto me afastava de cabeça alta, Joana era uma chama. *Populus,
qui ambulabat in tenebris, vidit lucem magnam*" (Inside me, as I walked

away with my head high, Joana was a flame. *Populus, qui ambulabat in tenebris, vidit lucem magnam*) ("Retábulo" 113).

Joana Carolina may be here canonized in the priest-narrator's mind through the Latin reference to the Gospel of Matthew. But this canonization —indeed, Joana Carolina becoming a Christ figure—is achieved inconclusively, in heterodox fashion, with the priest walking away, obliquely and metaphorically so, through a fusion of astrological and aesthetic elements that connote the text's quality as an artifact and as a shifting semiotic map that defers the sedimentation of sense or representational closure.

I am suggesting that Lins's will *to ornament the subaltern* entirely rewrites the subaltern problematic. The subaltern, in Lins, becomes *an affective site of multiple writings*. More specifically, the ornament displaces the logocentrism and coloniality inherent in the realist premise. The ornament, in this regard, serves an epistemological purpose: layering objects of representation with a second level of signification that suggests the text's artificial structuring— like the metaliterary references to writing, weaving, and semblance that frame Joana Carolina in the moment of her canonization as a "form announced" that "must be for an artist"— highlights the multiplicity of Lins's writing procedures, tracing their limits as potential political tools (113). Similar to Lispector, Viñas, Andrade, and the concretes, I am suggesting that there is a critical force in laying bare Lins's system of writing.

Inverting the liturgical order, "Eleventh Mystery" also suspends the confessionary logic of discipline in the Foucaultian sense. This inversion sequence preserves Joana Carolina's status as an indeterminate object of art, a shifting ornamental signifier of contemplation that resists facile encapsulation or a violent "speaking for" in the name of administered institutions. She doesn't passively confess for us how she "agrees" with what has happened to her and the exploited multitude: "Padre, muitas vezes desejei matar" (Father, many times I've desired to kill) ("Retábulo" 111; Frizzi, "Retable" 158). She can't remember her "sins"; indeed, she is no noble "savage." Her canonization occurs at the level of an epistemic suspension and at the level of an accumulative unfolding metaphor. The text itself may be productively viewed as the way by which, as a sign for subaltern redemption, as well as a sign for art and writing, Joana Carolina is ambiguously woven across this plotting of borders and multiple readings. The giving of names, sanctification, and the mediation of this epistemic frontier that "Eleventh Mystery" explores thematically with the priest's phrase, "a priest must avoid the infiltration of things," occurs precisely in the text's suspension of sense with synesthetic flames and Latin. To the double-inquiry riddle-form that inaugurated "Eleventh Mystery," the naming of "it" ends in flames, naming *is* flames, and this is a properly aesthetic gesture, the political interface of the literary ornament in Osman Lins.[41] In this way, we could say with Slavoj Žižek that the subaltern remains a sublime object not of ideology but of aesthetic tensions.

ALTERNATIVE SCRIPTURES: SUBALTERNITY & REPRESENTATION

"There is, no doubt, something slightly disconcerting and perhaps not entirely welcome," writes Alberto Moreiras, in the "structural similarities between the superregionalist and the subalternist projects" (*Exhaustion* 170). The troubling link connecting the Boom to subalternist projects, Moreiras suggests, resides in the fact that the novel becomes "an appropriating machine" of cultural alterity, while subalternist theoretical practice is "born in willed opposition to" any such appropriative schematics (170).

Moreiras's observation finds pertinent echo with a host of pioneering theorists in the field: reflection on the interrelations between cultural forms and the state have become suspect. Herein lies the relevance of the question that pulses through this chapter: as exodus from state-centered accounts of culture, the subaltern problematic presents us with a challenging horizon that may very well hold an interpretative key for productively piecing together fragments of the past. Indeed, as we have shown throughout this volume, the subalternist frame remains especially pertinent in a cultural, critical, and political context averse to essentialism and statist ideology.

While trying to understand Lins in our time one never knows if one should read him solely from the vantage of form or from that of history and politics, "Final Mystery" in "Retábulo" presents us with a case that blurs these distinctions while problematizing normative conceptions of "literature." I want to read "Final Mystery" as a limit-text, as Lins's response to the impasse of representation provided in the case of the subaltern. I am not interested in unearthing Lins's technique solely in order to describe it. Rather, I am keen on demonstrating how the ornament implicates the reader in a critical relationship to this epistemological problem and how, at the very least, we may begin to reimagine the ways in which the limits of literary discourse were plotted in productive ways by Latin American intellectuals of the 1960s. If the aura was restored by the Boom, I argue, it was also questioned, critiqued, and profaned. Subalternity, in effect, was imagined by the literary otherwise.

"Final Mystery" is the account given by a multitude of "nobody" narrators who are carrying Joana Carolina's corpse to a mass burial ground. This throng of subalterns, represented by the semiotic indicator of infinity—∞— lets us know early on that they, like Joana Carolina, are the despised, downtrodden, and poor. How she belonged to the life-world of the "nobodies," a world that is described as dominated by the rich and powerful, is their topic.

Narrative develops along an axis of sweeping, musical descriptions rendered in the present tense, and along a parallel messianic register that paints Joana Carolina as a miracle worker and potential redeemer of the poor.

As in the Twelfth Station of the Cross, where Christ dies as a martyr and introduces into the world the principle of a new law and the Pentecostal speaking of tongues, "Mistério final" constitutes a challenging denouement. Not unlike the Mystery of the Cross, death, messianic apotheosis, and the bringing of a new law and language are its principal themes. And yet the text also points to a subset of themes bearing on literature, the arts, and politics. Insofar as narrative is chanted for the first (yet conclusive) time by a throng of dispossessed "nobodies" in the first-person plural, *nós*, the text foregrounds the problem of subalternity and solidarity.

The oscillation between prose, poetry, and theater in "Retábulo" is well documented.[42] And yet the infinity symbol denoting the narrator's choral speech suggests a larger anomaly. This is so because the "mystery" riddle that has prefaced each of the eleven previous tableaux—its stations or seasons akin to the messianic Via Crucis—is here removed. I want to suggest that the text's riddle and mystery become conflated in the choral host's narrative point of view.[43] Indeed, is it not the case that this infinite perspectivism of the subaltern chorus—designated by the signs ∞ and *nós*—implies an enigmatic breaking down, or shall we say, breaking out of the panel's representational scheme? Indeed, we recall that the titular "novena" commemorates the Christian Pentecost. Following Fredric Jameson's concept of the political unconscious, I want to argue that the messianic Pentecost serves as an allegorical horizon that introduces the promise of an "other" revolutionary language in Lins's "Retábulo."

And yet, Ángel Rama's concept of transculturation is curiously absent. Akin to Franco Moretti's reading of Gabriel García Márquez's *Cien años de soledad* (1967), language in "Retábulo" is strikingly neutral, monotone, and, above all, artificial. But unlike Moretti's critique of García Márquez, I want to stress the critical potential of this artificial discourse. Indeed, one could say that the narrative indicators—ornamental signs such as the cross or the sign of infinity—inscribe precisely a discursive problem concerning the nature and limits of literature.[44]

Put differently, the narrative indicator designates a sensory assemblage.[45] Drawn from astrology and alchemy, and similar to stage script, the indicators serve as visual frames to introduce narrative speech. Folding synthetic arrangements stretched to infinity, the indicators proliferate perspective while calling attention to writing's limits.

In "Final Mystery," the subaltern chorus utilizes a biblical register that transcends human knowledge: "nunca tivemos a impressão tão viva e tão

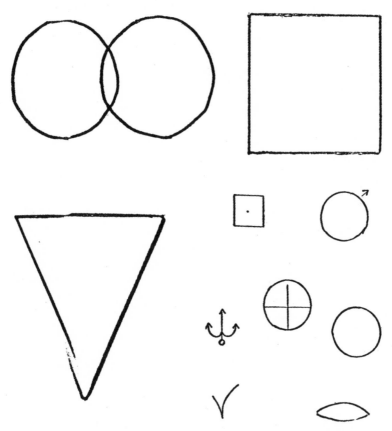

Esboço de alguns sinais identificadores das personagens feito por Osman Lins.

Fig. 5.7. Sketches of narrative indicators, by Osman Lins. Reprinted in Sandra Nitrini, *Poéticas em confronto: "Nove, novena" e o novo romance.* Courtesy of the estate of Osman Lins.

perturbadora de que esta é a arca do Próximo Dilúvio, que as novas águas vingativas tombarão sobre nós quarenta dias e quarenta noites . . . e que somente Joana sobrevivera" (we never had such a strong and disturbing feeling that this was the ark of the Next Great Flood, that the new vengeful waters would fall on us for forty days and forty nights) ("Retábulo" 114; Frizzi, "Retable" 163). Joana Carolina is inscribed as the "ark" announcing the advent of the "Next Flood." She is also described as a messianic maternal matrix and figure for redemption: "para depois gerar com um gesto os seres que lhe aprouver: plantas, bichos, Javãs, Magogs, Togarmas, Asquenazes" (to [later] give birth with a gesture to the creatures she pleased: plants, animals, Javans, Magogs, Togarmahs, Ashkenazes) ("Retábulo" 115; Frizzi, "Retable" 163).

The subaltern multitude also speaks from an accumulative register: "Hats in our hands, hard faces, rough hands, denim clothes, leather sandals, we greengrocers, market vendors, butchers, carpenters, middlemen in the cattle business, saddlers, sellers of fruits and birds, men of uncertain means and without a future, are taking Joana to the cemetery, we the nobodies of this town, because the others, the people with money and power, always ignored her" (Frizzi, "Retable" 161–62).[46] The force behind this distribution of class resides in the text's fragmentary mode of enunciation. Connoting the lack of agency and representative power in the polis, the absence of binding verbs, the breaking of the grammatical subject-object-predicate sequence is the hinge that binds these countless subalternized occupations divided by a long string of commas. Infinity—the sign of a "higher" cosmological order and the promise of messianic redemption—also seems to point to an infinite absence; call it subaltern agency or restitution, the infinity sign of the multitude configures the site of an interrogation and postponement of fulfillment.

Of the subaltern in "Mistério final" Lins wrote,

> In the final part, which is the burial, she is followed by the poor from
> the city, by the workers, the artisans, the small merchants, by the men
> with rough hands, and the whole burial is constructed in a highly violent
> rhythm. This narrative[,] which seems to be concerned with aesthetic
> problems, in reality, of all that I had written until that moment [1966], is
> the text with the most political problems. "Retábulo de Santa Joana Car-
> olina" is, in my view, political, and highly violent, although the majority of
> people tend to see in this text a quasi-religious narrative, beginning with
> the title, but the text is a narrative of a violent protest against the way that
> the poor are treated in my country.[47]

A political text, a violent text, yet one in which it is impossible to directly speak for the subaltern, Lins's "Mistério final" imposes a common strategy of the Latin American Boom: the reversion to myth. And yet, far from a procedure entailing the ultimate transcoding of heterogeneous discursive modalities and the imposition of a mythos to resolve intractable social contradictions, Lins's "Mistério final" is a halting, interruptive text that inscribes tension in the very myth and perspective encoding structures that inform it.

Far from a rote rewriting of a Christian saint's hagiography or the mythological trope of São Sebastião in the Brazilian Northeast, Joana Carolina functions as a *divided* ornamental signifier: "She lived her life with meekness, with humility and firmness, love and compassion. She died with reduced possessions and [a reduced number of] friends. Never did the plundering of others unleash any ambitions in her soul. Never did the evil suffered engender in her soul other evils" (Frizzi, "Retable" 165).[48] And yet, following Rancière, we would err in deducing the text's politics from such explicit moralizations on the part of the subaltern narrators.[49] This ethical sequence is part and parcel of the properly medieval, choral, and popular linguistic register that the text is self-consciously inhabiting: "Vamos carregando Joana para o cemitério, atravessando a cidade e seu odor de estábulos . . . entre Flores e Ruis, Glorias e Salvios, Hélios e Teresas, Isabeis e Ulisses, Josés e Veras" (We are carrying Joana to the cemetery, crossing the town and its smell of stables . . . among Floras and Ruis, Glórias and Sálvios, Hélios and Teresas, Isabels and Ulisses, Josés and Veras) ("Retábulo" 116; Frizzi, "Retable" 165).

Like Joana Carolina, the subaltern multitude becomes a shifting, accumulative signifier, a sign that proliferates and deterritorializes a central optical plane. But through the dispersion of their names that are also metonymies of the natural world, "um pomar generoso," a strange subjectivity of the poor is articulated:

> She died at the end of the winter. Will another like her be born in the next season? . . . Beneath the ground, beneath the plaster, beneath the weeds, the silent guests appear [*without words*]. Hawthornes and Myrtles, Hazels and Olives, Rosewoods and Laurels. They dressed them—why this [useless] generosity—in their Sunday suits, the finest dress, the best tie, the newest shoes. Strange reunion: all with their lips sealed, hands crossed, heads bare, all stiff, their eyelids closed and all facing the same direction, as if waiting, all alone, in front of a big portico in which someone was about to pass. A judge, an admiral, a harpist, a waiter with trays. Bringing what? . . . The Awaited One is tarrying, and the bodies of these mutes, of these immobile and speechless guests are being devoured. Humbly, in silence, Joana Carolina takes her place, her hands joined together, among Meadows, Wolfes and Burrs, among Lilies, Berries and Heathers, among Lambs, Quinceys and Amaryllis, among Roses, Lyons and Daisies, among Reeds, Crabs and Veronicas, among Martens, Jasmines, Irises, Hollies, Dales, Violets, Maples, Foxes, Ivies, among Cranes, and Fishes, and Ferns, in the dress she wore on Sunday afternoons and *enveloped [penetrada] by the silence that was her only companion.*[50] (Frizzi, "Retable" 165–66, emphasis added)

This "useless generosity" of naming that closes "Retábulo," the useless dispersion of proper names that bespeak of flora and fauna, rewrites the subaltern narrator chorus, sign of infinity, as metonymies of writing. The giving of names is, after all, emphasized.[51] As semiotic ornaments, the first letters

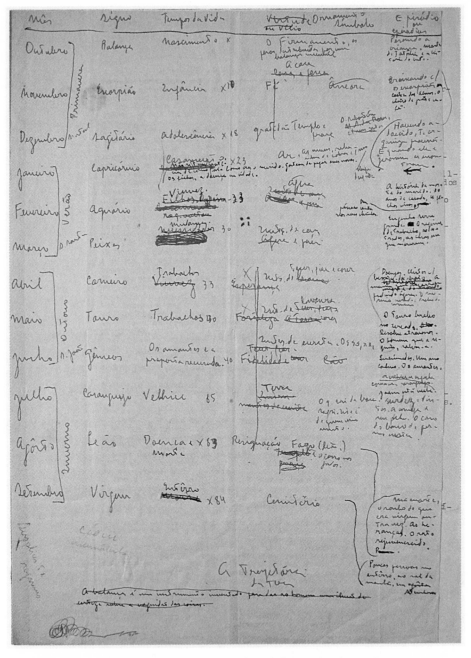

Fig. 5.8. Manuscript outline: charting from left to right, the twelve months, astrological signs, life phases, ornamental panels, and narratives of "Retábulo de Santa Joana Carolina," by Osman Lins. Photograph by author. Courtesy of the estate of Osman Lins.

of their names suggest the letters of the alphabet even as they burst across the commas in plantlike offshoots, in symphonic crescendo.[52] But this scriptural economy that lines the text's denouement and Joana Carolina's burial in a mass gravesite presents us also with a threshold, the contours of which delimit the problem of final meaning and redemption.

In charting this frontier, we should note that narrative voice here abruptly warps into omniscience. This deus ex machina voice from the outside interrupts the burial passage with questions concerning the arrival of an "Awaited" (*Tarda o Esperado*). Everything happens as though this authorial bird's-eye perspective were framing Joana Carolina's burial for us on the final partition of the retable tableau.

According to Maria Balthasar Soares, such abrupt shifts in perspective "accentuate the movement of writing in the story" (174). Dissonant closure, yet connoting a messianic horizon of redemption, what follows is yet another proliferation of signifiers. To the question, "why the useless generosity?"—of writing, of art, of naming?—Joana Carolina *and* the narrative point of view cross over into the "silent" horde and deathbed from a plane of omniscience.

Put differently, the "generous garden," in Lins, becomes an allegorized system of writing, a politics of aesthetics, that simultaneously displaces and fractures the transcendence of sense in the Saint signifier, and names and distributes its objects as ornaments that burrow under an epistemic ground in crisis: the writing of violence at the epistemological limits of literature and subalternity.[53]

To the extent that, following Benedito Nunes, Lins's text endeavors to "subject" the experience of entropic life to the "discipline of a poetic order," it is my contention that his narrative system presents us with, as in the baroque, a de-disciplined object ("Narration" 203). The object of representation and of social redemption is thus twice named and silenced: the story is cast, refracted, and suspended as a narrative modality of writing that calls attention to itself in its very finitude; that is, as an accumulative series of interlocking ornaments that serve as framing, refractory objects that call attention to the narrative's constructedness, and that also serve as the essential narrative components of the story: characters, narrators, and objects are also ornaments on the retable tableau. An inversion of Eden at the moment of Joana Carolina's burial, these ornaments warp into *metonymical figures of writing*, a poetic garden that points to a *critical function*: the overarching tableau frame that repositions, layers, and interrupts the story's objects and narrative structure. Joana Carolina's apotheosis, a figure of subaltern redemption, is ambiguously framed in silence and encircled by the nameless poor in the backlands, as though by an army of awaiting angels, flora, and creatures. Ornamental signs constituting an *alternative scripture*, this inversion of Eden culminates in the *becoming retable* and *politically problematic* of the narrative field. That is, far from positing the subaltern "other" as the object of transculturation and poetic discipline, as so many did in the 1960s, Lins's ornaments make this mediation critical as they constantly mediate the text's depictions of violence and subalternity: the subaltern is cast not so much as an object of ideology but as a figuration of accumulation and condensation, tension and textuality, principle for a new poetic and political word.

WRITING VIOLENCE

"To multiply the dimensions of the literary work," wrote Osman Lins in his widely distributed tract on the social function of the writer, was to establish a means of "connecting it more profoundly with reality" (*Guerra* 219). Lins's aesthetic of ornaments, inspired in Brazilian and European art forms, effectively articulated a multidimensional semantic field that he hoped would allow the reader to "see reality more globally" (Lins, *Evangelho* 214).[54] This "reality," of course, concerned Brazil in the context of the military dictatorship, and the problem of violence as it related to subaltern subjects in the Brazilian Northeast.

Toward the end of the 1960s, across the continent, literary writers begin to develop the idea of articulating a mode of counterviolence to the violence of the state and neocolonialism. If "stylization . . . activates the institutional memory," as Julio Ramos has argued concerning fin-de-siècle Latin American literature, the subject of an experimental style in the late 1960s became a fiercely contested discursive site for writers aligned with the Left (*Divergent* 180). For Lins, the construction of an innovative, personal style that responded to the political but which also met the demands of the market was a matter of performing a juggling act: on the one hand, as a professionalized writer who promoted and considered himself a servant to the craft of literature, Lins felt compelled to construct a literature that "re-integrated the word" with a public sphere he deemed fallen and passive, as well as intellectually "underdeveloped," due to invasion by the North American culture industry. The social task of the writer, in the context of Lins, was to engage the reader with a text of ornaments that revealed its very limits as text: "o romancista atual, contemporâneo, não quer mais iludir o leitor, ele segue uma linha que se aproxima da linha brechtiana, ele propõe ao leitor não um simulacro da vida, mas um texto, um texto narrativo, que se propõe como texto e propõe os personagens como personagens e não como figuras de carne e osso" (the actual, contemporary novelist does not desire to elude the reader: he follows a line that is close to Brecht; he proposes not a simulacrum of life, but a text, a narrative text, that proposes itself as text and its characters as characters and not figures of flesh and blood) (*Evangelho* 225). If the object was to make a text that revealed its limits as craft, and no longer be a vehicle of mimetic illusion, for Lins, this text was also importantly conceived as "um texto como detonador de percepções" (the text as a detonator of perceptions) (*Evangelho* 217).

The analogy of the text as a psychic laboratory and violent detonator of sensory perception takes us back to the historical avant-gardes of the 1920s.[55] In the case of Brazil, Mário de Andrade theorized the poetic act as a defamiliarizing "psychic realism" concerned with sensory perception in modernity and the unconscious (*Obra imatura* 292–94). And yet this avant-garde analogy in the 1960s should not be reduced to literary autonomization.[56] Neither should it be viewed as confined to the effervescent, iconoclastic terms of the avant-garde manifesto. Negotiating the problem of writing violence in the 1960s, as a matter of material politics and symbolic representation, effectively is the other side of the problem that Lins addressed on countless occasions, especially in interviews, in his correspondence, and in his essays. But then what exactly constitutes writing violence?

Following José Rabasa, I understand writing violence in two mutually interrelated modes. First, writing violence concerns representing such atrocities as exploitation of labor, political murder and ambush, and other forms of obvious "material terror" that contextualize the story and subaltern life-world of Joana Carolina in Pernambuco (Rabasa, *Writing* 22). Second, writing violence also concerns the power and force of writing as such, whereby writing serves as a codifying, appropriating apparatus that not only names and defines its objects of representation, but also has the capacity to expropriate the specificity and life-world of the referent, such as the subaltern "other" that Lins's text foregrounds. In the second, more thorny conception of representational violence, we should also recall that writing violence entails codifying legal and conceptual apparatuses that serve such ends as racism, facile stereotyping, and reductive, essentialist views of human perception and sense-making activity. Writing violence, in other words, is related to symbolic forms of violence.

While writing violence in the material, explicit sense is markedly tacit in "Retábulo de Santa Joana Carolina," as Lins liked to say, the ways in which the text negotiates symbolic violence through an aesthetic of ornaments demand a heightened attention to form. Following Deleuze and Guattari, I am referring to the ways in which the ornament in Lins is capable of simultaneously plotting and counteraddressing any reifying, essentialist apparatus of "royal science" that either subjugates, "overcodes," or congeals the specificity of a group or subject's "objective being" (*Anti-Oedipus* 27). And by "objective being," Deleuze and Guattari's decentering of Marx's classical definition of "living labor," and similar to Rabasa's notion of *elsewheres*, I understand a mode of existential, psychic, aesthetic, and productive dwelling, "irreducible to the State," that is posited as nonsubjugated by the conceptual apparatuses of domination and capture proper to idealistic categories and empire (Rabasa, "Elsewheres" 86; Deleuze and Guattari, *Thousand* 360). Like Lins's preferred image of the novelist as a master craftsman, Deleuze and Guattari describe the artist as a "master of objects" (*Anti-Oedipus* 32). According to this view, the artist distributes objects in dissonant modalities that serve "to short-circuit social-production and to interfere with the reproductive function of technical machines by introducing elements of dysfunction" (*Anti-Oedipus* 31). Accordingly, Deleuze and Guattari's vision of dissonant art constitutes a mode of writing (mapping) violence that works to dismantle symbolic violence from the standpoint that the normative conceptual apparatuses that structure and regulate social production are also powerful forms of symbolic violence.

With respect to the problem of addressing subalternity through literary style in Brazil during the 1960s, Deleuze and Guattari's point is well taken, and allows us to reconsider Lins's belief that the reader needed to be prodded into a more vital relationship with the text. The notion of constructing the *dynamic, concrete,* and *"vital" structure* in poetry and the visual arts was a major tendency in Brazil during the 1960s, as has been shown (Ramírez, "Vital" 193; Clüver, "Noigandres").[57] Lins's insistence that his literature of ornaments was not difficult but *direct* (*vai mostrando tudo ao leitor*) informs this general structure of feeling during the 1960s (*Evangelho* 149). To the extent that, for Lins, the Brazilian reading public was fallen and passive due to the "invasion" of the culture industry, engaging the reader became a central focus, because even *os leitores ilustrados* too often lacked the capacity to "ler as coisas em profundidade" (to read things deeply) (*Evangelho* 221).

We have shown how the ornament, in Lins, served to supplement the narrative field and the story of Joana Carolina's life with an array of poetic, religious, symbolic, cosmological, and astrological frames. These narrative points of view, such as the sign of infinity, ∞, for the subaltern chorus and the cross, †, to represent the priest, designate a cast of rotating narrators and serve as duplicitous signifiers that deterritorialize and reframe the entire economy of textual objects that make up the narrative.[58] These ornament-narrators also serve to call attention to the compositional fabric of the story insofar as they are narrator-symbols that project multiple connotations, and because of the fact that the entire narrative sequence is told in the present tense whereby the performative question of *writing* and the *process of signification* are reflected.

In concluding, I wish to stress that Lins was fascinated by the concept of aperspectivism and medieval art forms. With respect to Lins's preoccupation with perspective, it is useful to reconsider his programmatic voyage to Europe in 1961.[59] In an interview with Wladyr Nader, Astolfo Araújo, Hamilton Trevisan, and Gilberto Mansur for the literary review *Escrita* in 1976, Lins provides a remarkable portrait of this "aesthetic voyage."[60] Over the course of the interview, Lins highlights his scheduled trips to concerts, museums, and excursions to cathedrals. Of all the experiences, including his interviews with the leading figures of the French *nouveau roman*, such as Alain Robbe-Grillet and Michel Butor, Lins emphasizes the importance of observing medieval stained glass:

> I would say that the principal experience of my European voyage—the one that marked me and would mark me for the rest of my life—was my contact with stained-glass windows and Roman art, medieval art in general. With respect to stained-glass windows, I learned a fundamental lesson: I was able to carefully examine the degeneration of this art form. Insofar as the stained-glass resigned itself to its [compositional] limits, to lead and colored glass, it shone in all its force as an art form. But soon after the glassmakers started to find that insufficient, and they began to paint the stained glass; they brought to the art of stained-glassmaking the art of painting. From that moment the stained glass degenerates. This brought me to a belief of which I am firmly convinced: that things shine, let's say, in their limitations. Limitations are not necessarily a limitation in the common usage of the term, but a force. I mean to say that the stained glass was impacting insofar as it was limited, insofar as it accepted its limitation. Additionally, the stained glass, being an art form that is extremely synthetic, even rustic, proved to be a highly expressive art. It brought me to the conviction that a literature in the line of Proust is not necessary. It's funny that Proust thought of his art as closely related to the art in cathedrals, because his art was an art of the miniature, very minute, while stained-glassmaking is a synthetic art, extremely direct. Thus in my literature I really am looking for a work that is direct. . . . The other thing about my contact with medieval art is the aperspectival character of this art. . . . if the Renaissance had brought with it a perspectival vision of the world, naturally centered in the human eye, the Middle Ages brought the aperspectival vision, due to the fact that it was a theocentric age as opposed to anthropocentric; so artists, as a reflex to the general vision of the medieval man, tended to see things as though they were not fixed in a determinate place. This made the vision of the world much richer: it did not limit the vision of things to the human condition.[61]

This interview statement seems essential. Lins's aesthetic voyage to Europe has been interpreted as a turning point in his conception of narrative, which, until the voyage, was characterized as realist. While this interpretation remains valid, the interview statement permits us to connect the problem of aesthetic perspective to the problem of writing violence. Doubtless, Lins's insight regarding the observation of perspective in the cathedral's stained glass concerned the limiting of perspective. The relationship that is established between the depiction in the glass and the perceiving subject becomes more dynamic and multiple (*muito mais rica*) inasmuch as perspective in the stained glass becomes unfixed, freeing the perceptual field from a central focal point. This experience of a synthetic or multiple perspective (*sintética*), more than an articulation of Lins's fascination with medieval European art forms, registers for Lins the way unfixed perspective can frustrate mimetic figuration. Put differently, the unfixed, synthetic perspective produces a sphere of perceptual and cognitive mobility for the spectator.

This snapshot of Lins's illumination regarding unfixed perspective enables us to better conceive the complexity of Lins's preoccupation with narrative perspective and the problem of countermapping violence through literature. For inasmuch as narrative perspective, in Lins, provided a frame for writing violence in the Brazilian northeastern backlands in the explicit sense of naming, by unfixing narrative perspective through an array of ornaments, he made narrative perspective a dynamic field of perception that de-ontologized the unitary descriptive frame. In this regard, writing violence from an aesthetic of ornaments charts and responds to violence in two specific senses—the material and the symbolic. On the one hand, Lins's narrative charts the material violence that subaltern subjects suffer at the hands of land barons and a corrupt state. In this more explicit regard, the ornament supplements and enriches narrative perspective through a series of shifting signifiers that suggest various modalities and angles for understanding exploitation: through the trope of redemption (Joana Carolina as exploited subaltern who is recast as a saint represented on the ornament tableau painting), for example, or through the trope of a subaltern multitude that awaits the arrival in the backlands of a new heaven (revolution) that will overthrow the landowners (the subaltern narrator-chorus represented by the ornament sign of infinity).

On the other hand, writing against symbolic violence through an aesthetic of ornaments concerns displacing the unitary, epistemological perspective of naming with a multiplicity of perspectives that underscore the constructed quality of the text. In this way, Lins's ornament charts violence through narrative form, and simultaneously deconstructs the conceptual apparatus of capture and codification underlying symbolic violence and the language of "royal science." Accordingly, the ornament discloses and deflects the force and violence of writing proper.

Against the grain of Lins's self-proclaimed motive to lead the reader from a situation of chaos to cosmological order through the ornamental word, Lins's oft-repeated three-stage autobiographical, evolutionary model (*procura, transição, plenitude* [search, transition, plenitude]), I am making the counterclaim that the ornament inscribes the text's radical finitude in a double horizon: subalternity and the metaliterary.[62] It is not chaos, and it is not cosmos, but the finitude of literature and epistemological limits that are ultimately relayed across the ornament's field. Doubtless, critics are correct in asserting that there is geometrical symmetry and numberless references to the cosmos, the zodiac, and to writing and art forms in the narration of Joana Carolina's life. But these signs of positivity, closure, and semantic sedimentation, including any redeeming representation of subalternity, are interrupted, overlapped, suspended, and recoiled by the undoing of representation in two directions: forwards in terms of a text that constantly suspends, partitions, and redirects its representation as multiple, accumulative, and artificial, and backwards in terms of the inscription of subalternity as a *mark* of infinity, as the epistemic fissure and divide against which a counterpolitics could organize itself, as the nameless multitude that remains unredeemed in the hollow, artificial shell of the signifier ∞. Joana Carolina's apotheosis, at the text's close, is just this blending in with the infinite nameless, in the mass burial site, a profanized and poetic image—more interrogative than affirmative.

Yet we would be mistaken to think of Lins as advocating a devaluation of literature's voice in political and epistemological matters such as representing subalternity. This much is clear: Lins believed, as did Ángel Rama, that writing represented human culture's highest form of self-expression. In a letter written in 1975, Lins explains how in "Retábulo de Santa Joana Carolina" the themes of hunting, fishing, agriculture, fiction, and weaving are depicted in sequence in the tableaux in order to allegorize the march of *civilização*: "o homem partindo de um estagio primitivo e chegando (no quadro da narrativa) a sua conquista suprema, a escrita" (civilization: man advancing from a primitive stage and arriving [in the narrative frame] to his supreme conquest, writing) (letter to Sandra Nitrini, 25 March 1975). And it is not speculation to say that the highest form of writing, for Lins, was literature. In this sense, Idelber Avelar's thesis concerning the Latin American Boom's aesthetic compensation for politics is applicable to Lins.

And yet Avelar's thesis concerning the thematization of writing only partially hits the mark when applied to Lins's and the Boom's deeper textual characters. The metatextual dimension that I have been highlighting and conceptualizing in Lins charts the field of narrative representation in reverse as an apparatus of *ornamental writing*. In so doing, it inverts, counterfocalizes, and duplicates the chain of narrative objects, or characters and events, which become signs for this doubling writing modality. The problem of writing violence is counterwritten in this way. The force of writing and contesting symbolic violence by revealing writing's finitude takes on a more powerful dimension when its signifying chains duplicate, intercept, and overarch the interpretation and representation of the other limit of its horizon—subalternity. Accordingly, Lins's aesthetic of ornaments in "Retábulo de Santa Joana Carolina" articulates the deterritorialization of writing violence and an ethnographic gaze that posits no ideological, conceptual, or identitarian positivity or cultural identity, no ultimate universalization of the regional subaltern, but rather diagrams through its winding and interlocking array of artifices the suspension of all and any writing positivity so as to reveal the possibility of thinking through the horizons and conditions of writing's elsewheres: an infinity of nameless nobodies, the poor in the Brazilian backlands, whose redemption, delayed, never narrated, but promised in choral song, also configures a *writing grid*, which should be deciphered, across the death of the martyr-subaltern-saint, as an interrogation and inscription of the impasse of the literary in Latin America during the 1960s.[63]

WRITING SUBALTERN REDEMPTION & INSURGENCY

Haroldo de Campos's "The Left-Winged Angel of History"

WHAT IS at stake in the field of subversion proper to the anti-literary, if not, in the end, the laying down of an unlimited plane of justice as opposed to the shadows of an identitarian state? We will return to the question of justice and anti-literature's untimely secret later, but let us first lay down, in very broad strokes, a recap of our main arguments.

Throughout this book, I have posed the problem of writing: writing and its limits, writing and margins, writing and anti-literature. Paying heed to the historical specificity of literature as a cultural institution in Brazil and Argentina, I have theorized an anti-literary countertradition from an intensive engagement with form. Through an examination of the diverse projects of Clarice Lispector, Oswald de Andrade, the Brazilian concrete poets, Osman Lins, and David Viñas, our opening claim remains operative: whatever critical force to be extracted from the literary question in Latin American studies begins with a critique of what is meant today by "literature." Beyond representation, then, and beyond the identitarian imaginary that reduces the literary question in Latin American studies, this book proposes, for the first time, historical case studies of an anti-literary line. Such a line emerges with force in the 1920s and runs through the present.

Yet the theory of anti-literature will only be understood as untimely, following Nietzsche, as acting counter to our time and on it, for a future, it is hoped, to come. Conceiving of an untimely dimension of literature means thinking its heterogeneous modes of expression as forms of resistance. Creation requires the new and unforeseen. Writing as heterogenesis. That is, anti-literary writing will only be understood as the affirmation of new syntactic and affective powers. In their flight from dominant semiotic systems, including the reign of opinion and essentialist conceptions of writing and history, it could be said that anti-literary writers hook up writing to literature's outside, to nonwriting and egalitarian modes of imagining the community. What is at issue is precisely this: the concept of anti-literature need not restrict itself to an avant-garde, modernist paradigm of the arts. Rather, an approach to the anti-literary entails reconceptualizing the problem of writing as a sensory procedure and perceptual force.

The question of what is anti-literature can perhaps best be posed only in the wake of literature's exhaustion, when the arrival of defeatist accounts demands the time for speaking concretely. Indeed, bibliography on the nature of literature in the field is marginal. The question is always asked, but has remained in large part abstract, too burdened by representation, too overdetermined by epistemology and sociology. Theorists have not been sufficiently concerned with what I call writing's affective force and constituent power. They have preferred, in large measure, to conceptualize literature as a ready-made system, a cultural regime, as given knowledge. Yet the anti-literary medium is never given but produced. In its confrontation with nonwriting, with minorities, with multimedia, and the order of opinion, we can best visualize anti-literature as a polyphonic, open assemblage composed of diverse regimes of signs.

Literature constitutes a specific procedure of the sensible. Namely, it deals in perception and affects. Literature frustrates the dominant order of the sensible, that is, the common, habitual ways of seeing, making, and feeling in the community. Accordingly, I have sought to de-suture it from hegemonic conceptions of politics and all regimes of representation. De-linking literature from representation so as to rethink the subversive stakes of experimental writings from the 1920s to the present, I have historicized a countermemory of writing's legacies.[1] Going beyond traditional accounts that locate the Spanish American "Boom" as the homecoming and avatar of an evolved literary subject and golden age of "Latin American" literature, the studies in this volume make a case for expansion in the field by including Brazilian, relatively marginalized writers, and the late Argentine writer David Viñas, whose work is all too often reduced to propaganda. All of the texts in question offer new images of writing. Furthermore, I argue that an examination of anti-literature not only defies traditional notions of literature, but changes the larger discussion about the "nature" of Latin American literature and permits us to reconceptualize the question of writing the

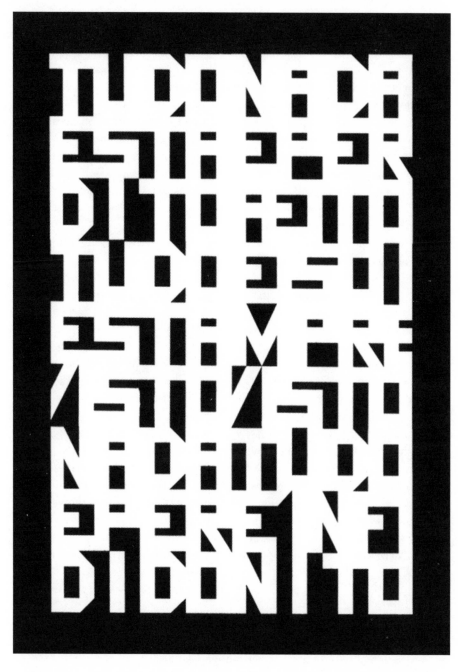

Fig. 6.1. "TUDO ESTÁ DITO," by Augusto de Campos. From *Viva vaia: Poesia 1949–1979*. Courtesy of Augusto de Campos.

subaltern, the feminine, literary politics, and the literary debate in Latin American studies today from a distinctly comparative and original Brazilian context. Reflection on Brazilian writers within Latin American studies is rare. To the extent that the divide persists, this book attempts to not only redirect the critique of literature in the field, but to work unexamined connections between Brazilian and Spanish American literature.

Let us now reaffirm the threads that constitute our plan of research: *Anti-Literature* examines the epochal crisis of literature and literature's constituent powers. Not content with marking literature's limits with respect to cultural representation, I consider writings that propose a new framework for writing, a new situation for thinking the sensible. If "literature" persists in crisis in our field, the task today is to reconstitute its critical force. Literature becomes anti-literature when it subverts itself. My contention is that it is only by bearing witness to this relation of non-essence, non-identity, and non-closure—literature is not literature—that we can begin to read anew. This book's examination of the different genres and media that Brazilian and Argentine anti-literary writers mobilize—nonverbal anti-poetry, feminine writing, film, painting, pop culture, subaltern affect, baroque ornamentation, and so on—expands our understanding of what is meant by "Latin American" literature.

In other words, like Augusto de Campos's video-poem, "TUDO ESTÁ DITO" (EVERYTHING'S SAID) (1979; 1996), by accounting for literature's nonrelation to identity, we witness how anti-literature proposes a new conception of form where the conventional literary "all said" becomes undone: "TUDO / ESTÁ / DITO / TUDO / ESTÁ / VISTO / NADA / É PERDIDO / NADA / É PER / FEITO / É SÓI / MPRE / VISTO / TUDO / É / INFI / NITO" (EVERY / THING'S / SAID / EVERY / THING'S / SEEN / NOTHING'S / LOST / NOTHING'S / PER / FECT / IT'S ONLY / UNFORESEEN / EVERYTHING'S / INFI / NITE) (249). In effect, through the anti-poem's zigzagging movement across the verbal and nonverbal, the poem and video, the straight line and labyrinth, we witness the idea of literary evolution and plenitude—EVERYTHING'S / SAID / EVERYTHING'S / SEEN—implode as a self-critical field of limitless verbal, vocal, and visual force.

AFTERIMAGES: AFFECT & LIMIT

Against totalization and fixed unitary subjects, Brazilian and Argentine anti-literature constitutes an affair with limits—with sensation and writing's powers of finitude. Yet according to influential critics, it would seem that the literary was always doomed in Latin America to an identitarian imaginary. Against the grain of this traditional view that presupposes a precarious social bond, concretized through the transculturating literary apparatus, this book has proposed an examination of the following problematic: that anti-literature never arises from representation, but with a specific concern with affect. In so doing, I have referred to the fact that anti-literary writing is involved in creating new modes of perception and feeling that challenge the habitual ways of seeing and sensing in the community. This includes generating fresh ways of understanding what is meant by "Latin American" literature today. In particular, I argue that Brazilian and Argentine anti-literature resists all genre fixity by cannibalizing multiple regimes of perception and artistic genres, from movies, radio, television, and the computer to subaltern life-worlds and concrete art.

Throughout this book we have discerned images of anti-literary writing. In so doing, we have studied the aesthetic, political, and historical bases of the anti-literary's generative powers of becoming. Our task has been to examine the possibilities and limits of the literary as a site of reflection and reaction to contemporary conditions. Against representation, we have called for assessing the problem of anti-literature from the framework of its constituent process. Such an approach entails restaging writing in terms of its radicalized medium, as a strange textual body (*corpo estranho*) that is generative of multilinear movements of creativity against all measure (Pignatari, "Marco" 149). In its most general conception, following Spinoza, we dissolve the impoverished form-content divide to conceive of form as a capacity and affective compositional milieu. To speak of writing's powers of resistance is to consider language as a generative semiotic assemblage. Yet it is also to rethink the *matter* of writing not as an organized system or fountainhead of the "real," to be sure, but as a sensory aggregate that affirms chance, play, and the untimely opening of the event of the text. Through syntactic configurations that oppose closure and fixity, writing constitutes a milieu of sensation that condenses multiple regimes of signs. Our notion of anti-literature, dismissive as it is of unity, breaks free from the form-content divide by conceptualizing form as a polyphonic capacity and constituent power. No doubt, our concern with affect over representation entails a paradigm shift.

The transformation of the discussion of "literature" today turns on the basis of anti-literature. To be sure, this is not a simple act of negation. Nor are we advocating an exclusive approach. We are announcing, rather, what the Brazilian and Argentine anti-literary works themselves have shown us: an exodus from the conceptual coordinates of traditional culturalist and philological approaches. Each chapter has offered a rethinking of the onto-logical bases of traditional vocabularies that confine literature and politics to the logic of representation. In invoking the force and relevance of Brazilian and Argentine anti-literature's legacy for our time, we are breaking free from all monological conceptions of writing, history, and culture, which includes revoking the illusion of modernist autonomy as progressive intransitivity. In the seams of our discourse it should be clear that we are also willfully exiting from antiquated, cut-and-dried conceptions that tend to prize monological formulations of literary genre and the projection of literature as a state form. What is one to make of the feminine, subalternist, multimedial assemblage in Lispector or the cybernetic anti-poetry of Augusto de Campos? The film-prose of Viñas, or the ornamental tableau narratives of Lins? We want nothing to do with literary purity and essence. Anti-literature is anti-institution and anti-state. *Accordingly, through an assessment of Brazilian and Argentine experimental limit-works and their relationship to nonwriting and nonhistory, we discover in anti-literature the conceptual basis for a powerful political syntax of the sensible that defies domination and state-logic.* We thereby discover a new conception of literary politics—a tide change, we argue, in a debate that has remained largely stagnant since the subalternist turn of the 1990s. In so doing, it should be clear that we are leaving the discourse of exhaustion toward a posthegemonic, affective, and untimely conception of experimental writing.

To comprehend the concept of anti-literature and its relationship to politics, we do well to contrast it with transculturation. In transculturating accounts of the literary, literature is conceived as a sovereign subject, a form modeled on the Romantic, national popular integrating functions assigned to the state. According to this view, literature's task is identitarian. It represents, integrates, and "crowns" the diversity of peoples into a single, national popular unity. The writer translates cultural difference and speaks for the "people." Difference is subsumed under sameness. Yet if it is true that the act of writing is always an act of thought that co-belongs with politics, then in the case of transculturation theory any thinking of the sensible shuts down. Transculturation cannot perceive literature's powers of texture, syntactic subversion, affect, and, crucially, the work's semiotic density. We rather work, so to speak, from the ground up, concerning the work's verbal, vocal, and visual materials as instruments of the sensible. What is more, identity stifles the intricate folds of composition and its zones of illiteracy. Anti-literature, by contrast, is never unified and is best imaged as a distributive milieu of affects. Deleuze and Guattari observe that the creation of unforeseen affects dissolves reified norms of perception.[2] *As a change of scale and flight from domination*, the affect has nothing to do with identity and majoritarian standards.

Through the lens of Brazilian and Argentine anti-literature, we create a new typology of the text. Like the affect, the work is produced through a multiplicity of registers. Accordingly, the multiplicity of regimes of signs reveals the work's productive relationship with the limit. Throughout this book, we have endeavored to examine literature's limit as a generative, polyvocal force. Whether grounded in the problem of writing the feminine, the subaltern, or sabotaging the technomediated reification of the sensible, our task has been to show how anti-literature articulates a freeing of writing from representation. Following Rancière, but highlighting Brazilian and Argentine anti-literature's specific historical concern with metaliterature, subalternity, and challenging the old, hierarchical view of literature, anti-literature intervenes by suspending and redistributing the common perceptual coordinates of the community. Brazilian and Argentine anti-literature therefore create a new sensorium, one that suspends the tyranny of opinions, clichés, and consensual standards. Its politics resides not in sticking to a party line, nor in the blind relay of message, but in the creation of an interface between mediums, between majoritarian standards of command and new forms of sense-making, sensation, and perception. Charting the limits of customary conceptions of literary politics, one could say that the protean works we have examined disrupt logics of domination. At the minimum, these works articulate events of writing that destroy state-centered thought. But in addition to these limit-works, centered as they are in modern Brazil and Argentina, we need to rethink the concept of anti-literature in light of the new challenges presented by our time. Such a conceptual rethinking is the goal of this chapter.

THE COMMON & LITERARY POLITICS

Writing at the limit of literature, we have focused at length on the problem of literary politics in twentieth-century Brazil and Argentina. In so doing, we have established the mutually defining relationship between anti-literature's radicalized medium and the production of affects. To the extent that we have noted anti-literature's task of subverting the sensible, as well as its multimedial and feminine modes of articulation, can anti-literature today construct a language adequate to the event of subaltern struggle? What is anti-literature's relationship to the ever-present contemporary death work of the state? And can we approach anti-literature's limit-texts as intermediaries between collective action and historical sense? What possible meaning can anti-literature have in today's world, where violence, state of exception, and perpetual war reign?

Confronted by the problem of anti-literature and its generative powers, our concluding reflection takes up the task contemporary poetry sets itself in regard to redeeming subalternity from the stranglehold of a violent present. As theoretical inquiry, denunciatory poem, and avant-garde experiment, Haroldo de Campos's "O anjo esquerdo da história" (The Left-Winged

Angel of History) (1996) suggestively restages the police massacre of nine-teen landless workers in Eldorado dos Carajás.[3] While critics have rightfully read the poem as the expression of Campos's indignation and solidarity, they have not addressed the arduous question of mediating affect and subaltern insurgency which configures the work's generative matrix. As will be shown in what follows, "O anjo" defies literary genre by configuring an untimely poetic space grounded in subaltern affect. In effect, it is a limit-work that approximates a liberated image for reframing the crisis of the social bond, as well as a means for gauging anti-poetry's productive relationship to subal-tern revolution. It is a radical work, then, about justice, and a contemporary form of subalternist, anti-literary force.

Composed in the aftermath of the military police's massacre of nineteen landless workers in the town of Eldorado dos Carajás, "O anjo esquerdo da história" problematizes the very notions of poetry, history, and writing sub-altern insurgency. While scholars such as Else R. P. Vieira and Maria Esther Maciel have examined the text's relationship to memory and a vast swath of historical intertexts, we lack a theoretical appraisal of "O anjo" in terms of affect, writing the subaltern, and what I will call Campos's commitment to the *untimely* materiality of anti-literature. Breaking with linear syntax and blurring the distinction between philosophy, poetry, and translation, accord-ingly, it is an anti-literary work that radically redistributes the conditions of intelligibility for what "literature" signifies in our present. Against populism and nation-centered discourse, yet summoning the memory of the massacre with all its might, it is a limit-work that frames the possibilities and limits of poetry as a site for reactivating a thinking of history from the vantage of an anti-literary "Left."

It is impossible to speak of the text in isolation, as the poem was com-posed in the context of international outcry. And as a palimpsestic configura-tion that parodically plays with photography, painting, music, film, the Bible, and classic texts from Brazilian and European literature, it is likewise diffi-cult to conceive of the text in the singular. To be sure, Campos will translate the poem into English in the year 2000 for the international journal of post-colonial studies, *Interventions*, to mark the five-hundred-year anniversary of Portugal's "discovery" of Brazil.[4] First published in the Workers' Party journal *PT Notícias* in 1996 and reedited in its current, definitive version in 1998, "O anjo" consists of four nonsequential stanzas and eighty-three fragmented verses varying from five to seven syllables in length. Demand-ing from the outset acute attention to semantic multiplicity, verse is struc-tured as a continuous flux of signs. Through minimalist, anti-ornamental versification, the poem pays tribute at once to Schönberg's tone row and the medieval popular *redondilha de arte menor*. Indeed, while it could be said that Campos's deployment of this fractured *arte menor* summons the popular northeastern minstrelsy and the politically charged verse of João Cabral de Melo Neto, we do well to observe that arte menor recalls the liturgical practice of *mística* by the Movimento dos Trabalhadores Rurais Sem Terra (MST, or Landless Workers Movement). According to Plínio de Arruda Sampaio, the mística is a storytelling performance that precedes workers' meetings. In fact, the mística configures a celebratory revolutionary space in which poetry and politics, socialism and Christianity converge:

> Meetings small, large and enormous always begin with a celebration. It's short at small meetings, long and elaborate at large ones. The elements of these celebrations are always the same: earth, water, fire, ears of corn, the student's notebook, the hoe, flowers. Not much is said. Poetically and convincingly, they reclaim the voices of popular poets and of the great Brazilian poets such as Haroldo de Campos, Drummond de Andrade, Pedro Terra. The expressions are meaningful and significant: canto, a closed fist signifying indignation, readiness for struggle, hope. Pure canto of popular troubadours from deep in the country, people like Ze Pinto, Ze Claudio, Marquinho. This is blended with canto, delicate as the finest flower, from Brazilian artists like Chico Buarque, Tom Jobim, Caymi, Milton Nacimento.
>
> Celebrations always occur against a backdrop of the great stories of those who have fought for the people. Here the syncretism of the landless erupts: Marighela, the communist guerrilla fighter is found next to the image of Paulo Freire, the revolutionary Catholic educator. Rosa Luxembourg is next to Madre Cristina, a Catholic nun. Florestan Fernandes, profound Marxist intellectual, is at the side of Padre Josimo, a monk murdered by the landholders' assassins. Karl Marx is found next to Jesus Christ.
>
> The truth is that those who are surprised by this mixture know very little about the mentality of the Brazilian people nor do they seem to understand the true dimensions of socialist humanism.
>
> All liturgy is pedagogy. The celebrations that precede the work meetings remind the participants of the meaning of their mística: solidarity, internationalism, readiness for struggle. This symbolism gives the group its identity and links it to the past. But at the same time it orients the group to the future with an image of a just Brazil, rich with milk and honey. (Sampaio, "Mística")

If millenarianism and music mark the mística performance as celebration, Campos's recourse to polyphony establishes a relationship with choral performance. In effect, "O anjo" will cannibalize multiple registers:

the messianic mística and the requiem form. Writing at history's limit, the poem will not only mourn but reactivate unrecognized subaltern affects. Having discerned this, renowned contemporary Brazilian composer Gilberto Mendes will construct a polyvocal interpretation for the poem with the Symphony Orchestra for the State of São Paulo in 2006. What is more, marking the first-year anniversary of the massacre, and coinciding with the MST's March on Brasília in April 1997, Campos will read the poem to the São Paulo House of Representatives in protest for the impunity granted the military police force.

To the extent that Campos's poem investigates the massacre from the perspective of affect and performance, we need to delve deeper into its historical layers, beginning with a recounting of the catastrophe itself. Portuguese novelist José Saramago succinctly relates that

> [o]n 17 April 1996, in the Brazilian state of Pará, near a town called Eldorado dos Carajás . . . 155 military policemen, armed with rifles and machine guns, opened fire on a demonstration of peasants who were blocking the roadway in protest against the delay in the legal proceedings to expropriate land. The proceedings concerned the rough draft or façade of a supposed agrarian reform in which, amid minimal steps forward and dramatic steps back, fifty years had already gone by without ever sorting out the grave problems of subsistence (it would be more correct to say survival) of the farmhands. That day, nineteen dead and fifty-seven wounded lay scattered on the ground at Eldorado dos Carajás. Three months after this bloody event, the Pará state police, arrogating to itself the role of judge . . . declared publicly the innocence of its 155 soldiers, alleging that they had acted in self-defence, and as if that were not enough, they brought criminal charges against three of the peasants for contempt, injuries and illegal possession of weapons. The protesters' arsenal consisted of three pistols, rocks and farm implements which were more or less capable of being brandished. (11)

There were fifteen hundred peasants occupying highway PA-150 that day. And as Saramago paints it for us, at stake was the overlong delay of state-sanctioned land reform. The event concerned, moreover, disparate modes of organization and the overflowing of limits: the desire to settle families on the Machacheira plantation, an unproductive, uncultivated space the MST had been occupying for months, and the "transcendent power" of the state (Beasley-Murray 227). In other words, closing off the MST as perpetual mass mobilization, the state suspended the law to violently capture the group's constituent process. In our reading of "O anjo," we will dwell in this perilous space of limits, overflow, and violence. The intention will be to

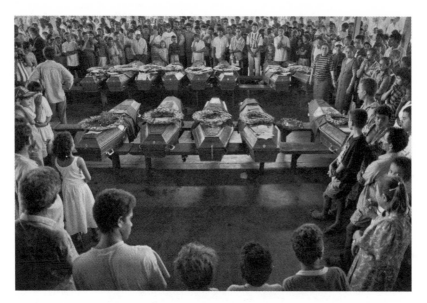

Fig. 6.2. MST Funeral Vigil, Eldorado dos Carajás, by Sebastião Salgado. From Salgado, *Terra: Struggle of the Landless.* © Sebastião Salgado/Amazonas/(Contact Press Images).

show how Campos hooks up poetry to the constituent process of the multitude, that is, to the MST's forms of creative resistance and organization. For "O anjo" will not shy from solidarity, nor will it flinch from subaltern memory work, but it will only do so by resisting representation. It will dwell with specters. In effect, through the construction of a free temporal structure that introduces the text as an incalculable body of affects, the poem will be concerned with creating a future for poetry rooted in experimentation, militancy, and justice. Seizing the creative moment of invention at each turn, Campos's poem problematizes linear logic and ushers in an untimely chance for poetry in relation to subversion, politics, and subalternist historical reflection.

Saramago's description of the massacre serves as preface for Sebastião Salgado's international exhibit and best-selling book, *Terra: Struggle of the Landless* (1997). To the extent that *Terra* establishes unforeseen links between photography, poetry, painting, politics, historical reflection, and subaltern affect, it will no doubt endeavor to perform an interruption of homogeneous nation-centered narratives of Brazilian "progress." As a multimedial assemblage of micro-texts, dramatized images, popular songs, and poems by renowned Brazilian composers, in many ways it could be said that "O anjo" is *Terra*'s microcosm and offshoot.[5] The dialogue between texts is immediately

Fig. 6.3. MST Occupation of Giacometi Plantation, by Sebastião Salgado. From Salgado, *Terra: Struggle of the Landless.* © Sebastião Salgado/Amazonas/(Contact Press Images).

tangible. Syntax in both is visual, spatial, and analogical and driven by intertexts. Indeed, reminiscent of a scene from *Terra*, "O anjo" begins not with verse but at poetry's limits, with a cropped newspaper photograph from the *Folha de São Paulo*: the MST funeral march at Eldorado dos Carajás on 20 April 1996. Let us first consider Salgado's exhibit for necessary context.

Containing 109 black-and-white images taken between 1980 and 1996, *Terra* portrays the plight of Brazil's downtrodden and includes afterimages of the now legendary Eldorado dos Carajás massacre.

Salgado's haunting images of the state's death-work configure an arrest in time, a stark meditative space of contrast through which the viewer may ponder the cooperative, living pulsation of a people. For beyond the state's death-space, beyond the blood-streaked faces of the victims, Salgado's exhibit attests to the fact that, even now, a rising multitude of landless is redeeming history. Through images of collective struggle, school construction, occupation marches, and the still shining glow of hope in the eyes of children, a new world of life with dignity emerges. Framed in the most miserable of desert conditions—in these underbelly spaces of the global South, in this landless dystopian Brazil where state violence, exception, and neglect of the poor reign—Salgado's photos bear witness to a new people and a new earth that is being produced in common. Through montage sequences that invoke the messianic, the landless appear before our gaze as giants. If we begin Salgado's exhibit with Edenic images of indigenous peoples inhabiting the earth without property, the book ends as an incalculable opening up of history, with the landless multitude marching in revolution, scythes raised high: in spite of the state's death-work, the landless are multiplying and re-settling a land without capital.

Similar to Campos's poem, *Terra*'s multivalent syntax replaces critical reason's absence. Indeed, Salgado's project inscribes what could be called a *logic of elsewheres*: a flight from and radical relativization of instrumental logic (Rabasa, "Elsewheres" 86; *Without* 274). Consider *Terra*'s captions. Located at the back of the book and framed through a sterilized language that strains for surgical precision, Salgado's explicative texts enhance, para-doxically, the scene of unaccounted-for affects. Salgado refuses to speak for the subaltern, even as he relates the forensic facts encircling the massacre in restrained, deadpan language:

> In the late afternoon, the commander of the military police of the state of Pará sent troops from two different barracks to the scene; they surrounded the protesters from both sides of the highway, immediately opening fire with rifles and machine guns. . . . The forensic pathologist Nelson Massini, a professor at the Federal University of Rio de Janeiro . . . confirmed that at least ten of the victims were summarily executed by bullets in the head and the back of the neck. Judging from the powder burns, the weapons were discharged at extremely close range. Seven of the bodies were hacked to pieces by blows from the scythe or large knife. Pará, 1996 (142)

Like Salgado, Campos saw the Landless Workers Movement's revolu-tionary promise. Yet as we have seen in the case of the *Galáxias* and con-crete poetry in general, Campos was wary of politically driven poems at the level of content. When asked about poetry's relationship to politics, Cam-pos liked to invoke the Russian poet Vladimir Mayakovsky's slogan: poetry without revolutionary form could never be revolutionary.[6] Accordingly, in writing "O anjo" in the immediate aftermath of the massacre, Campos felt the need to craft a poem-response that was adequate to the event of subal-tern tragedy and resistance. Crossing the threshold of verse, such a creation would require an investigation of the MST's material conditions; namely, it would demand a more profound understanding of the MST's "syntax," including its modes of resistance and life-world.

By most measures, Brazil boasts one of the largest gaps between rich and poor in the world. This is so in spite of Brazil's status as an economic powerhouse, the seventh largest economy on the globe: 50 percent of ag-riculturally suitable land is controlled by 4 percent of landowners (Wright and Wolford xv). Within this context, Campos perceived "two Brazils" in conflict—one European, rich and cosmopolitan, and the other peripheral, underdeveloped, and characterized by hunger, migrancy, and illiteracy. "In today's Brazil," Campos would note, "what tends to resolve the problem of misery are [not poems but] movements like the MST, which as far as I have followed, don't simply occupy unproductive lands, but have created a politics of literacy and instruction for its members" ("Entrevista" 38). To be sure, the MST is one of the largest and most powerful social movements in Brazilian history.[7] According to Wendy Wolford's authoritative account,

> The MST was officially founded in the southernmost states of Brazil in the mid-1980s. Its membership expanded dramatically in the years following, and by the late 1990s the MST was the most dynamic and well-organized social movement in Brazilian history. Since its formation, the movement has used Brazilian law to argue for the right to property that is considered unproductive and not fulfilling its social function according to Article 184 of the Federal Constitution. The MST's main tactic is large-scale land occupation, where movement activists organize recruits to enter an un-productive property (as defined by the Constitution), usually late at night to avoid preemptive violent action from landowners and the government. The activists lead the new MST members in building temporary tents and squatting there until the government comes to assess their claim to the land. If the occupation is successful, usually after many months of nego-tiation, the government expropriates the property, divides it among the landless poor, creating what comes to be called the land reform settlement. Today, more than twenty years after the MST first came together, more than 250,000 families have occupied land through the movement, and, in 2001, the MST was directly affiliated with an estimated 1,459 settlements in twenty-three of Brazil's twenty-seven states (including the Federal District of Brasília, the country's capital). . . .
>
> The necessity and possibility of joining the MST . . . were shaped by a set of structural transformations. The state-led modernization of agriculture, which intensified after the military took office in 1964, made it difficult for smallholders to compete in the marketplace and many lost their land or migrated to the cities for work. . . . [A]t the same time, progressive priests affiliated with the Catholic and Lutheran Churches and often inspired by Liberation Theology helped to provide movement activists and members with crucial resources . . . and the gradual withdrawal of the military from government in the early 1980s created political opportunities for organiza-tion that had not existed earlier. (1, 16)

Campos's solidarity with the MST is well documented. Indeed, he never hesitated to affirm that the MST was carrying out "uma segunda abolição"

Fig. 6.4. A school for the children of the Santa Clara encampment, by Sebastião Salgado. From Salgado, *Terra: Struggle of the Landless.* © Sebastião Salgado/Amazonas/(Contact Press Images).

(a second abolition) against modern forms of slavery ("Uma segunda" 190). Through hard-fought agrarian reform on multiple fronts, and through its open network structure that emphasizes education, democracy, and literacy, Campos saw the MST as resolving the structural violence of misery plaguing Brazil. What is more, through its internationalism and de-emphasis of the party as paternal figure, the MST incarnated for Campos the idea of a future Brazil beyond the closure of the state. Through land seizures and its campaign for literacy, in short, the MST was abolishing the underlying continuities of structural subalternity.

Building on his 1960s claim that without revolutionary form there could be no revolutionary poetry, Campos would argue in his essay, "Poesia e modernidade: Da morte da arte à constelação. O poema pos-utópico" (Poetry and modernity: From the death of art to the constellation. The post-utopian poem) (1984), that poetry could no longer aspire to be the vehicle of the cultural vanguard and the utopian. That is, poetry could no longer strive to create a "new common language" that could potentially integrate the impoverished subaltern into the larger Brazilian community (266). Campos will repeat this wager for the rest of his life, but in a conference in 1999 he will add to it an interesting twist: land reform could make possible a new collective language: "avant-garde will be possible again in other conditions, even in Brazil. For Brazil, the first condition is to make an effective, hard agrarian reform without restrictions—a real one" ("Haroldo de Campos in Conference" 256). Aware of the pitfalls of the avant-garde's totalizing logic in the age of the closure of metaphysics, Campos will call for a critical poetry of the present: "poetry today is a poetry of the 'now' (I prefer the expression 'nowness' / *Jetztzeit*, a term appreciated by Benjamin)" ("Poesia e moderni-dade" 268–69). If poetry has become a postvanguard practice of the now in the age of global capital, what is the critical force of Campos's poem in rela-tion to the MST? More specifically, what can postutopian poetry, as a form of anti-literature, concretely hear, say, and do regarding the massacre of the MST peasant activists in Eldorado dos Carajás? Is anti-literature capable of creating a common language to come? This brings us to the question of literary politics and the poem's contemporary reception.

Just as Brazil's Landless Workers Movement increasingly seeks an in-ternational platform through the support of activists and artists, Else R. P. Vieira has observed the poem's will to multiply "listening posts" ("Trans-lating"). Denoting a nonlinear sense of history, these listening posts form a proliferating network structure that includes Campos's self-translation, the poem's intermedia (CD and image), and its international dissemination through scholarship and artists who take up the MST's cause.[8] What is more, for Vieira, the poem "fuses historical horizons" through an impressive weave of intertexts ("Translating"). By referencing the poetry of João Cabral, Pig-natari, Drummond de Andrade, the Bible, and Milton, as well as the *Reti-rante* paintings of Portinari and Walter Benjamin's philosophies of history and translation, the poem multiplies listening posts to "provide symbolic capital to the *sem-terra*" ("Translating"). Accordingly, Vieira reads the poem as a verbal monument whose task is to translate history on the side of the downtrodden. Vieira concludes that the "poem, in fact, forms a constellation with the historically shifting and increasingly political representations of the burial of the dispossessed of Brazil" ("Weaving" 162). While Vieira's obser-vations are no doubt insightful, I wish to add to her contribution by focusing on the poem's highly textured medium and the task it assigns itself, follow-ing Benjamin, to bring to life the life-world, insurgency, and the affects of the subaltern dead.

In effect, there is a fissure within Vieira's discourse that we need to ad-dress: the extent to which she interprets the poem as a collective monument is the measure by which she assigns the text a vanguard subjectivity whose task is to translate and reintegrate the subaltern as the revolutionary subject of history. Accordingly, her reading falls within the telos of the literary regime of representation. Reading the portrayal of subaltern history through the lens of the victim turned subject, the poem's intervening potential becomes confined to a testimonial translation. In short, the performative, anti-representational, and affective character of the text is largely overlooked. What follows will show how "O anjo" functions not to give testimony to history's buried truth, but to signal zones of illiteracy, resistance, and creative force on the other side of hegemonic representation.

As this book has shown, there will be no unitary representation, no naming of the subaltern as transculturated subject. Indeed, Gareth Williams has observed that "any thought of subalternity supposes a critical practice that hesitates (perhaps necessarily) before its objects of analysis" (*Other* 174). For Williams, the subaltern radically relativizes state logic and designates not only the downtrodden, but a multilinear critical position that unworks state-centered narratives. Subalternist reflection hesitates because the inscription of subaltern configurations within social space denaturalizes conclusive logics. As soon as one inscribes subalternity, Williams relates, critical reflection is confronted with reason's finitude. In flight from dominant systems, assigning to critical inquiry the task of abolishing fixity and consensual measures, Williams's injunction helps us frame anti-literature's encounter with subalternity and minoritarian peoples.

What is more, Williams's insight places us at a crossroads: how does Campos's poem create a new language that is adequate to the event of subaltern struggle? If we are faced with reason's finitude, how can one think the subaltern past through the framework of (anti)literature without becoming mere witnesses? What is common between anti-literature and the subaltern?

To respond to this query, a flashback to chapter 4 is fruitful. In the politically charged galactic text, "circulado de fulô" (1965), we witness the staging of an ambiguous procedure of identification between the poetic voice and an impoverished subaltern minstrel from the Brazilian Northeast: "aquela música não podia porque não podia popular / . . . mas o povo cria mas o povo engenha mas o povo cavila / o povo é o inventalínguas . . . / . . . mas ouça como canta louve como conta prove como dança e não peça que eu te guie" (that music couldn't because it couldn't popular / . . . but the people create but the people invent but the people object the people are the languageinventor . . . / . . . but listen how he sings praise how he tells experience how he dances and don't ask that I guide you). Through the dissonant recollection of the subaltern's music that could never be "popular," the poetic voice inscribes the crisis of vanguard writing in the 1960s. Far from depicting the subaltern through the lens of victimhood or otherness, here the subaltern becomes a constituent force, a "languageinventor," a singularity and equal participant in a common affective exchange. If the poetic voice cannot speak for the indescribable music of the subaltern, he recognizes its singularity and expressive powers. In fact, it could be said that through the creation of such inventive procedures of identification, which ceaselessly call attention to the limits of writing, the expressive powers of the poetic voice and the subaltern converge in a common project of resistance to state-centered logic. In this passage, then, the polyphonic syntax of the *Galáxias* inscribes an alternative world to capital and the state: an alternative means for imagining the relationship between literature, history, and the subaltern. Such a world and such a language, it is suggested, is to be produced, perhaps, in common. At the limit of reason, writing *with* subaltern affect: literature becomes an open, generative structure that does not represent but creates plurivocal worlds of sense.

If representation of the subaltern is the site of a transcendental illusion, in "O anjo" syntax begins as an act of affirmed difference. Unmasking history's postulates of progress and order (*ordem e progresso*), the poem testifies to a constituent power beyond measure whose task is to affirm problems:

> os sem-terra afinal
> estão assentados na
> pleniposse da terra :
> de sem-terra passaram a
> com-terra : ei-los
> enterrados
> desterrados de seu sopro
> de vida (H. Campos, "O anjo" 69)

> (the land-less at last
> are settled in the land
> pleni-possessedownership-land :
> from land-less they became
> landlords
> the with-land :   look at them
> in-earthed
> ex-earthed from their breath
> of life)

Within this movement of succession, writing hesitates. It will take the shape of a vigil, a form of mourning. Gazing at ruins, then: the massacred landless are "settled" (*assentados*) in the bowels of the unproductive estate, the latifundium.[9] As an ambiguous procedure of identification, the inscription of the murdered landless workers as "assentados" marks a repetition, a return,

Fig. 6.5. MST Occupation March, by Sebastião Salgado. From Salgado, *Terra: Struggle of the Landless.* © Sebastião Salgado/Amazonas/ (Contact Press Images).

a succinct "settling" of history that everyone knows. Paronomasia establishes a key narrative circuit: the adjectival term, *assentados*, refers at once to settlers, the settled, the assassinated, and to the act of settling accounts. Words configure a continuous, prismatic series. And stanza itself forms an alliterative, atonal circuit, a block of sensation that makes movement itself part and parcel of the work. Punctuation and irregular spacing produce a pictorial language. In effect, the proliferation of colons and hyphens—the dramatized dashes—summon an iconization of the event of the massacre. Typographic mimesis, as in the poetry of E. E. Cummings: punctuation represents, in other words, the passage of bullets, as well as the inexhaustible passage to an-other sense. In "O anjo," at stake is the very notion of crossing over the limit of poetry into the space of subaltern affect.

Writing between the lines, punctuation is flight and multiplicity of sense. It is a question of substituting direct signs, direct meanings, for mediate representations; it is a question, moreover, of producing semantic, pictorial, and aural constellations that induce the reader to perceive movement between signs and in continuous variation. Coming full circle, in effect, terms related to *terra*, to land concentration, and to settling accounts converge. And so is established the text's paradoxical genesis, which is truly an exodus. The poem's disparate network structure will undo linearity, the subject-object divide, and the subordination of objects to an enunciative subject: the landless, at last, have landed (*com-terra*) in a double movement, a double becoming. Like a rhizome, they are buried deeply in the scorched earth's bowels, as a constellation of terrified howls, in exile, struggling for "breath of life." "O anjo" is conceived entirely within poetry, but also entirely for its outside, as drama.

> com-terra : ei-los
> enterrados
> desterrados de seu sopro
> de vida
> aterrados
> terrorizados
> terra que à terra
> torna
> pleniposseiros terra-
> tenentes de uma
> vala (bala) comum :
> pelo avesso final ("O anjo" 69)

> (the with-land : look at them
> in-earthed
> ex-earthed from their breath
> of life
> terra-rized
> terrified
> from earth un-
> earthed they become
> pleni-possessors land-
> owners of a
> common (bullet) en-trenched :
> reverse in-verse finally)

In Campos's elegiac text, we experience time as a language that stutters and speaks in a foreign tongue, a Babelic language of pure forces and unforeseen readings. Inscribing another telos for historical reflection, dethroning literature as law of representation and speaking subject, how are we to come to terms with the poem's expressive powers? Such questions take us to our core inquiry: the problem of creating a language adequate to the monstrosity of the massacre. And what are we to make of the poem's prophetic denouement centered in justice and a messianic time to come, in which the titular angel of history "will one day . . . / convoke from the nebulous / roar that com-/ ing golden day / that at last supervenient / j u s t / s e t t l i n g / of accounts" (trans. from "O anjo" 71–72). In other words, what kind of future justice and language is the text summoning?

In countless instances, Campos will insist that poets worthy of the name work with the materiality of language. Eschewing his programmatic vanguard position of the 1950s and 1960s, Campos will later clarify in an interview what such materiality means: "Form is still the fundamental problem; one has always to invent a new form. How? There can be no 'programming' today. I can no longer have a 'Pilot Plan,' but I can know what I must not do. I must not give in to facility, or relapse into nostalgia for a lost paradise. I cannot program the future paradise, but the 'paradise lost' is of no interest. I must seek the sanction for what I do in the present moment, somewhere between critique and tradition, and that can provide my new contribution to poetry" ("Haroldo de Campos in Conversation" 281). Resisting formula, facility, and idealism, Campos's postutopian poetics opens us to a consideration of materiality, not beyond the boundary of poetry and critique but to a space between them, grounded in the line of flight of affect:

> pelo avesso final
> entranhados no
> lato ventre do
> latifúndio
> que de im-
> produtivo re-
> velou-se assim u-
> bérrimo : gerando pingue
> messe de
> sangue vermelhoso ("O anjo" 69)

> (reverse in-verse finally
> ingrained
> in the latiwomb
> of the latifundium
> which from im-
> productive re-
> vealed itself as u-
> berhythm-fecund : pinguid
> mass harvest
> galls blood-vermillion)

Marked by suspended reference and alliterative per-mutation, "O anjo" will welcome chance and the incalculable. For example, the technique of enjambment, coupled by the breaking open of words from the middle, refers

Fig. 6.6. Photographic image of the Landless Workers' Movement, in "O anjo esquerdo da história." Courtesy of the *Folha de São Paulo*, 20 April 1996. Photograph by Juca Varella. © FOTOGRAFIA/ FOLHAPRESS.

us to the continual passage to an-other sense, an-other form of doing poetry: to the cannibalization of new regimes of signs and to the intensive, constituent power of words. Indeed, as already indicated, the poem begins with a photograph of the MST's funeral march. More than testimonial evidence or tribute to Sebastião Salgado, the photograph is co-informational and converges with syntax. In other words, to the extent that continuous experimentation ensures the expansion of the text into multiple points of view, the poem will demand the dramatization of its materials, including the montage-becoming of words as condensed ensembles of sensation, semantic

MULTITUDE

WAR AND DEMOCRACY
IN THE AGE OF EMPIRE

"BRILLIANT." —THE VILLAGE VOICE

MICHAEL HARDT
AND ANTONIO NEGRI

AUTHORS OF EMPIRE

Fig. 6.7. Cover image of Michael Hardt and Antonio Negri's *Multitude* (2004).

tension, and subaltern affect. Putting the literary law of the word-center in question, accordingly, it is impossible not to view the enjambing flow of images, the serpentine structure of stanza, the breaking open of words in open polyphonic distributions, the lack of periods, as an iconization of the MST multitude march.

Constituting an opening to the other, the poem's vortex of signifiers inscribes the idea of singularities resisting the land problem in common. Indeed, they announce visually, affectively, and semantically the "messeanic" promise of the poem's prophecy: the "multigirante" angel of history to come. This minoritization of language marks a becoming of writing with that which is nonwriting. More crucial, perhaps, is the fact that the chance structure of syntax refers us to the radically other as *à-venir* and constituent process; namely, to the event of a form to come that cannot be anticipated. This is poetic concretion for Campos: a polyvalent process of sensation without program or central speaking subject. Such a procedure of the sensible renders explicit the verbal, vocal, and visual elements of the poem. And doubtless, as an "open, combinatorial form" for a form of art "without closure or completion," such a strategy of textual work overturns representation and will welcome, following Derrida, history's unforeseen other, the angel, as event of the incalculable ("Haroldo de Campos in Conversation" 280–81). This is significant. The problem of the poem's chance structure, *which inscribes, like a dice throw, the text as an incalculable power that multigenerates meanings, at once simultaneous, spatial, and multitudinous*, returns us to the question of form and materiality: concretion marks a graphic, spatial, nonlinear structure of resistance to the traditional conception of literature. It is here, against literature, that we broach the matter of politics. Following Michael Hardt and Antonio Negri's conception of the multitude as a collective power of resistance that singularities produce in common, one will consider "material" not merely the exploited dead in their graves as an external referent, as a "real," but all the constituents of the poetic signifier in an open, multitudinous, swarm intelligence: graphic, spatial, physical, sound, and semantic *as an untimely affair of politics*.

Accordingly, as a "multigenerative" form of writing, "O anjo" structurally pivots on paronomasia and paramorphism. The text will therefore inscribe, through wordplay and visual syntax, an anti-literary thought of the subaltern. The subaltern becomes not the figure for a collapsed state, not the representation of a passive victim, but a *co-constituent power*, a form of flight that resists state logic. Breaking with binaries, the subaltern is raised from the bowels of the earth as a new seed of time, a "larval" form, a *forma de fome* (form of hunger).

lavradores sem
lavra ei-
los : afinal con-
vertidos em larvas
em mortuá-
rios despojos :
ataúdes lavrados
na escassa madeira
(matéria)
de si mesmos : a bala assassina
atocaiu-os
mortiassentados
sitibundos
decúbito-abatidos pre-
destinatários de uma
agra (magra)
re(dis)(forme) forma
— fome — a-
grária : ei-
los gregária
comunidade de meeiros
do nada : ("O anjo" 70)

(laborless laborers-
look at them :
at last con-
verted into larvas
in mortua-
rivers castaways :
the coffins handcrafted
out of scarce
(material)
like themselves : -the bullet assassinates
ambushed them
death-settled
deaththirst
decumbent-driven even
pre-
destined for an

agra- (less)
re (dis) (formed) form
— hunger — rare-
ian : look-
at them gregarious
squatter community
now nothingness :)

Every poem, every text must achieve its own manner of speaking about its objects, as though it formed an alliance with them. As a gesture of approximation and alliance, Campos deploys polyvocal signs that are at once visual, semantic, and political: the proliferation of parentheses stages the MST's territorial occupations of the latifundia, graphically signals the coffins of the massacred, and portrays, in dissonance, the delay and deferral of agrarian reform:

agra (magra)
re(dis)(forme) forma
— fome —a-
grária : ei-
los gregária ("O anjo" 70)

(agra (less)
re (dis) (formed) form
— hunger —rare-
ian : look-
at them gregarious)

Like a Chinese character, syntax morphs into an ideogrammatic structure of analogical relationships that induce the imagination to read spatially. The parentheses signal a difficulty, a hesitation, an arrest of writing. Suspending linear history through *formas de fome*, Campos's parenthetic procedure moreover articulates a system of linkages. Co-operational, marking the poem as the site of a confluence and kinship between distinct regimes of signs—between Campos's strategy of material concretion and the MST's occupations of the great estates—in "O anjo," to write is to occupy and redistribute signs as affective assemblages. As a polysemic condensation of the conflict, the parentheses take us to history's underbelly, to its silenced voices. To the extent that enjambment and the pictorial language of punctuation configure syntax as the continuous passage to another sense, "O anjo" marks the between space as the site of anti-literature.

enver-
gonhada a-
goniada
avexada
— envergoncorroída de
imo-abrasivo re-
morso —
a pátria
(como ufanar-se da?)
apátrida
pranteia os seus des-
possuídos párias —
pátria parricida : ("O anjo" 71)

(inverse-
ashamed a-
gonenothingleft
vexed
— inversegonecorroded from
inmost-abrasive re-
moreso—
fatherland
(oh say can you sing?)
fatherless
mourns its dis-
possessed pariahs —
parricide fatherland :)

    The poem will be concerned with destabilizing values associated with property and the proper. Everything turns on the question of articulating a *just means*, of constructing a new language for addressing oneself to the singularity of the other before any social contract. Such a space will emerge only in the undermining of stately presence: through its dis-joining modes of address the poem will recreate the veiled, false, abrasive remorse of the "parricide state." Linguistically, compound words stage the image of the corrupt state's "mourning," as a falsified ritual of Orwellian duckspeak. The proliferation of compound words also inscribes the becoming-foreign of Campos's Portuguese; they constitute an implicit homage to Benjamin's German, as well as to e. e. Cummings's typographic idiolect.

que talvez só afinal a
espada flamejante
do anjo torto da his-
tória cha-
mejando a contravento e
afogueando os
agrossicários sócios desse
fúnebre sodalício onde a
morte-marechala comanda uma
torva milícia de janízaros-ja-
gunços :
somente o anjo esquerdo
da história escovada a
contrapelo com sua
multigirante espada po-
derá (quem derá!) um dia
convocar do ror
nebuloso dos dias vin-
douros o dia
afinal sobreveniente do
j u s t o
a j u s t e de
contas ("O anjo" 71–72)

(that perhaps only at last
the flaming sword
of the crooked angel of history flame-
pissing counterwind and
inflaming the
agrohitmen associates of
this funereal soldiery where
the death-marshal commands a
terrible militia of triggerhappy-gun
guards :
only the left-
winged angel of history
brushing history inverse
against the grain avenger
with his multi-

generative sword will-
one day (oh that it be such!)
convoke from the nebulous
roar that golden day
to come
that at last supervenient
j u s t
s e t t l i n g of
accounts)

Across the spatialized words, "j u s t o / a j u s t e de / contas"—an explicit cannibalization of Benjamin's technique for highlighting words—we are re-layed an enigmatic notion of justice. Settling history's score yet refusing to speak in the subaltern's name, justice will not be served by law or social compact. Nor will justice issue from solidarity and indignation: through representational testimony or intertextual listening posts for the downtrodden as the prevailing reading of the text would have it. Rather, what is at stake in "O anjo" is an untimely attending to the convergence between affect and chance, poetry and subaltern history, politics and multitude. It is, moreover, a question of producing, in common, multitudinous forms of resistance, even as "literature" opens up to its radical other. Writing as heterogenesis and chance for a future to come: such is the final image that emerges from Campos's rewriting of the massacre. We are here broaching the untimely secret of anti-literature.

CONCLUSION

The Untimely Secret
of Anti-Literature

SINCE THE 1950s, reproaches concerning the apolitical nature of Haroldo de Campos's poems and Brazilian concrete poetry are widespread. In many respects, they recall the accusations that the Marxist cultural critic Roberto Schwarz made against Campos and his brother, Augusto, regarding the "reactionary" implications of their writing for political action. In Campos's rejoinder to Schwarz, as well as in his writings concerning the political implications of poetry and literary theory, Campos rejects the notion that concrete poetry lacks a political dimension, or what Schwarz will call a "déficit de empiria" (a deficit of empirical data) ("Marco" 64). Writing against Schwarz's conception of matter as external presence, Campos emphasized that his lifelong engagement with politics never constituted an ideology or an ontotheological conception of politics; rather, it concerned the problem of creating revolutionary forms for the present during the postutopian epoch of the closure of metaphysics.[1] At stake is an anti-foundational delimitation of literature and politics that centers on Campos's conception of materiality:

> To be a Postutopian poet working on the concrete materiality of language does not mean to have renounced the critical dimension of the poetical task, neither to have forgotten the technical conquests of Modernity. *Even committed poems continue to be possible and necessary* (as for instance my

recent "The Left Angel of History," protesting against the massacre of the SEM-TERRA/*without-land* in Pará, north of Brazil). No nostalgic, regressive orientation is being aimed at. What is different is that I have substituted the optimistic-futuristic-millenarian project of the fifties with a more realistic and effective one, based on the urgent needs (either aesthetic or ideological) of the present. ("Brazilian Jaguar" 85, emphasis added)

In writing this book, I have attended to works that mark the collapse and limits of "literature" as classically understood. It goes without saying that anti-literary texts such as these blur the boundaries between literature, the other arts, historical reflection, and the avatars of intermedia, and escape exhaustive, unitary analysis. In responding to the problem of form as a complex of creative forces, what this book will have made apparent are new procedures of the sensible that introduce writing's untimely force. In our exodus from teleological conceptions of "literature," we discover protean works that violently undermine final meanings. Anti-literature is anti-closure.

As we have seen throughout the case studies, anti-literature contests foundational constitution. And it is precisely through this injunction, this matter of a politics of literature, that we bring together, in a final constellation, the threads of our research. This book has proposed a rethinking of the fundamental concepts of what is meant by "literature" in contemporary Latin American studies. If anti-literature tends toward an egalitarian intersemiotic practice that wages war against a conformist, majoritarian distribution of the sensible, it does so as a struggle and configuration of experience that suspends forms of domination. Yet skepticism concerning the importance of literature for political thinking remains widespread. The trenchant series of questions that the cultural theorist John Beverley asks at the beginning of his landmark book, *Against Literature* (1993), is representative: "The animus against literature . . . is due above all to literature's connection with the modern state" (xiii). "Is there not in fact," he asks, "a way of thinking about literature that is extraliterary, or as I prefer here, 'against' literature?" (2). "The problem," he concludes, "is that Latin American left cultural politics is still founded on a model of cultural authority and pedagogy in which . . . literature is positioned as the discourse that is crucially formative of Latin American identity and possibility" (5).[2]

Beverley's rejoinder against literature remains pertinent. The literary question in Latin American studies has reached a state of impasse. Redirecting our framework from representation and the subject to the problem of sensation and literature's limits, we uncover the power of Brazilian and Argentine pariah texts that challenge the literary institution and its idealist conception of culture. We uncover, what is more, how Brazilian anti-literature in particular creates the generative interval: not beyond the boundary of literature and politics but to a space between them. As an intervening procedure of the sensible, anti-literature interrogates literature's border spaces. We have dwelled in such interstitial, affective, and multimedial sites to engage some of the more pressing problems facing the question of experimental writing and its inexorable relation to politics: thus emerge, through a constellatory method, the themes of subalternity, writing the feminine, the minoritarian, anti-poetry, and literary politics, even as "literature" wrestles against itself as an institution of conformity and markets. For as we have insisted throughout concerning the interdisciplinary scope of our research, resistance, like creation, always takes place in the middle. As with the limit-case of "O anjo," our case studies explore the crossing of literature into uncharted semiotic, historical, and theoretical territories. Against traditional conceptions that call for the strict separation between the political and literary spheres, I have shown that the question of literary politics remains poorly posed. In order to counter this view, I have shown how anti-literature recaptures form as an assemblage of expression, an interplay between media, that effectuates subversions of the sensible. Finally, reflection on Brazilian writers within the framework of Latin American studies remains rare. To the extent that the divorce persists, this book endeavors to not only reenergize and redirect the critique of literature in the field, but to work the unexamined connections and intervals between Brazilian and Spanish American literature.

To the extent that this book is organized around the problem of anti-literature and the sensible, let us close our reflection on the multifarious ways in which "O anjo" intervenes in politics and historical memory work. Against identity, it is precisely the problem of time and the affect—the poem as the site of a politics of the sensible—that will allow us to carve out a fresh critical perspective for literature, beyond impasse and representation, into the folds of our politically charged present.

No doubt, the poem's final stanza constitutes a play on the idea of redeeming time from an untimely perspective of the Left. Recalling the poem's parenthetic series that are at once epistemological and pictographic, I hasten to delimit such substantive terms. Concerned with constructing a critical, postutopian poetry for the present, there will be no literary idealism in Campos, no falling back onto a transcendental signified. To be sure, the titular "anjo" recalls the materialist angel of history referenced in Walter Benjamin's ninth thesis on the philosophy of history. Benjamin's angel—derived from Paul Klee's painting *Angelus Novus*—is depicted with face turned toward the past. With wings caught by the stormy winds of "paradise," the angel perceives the catastrophe of so-called "progress": the angel wishes to stay, place time at a standstill, "awaken the dead and make whole what has been smashed" ("Theses" 257).

Retaining this image of disaster, history's specters, and the allegory of the angelic function of the historian who would brush official history against the grain to wake the dead, it is important to note that the redemptive angel's coming is described as "torto" ("O anjo" 71). "Torto" is a pun that refers to unevenness, the crooked, the unorthodox, and to the Left. Anarchical idiolect, the crooked angel signals the poem's zigzagging typographic procedures of spatialization as a power of becoming. The crooked syntax of "O anjo" reconstitutes the flight, the occupations, the encampments, and sensorial experience of the MST, even as it frames the difficulty and dissonance inherent in such multitudinous writing. As a self-reflexive inquiry that refracts the limits of poetry, the crooked inscribes subaltern affect as a constitutive fissure in history: the arrest of official discourse. Yet the crooked is also an incalculable figure that inscribes the circuitous, transcreating path through which the poem seeks convergence and kinship between its materials and the modes of resistance of the MST.

Sifting through Benjamin's "Theses," we perceive where Campos drew his inspiration:

> Like every generation that preceded us, we have been endowed with a
> *w e a k* messianic power, a power to which the past has a claim.
>
> . . .
>
> A chronicler who recites events without distinguishing between major
> and minor ones acts in accordance with the following truth: nothing that
> has ever happened should be regarded as lost for history. To be sure, only
> a redeemed mankind receives the fullness of its past—which is to say, only
> for a redeemed mankind has its past become citable in all its moments.
> Each moment it has lived has become a *c i t a t i o n   à   l'o r d r e   d u*
> *j o u r*—and that day is Judgment Day. (254)

For Giorgio Agamben, "these spaced words are, in a certain way, hyper-read: they are read twice, and as Benjamin suggests, this double reading maybe the palimpsest of citation" (*Time* 139). Agamben's achievement is to have located unforeseen textual correspondences in Benjamin's spatialized words, such as "w e a k," with the messianic writings of Paul, most notably in 2 Corinthians. There, Paul asks the Messiah "to free him from that thorn in his flesh, [and] hears the answer, *he gar dynamis en astheneia teletai,* 'power fulfills itself in weakness'" (140). Having identified this, Agamben demonstrates the importance of Benjamin's concept of image, *Bild,* which appears several times in the "Theses." For Agamben, *Bild* constitutes a methodological premise according to which the historian interweaves the past and present "in a constellation where the present is able to recognize the meaning of the past and the past therein finds its meaning and fulfillment" (142). There is no question that the enjambing, montage sequence of images in "O anjo" draws inspiration from Benjamin's concept of *Bild*. As typographic rarities that are emancipated, like punctuation, from traditional contexts, the spatialized words "j u s t o" and "a j u s t e" configure iconic images in their own right. They provide a close-up shot of the poem's core inquiry: the problem of justice and restitution of subaltern memory, which of a sudden converges, as encounter and design, with Benjamin's "Theses." Read through these terms, the "j u s t" (*j u s t o*) condenses a conception of writing subaltern massacre as an unlimited field of reading, relating, and co-creating. Such a field no doubt defies the logic of domination. Justice as a continuous line of singularities: blurs, bends back, and breaks up the reified character of social relations, as well as the banal accounts of "progress" that fail to count the part that has no part in society. Citable in all their moments, as freed expressions that articulate the desire to be in the exception, to think the relationless relation, the affective dimensions of Campos's text inscribe the crisis of poetry in the wake of subaltern tragedy.

On the border of literature and politics, the play with line in "O anjo" constitutes a phenomenology of composition in which each word, each punctuation mark, can be imagined in a performative sequencing, or a dice throw of limitless semiosis. In this regard, the poem is revolutionary in its seeking of new connections—new lines of concretion. This is a collective problematic in its own right. To the extent that the narrow, skeletal, hyphen-inflected, stanza-line articulates subaltern destituteness, the tracing of a limit-line separating the MST from the state, it also serves as the connective tissue, the contour of a poetic architecture, that sets up a compositional plane of immanence where nothing settles. Minoritarian becoming of language that images a community to come, the poem takes up the codified, segmented words of the social, provides a close-up of the materiality and social relations that underwrite them, and sets them off in flight. This is far from a mere flight into the imaginary or literary sphere. In other words, Campos, like the cameraman, penetrates the image, and makes of it a configuration of differential expressive relationships. Granting poetry its chance, leaving behind impasse and discourses of literary exhaustion, the anti-poem creates the interface between literature, revolutionary praxis, and subaltern tragedy. As a form of multitudinous concretion that attends to the aleatory sequence of desire as one reads, the aesthetic dimensions of "O anjo esquerdo da história" articulate a countermovement to Brazilian history. Poetry's relation to justice is only inscribed where the multitude of signs swarm in heterogenesis. We are broaching a rethinking of the question of form as the site of constitutive dislocation. To explore the materiality of poetic language, to materialize and make explicit all the constituents of the signifier, for Campos implies affirming the value of chance and suspension of reference. Such an exploration of materiality refers us to the coming of the radical other—the incalculable, inexhaustible textual body—as an opening to a future of writing beyond the looking glass of literature and the state. Such a secret, such an untimely experience of the literary letter become other, implies, doubtless, an alliance with other regimes of signs, including those of subaltern insurgency, and a corresponding hospitality for the experience of radical alterity: on condition that each sign, each stanza, each medium has reached a state of excess, beyond closure.

NOTES

INTRODUCTION

All translations not otherwise credited are my own.

1. Fernando J. Rosenberg examines the ways in which the Latin American avant-gardes powerfully undermine the teleology of modernity as a single temporality. See Rosenberg, *Avant-Garde*; and Rosenberg, "Cultural Theory." By the same token, Vicky Unruh's study of avant-garde women writers' work "as a multifaceted art of living" offers a case of expansion in the field (*Performing* 7–8). No doubt, the avant-garde experience in Latin America inscribes a fundamental event within the historical discursive formation of the literary field. With respect to recent scholarship, thinkers such as Francine Masiello, Mari Carmen Ramírez, Héctor Olea, Vicky Unruh, Fernando J. Rosenberg, Viviane Mahieux, and Gonzalo Aguilar point to the avant-garde's highly "self-critical attitude" due to its contentious encounters with European avant-garde proposals, its "pivotal relationship to the past," and the dilemma of engaging the reader and spectator with the problem of the present, national identity, cultural syncretism, and experimental art in an international context (Ramírez, "Highly Topical" 2; Unruh, *Vanguards* 6). These thinkers have issued a challenge to rethink the legacy of the Latin American avant-gardes and how the avant-gardes proposed, questioned, and disseminated engaged functions for art. Accordingly, Ramírez and Olea's essays and exhibition have called for a "nonlinear" and "generative, dialectical understanding of [vanguard] art," including reopening the discussion on vanguard practices and procedures carried out by groups and individuals of the 1950s and 1960s (Ramírez, "Prologue" xvi), while Unruh and Aguilar have pinpointed the need to focus on the avant-garde's modes of "non-conciliatory" intervention with the social, the tradition, the mimetic, and the international (Aguilar, "Formas" 34). For further elaboration of the problem of experimentation in Latin American avant-garde writers, see Shellhorse, "Radical Reinventions."

2. The state-sanctioned process of cultural "transculturation" in Latin America arises in tandem with the national-popular task of integration assigned to the literary during the first two decades of the twentieth century, and constitutes, according to Horacio Legrás, "the most influential term in the history of Latin American cultural criticism" (*Literature* 10). Rama's theory of literary transculturation finds its expression in what he calls "critical regionalism," a narrative modality centered in the incorporation of popular, indigenous voices and subjectivities. Exemplified in the novels of Gabriel García Márquez, Juan Rulfo, João Guimarães Rosa, and José María Arguedas, critical regionalism emerges, on the one hand, as a reaction to rationalization and Eurocentrism and, on the other, as the Latin American literary's ongoing will to autonomy, "representation" (*representatividad*), and "originality." For Rama, the regionalist writer is charged with the task of managing "authentically the symbolic languages developed by American men" (*Transculturación* 19). The concept of transculturation has been thematized and widely critiqued from different quarters. For some of the more notable contributions, see Williams, *Other Side*; Moreiras, *Exhaustion*; Beverley, *Against Literature* and *Subalternity*; Legrás, *Literature*; A. Johnson, *Sentencing*; Levinson, *Ends*; Dove, *Catastrophe* and *Literature*; de la Campa, *Latin Americanism*; Lund, *Impure Imagination*; and Sommer, *Proceed*. In

diverse ways, underwriting these interventions is a forceful critique of the subject, as well as a debate on the uses of theory and history in the field. For a trenchant critique of the subject in Latin American studies today, see D. Johnson, "How (Not)." See also Graff Zivin's illuminating call for an anti-identitarian, "an-archaeological," and "marrano" critical practice in "Beyond Inquisitional Logic."

3. In *Literature and Subjection*, Legrás makes the same claim, calling the Latin American literary regime a "historical formation": "[T]he formation that interests me may be termed the historical project of Latin American literature. Briefly, this project entailed the symbolic incorporation of peoples and practices persisting in the margins of society or the nation into a sanctioned form of representation" (4). See also Shellhorse, "Latin American."

4. For a pivotal discussion of the Latin American subaltern studies debate that raises the issue of art as a sore point, see Bosteels, "Theses." Indeed, if we are to traverse the problematic of subalternity in regard to a possible politics of literature, for Bosteels there arises the necessity of de-suturing art from politics (against transculturation) so as to rethink both art and politics "as singular thought procedures" (158). Without a doubt, John Beverley's *Against Literature* could be seen as an inaugural theoretical articulation that announces, in the words of Alberto Moreiras, "the possibility of a new paradigm for Latin Americanist reflection in the humanities" (*Exhaustion* 310). For an overview of the Latin American subaltern studies debate, see Rodríguez, "Reading Subalterns," as well as the diverse essays contained in *The Latin American Subaltern Studies Reader*. See also the special issue of *Dispositio*, *Latin American Subaltern Studies Revisited*, edited by Gustavo Verdesio. The issue contains numerous interventions and a conversation with John Beverley.

5. On literary posthegemony, see Shellhorse, "Literature"; Gareth Williams's superb *Other Side*; and Beasley-Murray's online writings in *Posthegemony*. For further elaboration and debate on posthegemony as a theoretical practice, see Alberto Moreiras's "Posthegemonía," and his special edited volume, *Infrapolítica y posthegemonía*; and Castro Orellana's edited volume, *Poshegemonía*.

6. On the crisis of the evolutionary literary model and its relationship to historiography in Latin American studies, see Castro-Klarén's "'Writing.'"

7. In the *Politics of Aesthetics*, Rancière will have affirmed the radical co-implication of experience, perception, politics, and art. "If the reader is fond of analogy," Rancière writes, "aesthetics can be understood in a Kantian sense—re-examined perhaps by Foucault—as the system of *a priori* forms of what presents itself to sense experience" (*Politics* 13). Art intervenes as a struggle over experience: "[a]rtistic practices are ways of doing and making that intervene in the general distribution of ways of doing and making as well as in the relationships they maintain to modes of being and forms of visibility" (12–13). Consequently, if artworks can lay claim to a project of subversion, this will be so in terms of their anti-foundational vocation vis-à-vis "the sensible delimitation of what is common to the community, the forms of its visibility and of its organization" (18).

8. "Old Glory Blue" refers to the saturated blue in the American flag. Just as the colors red and green clearly signal to the Cuban Revolution and Brazil, I am suggesting Campos's symbolic use of the color to denote the United States.

9. See in particular the essays by Rama, Viñas, and Garrels in the collected volume *Más allá del Boom*, edited by Rama.

10. See in particular Moreiras, *Exhaustion*; Ramos, *Divergent*; and Legrás, *Literature*.

1. FIGURATIONS OF IMMANENCE

1. The interview was conducted on 20 October 1976 at the Museum of Image and Sound in Rio by writers Affonso Romano de Sant'Anna and Maria Colasanti, who were personal friends of Lispector. See Lispector, *Outros* 137–71.

2. In the original, "falar o menos possível" and "não altera nada." The final interview, produced in February 1977 by Panorama Especial on TV Cultura, is widely available on the Internet. For a transcription, see Lerner 62–69.

3. Charles A. Perrone's contribution on this topic remains essential (*Seven* 67–86). See also Affonso Romano de Sant'Anna's comprehensive *Música popular e moderna poesia brasileira* (1978).

4. On Lispector's exploration of urban poverty and the subaltern in her chronicle writing, in the novel *A paixão segundo G.H.* (1964), and in the posthumous story "A bela e a fera, ou a ferida grande demais," see Marta Peixoto's essay "'Fatos são pedras duras,'" 106–25.

5. For an overview of *A hora da estrela* and a careful consideration of its place within Lispector's oeuvre, see Fitz, "Point of View." See also the monographs by Fitz, *Clarice Lispector* and *Sexuality and Being*. With respect to bibliographical research, in addition to Moser, see also the insightful studies by Nádia Batella Gotlib and Teresa Cristina Montero Ferreira.

6. It is clear that Rodrigo's narrative modality is far from innocent, as Marta Peixoto and others have astutely noted. And yet, I am shifting the problematic beyond a logic of writing centered in victimization and representational violence to the consequences that follow from Lispector's radical compositional plane. That is, to the multiple, nonappropriative, and feminine events of writing that Lispector's novel unleashes. It is for this reason that a line of comparison between *A hora da estrela* and Lispector's late volume of short stories, *A via crucis do corpo* (1974), should be drawn. As Earl E. Fitz has demonstrated, *A via crucis do corpo* deconstructs normative notions of feminine and masculine identity and introduces a powerful new writing style that foregrounds the body, class, and sexuality: "[f]eaturing an overt if restrained sexuality, a stripped-down style that eschews the lyricism of earlier works (including *Stream of Life*, published only the year before), a self-consciousness that invites readerly participation, and a utilization of the fantastic or the improbable, these short, wryly humorous narratives parodically undermine many of the assumptions and conventions of androcentric society" (*Sexuality* 132). Indeed, with *A hora da estrela* and *A via crucis do corpo*'s emphasis on the body, sensuality, and class consciousness, one can also productively link Lispector's late writings to the work of David Viñas, as we will see in chapter 2. For an overview of *A via crucis do corpo*, see Fitz, *Clarice Lispector* 113–15.

7. Concerning the concept of the literary habitus or literary field, see Bourdieu, "Field of Power." Of course, in Bourdieu's affirmation, "the literary field is the economic world reversed" (164). The literary field's legitimacy is structured through the construction of values based on belief and what Bourdieu calls the literary law of "disinterestedness" (164). Unlike in Europe during the nineteenth century, the Latin American literary field's consolidation in the twentieth century was uneven and never fully "disinterested." Anchored by the rationalizing, national popular project of mapping the continent and expressing regional difference vis-à-vis North America and Europe, the Latin American literary field became a regime, political in scope, of representation. On this topic, see Legrás, *Literature*; J. Ramos, *Divergent*; Rama, *Transculturación* and *La ciudad letrada*; and Shellhorse, "Latin American."

8. With respect to debates in the field of Latin American studies centered in the literary as a regime aligned to the state and the problematic of subalternity, see the pioneering work of Beverley, in particular, *Subalternity* and *Against*; Moreiras, *Tercer* and *Exhaustion*; Williams, *Other*; and Bosteels, "Theses."

9. Concerning the relationship between poststructural thinking procedures and thinking the feminine, Fitz's *Sexuality and Being* has been insightful, as has his coauthored work with Judith A. Payne, *Ambiguity and Gender in the New Novel of Brazil and Spanish America*. See also Helena, "A problematização." With respect to criticism of Cixous's readings of Lispector, see Klobuka, "Hélène Cixous"; and Carrera, "Reception."

10. The essay was later published in Peixoto's influential *Passionate Fictions* (see 82–99).

11. See Irigaray, *This Sex* 106–18. "It behooves us," she writes, "to look into the 'exteriority' of this form that is 'constituent [more than constituted]' for the subject, into the way it serves as a screen to another outside . . . into the death that it entails but in a 'relief' that authorizes misapprehension, into the 'symmetry' that it consecrates (as constituent) and that will cause the 'mirage' of the 'maturation of its power' for the subject to be always tributary of an 'inversion,' . . . into the process of projection it puts in place—'a fictional direction, which will always

remain irreducible for the individual alone'?—and into the phantoms that it leaves as remains. . . . Thus fluid is always in a relation of excess or lack vis-à-vis unity. . . . That is, any definite identification" (117, Lacan qtd.).

12. Quoting from Marx's *Capital*, Irigaray argues, "'[T]he value of commodities is the very opposite of the coarse materiality of their substance . . . Turn and examine a single commodity, by itself, as we will. Yet in so far as it remains an object of value, it seems impossible to grasp it' (ibid). The value of a woman always escapes: black continent, hole in the symbolic, breach in discourse. . . . In order to have a *relative value*, a commodity has to be confronted with another commodity that serves as its equivalent. Its value is never found to lie within itself. . . . Its value is *transcendent* to itself, *super-natural, ek-static. In other words, for the commodity there is no mirror that copies it so that it may be at once itself and its 'own' reflection.* One commodity cannot be mirrored in another, as man is mirrored in his fellow man. . . . The mirror that envelops and paralyzes the commodity specularizes, speculates (on) man's 'labor.' *Commodities, women, are a mirror of value of and for man.* In order to serve as such, they give up their bodies to men as the supporting material of specularization, of speculation. They yield to him their natural and social value as a locus of imprints, marks, and the mirage of his activity" (*This Sex* 175–77).

13. "To achieve a gendered subjectivity is to become the whole of oneself," Irigaray observes, "with the condition of not being the whole of the subject, of consciousness, of being, etc. In this perspective, there is no longer a negation of the negation in the Hegelian sense but the constitution of another type of subject and culture. . . . The problem is that the subject, historically masculine, has a tendency to apprehend the negative as oppression, as external to oneself, and not enough as a process of existing in itself/himself and necessary for the construction of an interiority" (*Why Different?* 75).

14. Pheng Cheah's account of nondialectical materialism in the philosophical projects of Gilles Deleuze and Jacques Derrida has been illuminating. See Cheah, "Nondialectical Materialism" 143–57.

15. "Pois de uma maneira geral—e agora sem falar apenas de politização—a atmosfera é de vanguarda, o nosso crescimento íntimo está forçando as comportas e rebentará com as formas inúteis de ser ou de escrever. Estou chamando de nosso progressivo autoconhecimento de vanguarda. Estou chamando de vanguarda 'pensarmos' a nossa língua. Nossa língua não foi profundamente trabalhada pelo pensamento. 'Pensar' a língua portuguesa do Brasil significa pensar sociologicamente, psicologicamente, filosoficamente, lingüisticamente sobre nós mesmos. Os resultados são e serão o que se chama de linguagem literária, isto é, linguagem que reflete e diz, com palavras que instantaneamente aludem a coisas que vivemos; numa linguagem real, numa linguagem que é fundo e forma, a palavra é na verdade um ideograma. É maravilhosamente difícil escrever em língua que ainda borbulha; que precisa mais do presente do que mesmo de uma tradição, em língua que, para ser trabalhada, exige que o escritor se trabalhe a si próprio como pessoa. Cada sintaxe nova é reflexo indireto de novos relacionamentos, de maior aprofundamento em nós mesmos, de uma consciência mais nítida do mundo e de nosso mundo. Cada sintaxe nova então abre pequenas liberdades . . . A linguagem está descobrindo o nosso pensamento, e o nosso pensamento está formando uma língua literária e que eu chamo, para maior alegria minha, de linguagem de vida" (*Outros* 105–6).

16. Olga da Sá, in her study *A escritura de Clarice Lispector* (1979), observes that *A hora da estrela* "constitui o ultimo coágulo de uma escritura toda voltada para a pesquisa a respeito das correspondências entre ser e linguagem" (constitutes the ultimate inflection of a writing completely absorbed with researching the correspondences between being and language) (216). Invoking Roland Barthes's *Criticism and Truth* (1966), Sá conceptualizes Lispector's writing as one of a "radical engagement with language proper" such that it questions at the same moment that it affirms: "Clarice não é um filósofo, um pensador, mas uma escritora, fundamentalmente comprometida com o ser *sob linguagem*; ou, melhor, *com a linguagem*, espessura do *ser*" (Clarice is not a philosopher, a thinker, but a writer fundamentally engaged with being *as language*; or better, *with language*, density of *being*) (19). In the preface to Sá's book, Haroldo de Campos makes an important observation regarding the radicality of Lispector's project, linking it, as it

were, to his own concrete poetics that contextualize his work in the 1950s, 1960s, and 1970s: Lispector's work "se perfila e se desdobra como proposta questionante" (profiles and unfurls as a questioning proposal) (12). "A literatura praticada por Clarice não é, própriamente, da índole do que caberia designar, *prima facie*, como 'literatura do significante[.]' É antes uma 'literatura do significado,' mas levada à sua fronteira extrema, à tensão conflitual com um referente volátil, à figuras de indizibilidade, e mobilizando para tanto todo um sistema de equações metafóricas . . . instaurado a contrapelo do discurso lógico, mediante o qual são aproximadas ou contrastadas as regiões mais surpreendentes e imponderáveis do plano do conteúdo" (Clarice's literature is not, at first glance, what one could describe as a "literature of the signifier." It is a "literature of the signified," but carried to its extreme limit, to a conflictual tension with a volatile referent, to figures of anti-expressivity, and accordingly, mobilizing an entire system of metaphorical equations . . . against discursive logic, through which and by which, at the level of content, Clarice's writing attains to or contrasts the most surprising and imponderable regions) (14).

17. See Jean Franco's important study, "From Modernization to Resistance."

18. Concerning the problematic of thought and writing to nonwriting, Gareth Williams has argued that the subaltern's inscription within the socius "obliges us to commit to a thought of relationality and potential finitude. It is therefore the promise of a radical interruption within any given conceptual system, for it undoes the naturalized constitution of that system and thereby establishes the demand for other relations between critical reason and its cultural objects" (*Other* 11). In a recent article, Luciana Namorato derives a reading from one of the novel's thirteen titles, "Ela não sabe gritar." For Namorato, one may read the resistant, nonverbal, affective life of Macabéa—especially in terms of its "silences" and strangeness—as generative of the novel's writing procedure. See Namorato, "A tentação do silêncio." See also Tace Hedrick's reflections in "Mãe é para isso" on the oft-flawed character of English translations of Lispector's work, including Giovanni Pontiero's translation of *A hora da estrela*. Drawing on Walter Benjamin and Gayatri Spivak, Hedrick suggests that mistranslating Lispector's original "mode of signification," which would mean providing more literal translations, might cause readers to miss Lispector's "constant search for ways to express, in language, what she thinks of as the extralinguistic, essential, and generative nature of such (biologically) female experiences as fecundity, pregnancy, and maternity" (56, 62).

19. For a discussion on the metatextual in Lispector, see Fukelman, "Escreves estrelas." See also Nunes, "O movimento da escritura" 150–55. An overview of Lispector's critical reception can be found in Ferreira-Pinto Bailey, "Clarice Lispector e a crítica."

20. For a general reading of Lispector from a Jewish standpoint, see the essential contribution by Vieira, "Clarice Lispector" 100–150; as well as Lindstrom, "Pattern of Allusions."

21. For an examination of the question of the nation in the Brazilian literary tradition and in relation to *A hora da estrela*, see Medeiros, "Clarice Lispector."

22. And yet, unlike Graciliano Ramos in his novel *Vidas secas* (1938) and monumentalized as a Cinema Novo pioneering film of the same title by Nelson Pereira dos Santos in 1962—where both artists cast protagonist Fabiano in illiteracy, and whose access to the lettered city would seemingly serve as a condition of possibility for enfranchisement—Macabéa is spun as a porous, refractive figure whose relation to writing beckons the reader to reflect on the compositional strategies at play on the part of the narrator. Far from an external story of social types grounded in an unbreachable subject-object divide, the problem of the letter in relation to the subaltern becomes a generative, internal path, or compositional field, that the novel stages with force.

23. Concerning the textual layering of Macabéa's "retratos," Lesley Feracho provides an examination of the ways in which Rodrigo's depictions of Macabéa "reveal the stereotypes of northeastern inferiority" (94). See her "Textual Cross-Gendering."

24. It is clear that the narrative's compositional plane displaces emphasis from any subject-object dialectic, that is, from any reading of Rodrigo's writing project in the dichotomizing terms of phallocentrism and Eurocentrism. The image of writing at play in *A hora da estrela* becomes an impersonal force of lines in flux, of "words that appear as words," even as they

combine to narrate a story of writing over that of the representation of polarized social and gendered subjects.

25. *A hora da estrela* might be productively examined in terms of the modes through which it constructs a series of lines, an "inflexible pulsating geometry" (*A hora* [1998] 82), that negotiates the limits of figuration so as to arrive at an affirmative, alternative, problematical syntax related to a distribution of singularities, sensations, and an untimely present.

26. With respect to the feminine in Lispector, see Helena, *Nem musa nem medusa*; Barbosa, *Clarice Lispector*; and Feracho's two chapters dedicated to *A hora da estrela* in *Linking the Americas* (67–108).

27. "Macabéa separou um monte com a mão trémula: pela primeira vez ia ter um destino. Madame Carlota (explosão) era um ponto alto na sua existência. . . . E eis que (explosão) de repente aconteceu: o rosto de madama se acendeu todo iluminado. . . . Madama tinha razão: Jesus enfim prestava atenção nela. Seus olhos estavam arregalados por uma súbita voracidade pelo futuro (explosão)" (75–77).

28. "Ela era calada (por não ter o que dizer) mas gostava de ruídos. Eram vida . . . (Quanto a escrever mais vale um cachorro vivo). . . . (É paixão minha ser o outro. No caso a outra. Estremeço esquálido igual a ela). . . . (Com excesso de desenvoltura estou usando a palavra escrita e isso estremece em mim que fico com medo de afastar da Ordem e cair no abismo povoado de gritos: o Inferno de liberdade. Mas continuarei.) . . . (Vejo que tentei dar a Maca uma situação minha: eu preciso de algumas horas de solidão por dia senão me muero). . . . (Como é chato lidar com fatos, o cotidiano me aniquila, estou com preguiça de escrever esta história que é um desabafo apenas. Vejo que escrevo aquém e além de mim. Não me responsabilizo pelo que agora escrevo.) . . . (Vejo que não dá para aprofundar esta história. Descrever me cansa" (33, 35, 37, 69, 72, 72).

29. I owe this formulation to Alberto Moreiras's paper "From Melodrama to Thriller," presented at LASA 2012. Moreiras's talk was part of a larger panel discussion, organized by Erin Graff Zivin, on Moreiras and José Luis Villacañas's Iberian Postcolonialities Encyclopedia Project.

30. Of melodramatic consciousness, Louis Althusser writes, "[M]elodramatic consciousness can only be dialectical if it ignores its real conditions and barricades itself inside its myth. Sheltered from the world, it unleashes all the fantastic forms of a breathless conflict which can only ever find peace in the catastrophe of someone else's fall. . . . In it, the dialectic turns in a void, since it is only the dialectic of the void, cut off from the real world forever. This foreign consciousness, without contradicting its conditions, cannot emerge from itself by itself, by its own 'dialectic.' It has to make a rupture—and recognize this nothingness, discover the non-dialecticity of the dialectic" (140). My thanks to Gareth Williams for this reference.

31. Referring back to the ideogrammatic title page, in the very middle, beneath Clarice Lispector's signature, we read, ".QUANTO AO FUTURO." Framed by two periods, like a subtle parenthesis that is nonetheless definite, trenchant, the fragment's futuricity as title over sense is suspended, just as the gesture of any imposed representation in Lispector is undone at the textual surface.

32. See Deleuze and Guattari's account of the percept, affect, and concept in *What Is Philosophy?* 163–99.

33. On the present in Lispector, Silviano Santiago has written the following statement: "O esforço da narrativa ficcional de Clarice Lispector é o de surpreender com minúcia de detalhes o acontecimento deconstruido. Ele é um quase nada que escapa e ganha corpo, é esculpido matreiramente pelos dedos da linguagem" (The impetus at stake in Clarice Lispector's narrative fiction is to astonish, with utmost detail, the deconstructed event. This event is an almost nothing that escapes and takes on a body: it is sculpted most skillfully through the fingers of language) ("A aula inaugural" 237).

34. See Spivak, *Death of a Discipline*, 71–102. "I have suggested that literary studies must take the figure as its guide. The meaning of the figure is undecidable," writes Spivak, "and yet we must attempt to dis-figure it. . . . And to learn to read is to learn to dis-figure the

undecidable figure into a responsible literality, again and again" (71–72). The "undecidable figure" for Spivak is underwritten by a notion of cultural planetarity over globalization, to a process of "othering" over an identitarian, dialectical viewpoint. This radical alterity that takes place in the textual act of responsible, nondominating dis-figuration allows one to relate, respond, and read in a nondialectical but planetary way, to the "vast precapitalist cultures of the planet" (101). The undecidable figure would no doubt share a relation with "the immense heterogeneity of subaltern cultures of the world" (16).

35. "For me," notes Irigaray, "questioning the patriarchal world has been possible from the discovery of the fabricated character of my feminine identity" (*Conversations* 3).

2. THE LETTER'S LIMIT

1. See the reaction to Viñas's anti-literary remarks in Jitrik, *El escritor argentino* 11–22. Jitrik writes, "Pocas semanas después de publicar *Dar la cara*, su autor, David Viñas, hizo declaraciones que en su momento me molestaron. Proclamaba la necesidad de abandonar la literatura si se quería llevar a términos de acción los proyectos que habían dado lugar, justamente, a una obra literaria encarada en cierta dirección. Definía la literatura casi como una distracción impotente e, implícitamente, condenaba a quienes ponían en ella algún tipo de esperanza" (11). No doubt Jitrik's resistance to Viñas's anti-literary proclamations will shift to a common politics the writers share: the problematic of dependency. Jitrik observes, "[M]e doy cuenta de que tanto [Viñas] entonces como yo en este momento estamos hablando de otra cosa, simplemente la angustia latente y manifiesta pero permanente que cargamos sobre nosotros, escritores argentinos, y que proviene del hecho de haber apostado a la carta de la literatura en un país dependiente" (11–12).

2. See Sarlo,"¿Qué hacer con las masas?," 15–55; and the comprehensive study by Gilman, *Entre el fusil y la pluma*.

3. This seems to be a principal theme in William Katra's interpretation of the *Contorno* project. For Katra, Sartre served as a mentor-guide that the *Contorno* writers did not always fully grasp: "Their writings reveal that they passionately embraced [Sartre's] principal ideas on engagement, even though at times they failed to capture entirely the spirit of his message" (34).

4. See Sarlo, "Los dos ojos de *Contorno*," 3–8. See also Katra, *Contorno*, esp. 63–67. While I disagree with Katra's historical assessment of the *Contorno* generation, which, according to him, begins with their "confusion" and "misplaced priorities" regarding their "political orientation," he offers an informative mapping of the cultural field in the 1950s and an extensive interpretation of Sartre's impact on Viñas and the writers of *Contorno* (63–67).

5. Emir Rodríguez Monegal's interpretation is symptomatic: "[L]as novelas de David Viñas carecen de una estructura nacida desde adentro; él se propone una tesis como cosa previa y, de acuerdo con ella, va manejando situaciones, personajes, hechos. Todo está movido en función de la tesis que sustenta y que va a demostrar en las páginas de sus novelas" (*El juicio* 73). Pilar Roca's book on Viñas's novels provides an interpretation that is more nuanced but still anchored in a discourse tied to theses and Viñas's personal positions: "es cierto que la novela de Viñas es una novela de tesis y ello implica una serie de limitaciones previas, pero no lo es menos que suele demostrar una enorme capacidad de autocrítica para señalar sus carencias" (14). According to Marcela Croce's reading of Viñas's critical project, as postulated in the pages of *De Sarmiento a Cortázar*, "[E]n Viñas la literatura—representación desde la perspectiva lukacsiana—es confirmatoria de una dominante orden política: la literatura argentina da cuenta del proceso de la construcción de una ideología dominante" (*David Viñas* 58). While Viñas certainly championed a self-reflexive and critical Marxian politics in his assessment of the Argentine literary tradition, he also called for a literature of "violence" against schemes and any sort of "sanctified" book. Accordingly, his literary production cannot and should not be reduced to a Lukacsian "science," or ideological thesis. For a nuanced reading of Viñas's critical production, see Crespi, *El revés y la trama*, which possesses the virtue of highlighting the continuity, and indeed, constant crossover between critique and creation in all of Viñas multifarious writings: "la separación entre 'crítica' y 'creación' aparece radicalmente cuestionada en el seno mismo

de esa obra que incluye ensayos signados por una importante carga ficcional, pero también relatos, novelas, aguafuertes, piezas de teatro, guiones de televisión o de cine en que la dimensión crítica es asumida sin tapujos" (9). See also, in particular, retrospective essays by Legrás ("David Viñas"), Ludmer ("David Viñas"), and Muñoz ("David Viñas"), as well as the splendid collection of essays in Rinesi et al., *David Viñas*.

6. "*Contorno* was the fundamental review," writes Francine Masiello, "that turned the tide of contemporary Argentine criticism, reversing the impressionistic explications that had dominated previous theories of writing. Following the initiatives of *Contorno*, the editors of subsequent literary journals continued to raise questions about the social responsibility of the writer" ("Argentine" 41). On *Contorno*, see especially Rodríguez Monegal, *El juicio*; Orgambide and Seiguerman, "Encrucijada"; Sarlo, "Los dos ojos" and "¿Qué hacer con las masas?"; Katra, *Contorno*; Croce, *Contorno*; Romero-Astvaldsson, *La obra narrativa* 31–74; Valverde, *David Viñas* 68–91; Masiello, "Argentine"; Terán, *En busca* 195–253; and Crespi, *El revés* 13–21. In his essay manifesto for the first issue of *Contorno* in November 1953 entitled "Los martinfierristas: Su tiempo y el nuestro," Juan José Sebreli invokes a new generational struggle and provides a sociological and existentialist critique of the vanguard Martinfierristas of the 1920s, claiming that the postwar years in Argentina mark "the age of commitment" and "responsibility" and not that of "metáforas y exclamaciones [creacionistas]" and liberal, author-centered politics (1). For Sebreli and the contributors to *Contorno*, the intellectual's responsibility hinges on mediating not only the literary and the cultural but also the advent of the Peronist masses in the Argentine public sphere, and reassuming the national as a political and not solely aesthetic or identitarian problem for authors and poets of talent. I am suggesting that the vanguard context of the 1950s and 1960s progressively witnesses the move from the dynamism of the subjective and the construction of a powerful poetic *I* capable of manipulating "the new" (Girondo 25–26), the structure of feeling of "authorial" talent and iconoclasm (M. Andrade, "O movimento" 252–53), and the concomitant consolidation of a national literary tradition and language capable of cannibalizing the "fashionable" European modernist techniques of the 1920s (Viñas, "El escritor vanguardista" 61), to calls for invention and intervention that negotiate the alienation of writers from a public sphere marked by the culture industry and the discourse of neocolonialism. Following Oscar Terán, if "the new was promoted again" in the 1960s, artists and writers sought "new legitimizing agencies" that generally hinged on looking to politics, the crisis of the masses, and the Cuban Revolution ("Culture" 271). "The early avant-garde artists did not suffer the conflict between art and politics, inasmuch as they believed that art itself transformed the social order" (272). According to Andrea Giunta, "Art was increasingly both representation and action" in the post-Peronist years of the late 1950s and 1960s in Argentina (16).

7. Yet from the very beginning, it is clear that Viñas's statements on literature are nothing less than anti-literary. For example, following the major box-office success of *El jefe*, Viñas was asked by a leading cultural supplement, *Gaceta Literaria*, to write his position on the relation between cinema and literature. Viñas writes, "No me interesa hablar de literatura y cine en general. Prefiero hacerlo circunscribiendo el problema a mi situación, a mi comunidad. Y por extensión a América Latina: 1) Los escritores argentinos corremos el riesgo de ser tan inoperantes que podamos vivir en paz. Es decir, convertirnos en algo decorativo para que se ocupen los zurcidores de historias literarias y nos decoren con algún epitafio y con un par de fechas, que bien puede ser la de nuestro nacimiento y de nuestra muerte. Porque no se trata de escribir para que nos llamen 'caballeros de castellano' o 'señores del idioma,' ni para que algún esforzado profesor de literatura escoja una página de cualquiera de nuestros libros y les proponga a sus alumnos: 'Tema: subrayar los adjetivos cinestésicos en la pág. 37 de la obra equis del malogrado escritor nacional' . . . Y mucho menos para llevar a cabo esa sórdida y melancólica que se conoce con el nombre de la 'carrera literaria' que generalmente termina con el ingreso en la mesa directiva de alguna revista literaria . . . No. Nuestra literatura tendrá algún sentido cuando sea una literatura de agitación. Y por dos razones fundamentales: porque la única literatura válida que hemos hecho ha sido de agitación (desde el viejo Sarmiento a Roberto Arlt pasando por Cambaceres), y porque esa actitud literaria presupone el enfrentamiento de una

comunidad con los problemas que le inquietan . . . Lo demás . . . son libros, muchas páginas escritas con mayor o menor destreza . . . pero nada más. 2) Y el cine puede ser el gran aliado de esa literatura de agitación, en tanto enfrentamiento, denuncia. Y difusión. O lo que es lo mismo, negación de la dulce y respetada inoperancia del escritor" ("Escribe" 15).

8. See in particular Viñas, *De Sarmiento* 15–21.

9. Even so, already in 1959 in a review of *Los dueños de la tierra*, Pedro Orgambide registers the filmic style of Viñas's prose, especially at the novel's opening (19). Daniel Link observes in 1994 that *Los dueños de la tierra* "[es] una de las primeras manifestaciones de la canibalización de las tecnologías audiovisuales en la literatura argentina" (38). Even if the inherent relationship between cinema and literature remains underappreciated, critics persist in claiming that Viñas's writings fall into "tipismo": "En Viñas, se dirá, habrá de caerse," writes Adriana A. Bocchino, "en lo se llamó tipismo . . . un verdadero problema de esquematismo para la literatura" (300).

10. While the original idea and writing of the text was Viñas's, it is important to underscore that the *Dar la cara* script was assiduously edited, discussed, and composed "de a dos" with the now legendary director José Martínez Suárez. Indeed, in a give-and-take worthy of legend, Viñas and Martínez Suárez went through twelve drafts over the span of two and a half months, reaching an impasse that would be resolved only through the intervention of another director, Leopoldo Torre Nilsson: "Hicimos doce versiones del guión. Fue entre la séptima y octava versión cuando David me dijo que, para él, el guión ya estaba finalizado. Le dije que no, que todavía faltaba corregir cosas, que había ciertas debilidades que se podrían modificar. . . . Se creó con esto una situación conflictiva: ninguno aceptaba la posición del otro. Entonces, lo que tuvimos que hacer fue tratar de buscar una tercera persona para que lo leyera y dijera lo que le parecía. Unos cinco minutos después de salir de la casa, David me llamó desde un café y me propuso que le pasáramos el libro a Torre Nilsson. Acepté y enseguida fuimos a la casa de Torre Nilsson. Le dijimos que teníamos una duda en cuanto al guión. Se lo entregamos y en dos, tres días nos llamó por teléfono . . . y seguimos trabajando hasta alcanzar la versión final" (Valles 164–65). On the collaborative writing process, Martínez Suárez adds, "Escribíamos de a dos en la casa de él que vivía con sus suegros, mujer e hijos en San Fernando, provincia de Buenos Aires casi hasta la madrugada, o en mi casa frente al Jardín Botánico (Malabia y Las Heras, ciudad de Buenos Aires) también hasta las altas horas de la noche. Yo calculo que un 60% en Palermo y el resto en San Fernando, en una Olivetto Lettera con copia a carbónico" (email to author, 29 February 2016). With respect to the genesis of the script, according to Martínez Suárez, "Fue Viñas quien me llamó a mí junto a su amigo Hernst Kehoe Wilson. Habían visto mi anterior película, o mejor dicho, mi primera película *El crack* (1960) y les gustó la forma de manejar personajes porteños, el uso de exteriores, en no entrar a estudios para rodar y una temática desarrollada con perspectivas precisas de la realidad porteña . . . Nos habíamos [ya] conocido pues éramos habitués al Cine Club Núcleo que daba sus funciones en el cine Dilecto, en Avenida Córdoba casi Paraná. [Era] [u]na amistad circunstancial hasta ese momento" (email to author, 29 February 2016). In a 2014 interview, Martínez Suárez further elaborates on why Viñas and Kehoe Wilson sought him out as director for the project: "al ver *El crack* advirtieron que tenía un lenguaje porteño y natural, y a raíz de ello determinaron quién podría realizar este guión que había escrito David. Entonces me llamaron, hablaron conmigo y me ofertaron ese trabajo. Yo les dije que antes quería que tocáramos el libro, lo estudiáramos, lo modificáramos. David aceptó y empezamos a trabajar juntos en el guión" (Valles 163). Regarding realism in his first feature, *El crack (una película argentina)* (1960), Martínez Suárez observes, "[T]ratamos [con el dramatúrgo y guionista, Carlos Alberto Parilla y Solly] que el filme fuera de obligatoria necesidad de visionamiento cuando se quisiera saber qué pasaba en la Argentina en 1960. No sólo con la problemática natural de un país en cualquier momento de su historia, sino que reflejara cómo se hablaba, cómo se vestía la gente, qué comía, qué ocurría en los niveles cotidianos cada día de la semana. Un verdadero fresco donde dije lo que quería decir y lo que me interesaba mostrar" (qtd. in Gallina 66). Martínez Suárez affirms the same in regard to the realist project of *Dar la cara* in Valles, *Fotogramas* 164, and Copetes Filmoteca, "Filmoteca."

11. On this topic, see especially Terán, *En busca* 195–253.

12. Edmundo Eichelbaum's emblematic essay, "Primer festival de cine argentino," includes an analysis of *El jefe*: "Con 'El Jefe,' tema de aguda crítica social, quedan definitivamente atrás el naturalismo fotográfico y el pintoresquismo sainetero, los sentimentalismos sobre la barra de la esquina, tantas veces desvirtuada en nuestros films. . . . Cada vez con mayor certeza los cineastas comprenden que el cine, como expresión artística, exige la interinfluencia o el acompañamiento de otras artes" (19). For an early article on the shift in emphasis from the folkloric and mythic to the urban, see also Couselo, "Literatura y cine argentino." No doubt *Dar la cara* parodies the old-guard cinema of national existence with Basilio Carbó's feature, *La isla negra*—a film that Viñas's protagonists Pelusa and Mariano reject for being formulaic and which, in turn, launches Mariano on the path to independent cinema.

13. Laura Podalsky explains: "The government encouraged the growth of independents through the 1957 Ley Cinematográfica. Promulgated under the Revolución Libertadora, the law established the first state film institute, the Instituto Nacional de Cinematografía (INC), to reinvigorate Argentine filmmaking. Through the INC, the state oversaw the obligatory exhibition of all Argentine films . . . and the rating of all films and theatres. . . . The INC also collected a new tax on film tickets and used those funds to support the production of Argentine films through grants and prizes" (85). See also the video interview in Viñas and Olivera, "*El jefe* medio siglo después."

14. Scholarship on Viñas's relation to cinema remains scant. The most extensive analysis to date is Bernini's "Viñas y el cine." See also, in particular, Bocchino, "Empecinada lucidez"; and Pérez Llhaí, "El cine." For a superb reading of *El jefe* against the wider cultural context of film production in the city of Buenos Aires, see Podalsky, *Specular* 84–99. For an indispensable source on Héctor Olivera's cinematography, see Landini, *Héctor Olivera*. For Fernando Ayala, in addition to Tomás Eloy Martínez, *La obra*, see Rapallo, *Fernando Ayala*.

15. Undoubtedly linked to the allegorical specter of the strong leader figure of Perón, the Viñas-Ayala-Olivera collaborations investigate the problem of the authoritarian strongman. In effect, both *El jefe* and *El candidato* "explore the conditions that contribute to the rise and popularity of authoritarian leaders" (Podalsky 87). In an illuminating interview with the newspaper *La Nación*, on 16 April 1958 Viñas relates, "[V]elocidad, ansias urgentes y fáciles, superficialidad, irresponsabilidad, falta de afincamiento en las cosas y en los sentimientos, aturdimiento, cinismo, desorientación en suma. La gente quiere cosas . . . y no sabe qué hacer con su libertad. De ahí que todos estén dispuestos a enajenarla, a transferirla a alguien que dé, mande, y resuelva ese malestar profundo y angustioso que los provoca" (qtd. in Podalsky 87). See also Héctor Olivera's "Prólogo" for the recently published filmscript *El jefe*, 9–17. Olivera's text explains *El jefe*'s epochal importance for Argentine cinema in general and for Olivera and Ayala's legendary film company, Aries Cinematográfica Argentina SRL. On the genesis of *El jefe* and its connection to Viñas, Olivera writes, "Cuando [Fernando Ayala] leyó un cuento del joven escritor David Viñas titulado 'El jefe' sintió que su postura ante el cine argentino podía concretarse en una película basada en este cuento. Por intermedio de Beatriz Guido, se puso en contacto con David que, según sus propias palabras, 'estaba haciendo un viaje iniciático por Sudamérica—generalmente la meta era París'—cuando en Bolivia recibí un telegrama anunciándome que alguien quería filmar ese cuento'" (10). Citing critics Claudio España and María Sáenz Quesada, Olivera underscores the film's importance: "'*El jefe* es el film más representativo de aquellos años . . . Detrás de la figura del "jefe," el emergente emblemático es Perón y las fuerzas en juego la prepotencia y la sumisión acrítica. Difícil analizar la Argentina de entonces sin tener en cuenta este producto cinematográfico.' Justamente María Sáenz Quesada, en su *Historia argentina*, la señala como la más significativa de su época" (15). Special thanks to Héctor Olivera for this indispensable source.

16. In the novel version of *Dar la cara*, the headlines appear at the denouement, announcing Castro's successful taking of Havana (583).

17. In his televised interview with José Martínez Suárez, Fernando Martín Peña calls this lost generation "la generación, luego frustrada, del 58, del Frondizismo" (Copetes Filmoteca).

For fundamental sources on the Argentine generation of 1960 and José Martínez Suárez, see works by Feldman 65, 81, 118; Castagna 243–63; Martín Peña; Cerdá; Desaloms; and Kozak, *La mirada* (2013 ed.). Kozak's book, *La mirada cinéfila*, which provides a portrait of the Cineclub Núcleo of Buenos Aires, is currently being edited and republished by the Editorial Universitaria de Buenos Aires (Eudeba) in the Cosmos series, edited by Máximo Eseverri (forthcoming). The volume will include a digitally remastered DVD copy of *Dar la cara* and a DVD-ROM copy of all the issues of Cineclub Núcleo's influential review, *Tiempo de cine*. On the reasons for including *Dar la cara* with the volume, Eseverri relates, "Hubo varias razones, la principal es que detectamos una correspondencia generacional y política entre cineastas como José Martínez Suárez, escritores como David Viñas y quienes llevaron adelante iniciativas como el Cineclub Núcleo, que era un espacio de aglutinamiento, encuentro, intercambio, aprendizaje y mutuo apoyo para una nueva generación de artistas e intelectuales preocupados por su época, su país y caracterizados por gestos de innovación y la urgencia por intervenir y hacer oír su voz en sus diferentes ámbitos de pertenencia. Al igual que en la película, las nuevas generaciones del campo del arte, la academia y la intelectualidad tuvieron en medios como la revista y actividades como el Cineclub un espacio de encuentro y diálogo. El mismo José [Martínez Suárez], como he probado en el libro *Raab/Visconti: La Tierra Tiembla* (2010), participó activamente del Cineclub. Destacamos en el libro, además, la promoción que la revista hizo de películas como esta" (email to author, 14 March 2016). Special thanks to José Martínez Suárez, Máximo Eseverri, C. Adrián Muyo, and the Instituto Nacional de Cine y Artes Audiovisuales for these references.

18. See Deleuze and Guattari, *Thousand* 202–39; and *What Is* 85–113. For an outstanding discussion of affect, habitus, and politics in the context of Deleuze, Guattari, Bourdieu, and Spinoza as related to Chilean political processes of the twentieth century, see Beasley-Murray 174–225.

19. Estela Valverde explains the unorthodox compositional process: "Para escribir esta novela Viñas utiliza el libreto cinematográfico homónimo como punto de partida y 'procede por adición' adoptando un proceso inverso al que generalmente se sigue" (298).

20. See Martínez Suárez's televised interview with Fernando Martín Peña, in which the director asserts the movie's documentary thrust: "*Dar la cara* representa un momento exacto, hasta las palabras que estaban comenzando a utilizarse, las utilizamos en la película" (Copetes Filmoteca). Moreover, just as with *El crack*, he explains, "Si alguien necesita saber cómo se hablaba, cómo se vestía, cómo se comía, cómo se bailaba, cómo se hacía el amor en aquella época [en Buenos Aires], hay que ver *Dar la cara*" (Copetes Filmoteca). The interview is widely available on the Internet.

21. It is important to underscore that the novel is set in 1958 and ends with Fidel Castro's takeover of La Habana on 1 January 1959. In effect, the revolution is announced by newspaper delivery boys, Beto and Cholo (*Dar la cara* 583). In contradistinction, the movie begins with a similar newspaper delivery scene, this time announcing Castro's struggle in the Sierra Maestra, and spans four years (1958–62). Martínez Suárez relates, "Nos inspiramos más en los hechos históricos, por eso la película comienza con la noticia de que 'Fidel Castro lucha en la Sierra Maestra,' y termina con la noticia de que 'Argentina compró un portaaviones.' Así que, históricamente, es para que el espectador tenga noción de lo que pasó en el país, que sepa sobre el período histórico del que estábamos hablando, de 1959 a 1962" (qtd. in Valles 166).

22. On the change of title and origin of the novel project, José Martínez Suárez relates, "El caso fue que David me preguntó si me molestaba que él hiciera del argumento una novela pues se había abierto un importante concurso literario [Primer Premio Nacional de Literatura]. Yo le respondí que me parecía una idea excelente. Y David escribió esa novela que tiene notables variantes con respecto al guión original. Y hablando del guión original: cuando estábamos trabajando el argumento el título de la película era *Salvar la cara*. Pensando en ese título advertí que la palabra 'salvar' era como esquivar el enfrentamiento mientras que tenía más potencia 'dar' la cara. Se lo comenté a David, lo pensó unos minutos y aceptó la sugerencia" (email to author, 26 February 2016).

23. For an influential account of Latin American foundational fictions of the nineteenth century, see Sommer, *Foundational Fictions*.

24. See Sartre's *What Is Literature?*, 141–238.

25. As Deleuze said of the writer, Viñas will provide an intensive symptomatology of history and of the act of writing proper (*Essays* 3). In effect, Mariano's exodus from Basilio's studio to film the streets and slums of the "real Buenos Aires" parallels a larger historical phenomenon. "[I]n the late 1950s," Podalsky observes, "Argentine filmmakers began to move out of the studio to shoot on location with greater frequency. Until then, on-location shoots were relatively rare. . . . Encouraging this interest in depicting urban life in new ways were contemporary Italian films about city life like *Roma, cittá aperta* [Rome, open city], *Ladri di bicicletti* [Bicycle thieves], and *Umberto D* from the mid to late 1940s and early 1950s. Their harsh, if sentimental portrayals of the petty miseries of daily life in postwar Italy resonated with Argentine audiences" (84–86).

26. Quoted *s.v.* "infra," *Online Etymology*.

27. In April 1959, *Contorno* dedicated its final issue to Frondizi. See articles by the *Contorno* Editorial Board, Ismael Viñas, and León Rozitchner. See also Ismael Viñas's study, *Análisis del Frondizismo*. Elsewhere, at a roundtable discussion in 1968 on twentieth-century Argentine literature and politics with Rodolfo Walsh and Francisco Urondo, Juan Carlos Portantiero has observed, "Arturo Frondizi parecía ser la síntesis ideal que podía combinar el brillo de la inteligencia, es decir, cierta herencia intelectual argentina, con una posición no extremista frente al peronismo, al contrario: el rescate del peronismo, del rescate de lo que el peronismo tenía como movimiento popular" (274).

28. See Viñas's important authorial declaration on the inside dustjacket flap of his book *Las malas costumbres* (1963).

29. As a leftist, Viñas offers recognition of Birri that is tacit and not simply corrosive. See the 1959 interview in Viñas, "11 preguntas." On October 31, 1958, *Tire dié* was first screened in Buenos Aires at the Faculty of Law in the National University of Argentina. Alongside Fernando Ayala, Ernesto Sábato, and other notable intellectuals, Viñas participated in a roundtable discussion on the significance of Birri's pathbreaking film. On the other hand, the numerous parodic dimensions in both film and novel are tacit. In fact, the reference to Birri unfolds in an explicit and implicit sense: through filming the *villas miserias* (*Tire dié*) and through the insertion of Birri in the film as an extra. Of the numerous directors included in the film, Martínez Suárez relates, "Fernando Birri está sentado junto a Adelqui Camusso en el bar herradura de los laboratorios Alex; Solanas es el dirigente estudiantil de gruesos anteojos; Adolfo Aristarain en tres o cuatro planos en el mitín estudiantil . . . Leonardo Flavio protagonizando; Lautaro Murua, político-dirigente deportivo (el que tiene la secuencia final en el velódromo con Nuria Torray) . . . Todos ellos dirigieron" (email to author, 29 February 2016). Finally, it is important to note that Martínez Suárez himself taught for several years at Birri's newfound Escuela Documental de Santa Fe, beginning with its inauguration in 1956: "[E]stuve dos o tres años. Eran clases nocturnas, daba Realización III, es decir la final. Concurríamos semana por medio desde Buenos Aires. Fernando llevó a todos sus amigos capacitados: Carlos Alberto Padilla, Antonio Ripolli, Adelqui Camusso, Juan José Saer, Humberto Ríos, etc. Yo le diría que ese acto de Fernando conmocionó a toda la juventud cinéfila de la República, ampliando su espectro" (email to author, 3 March 2016).

30. On Birri's project to capture the "real" of Latin American misery, see his "Manifiesto de Santa Fe," as well as his explanatory essay, "Tire dié." On Birri's populism, see his essays "Cinema and Underdevelopment" and "For a Nationalist, Realist, Critical and Popular Cinema." Indeed, Birri criticized *El jefe* for its "evasiveness" and for presenting images of the country that were not real enough: "[T]he evasiveness of the few intellectualized films . . . Ayala's *El Jefe* . . . made the cinematographic images of the country they presented to audiences equally alien and foreign. . . . Our objective was a realism that would transcend this tendentious dualism" ("Cinema" 89). For an early and notable Marxian reading of Arlt, see Larra. For Viñas's negative rejoinder against reading Arlt through a mechanistic Marxism, see "Arlt y los comunistas."

31. Scholars are unanimous in praising Birri's film, *Tire dié*, as a pillar for Latin American Third Cinema of the 1960s. For an account of Third Cinema, see Solanas and Getino, "Towards a Third Cinema"; and Getino, "Some Notes." See also Birri, "Manifiesto de Santa Fe"; and Aimaretti, Bordigoni, and Campo. For Birri's lecture at Stanford University on the legacy of *Tire dié*, see Birri, "Tire dié (1956–1960)" 17–36. Birri's "Manifiesto de *Tire dié*" may be consulted in his "Los cinco manifiestos." For an overview of *Tire dié*, see Rufinelli 387. For an overview of Birri's oeuvre, see Sendrós.

32. See Pablo Díaz's documentary-interview, *David Viñas: Un intelectual irreverente*, widely available on the Internet.

33. The Arlt-Viñas connection is well documented. As already mentioned, *Contorno*, known for its parricidal war with the Argentine literary "fathers," dedicated its second issue to Arlt and championed his project for a variety of reasons: "mentalidad fronteriza," Arlt's use of the *voseo* and *lunfardo*, his denouncing of the system, his existentially problematical characters that charted and traversed the marginal sectors of Buenos Aires, and his recourse to the popular *folletín*, his literary journalism, and his autobiographical confessions in a historical juncture that the *Contorno* writers deemed informed by literary criollismo all pointed to Arlt as a fundamentally "sincere" writer who captured modern Argentine reality as lived in the city (Viñas, "Roberto Arlt: Periodista" 10). Viñas and his brother Ismael wrote the majority of essays in that fundamental second issue of *Contorno* in 1954, many under pseudonyms, and his critical approach exemplifies a bibliographical mastery of the entirety of Arlt's production. At a deeper level, Viñas examines Arlt's writing from a historical, existential, and compositional standpoint. "Desde el punto de vista de la creación," writes Viñas, "Arlt pertenece a una estirpe particular de creadores: infunde en sus personajes su propio sentimiento, su opinión frente al mundo, declara en ellos su ánimo, sus sueños y sus problemas, y cargados de tal modo, experimenta con sus vidas, lanzándolos a vivir las consecuencias absolutas de ese punto de partida" ("Roberto Arlt: Periodista" 9). For his part, José Martínez Suárez explains one central dimension to the Arlt reference in *Dar la cara* the film: "[los] libros [de Arlt] se mencionaban a menudo como posibles próximas producciones, era advertir que estaba en la carpeta de varios futuros directores y así fue como se convirtieron con el tiempo en películas todas las nombradas, la nómina comienza con *Martín Fierro* y sigue con Payró" (email to author, 3 March 2016).

34. We should underscore the open-ended character of León Vera's film script. Indeed, Mariano will constantly pester León not only about the film's readability for the public but also about the absence of a fixed technical design, which parallels, to be sure, Birri's project. In the words of the filmmaker, "[Q]ueriendo aprehender la móvil realidad de un 'lumpenproletariat,' [*Tire dié*] no tuvo un 'guión de hierro' y su guión técnico fue extractado del mismo una vez concluido" (Birri, "Tire dié").

35. On the *villas miserias* of Buenos Aires in the 1960s, José Martínez Suárez relates, "Las villas miserias habían pasado a formar parte de la ciudad. Tengo entendido que la primera se constituyó en Retiro cuando a comienzos de los años 30 se construyó la Dársena Norte en el barrio de Retiro, posteriormente a la asunción de Perón a la presidencia se realizaban festivales festejando el 17 de octubre y todo tipo de vehículo, tren, colectivo, etc. traía gente desde lo más lejano del interior a la ciudad. Cuando se delumbran con ellas, sus luces, sus avenidas, sus vidrieras preferían construir un tinglado junto a la casa de un amigo o pariente y convertirse en porteño. Los vehículos regresaban a sus puntos de partida semi vacíos, casi todos los viajeros habían quedado en [Buenos Aires]. No era difícil conseguir trabajo y formar familia si ya no estaba formada. A eso se le comenzó a llamar villas miserias que se extendían por distintos y distantes sectores de la ciudad y sus alrededores. Quería filmarlas porque formaban parte del panorama típico de la ciudad. Algunas estaban a 10 minutos de la Plaza de Mayo" (email to author, 3 March 2016).

36. In her superb study of Buenos Aires from the 1950s to 1970s, Laura Podalsky writes, "In the early 1960s, villas miserias were in many senses still marginal features of the Buenos Aires cityscape. In 1963, the approximately 230,962 people living in villas accounted for about 3.3 percent of the total population of the entire metropolitan area. The modernization projects

of the Revolución Libertadora and the subsequent Frondizi administration largely ignored these growing neighborhoods of makeshift homes built with found materials (wood, bricks, stones, corrugated tin). As suggested in David Kohon's short film, *Buenos Aires*, the patchwork construction of the dwellings contrasted sharply with the upwardly mobile aesthetic of new skyscrapers modeled on the steely glass skyscrapers in the United States and Europe. In sum, the villas didn't fare in plans to develop Argentina through the influx of foreign capital and technological renovation nor in attempts to refashion Buenos Aires as a cosmopolitan signpost of the new, modern society. . . . The villas mushroomed in unused spaces along railroad tracks, highways, and the Riachuelo—without clearly defined streets, access to water, or sewer hook-ups" (100–101).

37. Regarding fascist domination, Tealdi reads *Dar la cara* allegorically and thematically through the lens of an implicit anti-fascism: "El Poder político en *Dar la cara* ha de buscarse por ello en la aparición de grupos fascistas como manifestación del repliegue liberal después de la etapa peronista. Fascismo que encarna en grupos civiles en un primer momento y en militares a partir del '66. *Dar la cara* es entonces, aún con el predominio de lo interior-subjetivo, una denuncia del carácter fascista del poder político" (125).

38. See Moreiras, "Common Political Democracy." Working against identitarian ideology and the order of representation, Moreiras calls for a renewal of a thinking of political democracy through a *marrano* register. Like Viñas's radicalized medium, the marrano register is defined as "always open to exposure, or rather: it requires exposure for its self-constitution" ("Common"). See also Graff Zivin, "Aporias of Marranismo." Through a reading of Derrida's discussion of the generalized figure of the marrano, Graff Zivin provides an illuminating analysis of the marrano and its representations in contemporary Latin American literary production. Writes Graff Zivin, "At stake in the analysis of the marrano and its representations, I argue, is nothing less than the exposure of the limits of modern subjectivity, sovereignty, and hegemony" (191). For further elaboration on the volatility and force of the signifier "marrano" as aporetic figure, see Graff Zivin, *Figurative Inquisitions,* and her edited volume, *The Marrano Specter* (forthcoming).

39. See Viñas's declaration on the dustjacket flap of his book *Las malas costumbres* (1963).

3. SUBVERSIONS OF THE SENSIBLE

1. See Lévi-Strauss 16–23; and H. Campos, "Serafim" 5–28. In his introductory essay to *Serafim Ponte Grande* (1933), Haroldo de Campos compares Andrade's narrative technique to the hybrid repertoire of Lévi-Strauss's "bricoleur" ("Serafim" 9). The analogy concerns Andrade's use of the ready-made. "Bricoleur" has no precise equivalent in English, connoting deviousness, as well as the notion of the handyman and jack of all trades. For Lévi-Strauss, the notion of the improvising bricoleur, with his heterogeneous repertoire, can help one understand "primitive" mythical thought, as well as the artist: "[the bricoleur's] universe of instruments is closed and the rules of his game are always to make do with 'whatever is at hand.' . . . It is common knowledge that the artist is both something of a scientist and a 'bricoleur'" (17, 22).

2. With the publication of Carlos A. Jáuregui's *Canibalia* (Premio Casa de las Américas, 2005), Luís Madureira's *Cannibal Modernities*, and the voluminous critical anthology *Antropofagia hoje?*, edited by Jorge Rufinelli and João Cezar de Castro Rocha, there is no question that Andrade enjoys a privileged position in Latin American studies. And yet, the Brazilian concrete poets' pioneering efforts to revive Andrade's work have been, with few exceptions, relegated to bibliographic indexing. See Aguilar, *Poesía* 115–30, 275–302; and Jáuregui, *Canibalia* 543. The same can be said regarding the lack of scholarly reflection on the modes of expression that Andrade introduces into Brazilian poetry: the aphorism and the ready-made poem. Antonio Candido underscores the difficulty of defining anthropophagia: "É difícil dizer no que consiste exatamente a Antropofagia que Oswald nunca formulou, embora tenha deixado elementos suficientes para vermos embaixo dos aforismos alguns princípios virtuais, que a integram numa linha constante de literatura brasileira desde a Colônia: a descrição do choque das culturas, sistematizada pela primeira vez nos poemas de Basílio da Gama e Santa Rita Durão"

(84–85) (It's difficult to say exactly what anthropophagia is, since Oswald never formulated it, although he left enough elements to see some virtual principles under the aphorisms, which integrates it in a constant, Brazilian literary line since colonial times: the description of cultural shock, systematized for the first time in the poems of Basílio da Gama and Santa Rita Durão). Recently, Jáuregui described the aphorism as "surrealist phrases that work against rational argumentation" ("Anthropophagy" 25). The Brazilian concrete poets' theoretical reflections on Andrade's anti-literary modes of expression remain invaluable. See Pignatari ("Tempo"; "Marco"); A. Campos, *Poesia* (1978 and 2015) 1–7; *À margem* 143–57; "Oswald, Livro Livre"; and H. Campos, "Miramar," "Lirismo," and "Da razão". Accounts of Andrade's fragmentary style are abundant. Lacking is a theorization that connects it to the politics and crisis of representation. For an overview, see Boaventura, *A vanguarda*; Jáuregui, "Anthropophagy" 22–28; Jackson, "Literature" 1–16; Perrone, *Seven* 9–12; Lima 21–97; Schwartz, *Vanguardia* 175–231; Silva Brito 55–76; Larsen 72–97; Mendonça 72–92; Mendonça and de Sá 33–51; and Shellhorse, "Radical Reinventions."

3. In an edited version of the article "Marco Zero de Andrade," Pignatari underscores Andrade's break with literature (*disidentificação*) by altering his original wording of "Poesia em versos pondo em crise o verso" (46, 52), to "*Poesia em versus, pondo em crise o verso*" (*Contra-comunicação* 163, emphasis added).

4. See Nunes, *Oswald* 75–77: "Não devemos, porém, incriminar Oswald de Andrade, que não foi um filósofo puro, nem sociólogo ou historiador, por esses pecados de inconsistência lógica e de improvisção intelectual" (We should not, however, incriminate Oswald de Andrade, who was not a pure philosopher, nor a sociologist or historian, for his sins of inconsistent logic and intellectual improvisation) (76). See also Lucia Helena's influential study (*Totens* 179–99). On multiple occasions, the Campos brothers and Pignatari make the countercase. See Pignatari, "Tempo" 7–10; and A. de Campos, "Pós-Walds."

5. For example, see the interdisciplinary discussions on anthropophagia's relationship to Cinema Novo and Tropicália in Jáuregui, *Canibalia* 538–604; Madureira 111–30; and Aguilar, *Poesia* 117–57. Indeed, following João Cezar de Castro Rocha's call for the creation of new theoretical horizons to recover anthropophagia's "potência" from a non-identitarian framework, this chapter examines the concrete poets' revival of Andrade's poetics by charting the ways in which both Andrade and the concretes subvert the sensible (Castro Rocha, "Uma teoria" 663, 659).

6. See Pound's *Make It New* 5–8; and *Guide to Kulchur*, particularly 23–34, 44–50.

7. The radical language work of Mallarmé, Cummings, Joyce, and Pound figures predominantly in the poets' theoretical writings of the 1950s and 1960s. In the 1960s, notable Brazilians would include Oswald de Andrade, João Guimarães Rosa, Joaquim Sousândrade, and Pedro Kilkerry. Haroldo de Campos's manifesto, entitled "olho por olho à olho nu" (1956), provides a first portrait of the paideuma: "PAIDEUMA / elenco de autores culturmorfologicamente atuantes no momento / histórico: evolução qualitativa da expressão poética e suas táticas" (PAIDEUMA / cast of authors culturemorphologically actual in the historical / moment: qualitative evolution of poetic expression and its tactics) (74). In the essay "How to Read," Pound addresses what would make a "best history of literature": "the best history of literature, more particularly of poetry, would be a twelve-volume anthology in which each poem was chosen not merely because it was a nice poem . . . but because it contained an invention, a definite contribution to the art of verbal expression" (17).

8. The idea of participating in the syntax of its time is a mainstay in Brazilian concrete poetry from its origins in the 1950s. For this reason, Haroldo de Campos will write that concrete poetry "é a linguagem adequada à mente criativa contemporânea / permite a comunicação em seu grau + rápido / prefigura para o poema uma reintegração na vida cotidiana" (is the language adequate to the contemporary creative mind / it permits communication to the grain + rapid / it prefigures the poem reintegrated in quotidian life) ("olho" 75–76). In a letter to João Cabral de Melo Neto describing concrete poetry, Augusto de Campos will write "a defesa de uma arte que reduza ao mínimo o subjetivo, e que participe da sintaxe de seu tempo" (the defense of an art that reduces to the minimum the subjective, and which participates in the syntax of its

time) (2). Moreover, in the manifesto "plano-piloto para a poesia concreta" ([1958] 2006) Décio Pignatari and the Campos brothers proclaim concrete poetry's "realismo total" (218).

9. See Pignatari, *Errâncias* 44–47. Elsewhere in 1969, Pignatari will call for a nonlinear, interdisciplinary poetics, or "new barbarism," as a means of intervening in the sensible order established by the society of the spectacle: "Só a NOVA BARBÁRIE abre a sensibilidade aos contatos vivos . . . A tecnologia chega a um tal ponto de requinte que passa a requerer o marco zero de uma NOVA BARBÁRIE para desobstruir os poros" (Only the NEW BARBARISM opens sensibility to alive new encounters . . . technology has reached such a point of sophistication that one needs the zero degree of a NEW BARBARISM to clear the pores) (*Contracomunicação* 31).

10. Jorge Schwartz traces a parallel between Andrade's "rediscovery of Brazil" upon returning from Europe and his poetic "valorization of the national language": "Em Oswald de Andrade, a valoração da língua nacional aparece através do uso sincrético de africanismos, do tupi e do macarrônico ítalo-paulista fluxo migratório dos anos vinte. O retorno ao primitivismo, no caso da língua, deu-se não pela relevância do tupi como língua materna, mas pelo exorcismo das formas cultas e a apropriação da linguagem cotidiana como norma." (In Oswald de Andrade, the valorization of national language appears in the syncretic use of Africanisms, of the Tupi and the macoronic Italian-Paulista migratory flux of the 1920s. The return to primitivism, in the case of language, took place not because of the relevance of Tupi as a maternal language but due to the exorcism of elite forms and the appropriation of quotidian language as norm.) ("Um Brasil" 56). Benedito Nunes writes, "A imagem antropofágica, que estava no ar, pertencia ao mesmo sistema de idéias, ao mesmo repertório comum, que resultou da primitividade descoberta e valorizada, e a que se integravam, igualmente, na ordem dos conceitos, a mentalidade mágica, de Levy-Bruhl e o inconsciente freudiano" (The anthropophagic image, which was in the air, pertained to the same system of ideas, to the same common repertory, which resulted from the discovery and valorization of primitivism, and which [in turn] became integrated, likewise, at the level of concepts, to the [primitive] magic mentality of Levy-Bruhl and to the Freudian unconscious) (*Oswald Canibal* 18). See also Castro Rocha, "Uma teoria" 647–68. As for primitivism and its relation to the historical avant-gardes, it should be recalled that the Italian futurists referred to themselves as "the primitives of a new, completely transformed, sensibility" (Taylor, *Futurism* 11). In "Prefácio interessantíssimo," in his landmark book of poetry, *Paulicéa desvairada* (1922), Mário de Andrade called the Brazilian modernists "os primitivos duma era nova" (primitives of a new era) (34–35). See Justin Read's chapter on Mário de Andrade's *Paulicéa desvairada* ("Reversible" 59–102); but see also Perrone, "Presentation." For an account of anthropophagia in relation to Mário de Andrade's modernist novel, *Macunaíma*, see Rosenberg, *Avant-Garde* 77–105. See also, in particular, Unruh, *Latin American Vanguards* 42–50, 114–24, which includes outstanding analyses of both Oswald and Mário de Andrade's experimental writings; and Mahieux, *Urban Chroniclers* 64–92.

11. On Andrade's assimilation of European ideas and his various travels to Europe, see Schwartz, *Vanguardia* 179–87. Like Haroldo de Campos and Pignatari, Schwartz locates parody at the core of Andrade's poetry (224).

12. For wider context with respect to Latin America, see Gilman 35–96. See also Halperín Donghi 310–11.

13. "El primer número de *Invención* . . . marcaba el inicio de una nueva etapa del movimiento que denominaron 'salto participante.' Pero *los criterios modernistas fueron tan persistentes* que resulta mucho más adecuada la figura del *viraje* — antes que la del 'salto' — para describir este cambio, ya que los integrantes del grupo no cuestionaron sus supuestos sino que más bien se preocuparon por integrar — desde su poética — los cambios del entorno. . . . El salto participante fue, más que un aporte a una revolución que finalmente no tuvo lugar, la experiencia de *una colisión entre los paradigmas del modernismo y de la experiencia política*. . . . La falta de una resolución para esta tensión entre situación específica del campo y recepción extraartística hizo que la etapa 'participante' no haya tenido la continuidad y la persistencia necesarias en la obra de los concretistas. Ya en el tercer número de la revista, *la poesía comprometida parece cosa del pasado*, y en el cuarto, la presencia de Oswald de Andrade eclipsa

las posiciones anteriores a la vez que las redefine" (*Poesía* 99–103, emphasis added, except "viraje").

14. William Rowe writes eloquently of the "inner life" of poetry. Against the grain of set-in-stone systems of interpretation imposed on texts, Rowe calls for examining poetry as a "means of active discovery, and not simply a fulfilment, however well expressed, of what has been theorized already" (5).

15. In a 2008 article, Aguilar writes, "There is no politics without intervention upon contingency, without working the miracle of action. . . . It is a matter of shaking off subtraction, of abandoning negativity and returning to the positivity political action requires. It would seem that Augusto and Décio preferred to stick to the power of contradiction: the poem affirms a negative exteriority, in the case of Augusto, or an organic wear and tear, in the case of Décio. Haroldo, however, pushed beyond the limits, surpassed himself and worked with everything from party-political campaign songs to the banal language of the public authorities" ("Some Propositions" 190).

16. See Deleuze, *Essays* v–vi, 1–6.

17. On Brazil as "tropical Eden," see Sadlier 9–62. José Luiz Passos has shown quite clearly the importance of Caminha's "Carta" for Mário de Andrade's novel, *Macunaíma* (101–22).

18. For an overview, see Schwartz, "Um Brasil" 53–65, and his well-regarded book, *Vanguardia e cosmopolitisimo*. "*Pau-Brasil* lança as bases de uma brasilidade que procura a expressão estética em suas próprais raízes, apostando numa modernidade futurista inerente às vanguardas históricas. Uma nova linguagem, uma nova imagem poética" (*Pau-Brasil* establishes the bases for a Brazilianness that procures an aesthetic expression from its own roots, vying for a futurist modernity inherent to the historical avant-gardes. A new language, a new poetic image) ("Um Brasil" 61). For wider context regarding the Week of Modern Art in São Paulo, see Jackson, "Literature" 1–16.

19. It is clear that the Brazilian concrete poets follow Andrade's call, first announced in "Manifesto da Poesia Pau Brasil" (1924), for the exportation of Brazilian poetry. Beginning with the second volume of *Invenção* (1963), the poets will dedicate a concluding segment to the review, entitled "Móbile," that is dedicated to all things related to the exportation and diffusion of concrete poetry on the international and national fronts in the 1960s. In a cannibalization of Andrade worthy of the name, one of the subsections of "Móbile" will be called "Poetry of Exportation" ("MÓBILE" 92).

20. See Badiou, "Avant-Gardes" 131–47.

21. "Éste número de INVENÇÃO — o quarto — surge deliberadamente sob a invocação de Oswald de Andrade. A Oswald — a maior figura de nosso modernismo literário e o principal criador de nossa nova literatura — dedicamos, neste ano em que se comemorou o décimo aniversário de sua morte, uma secção especial" ("Foreword," *Invenção* 3).

22. Pignatari explains: "A poesia concreta é a primeira grande *totalização* da poesia contemporânea, enquanto poesia 'projetada.' . . . Considerando-se projeto a mediação entre dois momentos de objetividade" ("Situação" 65). Haroldo de Campos makes a similar claim in 1960: "A poesia concreta fala a linguagem do homem de hoje. . . . Pela primeira vez — e diz-se isto como verificação objetiva, sem implicação de qualquer juízo de valor — a poesia brasileira é totalmente contemporânea, ao participar na própria formulação de um movimento poético de vanguarda em termos nacionais e internacionais" ("contexto" 210–11). It should be noted, however, that in 1957 Augusto de Campos already speaks of concrete poetry's "realismo absoluto" insofar as "a poesia concreta começa por assumir uma responsabilidade total perante a linguagem . . . recusa-se a absorver as palavras como meros veiculos indiferentes" ("poesia concreta" 71).

23. My thanks to Augusto de Campos for providing this reference.

24. Far outstripping the purposes of this chapter, further distinctions should be drawn regarding the original idea of concrete poetry and the term's diverse historical meanings from an international context. Beginning in the 1950s, concrete poetry is launched by the Noigandres group and the Swiss poet Eugen Gomringer. "From this purposefully international gesture,"

writes Charles A. Perrone, "a calculated poetic practice emerged. Since about 1960, however, 'concrete' often also refers to numerous experiments on the printed page—typographical designs (often nonsemantic), pattern poems . . . which are not comparable to Gomringer's foundational texts nor to what the Brazilians called the 'verbivocovisual ideogram.' Concrete poetry was not conceived as figured word-designs but rather as a spatiotemporal juxtaposition of verbal material" (*Seven* 27). For an overview, see J. Bandeira and Barros 13–68; J. Bandeira 120–89; Perrone, *Seven* 25–66; H. de Campos, "Da poesia" 15–58; Camara, *Grafo-sintaxe*; Clüver, "Noigandres"; Mendonça, "A poesia concreta"; Barbosa, "Concretismo"; and Franchetti, *Alguns*. For the international projection of the concrete project, see the works by Solt, "World"; Clüver "'Ruptura'"; Erber, "Word" and *Breaching*; Price, *Object*; and the collection of articles in *Poetics Today* (June 1982). For a special issue dedicated to Brazilian concrete poetry, with articles by K. David Jackson, Irene Small, Marjorie Perloff, Claus Clüver, Antônio Sérgio Bessa, Willard Bohn, and Chris Funkhouser, see *Sección especial: Poesía concreta* in *Ciberletras 17* (2007). On material, "concrete" poetry from the Renaissance to the postmodern age as a transhistorical phenomenon, see Greene, "Concrete Historical." Greene's essay serves as the introduction to the special edition of the *Harvard Library Bulletin* he edited, entitled "Material Poetry of the Renaissance / The Renaissance of Material Poetry," which contains an interview with Augusto de Campos, additional essays by Charles A. Perrone, Marjorie Perloff, and Kevin Young, as well as an informative exhibit of material poetry from the age of the Renaissance to the present. Special thanks to Roland Greene for providing a copy of this source.

25. In his essay "Situação atual da poesia no Brasil," Pignatari calls Sartre's ban on poetic commitment a "curse" (*maldição sartreana*) (66).

4. THE UNTIMELY MATTER OF ANTI-LITERATURE

1. All citations from Haroldo de Campos's *Galáxias* (1963–76) come from the second edition, which was edited by Trajano Vieira and published in São Paulo by Editora 34 in 2004.

2. See especially Aguilar's pioneering contribution, *Poesía concreta brasileña* (355–70), and Bessa, "Ruptura," for a description of *Galáxias*'s decentered, global style. As Aguilar underscores elsewhere ("Haroldo" and "Some"), the problem of politics in Brazilian concrete poetry has been largely overlooked. Concerned with the problem of plural styles in the *Galáxias*, Bessa, for his part, reads Campos's appropriation of northeastern, subaltern forms not in terms of subversion, resistance, and politics but in terms of intellectual and affectionate "rediscovery of Brazil": "A consideração de Campos para esse tipo de literatura, aliás, é ao mesmo tempo afetuosa e intelectualizada. Em certo sentido, ele está 'rescobrindo o Brasil' via Pound" ("Ruptura" 20).

3. The fifty textual fragments that constitute the *Galáxias* are without pagination. Accordingly, for all subsequent references, including the final fragment here cited as "fecho encerro," I refer to the index of titles that appear in the first and second editions of *Galáxias* in 1984 and 2004.

4. See Sarlo, "¿Qué hacer con las masas?" 15–55.

5. "El poemario en su conjunto," writes Aguilar, "puede ser leído como la lucha — en el escenario de la página — entre la acción directa y la restringida, entre la búsqueda de un fuera-de-texto y el repliegue hacia sus potencialidades inmanentes" (*Poesía* 359). Aguilar makes a similar argument in a more recent work ("Some Propositions for Reflection" 175–92).

6. "Existe, desde el inicio del proyecto, un vaivén entre la historia (épica) y la acción restringida (pero epifánica) que se resuelve a favor de la segunda. . . . El gesto evolutivo se combina aquí con una prática que pone la autonomía de la escritura poética en los límites, aunque finalmente predomine un movimiento de búsqueda de lo epifánico en la escritura poética. Este repliegue hacia lo epifánico (a la luz autónoma que irradia un texto) es la otra cara de la frustración de la salida política. Entre 1963 y 1976, años en que se escriben estos poemas en prosa, la derrota de los movimientos progresistas y el endurecimiento de la dictadura militar en el Brasil frustran esas 'insinuaciones épicas' o utópicas" (*Poesía* 359).

7. "En esta constelación lingüística del pensamiento, la poesía aporta todos los recursos

de su materialidad y adquiere hasta cierto valor paradójico al desacralizar los textos canónicos a la vez que *sacraliza el trabajo poético*. Es por eso que el *paraíso* haroldiano se nutre de la poesía de Dante como presencia configuradora de sentido paradísico o epifánico. Sin embargo, este paraíso no es una realidad transcendente sino una iluminación inmanente que surge en el momento en que lengua y pensamiento devienen galaxia, constelación. . . . El trabajo poético agrupa sus materiales (discursos, libros, mente) y los relaciona abriendo en su inmanencia *el paradiso del poema*" (*Poesía* 366–67, emphasis added, except "paraíso").

8. In 1992, Campos will create a CD of sixteen "galactic" readings, in which his voice is accompanied by Alberto Mariscano playing the sitar. In the disc's explanatory note, he will speak of the scorelike quality of his galactic texts (*meu texto-partitura*) and cite his inspiration in the "mobility" of the Indian ragas, where chance is controlled through "structures of repetition" (*Galáxias* 119). The *Galáxias* are designed as an oral audition as much as a permutating reading space.

9. On the idea of poetic concretion, Campos affirms, "I changed from the limited problem of concrete poetry to the larger problem of concretion in language. The poet, in my opinion, has to deal with the concrete face of the language, the materiality of the signifier. . . . Each poet is by nature a concrete poet . . . since its beginning poetry has been dealing with concretion . . . the point is the materiality of language, the paronomasias, all the elements of the poetic function" (Perloff, "Brazilian" 168).

10. In the explicative appendix to the anthology *Concrete Poetry: A World View* (1967), Augusto de Campos describes his poem "sem um numero" in the following terms: "Social protest poem about the Brazilian peasant" ("Augusto" 254).

11. "I myself," states Haroldo de Campos, "from the time I was very young, was always for socialism, but for a democratic socialism. I was always against Stalinism. We as a group believed in socialism and so we were attacked by the Socialist realist poets of Brazil, who called us formalists. Even though our public position was clearly defined as a left-wing position" (Perloff, "Brazilian" 177).

12. Campos liked to speak of his "rediscovery of Brazil" upon returning from Europe in 1959 (*A educação* 113–14). His return to Brazil begins via a visit to the Northeast (Recife, Salvador), where he meets João Cabral de Melo Neto, who had recently composed his own politically charged homage to the northeastern minstrelsy, *Morte e Vida Severina: Auto de Natal pernambucano* (1954–55). On the crisis of poetry and representation in *Morte e Vida Severina*, see Shellhorse, "Explosion."

13. On Campos's homage to the northeastern minstrelsy, Antônio Sérgio Bessa relates, "It is believed that the Northeastern troubadour tradition, or minstrelsy, has roots in the Provençal tradition through Portugal and the poet-king, Lord Diniz, with his *cantigas* on friendship and love. Like their medieval European counterparts, the Brazilian troubadours are very respected and admired itinerant artists, whose communities guarantee their survival. . . . The passage cited originally by Campos seems to be written in the popular *sextilha* style, a stanza composed of six verses, each containing seven syllables. Our poet emulates the minstrel in those parts of the text that present a free flux of internal rhymes. But, although he mentions a specific style—*o martelo galopado*, in homage to its inventor, Jaime de Martelo, in the second half of the seventeenth century—his free style comes close to *mourão* verse, the style of choice for the *desafio*, or the duel between two minstrels" ("Ruptura" 27). For an introduction and translation in English of "circulado de fulô," see Bessa, "Circuladô." For a superbly translated volume in English of almost one hundred poems and several fundamental essays, see Campos, *Novas*.

14. See Deleuze's interview with Parnet in Deleuze, *Gilles Deleuze from A to Z*.

15. Campos affirms, "I am today making poetry, as Octavio Paz says very well, not of the future but of the present, and that poetry has the possibility of all the instruments of modernity and has to select in a precise moment what thing to do. There is no program for poetry. We had in the past the pilot plan for concrete poetry. We were programming the future. Now, it's not possible to program the future, so I am writing poetry that is dealing with the possibilities of modernity, not in a programmatic, but in a critical way. I'm trying to preserve that which

remains from utopian thinking, but now from the point of view of critique" (Perloff, "Brazilian" 169).

16. I owe the apt expression, "force of materiality," to Pheng Cheah ("Nondialectical" 156). For further discussion, see Cheah's trenchant analysis of Derrida's gift ("Obscure Gifts").

5. THE ANTINOMIES OF ANTI-LITERATURE

1. In an iconic manifesto-text, Campos writes, "a POESIA CONCRETA é a linguagem adequada à mente criativa contemporânea . . . TENSÃO para um novo mundo de formas / VETOR / para / o / FUTURO" (CONCRETE POETRY is the language adequate to contemporary creative consciousness . . . TENSION for a new world of forms / VECTOR / for / the / FUTURE) ("olho" 76).

2. From the beginning, Lins detected the tendency of critics to interpret his work as spiritualist. He would vehemently warn against it. Highlighting the mediation of subalternity in his writing, Lins writes, "Eu não pretendi colocar Joana Carolina lutando contra 'as adversidades da vida,' mas contra as adversidades de uma estrutura cruel, que ignora os pobres, inteiramente desprotegidos. O ritmo que rege o mistério final, a presença dos 'ninguens' que conduzem são uma prova disso" (I did not place Joana Carolina in a struggle against "the adversities of life," but against the adversities of a cruel structure, which ignores the poor, who are entirely unprotected. The rhythm that governs the final mystery, the presence of the "nobodies" that are carrying her is proof of this) (letter to Nitrini, 25 March 1975). On the Brazilian Northeast's deep-seated structural poverty, as well as the prevalence of folk Catholicism and messianism at the time of the composition of "Retábulo," see Gross. I mention this because the rural poor and peasants, including Joana Carolina, "the nobodies" in Lins's far from spiritualist formulation, constitute something like the subject matter of "Retábulo." Analyzing the situation in 1968, Gross writes, "Other than religion there was almost nothing of a cultural nature that the rural poor shared among themselves. Schooling was virtually nonexistent. As late as 1950, 74 percent of the population over five years of age, including [those on] the more prosperous coast, was illiterate. Until recently the *sertão* was one of the most isolated regions of Brazil. All-weather roads connecting it with the coast were not built until World War II. . . . The system of dependency on the family clans was the only secular institution of any import to the peasant, but the rich landowner was a protector of the rural poor insofar as it served his interests. Social and economic gulfs separated the rural oligarchy from the masses of the peasantry. Under these conditions, it is not surprising that the 'revitalization movements' in the *sertão* have taken a religious form" (381–82). Regarding the conditions of subalternity, one recalls the importance of the landed family clans in "Retábulo" as agents of violence and employment. And one further recalls, in "Sixth Mystery," the landowner puzzled by his father's decision to bring in a teacher for the plantation, namely Joana Carolina, who will become teacher-saint of the poor: "Bobagem de meu pai, coisas de velho, aceitar professora em nossas terras. Para ensinar a esses desgraçados?" (Stupidity of my father, the musings of an old man, to accept a teacher in our lands. To teach these unfortunate bastards?) (Lins, "Retábulo" 85; my translation). Joana Carolina's mother will describe her people under strictly subaltern conditions—as lacking property and letters: "Éramos gente sem posse, de poucas letras" (We were people without property, without writing) ("Retábulo" 80; my translation). Instances of violence and exploitation, as well as verbal, physical, and psychological abuse, including belligerent racism, are widespread in the work.

3. On the relationship between painting and Lins's poetics, see Nitrini, *Transfigurações* 161–77.

4. Lins, like Lispector and the concrete poets, has long been viewed through the lens of formalism, to the almost complete detriment of his explicit political concerns. See Armstrong, "Brazilian Novel."

5. "Professor Haroldo de Campos,

Vi a referência, não digo desfavorável, mas áspera, feita por você ao meu *Avalovara*, em entrevista à *Textura*. . . .

[P]ermito-me lembrar que cada um faz a própria literatura e que não pode fazer a de ninguém. Eu, por exemplo, não posso—e não desejaria—fazer a sua. Tenho a minha biografia, minha formação, minhas preocupações, venho de outro ponto do Brasil, etc. . . . Somos diferentes. Há mal nisso? A variedade nas buscas, eis uma das forças, talvez a maior, da literatura. Pensar de outro modo; fixar-se numa via única, não parece adequado ao escritor. . . .

Infelizmente, há hoje pessoas, no campo das artes, cuja posição deliberadamente pioneira acaba tornando-se limitadas e, o que é pior, intolerantes. Não vêem outra via, senão a que trilham ou imaginam trilhar. . . .

Mas se lhe escrevo, não é por nada disso. São tão ridículas, meu Deus, tão ridículas as disputas literárias! . . . Se me dirijo a você, é devido a outra assertiva—grave, a meu ver—, segundo a qual (como terá descoberto isto?) haveria eu efetuado, no meu romance, um 'remanejamento à la mode.' Já não se trata, aí, de uma opinião, mas de acusação um tanto séria, envolvendo a minha honestidade como escritor" (letter to Haroldo de Campos, 4 October 1974).

6. "Com Rosa acabou-se a prosa. Só *texto* pode agora interessar. Por isso não levo em conta as pretensões de 'vanguarda do meio-termo,' que sugestiona e satisfaz a alguns. Exemplo recentíssimo: o AVALOVARA, de Osman Lins. Trata-se de uma escrita fundamentalmente acadêmica e de um esquema romanesco tradicional, aos quais se impôs *de fora*, mecanicamente, sem qualquer critério, de necessidade intrínseca, um remanejamento 'à la mode'" (Campos, "Haroldo," *Textura* 16).

7. On this point, Charles A. Perrone observes, "The [Pilot-Plan for Concrete Poetry's] opening salvos are probably the two sorest points, since they do not regard the poetry per se but are put in larger historical terms. These points are the assertion of concrete poetry as the 'product of an organic evolution of literary forms' and the assumption of the death of verse. . . . [However,] [c]oncrete poetry was not the product of natural evolution but rather a *planned adventure* of contrived invention. The conscious elaborations of the Noigandres poets were a synchronic intervention that does not, in and of itself, justify their diachronic claims" (*Seven* 47).

8. See also Augusto de Campos's intervention on this topic in "Do Concreto ao Digital" and Décio Pignatari's interview in *A cultura pós-nacionalista*. Pignatari observes, "O que se conhece melhor da poesia concreta é, particularmente, esse momento da ortodoxia. Depois disso, muitas outras coisas se foram desenvolvendo. A poesia concreta não se fixou em uma simples questão da ortodoxia, de simplesmente defender palavras no espaço, não" (115). Special thanks to Augusto de Campos for providing a copy of the latter text.

9. Rebuffing the idea that he drew principal inspiration from the French *nouveau roman* and highlighting a fundamental political concern at the core of his "intellectual formation," in a letter to Sandra Nitrini dated 25 March 1975, Lins writes, "Acresce que, com as minhas leituras, não dexei de ser um primitivo. Sou um primitivo, um homem ligado ao mundo e aos mitos. Grillet, Sarraute, etc. são intelectuais. São 'homens de letras.' Eu tenho letras. Mas sou apenas um homem, encravado, alem disso, no mundo subdesenvolvido, com todos os seus dramas. A diferença é fundamental e deve ser levada em conta, sob pena de a sua visão do problema ficar prejudicada." (Add to that, for all my reading, I have never ceased being a primitive. I'm a primitive, a man linked to the world and to myths. Grillet, Sarraute, etc. are intellectuals. They are "lettered." I have letters. But really I'm merely a man, embedded in the underdeveloped world with all its dramas. The difference is fundamental and should be taken into account; otherwise, your perspective of the problem would end up flawed.)

10. Charting an unsuspected connection with Brazilian concrete poetry, in an important interview Lins will compare his concern with nonlinear, unfixed perspective with the writings of Mallarmé and Apollinaire: "Eu veria o início desta visão da literatura nos poetas, no Apollinaire, no Mallarmé. Principalmente no Apollinaire, a gente vê os caligramas que dão uma visão aperspectívica do mundo e mesmo da palavra" (I would perceive the origin of this vision of literature in poets, especially in Apollinaire, in Mallarmé. Principally in Apollinaire, one sees the calligrammes providing an unfixed vision of the world and even of the word itself) (*Evangelho* 214). Of course, the concrete poets thought less of Apollinaire than Mallarmé. Yet they always recognized the importance of Apollinaire's dictum: "Il faut que notre intelligence s'habitue à comprendre synthético-ideographiquement" (It is necessary for our intelligence to become

used to comprehending synthetic-ideographically) (Apollinaire, qtd. in Campos, Pignatari, and Campos, "Plano-piloto" 215). The quote comes from Apollinaire's *Le Guetteur mélancolique* (1952): "Révolution: parce qu'il faut que notre intelligence s'habitue à comprendre synthético-idéographiquement au lieu de analytico-discursivement" (144).

11. On the centrality of the baroque in Latin American studies and Hispanism, see Beverley, "On the Spanish" and "Baroque"; Moraña, "Barroco" and "Baroque/Neobaroque"; and Moreiras, "Mules." With respect to the baroque and the writers of the Boom, see Sarduy, "El barroco." See also Sarduy's philosophical essay, *Barroco*.

12. Carlos Fuentes wrote in 1969 that "[r]adical in the face of his or her past, the new Latin American writer sets out to revise it from this evidence: the lack of a language" (30). Fuentes thus inscribes a continent-wide problematic and identity discourse that privileged the new Boom novel as harbinger of a revolutionary and "authentic" language and consciousness (30).

13. During the 1960s, the "novela de la tierra" was primarily read through a stagist optics and was considered stylistically obsolete. In this view, the novel form had to "develop" a new language, "more universal" in style, while the nation-state teleologically advanced into a more "universal" form from a state of economic backwardness and dependency. According to Fuentes, "la novela tradicional aparece como una forma estática dentro de una sociedad estática" (14). For a reexamination of the legacy of the novela de la tierra, see Alonso, *Spanish American Regional Novel*.

14. See Lindstrom, "Autonomy and Dependency," for an insightful account of this topic. On the cultural Cold War in Latin America, see Franco's superb *Decline and Fall of the Lettered City*. See also Sorensen, *Turbulent Decade Remembered*.

15. With respect to the problem of the international market, a comprehensive reading of the activities and functions of the Boom novelist can be consulted in Ángel Rama's critical anthology, *Más allá del boom*. Literature's so-called achieved "authenticity" and autonomy were often juxtaposed and contrasted with the "falsity" of the language of consumer culture.

16. "That literature in our day is fascinated by the being of language," writes Foucault in 1966, "is neither the sign of an imminent end nor proof of a radicalization: it is a phenomenon whose necessity has its roots in a vast configuration in which the whole structure of our thought and of our knowledge is traced" (383).

17. See Sarlo, "¿Qué hacer con las masas?" While Sarlo's study concerns Argentina, her discursive mapping of the function of intellectual and political discourse may be juxtaposed against the case of Brazil, as well as to the general structure of feeling of the 1960s in Latin America. The examination of the writer's function in society, according to Sarlo, becomes progressively a discourse of transformation: "la cuestión pasaba por dos nudos: construir un intelectual que se convirtiera en sujeto material, corporal, de lo político, por una parte; evitar la oscilación de clase de los intelectuales para que, como bloque, se ubicaran definitivamente junto al proletariado" (*La batalla* 142–43). See also Gilman, *Entre la pluma y el fusil*.

18. See Levinson, "Ends of Literature as a Neoliberal Act."

19. According to Frizzi, "Surprisingly, little or nothing has been written about Lins in relation to other authors or movements outside Brazilian letters. Absent, for the most part, are references to the large and diverse number of Latin American writers often grouped under the umbrella of *literature of the boom*. . . . This problem of exclusion is common to most Brazilian authors, whose work is seldom included in the context of Latin American literature" ("Osman" 156). For a recent counterpoint, see Cariello.

20. Osman Lins, letter to Maryvonne Lapouge, 11 August 1969. Special thanks to Litânia Lins, Letícia Lins, Ermelinda Ferreira, Sandra Nitrini, Adria Frizzi, Claudio Vitena, and Leonardo Cunha for their invaluable assistance in my research.

21. According to Adria Frizzi, "Lins's poetics as conveyed in *Nine, Novena* constitutes the foundation of all his subsequent work and accounts for the way formal innovations serve his complex project: to return us to the mythic through the discourses of culture and the human arts" ("Osman" 157).

22. The notion of *heterotopia* that I read in Lins's ornament, understood as a radical procedure of textual de-ontologization that "stop[s] words in their tracks" and "contest[s] the very possibility of grammar at its source," is taken from Michel Foucault's reading of Borges's "La enciclopedia china" (Foucault xv–xxiv). In this way, I differ from Frizzi's dialectical understanding of narrative fragmentation in Lins. If, for Frizzi, "the fragmentation of discourse reflects the chaos of the world, and the geometric organization the cosmic order which can be achieved by art," my understanding of fragmentation and heterotopia hinges on the ways Lins's text traces and suspends its mimetic and referential dimensions with regard to the subaltern epistemological divide ("Introduction" 17).

23. While critics have amply charted the metaliterary dimension of Osman Lins's ornamental narratives, there has been little or no discussion on the ways his narratives negotiate the epistemological divide. For a reading of the metaliterary, understood as a perennial tension between the narration of history and the becoming literary of discourse in Lins, see Nitrini, *Poéticas*, 71–200.

24. Criticism rightfully points out the universal, mythic, and "cosmological" features in Lins's writing style. Lins actively promoted this vision in interviews and essays: "Se há alguma coisa de que é necessário o leitor estar consciente diante de um texto meu é de que eu não estou aspirando a dar uma visão apenas do homem brasileiro. Estou ligado ao meu país, ligado aos meus irmãos de infortúnio, mas o que procuro dar nos meus textos não é uma visão exclusiva do homem brasileiro, ou do Brasil, mas do cosmos" (If there is anything a reader should be aware about regarding my text it is that I am not merely aspiring to provide a vision of Brazilian man. I am bound to my country, bound to my brothers of misfortune, but the vision that I endeavor to provide in my texts is not an exclusive vision of Brazilian man, or of Brazil, but of the cosmos) (Lins, *Evangelho* 218). Few, however, have discussed his national popular politics or the pains he took to promote literature, both nationally and abroad, in his interviews, correspondence, essays, television scripts, and newspaper articles. In similar fashion, Lins was actively promoted by the Brazilian culture industry as a national figure who had achieved international success in magazine and newspaper supplements such as *Veja*, *Opinião*, and *O Estado de São Paulo*, as well as on TV Globo. For example, in 1976 the Brazilian magazine *Gente* reported, "Aos cinqüenta y dois anos, depois de trinta vivendo para a literatura, o pernambucano Osman Lins entra de sócio no clube mais fechado do Brasil: o dos escritores que vivem da literatura. Entrevistas com ele passam a ser constantes, e sempre transcorrem naturalmente, quase em tom bate-papo" (At fifty-two years old, after thirty years dedicated to living for literature, the Pernambucano Osman Lins has become a member of the most exclusive club in Brazil: writers who make a living from literature. Interviews with him have become frequent, and they always take place naturally, in conversational tone) (qtd. in *Evangelho* 201). For a discussion on Lins's publications abroad, see Godoy Ladeira, "Osman Lins" 186–95.

25. According to José Rabasa, it could be said that the force of subalternist reflection resides in providing "elements of self-critique" for Western modalities of discourse, including historiography and literature ("Elsewheres" 75). Accordingly, if the subaltern may be thought as "an elsewhere empty of positive characteristics," it provides a forceful and refractive mediation of traditional literary discourse in Latin America and its pitfalls (74).

26. With respect to the importance of self-reflexivity in addressing the subaltern problematic, Ileana Rodríguez writes, "Another goal [of Latin American subaltern studies] is to recognize that in history and culture of 'societies' Others' we can find, paradoxically, new ways of approaching some of the riddles created by the incapacity of bourgeois culture *to think about its own conditions of discursive production*" ("Reading Subalterns" 9, emphasis added). I am postulating that the metaliterary and the mapping of subalternity in Lins's ornamental texts not only calls attention to the literary artifact but, on the contrary, implicates the reader into a self-reflexive position to mediate the subaltern as a problem and not as an object. For further reflection on the scope of the Latin American Subaltern Studies Group, see Beverley, "Writing in Reverse." In the essay, Beverley writes at length about the productive divergence

of theoretical approaches in the Latin American Subaltern Studies Group, and about the group itself functioning "as a forum of discussions around a common concern" (624).

27. For a superb study on perhaps the most famous Brazilian "literary" work that is concerned with the Northeast and the problem of writing, see A. Johnson, *Sentencing Canudos*.

28. On isolation and the lack of any shared culture save religion, see Gross, "Religious Sectarianism," 381, as quoted above in n. 2. As Gross indicates, "[f]ew notions of social reform, or progress for that matter, could have filtered through the barriers of isolation . . . to influence the thinking of the backlanders" (381).

29. On *Revista Civilização Brasileira* as a vehicle of resistance, see in particular the article by Czajka.

30. Special thanks to Erica O'Brien Gerbino for her brilliant discovery of the *cantiga* intertext in Lins.

31. In a letter to Maryvonne Lapouge dated 4 May 1969, Lins describes the Ninth Mystery's illumination as evocative of Picasso and Chagall. Further still, he adds that others "são concebidos a maneira de alguns mestres medievais e mesmo da Renaçensa, quando viamos, ao mesmo tempo e num só quadro, o mesmo personagem em várias situações" (are conceived in the style of Medieval and even Renaissance masters, when we see, at the same time and in the same painting, the same character in various situations).

32. According to Candace Slater, the ornamental partitioning of Lins's text "recall[s] such sequences as the signs of the zodiac and the months of the year" and "the narrative, while not strictly chronological, records the protagonist Joana Carolina's passage from childhood through marriage and childbearing to old age and death" such that "the story is thus united through her" (290).

33. The concept of "violence" is not being invoked here in a merely descriptive sense. Of violence Lins wrote, "Se vocês leram com determinada atenção, vamos dizer, *Retábulo de Santa Joana Carolina*, vão ver que se trata de um texto repassado de violência . . . vão ver que a luta da figura central, Joana Carolina, já não é contra um determinado indivíduo, é contra o mundo. É contra a terra onde ela vive, é contra o seu país" (If you read with careful attention, let's say, "Retable of Saint Joana Carolina," you will see that it's a text that is saturated with violence . . . you will see that the struggle of the central figure, Joana Carolina, is not against a determined individual, it's against the world. It's against the land where she lives, it's against her country) (*Evangelho* 220). Accordingly, following Nancy Scheper-Hughes, the term will be deployed to designate the more explicit "everyday violence" of the political economy of the Brazilian Northeast, with its "many traditional and semifeudal structures, including its legacy of local political bosses (*coroneis*) spawned by an agrarian *latifundista* class of powerful plantation estate masters and their many dependents" (220). On the other hand, the term will also refer, following José Rabasa, to the "scriptural economy" associated with *symbolic violence*: "writing entails power structures: writing as the memory of subordination, as the record of theft, as the erasure of culture, as the process of territorialization" (*Writing* 14).

34. Ana Luiza Andrade shows that the tableaux in "Retábulo" serve as symbolic temporal indices for mediating the past and modernity: "os *tableaux* colocam-se no limiar entre a recordação do passado agrícola e arcaico da vida nordestina do engenho colonial, e a percepção de um olhar presente, urbano e moderno. Desdobrado este limiar, os espaços sócias divididos entre o erudito e o popular se interrompem para dar lugar ao espaço democrático de 'massa'" (the tableaux are placed at the threshold between the memory of the archaic and agricultural past of plantation-based northeastern life and the perspective of a present gaze that is urban and modern. Once this threshold is traversed, the riven social spaces between the erudite and popular are interrupted so as to testify to the democratic space of "masses") ("Reciclando" 96). The traditional "auratic" tableaux of the Church, accordingly, become refunctionalized: the multitude of the poor and the barren backlands of the Brazilian Northeast are its subject matter.

35. See Acosta's important *Thresholds of Illiteracy*, in particular, 1–25 and 73–76. As a mode of analysis and concept, Acosta will assert that "illiteracy names irreducibly ambiguous

semiosis" (9). Accordingly, he states, "I use the term to express the condition of semiological excess and ungovernability that emerges from the critical disruption of the field of intelligibility within which traditional and resistant modes of reading are defined and positioned" (9).

36. According to Ana Luiza Andrade's reading of Lins's ornament, "[H]á um deliberado e constante retorno às artes plásticas [porque] . . . Osman Lins busca uma refuncionalização dos meios da produção entre artes plásticas e industrias a fim de problematizar as relações entre arte e mercadoria" (There is a constant and deliberate return to the plastic arts [because] . . . Osman Lins is attempting a refunctionalization of media between plastic and industrial art so as to problematize the relation between art and commodity) ("Reciclando" 81).

37. For this reason, Lins will stress the anti-representational, assemblage character of his work. For example, explaining the almost exclusive prevalence of first-person narrative in *Nove, novena*, Lins writes, "O EU que busco é de outra natureza. É um instrumento para a conjugação dos verbos, as articulações de frase, a agenciamento do texto. Existe como pronome, mas um pronome falso, ilegítimo, pois não está em lugar do nome" (The *I* that I am procuring is of another nature. It's an instrument for the conjugation of verbs, for the articulation of phrases, for the assemblage of the text. It exists as a pronoun, but it's a false pronoun, illegitimate, because it doesn't replace a name) (letter to Nitrini, 28 April 1975).

38. The two cited sources refer to Adria Frizzi's English translation, "Eleventh Mystery," in *Nine, Novena* 156–61, and Lins's original, "Décimo Primeiro Mistério," in "Retábulo" 109–13. Unless otherwise indicated, henceforward paired page citations will refer to the two versions, in whichever order they are presented.

39. "O que é, o que é? Leão de invisíveis dentes, de dente é feito e morde pela juba, pela cauda, pelo corpo inteiro. . . . é filho, às vezes, de dois pedernais. Ainda que devore tudo, nada recusando a seus molares, caninos e incisivos, simboliza a vida" ("Retábulo" 109).

40. "Sua voz, perdidas as últimas inflexões, era um velho instrumento corroído, clarineta com liquens e teias de aranha. Custava-lhe unir as poucas palavras, tal como se as escrevesse. . . . Resplandecia, no âmago desses fenômenos, uma frase, uma palavra, um semblante, alguma coisa de completo e ao mesmo tempo de velado, como deve ser para um artista a forma anunciada, pressentida, ainda irrevelada, ainda inconquistada" ("Retábulo" 111, 113).

41. See Rancière, "Is There a Deleuzian Aesthetics?" Rancière's central hypothesis regarding Deleuze's concept of art, notably in his book on Francis Bacon and his thesis in *What Is Philosophy?*, is that art is a mode of being that promotes a sensory experience that exceeds the discursive schemes of normative political and legal representation that structure experience: "Aesthetics is born as a mode of thought when the work of art is subsumed under the category of a greater, heterogeneous form of the sensible. . . . Aesthetics is the mode of thought that submits the consideration of works of art to the idea of this heterogeneous power, the power of the spirit as a flame that equally illuminates and burns everything" ("Is There" 10). The concept and experience of the aesthetic as a "mode of thought," in Rancière, is opposed to the discourses of science and the legalistic and political administration of society.

42. See Slater, "Play of Voices." See also Soares, "Retábulo de Santa Joana Carolina."

43. Another way of looking at the "mystery" structure in "Retábulo," of course, is through the lens of Joana Carolina's miracles. According to Ana Luiza Andrade, "Joana Carolina's transcendent acts are poetically framed by allusions to the signs of the zodiac, since her spiritual life is an active element of a transformative cosmos as she performs down-to-earth miracles to overcome adversity" ("Nine" 206).

44. Regarding the ornamental narrative indicators, Álvaro Manuel Machado has claimed that they suggest "nostalgia for a primordial language" (32).

45. Just as Joana Carolina is never the narrator of the story, she is one of the only characters in "Retábulo" who possesses no symbol indicator. She is, in this way, a deterritorialized signifier: an object of contemplation, reverence, and interpretation whose sense is accumulative and never finalized.

46. While Frizzi's translation is superb, in my view the final sentence of the quote should not include the conjunction "because." The "nobody" narrators speak more from a proliferating,

rhythmical, and descriptive register than one of explanation of cause and function. Consider the nonlinear, constellational structure of the original: "Chapéus na mão, rostos duros, mãos ásperas, roupas de brim, alpercatas de couro, nós, hortelões, ferreiros, marchantes, carpinteiros, intermediários do negócio de gado, seleiros, vendedores de frutas e de pássaros, homens de meio de vida incerto e sem futuro, vamos conduzindo Joana para o cemitério, nós, os ninguéns da cidade, que sempre a ignoravam os outros, gente do dinheiro e do poder" ("Retábulo" 113).

47. "Na parte final, que é a parte do enterro, ela é seguido pelos pobres da cidade, pelos homens do trabalho, pelos artesãos, pelos pequenos negociantes, pelos homens das mãos grossas, e tudo o enterro é construído num ritmo batido, altamente violento. Esta narrativa que parece característica de preocupações estéticas, na realidade, talvez de tudo o que escrevi até aquele momento, é a que tem mais preocupações políticas. *Retábulo de Santa Joana Carolina* é a meu ver política, e altamente violenta, enquanto a maioria das pessoas tende a ver naquele texto uma narrativa quase religiosa, a partir inclusive do título, mas ele é a narrativa de um protesto violento contra o modo de como o pobre é tratado no meu país" (Lins, *Evangelho* 220).

48. "Viveu seus anos com mansidão e justiça, humildade e firmeza, amor e comiseração. Morreu com mínimos bens e reduzidos amigos. Nunca de nunca a rapinagem alheia liberou ambições em seu espírito. Nunca o mal sofrido gerou em sua alma outras maldades" ("Retábulo" 116–17).

49. See Christensen, "Eric Fromm's *Escape from Freedom.*"

50. "Morreu no fim do inverno. Nascerá outra igual na próxima estação? . . . Sob a terra, sob o gesso, sob as lagartixas, sob o mato, perfilam-se *os convivas sem palavras*. Cedros e Carvalhos, Nogueiras e Oliveiras, Jacarandás e Loureiros. Puseram-lhes—*por que inútil generosidade?*—o terno festivo, o mais fino vestido, a melhor gravata, os sapatos mais novos. Reunião estranha: todos de lábios cerrados, mãos cruzadas, cabeças descobertas, todos rígidos, pálpebras descidas e voltadas na mesma direção, como expectantes, todos sozinhos, frente a um grande pórtico através do qual alguém estivesse para vir. Um julgador, um almirante, um harpista, um garçon com bandejas. Trazendo o quê? . . . Tarda o Esperado, e os pedaços desses mudos, desses imóveis convivas sem palavras, vão sendo devorados. Humildemente, em silêncio, Joana Carolina toma seu lugar, as mãos unidas, entre Prados, Pumas e Figueiras, entre Azuçenas, Pereiras e Jacintos, entre Cordeiros, Gamboas e Amarílis, entre Rosas, Leões e Margaridas, entre Junqueiras, Gallos e Verônicas, entre Martas, Hortências, Artemísias, Valerianas, Veigas, Violetas, Cajazeiras, Gamas, Gencianas, entre Bezerras, e Peixes, e Narcisos, entre Salgueiros e Falcões, e Campos, no vestido que era o das tardes de domingo e *penetrada do silêncio com que ficava sozinha*" ("Retábulo" 117, emphasis added).

51. Lins's letter to his French translator regarding the final scene is revealing. Lins writes, "Há, ali, nomes e prenomes brasileiros que são também nomes de animais, de flores, de frutas ou de árvores frutíferas, e também nomes como Veiga (planície cultivada e fértil), como prado, todos ligados a natureza, como o que procuro evocar nessa morte, nesse enterro, os nomes da criaturas que povoam o mundo de Joana Carolina e também o mundo natural. Seria uma pena que isso se perdesse na tradução. Assim, sugiro mais uma vez que faça uma peregrinação através da lista telefônica de Paris. Os nomes que escolher, não terão que corresponder exatamente as que estão no texto. PODEM SER OUTROS, desde que sejam ao mesmo tempo nome de gente e de coisas naturais . . . Gostaria apenas que o número de nomes fosse MAIS O MENOS o mesmo, de modo que a enumeração tivesse qualquer desses momentos finais de sinfonias, quando todos os instrumentos são convocados. . . . Tudo isto concorre para dar, a essa parte final, um tom orquestral, que cessa na palavra Campos, depois do que vem as últimas linhas, que já não falam de multidões, mas do silêncio, da solidão de Joana" (In this passage you will find family names and first names that are also names of animals, flowers, fruits or fruit trees, and also names like Veiga (cultivated and fertile land tract), like prado [meadow], all linked to nature, inasmuch as what I am attempting to evoke in this death, in this burial, [are] the names of creatures that populate the world of Joana Carolina [which] is also the natural world. It would be a shame if this were lost in the translation. Thus, I suggest once more that you take a pilgrimage through the Parisian telephone book. The names that you choose do not have to

correspond exactly to the names in my text. THERE CAN BE OTHERS, provided that, at the same time, they are names of people and of natural things . . . I would just ask that the number of names be MORE OR LESS the same, in such a way that the enumeration should express any one of these final symphonic moments [in the original] when all the instruments are convoked. . . . All of this comes together to give, in the final part, an orchestral tone, which ends in the word Campos, after which come the last lines, that no longer speak of multitudes, but of silence, of the solitude of Joana). Lins, letter to Maryvonne Lapouge, 4 May 1969.

52. See Soares, "Retábulo de Santa Joana Carolina" 174–75.

53. See Rancière, "Aesthetics as Politics." Like Lins's aesthetic of the ornament, art forms for Rancière fundamentally mediate and "suspend" "the ordinary forms of sensory experience," including how one perceives the poor and the voiceless from a position of privilege, typically framed by ideological state apparatuses and hegemonic forms of power (23).

54. In regard to European art forms: "Above all," writes Ana Luiza Andrade, "*Nine, Novena*'s novelty transposes the artistic traditions of the late medieval and baroque periods to Lins's modern style of combining ornament and geometry, which not only coincides with his time/space and political conceptions but is also contemporary with a society of mass culture, insofar as the readership is taken into account in the writing process" ("*Nine*" 205).

55. For a detailed analysis of the relationship of Lins's work to an avant-garde aesthetic and the architecture of Oscar Niemeyer, see Calhman, "Literatura e arquitetura."

56. "One can make the strong case, effectively," writes Lins, "that the [avant-garde] revolution of the Brazilian Modernistas took place at the level of the text and not at that of the book. Not between literature and the public" (*Evangelho* 58). See Adria Frizzi's introduction to *Nine, Novena*. Frizzi recalls that Lins's aesthetic of ornaments was a reaction to the fragmentary character of modern art: "The absence of ornamentation is a symptom of the fractioning of modern man, who has lost touch with the modern universe and is no longer capable of conceiving of the world in a global way" (12).

57. See also Perrone, "Imperative"; and Shellhorse, "Formas."

58. This seems to be a key metaphor in Ana Luiza Andrade's reading of Lins as a formal innovator working with archaic forms, and as an engaged writer with such media as television and the polemical periodical piece. See Andrade, "Reciclando o engenho."

59. For an excellent examination of Lins's voyage, see Nitrini, *Transfigurações* 65–89.

60. The concept of the Latin American "aesthetic voyage" is from Viñas's *De Sarmiento a Cortázar* 184–89. Whereas for Viñas the Latin American *viaje estético* is a problematical trope that underwrites Argentine literary production in the context of *neocolonialismo*, Lins viewed this trip as fundamental to altering his writing style.

61. "Eu diria que a principal experiência desta minha temporada, que me marcou e marcará o resto da minha vida, foi o contato com os vitrais e com a arte românica, a arte medieval em geral. No que se refere aos vitrais, eu tomei uma lição fundamental: pude examinar detidamente a degenerescência dessa arte. Enquanto o vitral se resignava às suas limitações de vitral, ao chumbo e ao vidro colorido, ele esplendia com toda a sua força. Mas aos poucos os vitralistas começaram a achar que aquilo era insuficiente e começaram a pintar o vidro, começaram a levar para a arte do vitral a arte da pintura. A partir daí o vitral degenera. Isto me levou a uma crença da qual estou firmemente convencido: de que as coisas fulguram, vamos dizer, nas suas limitações. As limitações não são necessariamente uma limitação no sentido corrente, mas uma força. Quer dizer que o vitral era forte enquanto estava limitado, e aceitava sua limitação. Além do mais, o vitral, sendo uma arte extremamente sintética, e até rústica, era uma arte altamente expressiva. Levou-me também à convicção de que não é necessário uma literatura na linha proustiana. Engraçado que o Proust aproximava muito a arte dele à das catedrais, porque era uma arte miniatural, muito minuciosa, enquanto que o vitral é uma arte sintética, extremamente direta. Então na minha literatura venho realmente buscando realizar uma obra que seja direta. . . . A outra coisa que nesse meu contato com a arte medieval é o caráter aperspectívico dessa arte. . . . enquanto o Renascimento havia levado a uma visão perspectívica do mundo, naturalmente centrado no olho carnal, humano, a Idade Média levava a uma visão aperspectívica,

devido ao fato exatamente de ser uma época não antropocêntrica mas teocêntrica, de modo que os artistas, como reflexo da visão geral do homem medieval, tendiam a ver as coisas como se eles não estivessem fixados num determinado lugar. Isso levava a uma visão do mundo muito mais rica, não limitava a visão das coisas à condição carnal" (*Evangelho* 212–14).

62. The evolutionary scheme of "procura" (search), "transição" (transition), and "plenitude" (plenitude) refers to Lins's personal statements about the development of his writing style: "*Nove, Novena* inaugura uma fase de maturidade, talvez de plenitude, em minha vida de escritor" (*Nine, Novena* inaugurates a new phase of maturity, perhaps of plenitude, in my life as a writer) (*Evangelho* 141). See also A. Andrade, *Osman Lins*; and Igel, *Osman Lins*.

63. I am alluding to the subaltern "nameless" (*nós, os ninguéns da cidade*) narrators of "Mistério final," who are suggestively designated by the ornamental sign of infinity, ∞ (Lins, "Retábulo" 113). I would like to recall that the subaltern narrators blend at text's close into what is described as a "generous garden" (*pomar generoso*) (116). This "generous garden," an excessive signifier, is a mass burial site and a "garden," like Eden, of proliferating names that inscribes those of the downtrodden and exploited. The "generous garden" constitutes an ambiguous opening up of the subaltern chorus, one that bespeaks of the letters of the alphabet and connotes flora and fauna. Following the overarching "retable" tableau structure that frames the narrative, these names also configure the baroque backdrop of creatures and the poor who encircle and frame, like angels, the apotheosis "panel" scene of Joana Carolina's death. As ornaments, they are inscribed as a grid of polysemic writing *elements* connoting the redemption of the poor and cyclical, cosmic, and, above all, *poetic* rebirth.

6. WRITING SUBALTERN REDEMPTION AND INSURGENCY

1. As has been stressed throughout this book, particularly in chapter 1, where I discuss the formation and consolidation of the Latin American literary regime of representation, the importance of deep cultural contextualization for literary reflection is unquestionable. On this point, Julio Ramos's rejoinder against abstract "poststructuralist" conceptions of the literary remains relevant. See J. Ramos, *Divergent Modernities* 108. But also see Williams, "Hear Say Yes in Piglia," which dismantles nihilist interpretations of deconstruction in the field. On the importance of deep cultural contextualization, see Sara Castro-Klaren's lucid introductory essay to her edited volume, *A Companion to Latin American Literature and Culture*.

2. See Deleuze and Guattari, *Thousand* 268–71; and *What Is?* 163–99.

3. "The Left-Winged Angel of History" is Campos's own translation of the title.

4. For superb analysis of the two English translations of the poem, one by Campos and the other by Bernard McGuirk, see Vieira, "Translating History"; and McGuirk, "Laughin'."

5. The book, *Terra: Struggle of the Landless* (1997), was conceived and designed by Salgado's wife, Léila Wanick Salgado. On points of comparison between Salgado's and Campos's projects, see Maciel, "Utopian Remains."

6. Alongside his brother, Augusto, Haroldo de Campos translated Mayakovsky's work in 1961; with the assistance of Boris Schnaiderman, the poets published a collected volume of Mayakovsky's poems, entitled *Poemas*, and an anthology of Russian poetry in 1967. Indeed, in the 1961 appended postscript to the "Plano-piloto para poesia concreta" (1958) the concrete poets included Mayakovsky's slogan: "sem forma revolucionária não há arte revolucionária" (without revolutionary form there is no revolutionary art) (Campos, Pignatari, and Campos, *Teoria* 218).

7. For detailed elaboration of the MST's history and its modes of resistance, see Wright and Wolford, *To Inherit the Earth*, and Fernandes's online article. See also Vieira's impressive multimedia database, *The Landless Voices Web Archive*, which is housed at the University of Nottingham and widely available on the Internet. On the music, art, and poetry of the MST, see E. Vieira and McGuirk, *Landless*.

8. De Campos's "O anjo esquerdo da história" is multimedial on several fronts: (1) there is a CD recording of the poem in *Crisantempo: No espaço nasce uma curva* (1998); (2) the poem

literally begins with a photograph of the MST march; and (3) the original publication of the poem in *PT Notícias* (1996) includes a visual representation of a tree surrounded by angels in flight. For an interpretation of that image, see E. Vieira, "Weaving."

9. As "the site of competing cultural stories," of course, the ruin is a problem that has plagued the study of Latin America for decades (Unruh and Lazzara 4). See Vicky Unruh and Michael J. Lazzara's edited volume dedicated to the topic, *Telling Ruins in Latin America*, as well as the editors' introductory essay.

CONCLUSION

1. Gonzalo Aguilar suggestively observes that Campos's conception of political poetry turns not on ideology but on the poet's investigation of the "links between language and community" such that "lo central es darle forma al lenguaje de la comunidad" ("Haroldo" 9).

2. Regarding the impact of Beverley's questions for a future of Latin American studies, Alberto Moreiras writes, "I consider John Beverley's *Against Literature*, in all the richness of its self-conscious ambiguity, the inaugural text preparing and announcing the possibility for a new paradigm for Latin Americanist reflection in the humanities" (*Exhaustion* 310).

WORKS CITED

Acosta, Abraham. *Thresholds of Illiteracy: Theory, Latin America, and the Crisis of Resistance.* New York: Fordham UP, 2014.

Adorno, Theodor W. *Aesthetic Theory.* Trans. Robert Hullot-Kentor. Minneapolis: U of Minnesota P, 1997.

Adorno, Theodor W., and Max Horkheimer. *Dialectic of Enlightenment.* Trans. John Cumming. 1944. New York: Continuum, 1998.

Agamben, Giorgio. *The Time That Remains: A Commentary on the Letter to the Romans.* Trans. Patricia Dailey. Stanford: Stanford UP, 2005.

Aguilar, Gonzalo. "Formas de las vanguardias." *Poesía concreta brasileña: Las vanguardias en la encrucijada modernista.* Rosario: Beatriz Viterbo, 2003. 27–47.

Aguilar, Gonzalo. "Haroldo de Campos: La poesía como sabiduría." *El ángel izquierdo de la poesía: Poética y política antología.* Ed. Gonzalo Aguilar. Buenos Aires: Eloisa Cartonera, 2003. 5–13.

Aguilar, Gonzalo. *Poesía concreta brasileña: Las vanguardias en la encrucijada modernista.* Rosario: Beatriz Viterbo, 2003.

Aguilar, Gonzalo. "Some Propositions for Reflection on the Relation between Poetry and Politics." *Poesia concreta: O projeto verbovocovisual.* Ed. João Banderia and Leonora de Barros. São Paulo: Artemeios, 2008. 175–92.

Aimaretti, María, Lorena Bordigoni, and Javier Campo. "La Escuela Documental de Santa Fe: Um cuiempiés que camina." *Una historia del cine político y social en Argentina: Formas, estilos y registros (1896–1969).* Buenos Aires: Nueva Librería, 2009. 359–94.

Alonso, Carlos. *The Spanish American Regional Novel: Modernity and Autochthony.* Cambridge: Cambridge UP, 1990.

Althusser, Louis. "The 'Piccolo Teatro': Bertolazzi and Brecht; Notes on a Materialist Theater." *For Marx.* Trans. Ben Brewster. London: Verso, 2005. 130–51.

Altieri, Charles. *The Particulars of Rapture: An Aesthetics of the Affects.* Ithaca: Cornell UP, 2003.

Amaral, Suzana, dir. *A hora da estrela.* Photography and camera, Edgar Moura. 1985. New York: Kino on Video, 2005.

Amaral, Tarsila do, illus. "História do Brasil." O. de Andrade, *Pau Brasil* 23.

Amaral, Tarsila do, illus. "Pau Brasil." O. de Andrade, *Pau Brasil* n. pag.

Andrade, Ana Luiza. "Nine, Novena's Novelty." *Review of Contemporary Fiction* 15.3 (Fall 1995): 198–203.

Andrade, Ana Luiza. *Osman Lins: Crítica e criação.* Editora Hucitec: São Paulo, 1987.

Andrade, Ana Luiza. "Reciclando o engenho: Osman Lins e as constelações de um gesto épico." *Osman Lins: O sopro na argila.* Ed. Hugo Almeida. São Paulo: Nankin Editorial, 2004. 69–111.

Andrade, Mário de. *Obra imatura.* 1925. São Paulo: Livraria Martins Editora, 1980.

Andrade, Mário de. "O movimento modernista." *Aspectos da literatura brasileira.* São Paulo: Livraria Martins, 1978. 231–55.

Andrade, Mário de. "Prefácio interessantíssimo." *Paulicéa desvairada.* São Paulo: Casa Mayença, 1922. 7–39.

Andrade, Oswald de. "A crise da filosofia messiânica." *A utopia antropofágica*. São Paulo: Secretaria de Estado da Cultura de São Paulo / Editora Globo, 1990. 138–215.

Andrade, Oswald de. *A utopia antropofágica*. São Paulo: Globo, 2011.

Andrade, Oswald de. "crônica." *Primeiro caderno do aluno da poesia Oswald de Andrade*. São Paulo: Editora Globo, 2008. 70.

Andrade, Oswald de. "Diario confessional (fragmentos—1948/1949)." *Invenção: Revista de Arte de Vanguarda*, no. 4 (1964): 49–51.

Andrade, Oswald de. *Estética e política: Obras completas de Oswald de Andrade*. São Paulo: Globo, 1992.

Andrade, Oswald de. "Hip! Hip! Hoover!" *Poesias reunidas: Oswald de Andrade*. Ed. Haroldo de Campos. São Paulo: Círculo do Livro, 1976. 198–99.

Andrade, Oswald de. "Manifesto antropófago." O. de Andrade, *A utopia antropofágica* 67–74.

Andrade, Oswald de. "Manifesto da Poesia Pau-Brasil." O. de Andrade, *A utopia antropofágica* 59–66.

Andrade, Oswald de. *Os dentes do dragão*. São Paulo: Editora Globo, 2009.

Andrade, Oswald de. *Pau Brasil*. Paris: Sans Pareil, 1925.

Andujar, Claudia. *Clarice Lispector*. 1961. In *Clarice, uma biografia*. By Benjamin Moser. São Paulo: Cosac Naify, 2009.

Apollinaire, Guillaume. "Devant l'idéogramme d'Apollinaire." *Le Guetteur mélancolique: Poèmes inédits*. Paris: Gallimard, 1952. 142–44.

Arlt, Roberto. *El juguete rabioso*. Ed. Rita Gnutzmann. 5th ed. Madrid: Ediciones Cátedra, 2001.

Armstrong, Piers. "The Brazilian Novel." *The Latin American Novel*. Ed. Efraín Kristal. Cambridge: Cambridge UP, 2005. 105–24.

Avelar, Idelber. "Modernization and Mourning in the Spanish American Boom." *The Untimely Present: Postdictatorial Latin American Fiction and the Task of Mourning*. Durham: Duke UP, 1999. 22–38.

Badiou, Alain. "Avant-Gardes." *The Century*. Trans. Alberto Toscano. Cambridge: Polity Press, 2007. 131–47.

Badiou, Alain. *Second Manifesto for Philosophy*. Trans. Louise Burchill. Cambridge: Polity Press, 2011.

Bandeira, João. "Words in Space-Poetry at the National Exhibition of Concrete Art." *Concreta '56: A raíz da forma*. Ed. Lorenzo Mammì, João Bandeira, and André Stolarski. São Paulo: Museu de Arte Moderna de São Paulo, 2006. 120–89.

Bandeira, João, and Leonora de Barros. "Introdução." *Poesia concreta: O projeto verbivocovisual*. São Paulo: Artemeios, 2008. 9–68.

Bandeira, Manuel. *Apresentação da poesia brasileira*. 3rd ed. Rio de Janeiro: Livraria Editora, 1957.

Barbosa, Frederico. "Concretismo: São Paulo na literatura." *A poesia de Frederico Barbosa*. 9 October 2016. <https://fredericobarbosa.wordpress.com/tag/poesia-concreta/>

Barbosa, María José Somerlate. *Clarice Lispector: Des/fiando as teias da paixão*. Porto Alegre: EDIPCRS, 2001.

Barthes, Roland. *S/Z*. Trans. Richard Miller. New York: Hill and Wang, 1974.

Beasley-Murray, Jon. *Posthegemony: Political Theory and Latin America*. Minneapolis: U of Minnesota P, 2010.

Beasley-Murray, Jon. *Posthegemony: Something always escapes!* 28 August 2016. <https://posthegemony.wordpress.com/>

Benjamin, Walter. "Theses on the Philosophy of History." *Illuminations: Essays and Reflections*. Ed. Hannah Arendt. Trans. Harry Zohn. New York: Schocken Books, 1998. 253–64.

Bernini, Emilio. "Viñas y el cine." *Revista No Retornable* (November 2010). 15 July 2014. <http://www.no-retornable.com.ar/v7/popcorn/bernini.html>

Bessa, Antonio Sergio. "Introduction." *Novas: Selected Writings*. Evanston: Northwestern UP, 2007. xiii–xxxv.

Bessa, Antonio Sergio. Introduction to "circuladô de fulô." By Haroldo de Campos. *Ubuweb Ethnopoetics: Poems.* 4 March 2016. <http://www.ubu.com/ethno/poems/decampos_galaxias.html>

Bessa, Antonio Sergio. "Ruptura de estilo em *Galáxias* de Haroldo de Campos." Trans. Renato Rezende. *Transluminura* 1 (2014): 12–29.

Beverley, John. *Against Literature.* Minneapolis: U of Minnesota P, 1993.

Beverley, John. "Baroque Historicism, Then and Now." *Revista de Estudios Hispánicos: La Constitución del Barroco Hispánico; Problemas y Acercamientos* 33.1 (Fall 2008): 65–75.

Beverley, John. *Latinamericanism after 9/11.* Durham: Duke UP, 2011.

Beverley, John. "On the Spanish Literary Baroque." *Against Literature.* Minneapolis: U of Minnesota P, 1993. 47–65.

Beverley, John. *Subalternity and Representation: Arguments in Cultural Theory.* Durham: Duke UP, 1999.

Beverley, John. *Testimonio: On the Politics of Truth.* Minneapolis: U of Minnesota P, 2004.

Beverley, John. "Writing in Reverse: On the Project of the Latin American Subaltern Studies Group." *The Latin American Cultural Studies Reader.* Ed. Ana del Sarto, Alicia Ríos, and Abigail Trigo. Durham: Duke UP, 2004. 623–41.

Birri, Fernando. "Cinema and Underdevelopment." Trans. Malcolm Coad. *New Latin American Cinema.* Ed. Michael T. Martin. Vol. 1. Detroit: Wayne State UP, 1997. 86–94.

Birri, Fernando. "For a Nationalist, Realist, Critical and Popular Cinema." Trans. Michael Chanan. *New Latin American Cinema.* Ed. Michael T. Martin. Vol. 1. Detroit: Wayne State UP, 1997. 95–98.

Birri, Fernando. *La Escuela Documental de Santa Fe.* Rosario: Prohistoria Ediciones / Instituto Superior de Cine y Artes Audiovisuales de Santa Fe, 2008.

Birri, Fernando. "Los cinco manifiestos." *Fernando Birri—El alquimista poético político: Por un nuevo nuevo nuevo cine latinoamericano 1956–1991.* Madrid: Filmoteca Española/ Ediciones Cátedra, 1996. 15–35.

Birri, Fernando. "Manifiesto de Santa Fe." *La Escuela Documental de Santa Fe.* Santa Fe: Editorial Documentos del Instituto de Cinematografía de la Universidad del Litoral, 1964. 12–13.

Birri, Fernando. "Tire dié." 11 December 2014. <http://comunicacionymedios.files.wordpress.com/2007/09/birri-pionero-y-peregrino.pdf>

Birri, Fernando. "Tire dié (1956–1960)." *Soñar con los ojos abiertos: Las treinta lecciones de Stanford.* Buenos Aires: Aguilar, Altea, Taurus, Alfaguara, 2007. 17–36.

Boaventura, Maria Eugênia. *A vanguarda antropofágica.* São Paulo: Editora Ática, 1985.

Bocchino, Adriana A. "Empecinada lucidez: David Viñas en blanco y negro." *CELEHIS-Revista del Centro de Letras Hispanoamericanas* 23 (2012): 289–306.

Boone, Elizabeth Hill. "Introduction: Writing and Recording Knowledge." *Writing without Words: Alternative Literacies in Mesoamerica and the Andes.* Ed. Elizabeth Hill Boone and Walter D. Mignolo. Durham: Duke UP, 1994. 3–26.

Borelli, Olga. *Clarice Lispector: Esboço para um retrato possível.* Rio de Janeiro: Nova Fronteira, 1981.

Borges, Jorge Luis. "The Argentine Writer and the Tradition." *Labyrinths: Selected Stories & Other Writings.* Trans. James E. Irby. Ed. Donald A. Yates and James E. Irby. New York: New Directions, 1964. 177–85.

Bosteels, Bruno. "Theses on Antagonism, Hybridity, and the Subaltern in Latin America." *Dispositio* 52.25 (2005): 147–58.

Bourdieu, Pierre. "Field of Power, Literary Field and Habitus." *The Field of Cultural Production: Essays on Art and Literature.* Ed. Randal Johnson. New York: Columbia UP, 1993.

Calhman, Adelaide. "Literatura e arquitetura: 'O Retábulo de Santa Joana Carolina' e a Catedral de Brasília." *Osman Lins: O sopro na argila.* Ed. Hugo Almeida. São Paulo: Nankin Editorial, 2004. 201–23.

Camara, Rogério. *Grafo-sintaxe concreta: O projeto Noigandres*. Rio de Janeiro: Rios Ambiciosos, 2000.

Caminha, Pêro Vaz de. "Carta do achamento do Brasil, de Pêro Vaz de Caminha, dirigida a D. Manuel (Porto Seguro, da Ilha de Vera Cruz, 1 de Maio de 1500)." *Os sete únicos documentos de 1500 conservados em Lisboa referentes à viagem de Pedro Alvares Cabral*. Ed. Abel Fontoura da Costa and Antônio Baião. Lisbon: Agência-Geral Do Ultramar, 1968. n. pag.

Campos, Augusto de. *À margem da margem*. São Paulo: Companhia das Letras, 1989.

Campos, Augusto de. "América Latina: Contra-boom da poesia." *O anticrítico*. São Paulo: Companhia das Letras, 1986. 159–63.

Campos, Augusto de. "Augusto de Campos: Brazil/Brasil." *Concrete Poetry: A World View*. Ed. Mary Ellen Solt. Bloomington: Indiana UP, 1967. 254–57.

Campos, Augusto de. "cidade." *Invenção: Revista de Arte de Vanguarda*, no. 4 (1964): 103.

Campos, Augusto de. "cubagramma." *Invenção: Revista de Arte de Vanguarda*, no. 2 (1962): 9.

Campos, Augusto de. "Da Antiode à Antilira." *Poesia antipoesia antropofagia & cia*. São Paulo: Companhia das Letras, 2015. 62–69.

Campos, Augusto de. "Do Concreto ao Digital." *Poesia antipoesia antropofagia & cia*. São Paulo: Companhia das Letras, 2015. 313–22.

Campos, Augusto de. Letter to João Cabral de Melo Neto, 24 October 1957. Acervo de João Cabral de Melo Neto. Fundação Casa de Rui Barbosa, Rio de Janeiro.

Campos, Augusto de. *Linguaviagem*. São Paulo: Companhia das Letras, 1987.

Campos, Augusto de. "mercado." 2002. *Não: Poemas*. São Paulo: Perspectiva, 2008. 116–17.

Campos, Augusto de. *O anticrítico*. São Paulo: Companhia das Letras, 1986.

Campos, Augusto de. "OLHO POR OLHO." *Invenção: Revista de Arte de Vanguarda*, no. 4 (1964): 103.

Campos, Augusto de. "Oswald, Livro Livre." *Poesia antipoesia antropofagia & cia*. São Paulo: Companhia das Letras, 2015. 193–204.

Campos, Augusto de. *Poesia, antipoesia, antropofagia*. São Paulo: Cortez e Morães, 1978.

Campos, Augusto de. *Poesia antipoesia antropofagia & cia*. São Paulo: Companhia das Letras, 2015.

Campos, Augusto de. "poesia concreta (manifesto)." Campos, Pignatari, and Campos 71–72.

Campos, Augusto de. "pontos-peiferia-poesia concreta." *Teoria da poesia concreta: Textos críticos e manifestos 1950–1960*. Cotia: Ateliê Editorial, 2006.

Campos, Augusto de. "Pós-Walds." *O Estadão de São Paulo* (2 July 2011). 28 May 2014. <http://www.estadao.com.br/noticias/impresso,pos-walds,739633,0.htm>

Campos, Augusto de. "Revistas re-vistas: Os antropófagos." Edição fac-similar. São Paulo: AbrilCultural/Metal, 1975. 1–13.

Campos, Augusto de. "sem um numero." *Antologia Noigandres do verso à poesia concreta*. São Paulo: Massao Ohno Editora, 1962. 113.

Campos, Augusto de. "TUDO ESTÁ DITO." *Viva vaia: Poesia 1949–1979*. Cotia: Ateliê Editorial, 2001. 248–49.

Campos, Augusto de, and Cid Campos. *Poesia é risco*. Phillips, 1995. CD.

Campos, Augusto de, and Haroldo de Campos. "Poesia concreta." *Diário Popular*, 22 December 1956. n. pag.

Campos, Augusto de, Haroldo de Campos, and Boris Schnaiderman. *Maiakóvski: Poemas*. São Paulo: Perspectiva, 2011.

Campos, Augusto de, Décio Pignatari, and Haroldo de Campos. *Teoria da poesia concreta: Textos críticos e manifestos 1950–1960*. São Paulo: Ateliê Editorial, 2006.

Campos, Augusto de, Décio Pignatari, and Haroldo de Campos. "Plano-piloto para poesia concreta." 1958. *Teoria da poesia concreta: Textos críticos e manifestos 1950–1960*. São Paulo: Ateliê Editorial, 2006. 215–18.

Campos, Haroldo de. *A educação dos cinco sentidos*. São Paulo: Brasiliense, 1985.

Campos, Haroldo de. "a obra de arte moderna." *Teoria da poesia concreta: Textos críticos e manifestos 1950–1960*. Cotia: Ateliê Editorial, 2006. 49–53.

Campos, Haroldo de. "Arte pobre, tempo de pobreza, poesia menos." *Metalinguagem e outras metas*. São Paulo: Editora Perspectiva 34, 1992. 221–30.

Campos, Haroldo de. "The Brazilian Jaguar." *boundary 2* 26.1 (1999): 83–85.

Campos, Haroldo de. "contexto de uma vanguarda." Campos, Pignatari, and Campos 209–14.

Campos, Haroldo de. "Da poesia concreta à *Galáxias* e *Finismundo*." *Depoimentos de oficina*. São Paulo: Unimarco Editora, 2002. 15–58.

Campos, Haroldo de. "Da razão antropofágica: Diálogo e diferença na cultura brasileira." *Metalinguagem e outras metas*. São Paulo: Editora Perspectiva 34, 1992. 231–55.

Campos, Haroldo de. "Do epos ao epifânico (gênese e elaboração das *Galáxias*)." *Metalinguagem e outras metas*. São Paulo: Editora Perspectiva 34, 1992. 269–88.

Campos, Haroldo de. "Dois dedos de prosa sobre uma nova prosa." *Invenção: Revista de Arte de Vanguarda*, no. 4 (1964): 112.

Campos, Haroldo de. "Entrevista: Haroldo de Campos." With Armando Sergio Prazeres et al. *galáxia* 1.1 (2001): 29–47.

Campos, Haroldo de. "The Ex-Centric's Viewpoint: Tradition, Transcreation, Transculturation." *Haroldo de Campos: A Dialogue with the Brazilian Concrete Poet*. Ed. K. David Jackson. Oxford: Centre for Brazilian Studies, 2005. 3–13.

Campos, Haroldo de. *Galáxias*. 2nd ed. Ed. Trajano Vieira. São Paulo: Editora 34, 2004.

Campos, Haroldo de. "Haroldo de Campos." *Textura* 3 (May 1974): 10–17.

Campos, Haroldo de. "Haroldo de Campos in Conference with Nicholas Zurbrugg, et al." McGuirk and Vieira 254–63.

Campos, Haroldo de. "Haroldo de Campos in Conversation with Jacques Donguy." McGuirk and Vieira. 264–81.

Campos, Haroldo de. "The Left-Winged Angel of History." Trans. Haroldo de Campos. *Interventions* 2.3 (2000): 328–29.

Campos, Haroldo de. "Lirismo e participação." Foreword. *O santeiro do mangue e outros poemas*. By Oswald de Andrade. São Paulo: Editora Globo, 1991. 47–53.

Campos, Haroldo de. "Miramar na mira." Foreword. *Memórias sentimentais de João Miramar*. By Oswald de Andrade. São Paulo: Editora Globo, 1990. 5–33.

Campos, Haroldo de. "nascemorre." *Concrete Poetry: A Worldview*. Ed. Mary Ellen Solt. Bloomington: Indiana UP, 1971. 103.

Campos, Haroldo de. *Novas: Selected Writings*. Ed. Antônio Sérgio Bessa and Odile Cisneros. Evanston: Northwestern UP, 2007.

Campos, Haroldo de. "O anjo esquerdo da história." *Crisantempo: No espaço nasce uma curva*. São Paulo: Perspectiva, 1998. 68–72.

Campos, Haroldo de. "olho por olho à olho nu." Campos, Pignatari, and Campos 73–76.

Campos, Haroldo de. *O sequestro do barroco na formação da literatura*. São Paulo: Iluminuras, 2011.

Campos, Haroldo de. "Poesia e música." *Metalinguagem e outras metas*. São Paulo: Editora Perspectiva 34, 1992. 279–88.

Campos, Haroldo de. "Poesia e modernidade. Da morte da arte à constelação. O poema pos-utópico." *O arco-iris branco: Ensaios de literatura e cultura*. Rio de Janeiro: Imago, 1997. 243–69.

Campos, Haroldo de. "Poesia y modernidad: De la muerte del arte a la constelación. El poema postutópico." *De la razón antropofágica y otros ensayos*. Trans. Rodolfo Mata. Mexico City: Siglo Veinituno Editores, 2000. 24–47.

Campos, Haroldo de. "Prefácio." *A escritura de Clarice Lispector*. By Olga da Sá. Petrópolis: Editora Vozes, 1979. 11–15.

Campos, Haroldo de. "Serafim: Um grande não-livro." Foreword. *Serafim Ponte Grande*. By Oswald de Andrade. São Paulo: Globo, 1990. 5–28.

Campos, Haroldo de. "Servidão de passagem 4 fragmentos." *Invenção: Revista de Arte de Vanguarda*, no. 2 (1962): 4–7.

Campos, Haroldo de. "Uma poética de radicalidade." Foreword. *Poesias reunidas: Oswald de Andrade*. By Oswald de Andrade. São Paulo: Círculo do Livro, 1976. 7–72.

Campos, Haroldo de. "Uma segunda abolição." Vieira and McGuirk 190–91.

Campos, Haroldo de. "A Word in Response to the Debate on Cultural Dependency in Brazil." McGuirk and Vieira 293–96.

Candido, Antonio. "Digressão sentimental sobre Oswald de Andrade." *Vários escritos*. São Paulo: Duas Cidades, 1970. 57–87.

Candido, Antonio. *Formação da literatura brasileira (Momentos decisivos)*. Vol. 1. Belo Horizonte: Editora Itatiaia, 1993.

Candido, Antonio. "Literatura e subdesenvolvimento." *Argumento* 1.1 (1973): 7–24.

Candido, Antonio. *Vários escritos*. São Paulo: Duas Cidades, 1970.

Cariello, Graciela. *Jorge Luis Borges y Osman Lins: Poética de la lectura*. Rosario: Laborde Libros Editor, 2007.

Carrera, Elena. "The Reception of Clarice Lispector via Hélène Cixous: Reading from the Whale's Belly." *Brazilian Feminisms*. Ed. Solange Ribeiro de Oliveira and Judith Still. Nottingham: University of Nottingham, 1999. 85–100.

Castagna, Gustavo J. "La generación del 60: Paradojas de un mito." *Cine argentino: La otra historia*. Ed. Sergio Wolf. Buenos Aires: Ediciones Buena Letra, 1992. 243–63.

Castro-Klarén, Sara. "Introduction." *A Companion to Latin American Literature and Culture*. Ed. Sara Castro-Klaren. West Sussex: Wiley-Blackwell, 2008. 1–11.

Castro-Klarén, Sara. "'Writing with his thumb in the air': Coloniality, Past and Present." *The Narrow Pass of Our Nerves: Writing, Coloniality and Postcolonial Theory*. Madrid: Iberoamericana, 2011. 363–89.

Castro Rocha, João Cezar de. "Oswald em cena: O Pau-Brasil, o Brasileiro e o Antropófago." Rufinelli and Castro Rocha 11–18.

Castro Rocha, João Cezar de. "Uma teoria de exportação? Ou: 'Antropofagia como Visão do Mundo.'" Rufinelli and Castro Rocha 647–48.

Centro de Documentación e Investigación de la Cultura de Izquierdas en la Argentina. "Flyer for *Contorno*, Number 2 dedicated to Roberto Arlt (May 1954)." Buenos Aires: CeDInCI, 2001.

Cerdá, Marcelo. "Los directores de la Generación del 60 y las relaciones permeables frente al contexto político y social." *Una historia del cine político y social en Argentina: Formas, estilos y registros (1896–1969)*. Buenos Aires: Nueva Librería, 2009. 311–46.

Cheah, Pheng. "Nondialectical Materialism." *Diacritics* 38.1–2 (Spring–Summer 2008): 143–57.

Cheah, Pheng. "Obscure Gifts: On Jacques Derrida." *Differences: A Journal of Feminist Cultural Studies* 16.3 (2005): 41–51.

Christensen, Peter G. "Eric Fromm's *Escape from Freedom*: A Reference Point for Osman Lins' *Nove, novena*." *Chasqui: Revista de Literatura Latinoamericana* 23.2 (November 1994): 30–38.

Cixous, Hélène. *Reading with Clarice Lispector*. Trans. Verena Andermatt Conley. Minneapolis: U of Minnesota P, 1990.

Clüver, Claus. "The Noigandres Poets and Concrete Art." *Ciberletras 17* (July 2007). 11 March 2016. <http://www.lehman.cuny.edu/ciberletras/v17/cluver.htm>

Clüver, Claus. "The 'Ruptura' Proclaimed by Brazil's Self-Styled 'Vanguardas' of the Fifties." *Neo-Avant-Garde*. Ed. David Hopkins. Amsterdam: Rodopi, 2006. 161–96.

Contorno Editorial Board. "Análisis del frondizismo." *Contorno* 9–10 (April 1959): 1.

Copetes Filmoteca. "Filmoteca, temas de cine—Copete 'Dar la cara.'" Per. José Martínez Suárez and Fernando Martín Peña. Online video clip. Youtube (18 August 2015). 17 March 2016. <https://www.youtube.com/watch?v=cHN2bBroXtc>

Couselo, Jorge Miguel. "Literatura y cine argentino." *Gaceta Literaria* 20.1 (1960): 32.

Crespi, Maximiliano. *El revés de la trama*. Bahía Blanca: 17grises editora, 2009.

Croce, Marcela. *Contorno: Izquierda y proyecto cultural*. Buenos Aires: Ediciones Colihue, 1996.

Croce, Marcela. *David Viñas crítica de la razón polémica: Un intelectual argentino heterodoxo entre "Contorno" y Dios*. Buenos Aires: Suricata, 2005.

Czajka, Rodrigo. "A *Revista Civilização Brasileira*: Projeto editorial e resistência cultural 1965–1968." *Revista de Sociologia e Política* V 18.35 (February 2010): 95–118.

Dar la cara. Dir. José A. Martínez Suárez. Prod. Ernesto Kehoe Wilson, Saulo Benavente, David Swilich and Fernando Birri, 1962. Screenplay by David Viñas and José A. Martínez Suárez. Mus. Leandro "Gato" Barbieri. Perf. Leonardo Favio, Raúl Parini, Luis Medina Castro, Pablo Moret, Nuria Torray, Ubadlo Martínez, Daniel de Alvarado, Lautaro Murúa, Guillermo Bredeston, Susana Mayo, Mariela Reyes, Dora Baret, Walter Santa Ana, José María Fra, Corrado Corradi, Héctor Pellegrini, Manuel Rosón, Nelly Tesolín, Alberto Gorzio, Augusto Fernandes, Cacho Espíndola, Eduardo Vener, António Pérez Tersol, Orlando Marconi, Mario Benigno, María Vener, Claude Vernet, Rosángela Balbo, Fernando Solanas, Adolfo Aristarain, Fernando Birri, Adelqui Camuso. Instituto Nacional de Cine y Artes Audiovisuales/Director's Copy, 2016. DVD.

Debord, Guy. *The Society of the Spectacle*. Trans. Donald Nicholson-Smith. New York: Zone Books, 1995.

De la Campa, Román. *Latin Americanism*. Minneapolis: U of Minnesota P, 1999.

Deleuze, Gilles. *Difference and Repetition*. Trans. Paul Patton. New York: Columbia UP, 1994.

Deleuze, Gilles. *Essays Critical and Clinical*. Trans. Daniel W. Smith and Michael A. Greco. Minneapolis: U of Minnesota P, 1997.

Deleuze, Gilles. *The Fold: Leibniz and the Baroque*. 7th ed. Trans. Tom Conley. Minneapolis: U of Minnesota P, 2007.

Deleuze, Gilles. *Gilles Deleuze from A to Z with Claire Parnet*. Dir. Pierre-André Boutang. Trans. Charles Stivale. Cambridge: MIT P, 2012. DVD.

Deleuze, Gilles. *Proust and Signs*. Trans. Richard Howard. Minneapolis: U of Minnesota P, 2000.

Deleuze, Gilles. *Spinoza: Practical Philosophy*. Trans. Robert Hurley. San Francisco: City Lights Books, 1988.

Deleuze, Gilles, and Félix Guattari. *Anti-Oedipus: Capitalism and Schizophrenia*. 1972. Trans. Robert Hurley, Mark Seem, and Helen R. Lane. Minneapolis: U of Minnesota P, 2005.

Deleuze, Gilles, and Félix Guattari. *Kafka: Toward a Minor Literature*. Trans. Dana Polan. Minneapolis: U of Minnesota P, 1986.

Deleuze, Gilles, and Félix Guattari. *A Thousand Plateaus: Capitalism and Schizophrenia*. 8th ed. Trans. Brian Massumi. Minneapolis: U of Minnesota P, 2000.

Deleuze, Gilles, and Félix Guattari. *What Is Philosophy?* Trans. Hugh Tomlinson and Graham Burchell. New York: Columbia UP, 1994.

Deleuze, Gilles, and Claire Parnet. *Dialogues II*. Trans. Hugh Tomlinson and Barbara Habberjam. New York: Continuum, 2006.

Derrida, Jacques. *Given Time: I. Counterfeit Money*. Trans. Peggy Kamuf. Chicago: U of Chicago P, 1992.

Derrida, Jacques. *Positions*. Trans. Alan Bass. Chicago: U of Chicago P, 1981.

Derrida, Jacques. *Rogues: Two Essays on Reason*. Trans. Pascale-Anne Brault and Michael Naas. Stanford: Stanford UP, 2005.

Derrida, Jacques. *Specters of Marx: The State of the Debt, the Work of Mourning, and the New International*. Trans. Peggy Kamuf. New York: Routledge, 1994.

Derrida, Jacques. "'This Strange Institution Called Literature': An Interview with Jacques Derrida." Trans. Geoffrey Bennington and Rachel Bowlby. *Acts of Literature*. Ed. Derek Attridge. London: Routledge, 1992. 33–75.

Desaloms, Daniel. *Vidas de película: La generación del 60*. Buenos Aires: La Crujía/DAC Editorial, 2013.

Díaz, Pablo. *David Viñas: Un intelectual irreverente.* Per. David Viñas, Beatriz Sarlo, Susana Santos, Léon Rozitchner, et al. Prod. Luis I. Marsiletti and Pablo Díaz. 2008. Online video clip. Youtube (June 2, 2014). 21 March 2016.

Dove, Patrick. *The Catastrophe of Modernity: Tragedy and the Nation in Latin American Literature.* Lewisburg: Bucknell UP, 2004.

Dove, Patrick. *Literature and "Interregnum": Globalization, War, and the Crisis of Sovereignty in Latin America.* Albany: State U New York P, 2016.

Dunn, Christopher. *Contracultura: Alternative Arts and Social Transformation in Authoritarian Brazil.* Chapel Hill: U of North Carolina P, 2016.

Dunn, Christopher. "Desbunde and Its Discontents: Counterculture and Authoritarian Modernization in Brazil, 1968–1974." *The Americas* 70.3 (January 2014): 429–58.

Dunn, Christopher. "Experimentar o Experimental": Avant-Garde, Cultura Marginal, and Counterculture in Brazil, 1968–72." *Luso-Brazilian Review* 50.1 (2013): 229–52.

Dunn, Christopher. "Tropicália, Counterculture, and the Diasporic Imagination in Brazil." *Brazilian Popular Music and Globalization.* Ed. Charles Perrone and Christopher Dunn. New York: Routledge, 2001. 72–95.

Eichelbaum, Edmundo. "Primer festival de cine argentino." *Gaceta Literaria* 15.3 (1958): 18–19.

El candidato. Dir. Fernando Ayala. Prod. Héctor Olivera, 1959. Perf. Alfredo Alcon, Olga Zubarry, Duilio Marzio, Alberto Candeau, Iris Marga, Guillermo Battaglia, Héctor Calcaño. Screenplay by David Viñas and Fernando Ayala. Emerald Video/Aries Cinematográfica Argentina, 2008[?]. DVD.

El jefe. Dir. Fernando Ayala. Prod. Héctor Olivera and Fernando Ayala. 1958. Perf. Alberto de Mendoza, Duilio Marzio, Orestes Caviglia, Leonardo Favio, Luis Tasca, Graciela Borges, Ignacio Quirós, Ana Casares, Violeta Antier, Pablo Moret, Emilio Alfaro. Screenplay by David Viñas and Fernando Ayala. Emerald Video/Aries Cinematográfica Argentina, 2010. DVD.

Eloy Martínez, Tomás. *La obra de Ayala y Torre Nilsson en las estructuras del cine argentino.* Buenos Aires: Ediciones Culturales Argentinas, Ministerio de Educación y Justica, Dirección General de Cultura, 1961.

El Sabio, Alfonso X. "Alfonso the Learned Reading His Canticles." *Spanish Illumination.* Ed. Jesús Domínguez Bordona. Vol. 1. New York: Hacker Art Books, 1969. n. page.

El Sabio, Alfonso X. "Praises of the Virgin and of the Archangel Gabriel." *Spanish Illumination.* Ed. Jesús Domínguez Bordona. Vol. 1. New York: Hacker Art Books, 1969. n. page.

Erber, Pedro. *Breaching the Frame: The Rise of Contemporary Art in Brazil and Japan.* Berkeley: U of California P, 2015.

Erber, Pedro. "The Word as Object: Concrete Poetry, Ideogram, and the Materialization of Language." *Luso-Brazilian Review* 49.2 (2012): 72–101.

Eseverri, Máximo. Email to author, 14 March 2016.

Feldman, Simón. *La generación del 60.* Buenos Aires: Instituto Nacional de Cinematografía, 1990.

Félix, Moacyr. "Nota Introdutória." *Violão da Rua (II).* Ed. Álvaro Vieira Pinto and Ênio Silveira. Rio de Janeiro: Editora Civilização Brasileira, 1962. 9–11.

Feracho, Lesley. "Authorial Intervention in *A hora da estrela*: Metatextual and Structural Multiplicity." *Linking the Americas: Race, Hybrid Discourses, and the Reformulation of Feminine Identity.* Albany: State U of New York P, 2005. 67–84.

Feracho, Lesley. "Textual Cross-Gendering of the Self and the Other in Lispector's A hora da estrela." *Linking the Americas: Race, Hybrid Discourses, and the Reformulation of Feminine Identity.* Albany: State U of New York P, 2005. 85–108.

Fernandes, Bernardo Mançano. "The MST, Its Genealogy and the Struggle for Agrarian Reform in Brazil." *The Landless Voices Web Archive.* Trans. Malcolm K. McNee. Ed. Else R. P. Vieira. 30 November 2014. <http://www.landless-voices.org/vieira/archive-05.phtml?rd=MSTITSSG356&ng=e&sc=3&th=42&se=0>

Ferreira, Teresa Cristina Montero. *Eu sou uma pergunta: Uma biografia de Clarice Lispector*. Rio de Janeiro: Rocco, 1999.

Ferreira-Pinto Bailey, Cristina. "Clarice Lispector e a crítica." *Clarice Lispector: Novos aportes críticos*. Ed. Cristina Ferreira-Pinto Bailey and Regina Zilberman. Pittsburgh: Instituto Internacional de Literatura Iberoamericana, 2007. 7–23.

Fitz, Earl E. *Clarice Lispector*. Boston: Twayne, 1985.

Fitz, Earl E. "Point of View in Clarice Lispector's *A hora da estrela*." *Luso-Brazilian Review* 19.2 (1982): 195–208.

Fitz, Earl E. *Sexuality and Being in the Poststructuralist Universe of Clarice Lispector: The Différance of Desire*. Austin: U of Texas P, 2001.

Fitz, Earl E., and Judith A Payne. *Ambiguity and Gender in the New Novel of Brazil and Spanish America*. Iowa City: U of Iowa P, 1993.

Foreword. *Invenção: Revista de Arte de Vanguarda* 4 (December 1964): 3.

Foucault, Michel. *The Order of Things: An Archaeology of the Human Sciences*. 1966. New York: Vintage, 1994.

Franchetti, Paulo. *Alguns aspectos da teoria da poesia concreta*. 4th ed. Campinas: Editora da Unicamp, 1993.

Franco, Jean. *The Decline and Fall of the Lettered City: Latin America in the Cold War*. Durham: Duke UP, 2002.

Franco, Jean. "From Modernization to Resistance: Latin American Literature 1959–1976." *Critical Passions: Selected Essays*. Durham: Duke UP, 1999. 285–310.

Frizzi, Adria. "Introduction." *Nine, Novena*. By Osman Lins. Trans. Adria Frizzi. Los Angeles: Sun & Moon Press, 1995. 7–22.

Frizzi, Adria. "Osman Lins: An Introduction." *Review of Contemporary Fiction* 15.3 (Fall 1995): 155–60.

Frizzi, Adria, trans. "Retable of Saint Joana Carolina." *Nine, Novena*. By Osman Lins. Los Angeles: Sun & Moon Press, 1995. 107–66.

Frondizi, Arturo. *Mensajes presidenciales, 1958–1962*. Buenos Aires: Ediciones Centro de Estudios Nacionales, 1978.

Fuentes, Carlos. *La nueva narrativa hispanoamericana*. Mexico City: Cuadernos de Joaquín Mortiz, 1969.

Fukelman, Clarisse. "Escreves estrelas (ora, direis)." *A hora de estrela*. By Clarice Lispector. Rio de Janeiro: Record, 1984. 7–25.

Gallina, Mario. *Estoy hecho de cine: Conversaciones de José Martínez Suárez con Mario Gallina*. Buenos Aires: Prosa y Poesía Amerian Editores, 2013.

Garrels, Elizabeth. "Resumen de la Discusión." *Más allá del Boom: Literatura y mercado*. Ed. Ángel Rama. Buenos Aires: Folios Ediciones, 1984. 289–326.

Getino, Octavio. "Some Notes on the Concept of a Third Cinema." *New Latin American Cinema*. Ed. Michael T. Martin. Vol. 1. Detroit: Wayne State UP. 99–107.

Gilles Deleuze from A to Z. Pierre-André Boutang. Perf. Gilles Deleuze and Claire Parnet. Trans. Charles J. Stivale. Cambridge: MIT P, 2011. DVD.

Gilman, Claudia. *Entre la pluma y el fusil: Debates y dilemas del escritor revolucionario en América Latina*. Buenos Aires: Siglo Veintiuno, 2003.

Girondo, Oliverio. "Manifiesto de 'Martín Fierro.'" *Revista Martín Fierro 1924–1927: Edición facsimilar*. Buenos Aires: Fondo Nacional de las Artes, 1995. 25–26.

Giunta, Andrea. *Avant-Garde, Internationalism, and Politics: Argentine Art in the Sixties*. Trans. Peter Kahn. Durham: Duke UP, 2007.

Godoy Ladeira, Julieta de. "Osman Lins: Crossing Frontiers." Trans. Adria Frizzi. *Review of Contemporary Fiction* 15.3 (Fall 1995): 186–95.

Gotlib, Nádia Batella. *Clarice Fotografiada*. São Paulo: Edusp/Imprensa Oficial, 2007.

Gotlib, Nádia Batella. *Clarice: Uma vida que se conta*. São Paulo: Editora Atica, 1995.

Graff Zivin, Erin. "Aporias of Marranismo: Sabina Berman's *En el nombre de Dios* and Jom Tob Azulay's *O Judeu*." *CR: The New Centennial Review* 12.3 (2012): 187–216.

Graff Zivin, Erin. "Beyond Inquisitional Logic, or, Toward an An-archaeological Latin Americanism." *CR: The New Centennial Review* 14.1 (2014): 195–212.

Graff Zivin, Erin. *Figurative Inquisitions: Conversion, Torture, and Truth in the Luso-Hispanic Atlantic*. Evanston: Northwestern UP, 2014.

Greene, Roland. "The Concrete Historical." *Harvard Library Bulletin* 3.2 (Summer 1992): 9–18.

Greene, Roland. "Inter-American Obversals: Allen Ginsberg and Haroldo de Campos circa 1960." *Xul: Revista de Poesia, 5 +5, 2005*. 27 February 2014. <www.bc.edu/research/xul /5+5/greene.htm>

Gross, Sue Anderson. "Religious Sectarianism in the Sertão of Northeast Brazil 1815–1966." *Journal of Inter-American Studies* 10.3 (July 1968): 369–83.

Guimarães Rosa, João. *Grande Sertão: Veredas*. Rio: José Olympio Editora, 1971.

Gullar, Ferreira. "A Bomba Suja." *Violão da Rua (II)*. Ed. Álvaro Vieira Pinto and Ênio Silveira. Rio de Janeiro: Editora Civilização Brasileira, 1962. 43–45.

Gullar, Ferreira. "João Boa Morte." *Violão da Rua (II)*. Ed. Álvaro Vieira Pinto and Ênio Silveira. Rio de Janeiro: Editora Civilização Brasileira, 1962. 22–35.

Gullar, Ferreira. "Que Fazer?" *Violão da Rua (II)*. Ed. Álvaro Vieira Pinto and Ênio Silveira. Rio de Janeiro: Editora Civilização Brasileira, 1962. 40–42.

Halperín Donghi, Tulio. *The Contemporary History of Latin America*. Trans. John Charles Chasteen. Durham: Duke UP, 1993.

Hardt, Michael, and Antonio Negri. *Multitude: War and Democracy in the Age of Empire*. New York: Penguin, 2004.

Hedrick, Tace. "'Mãe é para isso': Gender, Writing and English Language Translation in Clarice Lispector." *Luso-Brazilian Review* 41.2 (2005): 56–83.

Helena, Lucia. "A problematização da narrativa em Clarice Lispector." *Hispania* 75.5 (1992): 1164–73.

Helena, Lucia. *Nem musa, nem medusa: Itinerários da escrita em Clarice Lispector*. Niterói: Editora da Universidade Federal Fluminense, 1997.

Helena, Lucia. *Totens e tabus da modernidade brasileira: Símbolo e alegoria na obra de Oswald de Andrade*. Rio de Janeiro: Universidade Federal Fluminense/CEUFF, 1985.

Houaiss, Antônio. *Seis poetas e um problema*. Rio de Janeiro: Tecnoprint Gráfica, 1967. 143–85.

Igel, Regina. *Osman Lins: Uma biografia literária*. São Paulo: T. A. Queiroz, 1988.

"Infra." *Online Etymology*. 31 December 2014. <http://www.etymonline.com/index.php?term =infra->

Infrapolítica y posthegemonía. Special issue of *debats* 128, no. 3 (2015): 6–93.

Irigaray, Luce. *Ce sexe qui n'en est pas un*. Paris: Les Éditions de Minuit, 1977.

Irigaray, Luce. *Conversations*. With Stephen Pluhácek, Heidi Bostec, Judith Still, Michael Stone, Andrea Wheeler, Gillian Howie, Margaret R. Miles, Laine M. Harrington, Helen A. Fielding, Elizabeth Grosz, Michael Worton, and Birgitte H. Middtun. New York: Continuum, 2008.

Irigaray, Luce. *This Sex Which Is Not One*. Trans. Catherine Porter. Ithaca: Cornell UP, 1985.

Irigaray, Luce. *Why Different? A Culture of Two Subjects*. Trans. Camille Collins. New York: Semiotext(e), 2000.

Jackson, K. David. *A prosa vanguardista na literatura brasileira: Oswald de Andrade*. São Paulo: Editora Perspectiva, 1978.

Jackson, K. David. "Literature of the São Paulo Week of Modern Art." *Texas Papers on Latin America*. Austin: Institute of Latin American Studies, University of Texas at Austin, 1987.

Jackson, K. David. "Music of the Spheres in *Galáxias*." *Haroldo de Campos: A Dialogue with the Brazilian Concrete Poet*. Ed. K. David Jackson. Oxford: Centre for Brazilian Studies, 2005. 119–28.

Jackson, K. David. "Traveling in Haroldo de Campos's *Galáxias*: A Guide and Notes for the Reader." *Ciberletras* 17 (July 2007). 4 January 2015. <http://www.lehman.cuny.edu /ciberletras/v17/jackson.htm>

Jameson, Fredric. *The Political Unconscious: Narrative as a Socially Symbolic Act*. Ithaca: Cornell UP, 1981.

Jáuregui, Carlos A. "Anthropophagy." *Dictionary of Latin American Cultural Studies*. Ed. Robert McKee Irwin and Mónica Szurmuk. Gainesville: UP of Florida, 2012. 22–28.

Jáuregui, Carlos A. *Canibalia: Canibalismo, calibanismo, antropofagia cultural y consumo en América Latina*. Madrid: Iberoamericana, 2005.

Jitrik, Noé. *El escritor argentino: Dependencia o libertad*. Buenos Aires: Ediciones del Candil, 1967. 11–22.

Johnson, Adriana Michéle Campos. *Sentencing Canudos: Subalternity in the Backlands of Brazil*. Pittsburgh: U of Pittsburgh P, 2010.

Johnson, David E. "How (Not) to Do Latin American Studies." *South Atlantic Quarterly* 106.1 (2007): 1–19.

Johnson, David E. "The Time of Translation: The Border of American Literature." *Border Theory: The Limits of Cultural Politics*. Ed. Scott Michaelson and David E. Johnson. Minneapolis: U of Minnesota P, 1997. 129–65.

Junkes Bueno Martha-Toneto, Diana. *As razões da máquina antropofágica: Poesia e sincronia em Haroldo de Campos*. São Paulo: Editora UNESP, 2013.

Katra, William H. *Contorno: Literary Engagement in Post-Peronist Argentina*. Rutherford: Associated UPs, 1988.

Klobuka, Ana. "Hélène Cixous and the Hour of Clarice Lispector." *SubStance* 23.1 (1994): 41–62.

Kozak, Daniela. *La mirada cinéfila: La modernización de la crítica en la revista Tiempo de Cine*. Mar del Plata: 28 Festival Internacional de Cine de Mar del Plata, 2013.

Kozak, Daniela. *La mirada cinéfila: La modernización de la crítica en la revista Tiempo de Cine*. Rev. and exp. ed. Buenos Aires: EUDEBA, forthcoming.

Landini, Carlos. *Héctor Olivera*. Buenos Aires: Centro Editor de América Latina, 1993.

Larra, Raúl. *Roberto Arlt: El torturado*. Buenos Aires: Ediciones Alpe, 1956.

Larsen, Neil. "Modernism as *Cultura Brasileira*: Eating the Torn Halves." *Modernism and Hegemony: A Materialist Critique of Aesthetic Agencies*. Minneapolis: U of Minnesota P, 1990. 72–97.

Latin American Subaltern Studies Group. "Founding Statement." *The Postmodernism Debate in Latin America*. Ed. John Beverley, José Oviedo, and Michael Aronna. Durham: Duke UP, 1995. 135–46.

Latin American Subaltern Studies Revisited. Ed. Gustavo Verdesio. Special issue of *Dispositio* 25.52 (2005): 1–404.

Legrás, Horacio. "David Viñas (Buenos Aires, 1929–2011)." *Revista de Crítica Literaria Latinoamericana* 37.73 (2011): 459–66.

Legrás, Horacio. *Literature and Subjection: The Economy of Writing and Marginality in Latin America*. Pittsburgh: U of Pittsburgh P, 2008.

Lerner, Julio. "A última entrevista de Clarice Lispector." *Shalom* (June–August 1992): 62–69.

Levinson, Brett. "The Bind between Deconstruction and Subalternity, or the Latin Americanist Nation." *The Ends of Literature: The Latin American "Boom" in the Neoliberal Marketplace*. Stanford: Stanford UP, 2001. 169–91.

Levinson, Brett. "The Ends of Literature as a Neoliberal Act." *The Ends of Literature: The Latin American "Boom" in the Neoliberal Marketplace*. Stanford: Stanford UP, 2001. 10–30.

Levinson, Brett. *The Ends of Literature: The Latin American "Boom" in the Neoliberal Marketplace*. Stanford: Stanford UP, 2001.

Lévi-Strauss, Claude. *La pensée sauvage*. Paris: Plon, 1962.

Lima, Luís Costa. "Oswald de Andrade." *Poetas do modernismo: Antologia crítica*. Ed. Leodegário Amarante de Azevedo Filho. Vol. 1. Brasilia: Instituto Nacional do Livro, 1972. 21–97.

Lindstrom, Naomi. "Autonomy and Dependency." *The Social Consciousness of Latin American Writing*. Austin: U of Texas P, 1998. 13–42.

Lindstrom, Naomi. "The Pattern of Allusions in Clarice Lispector." *Luso-Brazilian Review* 36.1 (1999): 111–21.

Link, Daniel. "Recorridos por Viñas: Tecnología y desperdicios." *La Chancha con cadenas: Doce ensayos de literatura argentina*. Buenos Aires: Ediciones del Eclipse, 1994. 36–40.

Lins, Osman. *Avalovara*. São Paulo: Melhoramentos, 1973.

Lins, Osman. *Evangelho na taba: Outros problemas inculturais brasileiros*. São Paulo: Summus, 1979.

Lins, Osman. *Guerra sem testemunhas: O escritor, sua condição e a realidade social*. 2nd ed. São Paulo: Ática, 1974.

Lins, Osman. Letters to Maryvonne Lapouge, 4 May 1969, 11 August 1969. Acervo de Osman Lins. Fundação Casa de Rui Barbosa, Rio de Janeiro.

Lins, Osman. Letters to Sandra Nitrini, 25 March 1975, 28 April 1975. Acervo de Osman Lins. Fundação Casa de Rui Barbosa, Rio de Janeiro.

Lins, Osman. Letter to Haroldo de Campos, 4 October 1974. Personal collection, Sandra Nitrini.

Lins, Osman. Manuscript Note, "Retábulo de Santa Joana Carolina." Acervo de Osman Lins. Fundação Casa de Rui Barbosa, Rio de Janeiro.

Lins, Osman. *Nove, novena*. 1966. São Paulo: Companhia das Letras, 1994.

Lins, Osman. *O ideal da glória: Problemas inculturais brasileiros*. São Paulo: Summus, 1979.

Lins, Osman. "Retable of Saint Joana Carolina." *Nine, Novena*. Trans. Adria Frizzi. Los Angeles: Sun & Moon Press, 1995. 107–66.

Lins, Osman. "Retábulo de Santa Joana Carolina." *Nove, novena*. 1966. São Paulo: Companhia das Letras, 1994. 72–117.

Lins, Osman. Typescript, "Nono Mistério." Acervo de Osman Lins. Fundação Casa de Rui Barbosa, Rio de Janeiro.

Lispector, Clarice. *Água viva*. Rio de Janeiro: Editôra Artenova, 1973.

Lispector, Clarice. *A hora da estrela*. 1977. Rio de Janeiro: Rocco, 1998.

Lispector, Clarice. *A hora da estrela*. 6th ed. Rio de Janeiro: Livraria José Olympio Editora, 1981. Title page.

Lispector, Clarice. *A via crucis do corpo*. Rio de Janeiro: Rocco, 1974.

Lispector, Clarice. "Literatura e Justiça." *A legião estrangeira: Contos e crônicas*. Rio de Janeiro: Editôra do Autor, 1964. 149–52.

Lispector, Clarice. "Macabéa quando vem para o Rio." Manuscript note by Clarice Lispector and Olga Borelli. 19 February 2014. <http://revistapiaui.estadao.com.br/blogs/questoes-manuscritas/geral/manuscrito-nedito-de-clarice-lispector>

Lispector, Clarice. "Morte de Maca." Manuscript notes for paragraphs 483, 484, and 488, *A hora da estrela*. Notes by Clarice Lispector and Olga Borelli. Instituto Moreira Salles. 19 February 2014. <http://claricelispectorims.com.br/v1/Ims/view/80>

Lispector, Clarice. *Outros escritos*. Rio de Janeiro: Rocco, 2005.

Ludmer, Josefina. "David Viñas: Una semblanza." *David Viñas: Tonos de la crítica*. Buenos Aires: Textos Institucionales, 2011. 15–21.

Lund, Joshua. *The Impure Imagination: Toward a Critical Hybridity in Latin American Writing*. Minneapolis: U of Minnesota P, 2006.

Machado, Álvaro Manuel. "Osman Lins e a nova cosmogonia latino-americana." *Colóquio Letras* 33 (September 1976): 30–39.

Maciel, Maria Esther. "Utopian Remains: The Matter of the Landless Peasants in Brazilian Contemporary Art." Trans. Thomas Burns. Maria Esther Maciel Homepage. 29 November 2014. <http://www.letras.ufmg.br/esthermaciel/landless.html>

Maddalena, Maestro della. *Retable of the Virgin with Infant*. Tempura on wood. *Les Arts Decoratifs*. Digital image. 6 December 2014. <http://www.lesartsdecoratifs.fr/francais/arts-decoratifs/collections-26/parcours-27/chronologique/moyen-age-renaissance/les-salles/le-gothique-international/retable-de-la-vierge-a-l-enfant-527>

Madureira, Luís. *Cannibal Modernities: Postcoloniality and the Avant-Garde in Caribbean and Brazilian Literature*. Charlottesville: U of Virginia P, 2005.

Mahieux, Viviane. *Urban Chroniclers in Modern Latin America: The Shared Intimacy of Everyday Life*. Austin: U of Texas P, 2011.

Martínez Suárez, José. "Dar la cara." *Cine Club La Rosa*. 10 December 2014. <http://cine clublarosa.blogspot.com/2013/09/martinez-suarez-habla-de-dar-la-cara.html>

Martínez Suárez, José. Emails to author, 26 February 2016, 29 February 2016, 3 March 2016, 14 March 2016.

Martín Peña, Fernando. *60 generaciones, 90 generaciones: Cine argentino independiente*. Ed. Fernando Martín Peña. Buenos Aires: Museo Latinoamericano de Buenos Aires-Colección Constantini / Instituto Torcuato Di Tella / Revista Film, 2003.

Martins, Sérgio B. *Constructing an Avant-Garde: Art in Brazil, 1949–1979*. Cambridge: MIT P, 2013.

Masiello, Francine. "Argentine Literary Journalism: The Production of a Critical Discourse." *Latin American Research Review* 20.1 (1985): 27–60.

Masiello, Francine. *El cuerpo de la voz: Poesía, ética y cultura*. Rosario: UNR Editora, 2013.

Masiello, Francine. *Lenguaje e ideología: Las escuelas argentinas de vanguardia*. Buenos Aires: Hachette, 1986.

Masotta, Oscar. "Explicación de *Un Dios cotidiano*." *Conciencia y estructura*. Buenos Aires: Editorial Jorge Álvarez, 1969. 120–44.

Material Poetry of the Renaissance / The Renaissance of Material Poetry. Special issue of *Harvard Library Bulletin* 3.2 (Summer 1992): 1–104.

McGuirk, Bernard. "Laughin' Again He's Awake: Haroldo de Campos *À L'Oreille de L'Autre Celte*." McGuirk and Vieira 126–52.

Medeiros, Paulo de. "Clarice Lispector and the Question of the Nation." *Closer to the Wild Heart: Essays on Clarice Lispector*. Ed. Cláudia Pazos and Claire Williams. Oxford: European Humanities Research Centre, 2002. 142–61.

Mendonça, Antônio Sérgio. *Poesia de vanguarda no Brasil: De Oswald de Andrade ao concretismo e o poema processo*. Rio de Janeiro: Editora Vozes, 1970.

Mendonça, Antônio Sérgio, and Alvaro de Sá. *Poesia de vanguarda no Brasil: De Oswald de Andrade ao Poema Visual*. Rio de Janeiro: Edições Antares, 1983.

Mendonça, Julio. "A poesia concreta de Augusto de Campos." *Carta Educação*. 9 October 2016. <http://www.cartaeducacao.com.br/aulas/medio/a-poesia-concreta-de-augusto -de-campos/>

Mignolo, Walter. "Signs and Their Transmission: The Question of the Book in the New World." *Writing without Words: Alternative Literacies in Mesoamerica and the Andes*. Ed. Elizabeth Hill Boone and Walter D. Mignolo. Durham: Duke UP, 1994. 220–70.

Mignolo, Walter. "Writing and Recorded Knowledge in Colonial and Postcolonial Situations." *Writing without Words: Alternative Literacies in Mesoamerica and the Andes*. Ed. Elizabeth Hill Boone and Walter D. Mignolo. Durham: Duke UP, 1994. 293–313.

"MÓBILE. Invenção 3: Informações." *Invenção: Revista de Arte de Vanguarda* 3 (June 1963): 87–94.

Moraña, Mabel. "Baroque/Neobaroque/Ultrabaroque: Disruptive Readings of Modernity." Trans. Gerardo Garza. *Ideologies of Hispanism*. Ed. Mabel Moraña. Nashville: Vanderbilt UP, 2005. 241–81.

Moraña, Mabel. "Barroco y transculturación." *Crítica impura*. Madrid: Iberoamericana, 2004. 19–54.

Moraña, Mabel. "Ideología de la transculturación." *La escritura del límite*. Madrid: Iberoamericana, 2010. 159–68.

Moraña, Mabel. "Postscríptum: El Afecto en la Caja de las Herramientas." *El lenguaje de las emociones: Afecto y cultura en América Latina*. Ed. Mabel Moraña and Ignacio M. Sánchez Prado. Madrid: Iberoamericana, 2012. 313–37.

Moreiras, Alberto. "Common Political Democracy: The Marrano Register." *Impasses of the Post-Global: Theory in the Era of Climate Change.* Ed. Henry Sussman. Vol. 2. Ann Arbor: Open Humanities Press, 2012. 23 September 2016. <http://quod.lib.umich.edu/o/ohp/10803281.0001.001/1:10/--impasses-of-the-post-global-theory-in-the-era-of-climate?rgn=div1;view=fulltext>

Moreiras, Alberto. *The Exhaustion of Difference: The Politics of Latin American Cultural Studies.* Durham: Duke UP, 2001.

Moreiras, Alberto. "From Melodrama to Thriller." Iberian Postcolonialities I: A Metahistory of the Practices of Material Power. LASA International Congress, San Francisco. 25 May 2012.

Moreiras, Alberto. "Infrapolitical Literature: Hispanism and the Border." *CR: The New Centennial Review* 10.2 (2010): 183–204.

Moreiras, Alberto. *Línea de sombra: El no sujeto de lo político.* Santiago: Palinodia, 2006.

Moreiras, Alberto. "Mules and Snakes: On the Neo-Baroque Principle of De-Localization." *Ideologies of Hispanism.* Ed. Mabel Moraña. Nashville: Vanderbilt UP, 2005. 201–29.

Moreiras, Alberto. "Newness, World Language, Alterity: On Borges's Mark." *Thinking with Borges.* Ed. William Egginton and David E. Johnson. Aurora: Davies Group, 2009. 121–40.

Moreiras, Alberto. "Posthegemonía, o más allá del principio del placer." *alter/nativas* 1 (2013): 1–21.

Moreiras, Alberto. *Tercer espacio: Literatura y duelo en América Latina.* Santiago: Universidad Arcis, 1999.

Moreiras, Alberto, and José Luis Villacañas. "Introduction: Latin American Postcolonialities." Iberian Postcolonialities: Proposal Document 2, August 2010, Copyright Department of Hispanic Studies, Texas A&M University. 19 July 2014. <http://hisp.tamu.edu/research/proposaldoc2.html>

Moretti, Franco. *Modern Epic: The World System from Goethe to García-Márquez.* Trans. Quintin Hoare. London: Verso, 1996.

Moser, Benjamin. *Why This World? A Biography of Clarice Lispector.* Oxford: Oxford UP, 2009.

Muñoz, Gerardo. "David Viñaz: literatura y materialismo." *Diario de Cuba,* 11 Sept. 2013. Web. 19 February 2017. <http://www.diariodecuba.com/de-leer/1378904441_4636.html>

Namorato, Luciana. "A tentação do silêncio em 'Ela não sabe gritar' (ou a 'A hora da estrela') de Clarice Lispector." *Hispania* 94.1 (2011): 50–62.

Nancy, Jean-Luc. *The Inoperative Community.* Ed. Peter Connor. Trans. Peter Connor, Lisa Garbus, Michael Holland, and Simona Sawhney. Minneapolis: U of Minnesota P, 1991.

Negri, Antonio. *Insurgencies: Constituent Power and the Modern State.* Trans. Maurizia Boscagli. Minneapolis: U of Minnesota P, 1999.

Nietzsche, Friedrich. *Untimely Meditations.* Ed. Daniel Breazeale. Trans. R. J. Hollingdale. New York: Cambridge UP, 1991.

Nitrini, Sandra. Letter to Maryvonne Lapouge, 4 May 1969. Acervo de Osman Lins. Fundação Casa de Rui Barbosa, Rio de Janeiro.

Nitrini, Sandra. *Poéticas em confronto: "Nove, novena" e o novo romance.* São Paulo: HUCITEC, 1987.

Nitrini, Sandra. *Transfigurações: Ensaios sobre a obra de Osman Lins.* São Paulo: Editora Hucitec, 2010.

Novo Aurélio Século XXI: O Dicionário de Língua Portuguesa. 3rd ed. Rio de Janeiro: Editora Nova Fronteira, 1999.

Nunes, Benedito. "Narration in Many Voices." Trans. Linda Ledford-Miller. *Review of Contemporary Fiction* 15.3 (Fall 1995): 198–203.

Nunes, Benedito. "O movimento da escritura." *O drama da linguagem: Uma leitura de Clarice Lispector.* São Paulo: Éditora Atica, 1989.

Nunes, Benedito. *Oswald Canibal.* São Paulo: Editora Perspectiva, 1979.

Olea, Héctor. "Versions, Inversions, Subversions: The Artist as Theoretician." *Inverted Utopias: Avant-Garde Art in Latin America*. Ed. Mari Carmen Ramírez and Héctor Olea. New Haven: Yale UP, 2004. 443–55.

Olivera, Héctor. "Prólogo." *El jefe*. By David Viñas and Fernando Ayala. Buenos Aires: Biblos Argentores, 2013. 9–17.

Orgambide, Pedro G. Review of *Los dueños de la tierra*. *Gaceta Literaria* 18.1 (1959): 19.

Orgambide, Pedro G., and Osvaldo Seiguerman. "Encrucijada y rebeldía." *Gaceta Literaria* 15.3 (1958): 1, 15–16.

Passos, José Luiz. *Ruínas das linhas puras: Quatro ensaios em torno a Macunaíma*. São Paulo: Annablume, 1998.

Pérez Llhaí, Adrián Marcos. "El cine: Una política de la ciudad." *David Viñas: Tonos de la crítica*. Los Polvorines: Universidad Nacional de General Sarmiento, 2011.

Perloff, Marjorie. "Brazilian Concrete Poetry: How It Looks Today; An Interview with Haroldo and Augusto de Campos." *Haroldo de Campos: A Dialogue with the Brazilian Concrete Poet*. Ed. K. David Jackson. Oxford: Centre for Brazilian Studies, 2005. 165–79.

Perloff, Marjorie. "Concrete Prose in the Nineties: *Galáxias* and After." *Haroldo de Campos: A Dialogue with the Brazilian Concrete Poet*. Ed. K. David Jackson. Oxford: Centre for Brazilian Studies, 2005. 139–61.

Peixoto, Marta. "'Fatos são pedras duras': Urban Poverty in Clarice Lispector." *Closer to the Wild Heart: Essays on Clarice Lispector*. Ed. Cláudia Pazos and Claire Williams. Oxford: European Humanities Research Centre, 2002. 142–61.

Peixoto, Marta. *Passionate Fictions: Gender, Narrative, and Violence in Clarice Lispector*. Minneapolis: U of Minnesota P, 1994.

Peixoto, Marta. "Rape and Textual Violence in Clarice Lispector." *Rape and Representation*. Ed. Lynn A. Higgins and Brenda R. Silver. New York: Columbia UP, 1991.

Perrone, Charles A. *Brazil, Lyric, and the Americas*. Gainesville: UP of Florida, 2010.

Perrone, Charles A. *Masters of Contemporary Brazilian Song: MPB 1965–1985*. Austin: University of Texas Press, 1989.

Perrone, Charles A. "Presentation and Representation of Self and City in *Paulicéia Desvairada*." *Chasqui* 31.1 (2002): 18–27.

Perrone, Charles A. *Seven Faces: Brazilian Poetry since Modernism*. Durham: Duke UP, 1996.

Perrone, Charles A., and Christopher Dunn. *Brazilian Popular Music and Globalization*. New York: Routledge, 2001.

Pignatari, Décio. *A cultura pós-nacionalista*. Rio de Janeiro: Imago Editora, 1998. 111–25.

Pignatari, Décio. "beba coca cola." *Antologia Noigandres do verso à poesia concreta*. Ed. Décio Pignatari, Haroldo de Campos, Augusto de Campos, Ronaldo Azeredo, and José Lino Grünewald. São Paulo: Massao Ohno Editora, 1962. 34.

Pignatari, Décio. *Contracomunicação*. São Paulo: Ateliê Editorial, 2004.

Pignatari, Décio. *Errâncias*. São Paulo: Editora Senac, 1999.

Pignatari, Décio. "Marco Zero de Andrade." *Letras* [ALFA, FFCL de Marília] 5–6 (March 1964): 41–56.

Pignatari, Décio. "nova poesia: concreta (manifesto)." Campos, Pignatari, and Campos 67–70.

Pignatari, Décio. "Situação atual da poesia no Brasil." *Invenção: Revista de Arte de Vanguarda*, no. 1 (1962): 51–70.

Pignatari, Décio. "stèle pour vivre n°3 estela cubana." *Invenção: Revista de Arte de Vanguarda*, no. 2 (1964): 11.

Pignatari, Décio. "Tempo: Invenção e inversão." Foreword. *Um homem sem profissão: Sob as ordens de mamãe*. By Oswald de Andrade. São Paulo: Editora Globo, 1990. 7–10.

Pignatari, Décio, and José Nania. "ESTELA AO PENSAMENTO BRUTO OSWALD DE ANDRADE." *Invenção: Revista de Arte de Vanguarda*, no. 4 (1964): 37.

Pignatari, Décio, and Luiz Angelo Pinto. "Nova linguagem, nova poesia." *Invenção: Revista de Arte de Vanguarda*, no. 4 (1964): 79–84.

Podalsky, Laura. *Specular City: Transforming Culture, Consumption, and Space in Buenos Aires, 1955–1973*. Philadelphia: Temple UP, 2004.

Poetics of the Avant-Garde. Special issue of *Poetics Today* 3.3 (1982): 137–209.

Pontiero, Giovanni. "Afterword." *The Hour of the Star*. Trans. Giovanni Pontiero. New York: New Directions, 1992.

Portantiero, Juan Carlos, Rodolfo Walsh, and Francisco Urondo. "Literatura argentina del siglo XX." *Panorama actual de la literatura latinoamericana*. Madrid: Editorial Fundamentos, 1971. 258–80.

Poshegemonía: El final de un paradigma de la filosofía política en América Latina. Ed. Rodrigo Castro Orellana. Madrid: Biblioteca Nueva, 2015.

Pound, Ezra. *Guide to Kulchur*. 1938. New York: New Directions, 1952.

Pound, Ezra. "How to Read." *Literary Essays of Ezra Pound*. Ed. T. S. Eliot. New York: New Directions, 1968. 15–19.

Pound, Ezra. *Make It New: Essays by Ezra Pound*. New Haven: Yale University Press, 1935.

Price, Rachel. *The Object of the Atlantic: Concrete Aesthetics in Cuba, Brazil, and Spain, 1868–1968*. Evanston: Northwestern UP, 2014.

Rabasa, José. "The Comparative Frame in Subaltern Studies." *Postcolonial Studies* 8.4 (2005): 365–80.

Rabasa, José. "Elsewheres: Radical Relativism and the Frontiers of Empire." *Qui Parle* 16.1 (Summer 2006): 71–94.

Rabasa, José. *Without History: Subaltern Studies, the Zapatista Insurgency, and the Specter of History*. Pittsburgh: U of Pittsburgh P, 2010.

Rabasa, José. *Writing Violence on the Northern Frontier: The Historiography of Sixteenth-Century New Mexico and Florida and the Legacy of Conquest*. Durham: Duke UP, 2000.

Rama, Ángel. "El 'boom' en perspectiva." *Más allá del boom: Literatura y mercado*. Ed. Ángel Rama. Buenos Aires: Ediciones Folios, 1984.

Rama, Ángel. *La ciudad letrada*. Hanover: Ediciones del Norte, 1984.

Rama, Ángel, ed. *Más allá del boom: Literatura y mercado*. Buenos Aires: Ediciones Folios, 1984.

Rama, Ángel. *Transculturación narrativa en América Latina*. Mexico City: Siglo Veintiuno, 1982.

Ramírez, Mari Carmen. "A Highly Topical Utopia: Some Outstanding Features of the Avant-Garde in Latin America." *Inverted Utopias: Avant-Garde Art in Latin America*. Ed. Mari Carmen Ramírez and Héctor Olea. New Haven: Yale UP, 2004. 1–15.

Ramírez, Mari Carmen. "Prologue." *Inverted Utopias: Avant-Garde Art in Latin America*. Ed. Mari Carmen Ramírez and Héctor Olea. New Haven: Yale UP, 2004. xv–xvii.

Ramírez, Mari Carmen. "Vital Structures: The Constructive Nexus in South America." *Inverted Utopias: Avant-Garde Art in Latin America*. Ed. Mari Carmen Ramírez and Héctor Olea. New Haven: Yale UP, 2004. 191–201.

Ramos, Julio. *Divergent Modernities: Culture and Politics in Nineteenth Century Latin America*. Trans. John D. Blanco. Durham: Duke UP, 2001.

Ramos, Julio. "The Other's Knowledge: Writing and Orality in Sarmiento's *Facundo*." *Divergent Modernities: Culture and Politics in Nineteenth Century Latin America*. Trans. John D. Blanco. Durham: Duke UP, 2001.

Rancière, Jacques. "Aesthetics as Politics." *Aesthetics and Its Discontents*. Trans. Steven Corcoran. Malden: Polity Press, 2009. 19–44.

Rancière, Jacques. *Aisthesis: Scenes from the Aesthetic Regime of Art*. Trans. Zakir Paul. New York: Verso, 2013.

Rancière, Jacques. *Dissensus: On Politics and Aesthetics*. Trans. Steven Corcoran. New York: Continuum, 2010.

Rancière, Jacques. "Is There a Deleuzian Aesthetics?" Trans. Radmila Djordjevic. *Qui Parle* 14.2 (Spring–Summer 2004): 1–14.

Rancière, Jacques. *Le partage du sensible: Esthétique et politique*. Paris: La Fabrique éditions, 2000.

Rancière, Jacques. *The Politics of Aesthetics*. Trans. Gabriel Rockhill. New York: Continuum, 2004.

Rapallo, Fernando. *Fernando Ayala*. Buenos Aires: Centro Editor de América Latina, 1993.

Read, Justin A. "Obverse Colonization: São Paulo, Global Urbanization and the Poetics of the Latin American City." *Journal of Latin American Cultural Studies* 15.3 (2006): 281–300.

Read, Justin A. "The Reversible World: America as Dissonance in Mário de Andrade's *Paulicéia Desvairada*." *Modern Poetics and Hemispheric American Cultural Studies*. New York: Palgrave Macmillan, 2009. 59–102.

Revista de Civilização Brasileira 11–12 (1967). Cover illustration. Unknown. Personal photograph by author.

Rinesi, Eduardo, et al. *David Viñas: Tonos de la crítica*. Los Polvorines: Universidad Nacional de General Sarmiento, 2011.

Roca, Pilar. *Política y sociedad en la novelística de David Viñas*. Buenos Aires: Editorial Biblos, 2007.

Rodríguez, Ileana. "Reading Subalterns across Texts, Disciplines, and Theories: From Representation to Recognition." *The Latin American Subaltern Studies Reader*. Ed. Ileana Rodríguez. Durham: Duke UP, 2001. 1–32.

Rodríguez Monegal, Emir. "David Viñas en su contorno." *Narradores de esta América*. Buenos Aires: Alfa Editores, 1974. 310–30.

Rodríguez Monegal, Emir. "Dos novelas de David Viñas: Los parricidas crean." *Marcha* 859 (1957): 21.

Rodríguez Monegal, Emir. *El juicio de los parricidas*. Buenos Aires: Editorial Education, 1956.

Romero-Astvaldsson, Angela. *La obra narrativa de David Viñas: La nueva inflexión de Prontuario y Claudia Conversa*. Bern: Peter Lang, 2007.

Rosenberg, Fernando J. *The Avant-Garde and Geopolitics in Latin America*. Pittsburgh: U of Pittsburgh P, 2006.

Rosenberg, Fernando J. "Cultural Theory and Avant-Gardes: Mariátegui, Mário de Andrade, Oswald de Andrade, Pagú, Tarsila do Amaral, César Vallejo." *A Companion to Latin American Literature and Culture*. Ed. Sara Castro-Klarén. West Sussex: Wiley-Blackwell, 2008. 410–25.

Rowe, William. *Poets of Contemporary Latin America: History and the Inner Life*. Oxford: Oxford UP, 2000.

Rozitchner, León. "Un paso adelante, dos atrás." *Contorno* 9–10 (April 1959): 1–15.

Rufinelli, Jorge. "Las películas." *Soñar con los ojos abiertos: Las treinta lecciones de Stanford*. Ed. Jorge Rufinelli and Fernando Birri. Buenos Aires: Aguilar, 2007. 387–98.

Rufinelli, Jorge, and João Cezar de Castro Rocha, eds. *Antropofagia hoje?* São Paulo: Realizações, 2011.

Sá, Olga da. *A escritura de Clarice Lispector*. Petrópolis: Editora Vozes, 1979.

Sadlier, Darlene J. *Brazil Imagined: 1500 to the Present*. Austin: U of Texas P, 2008.

Salgado, Sebastião. *Terra: Struggle of the Landless*. Trans. Clifford Landers. London: Phaidon Press, 1997.

Sampaio, Plínio Arruda. "The Mística of the MST." Trans. Plínio Arruda Sampaio. *The Landless Voices Web Archive*. Ed. Else R. P. Vieira. 21 November 2014. <http://www.landless-voices .org/vieira/archive-05.phtml?ng=e&sc=3&th=42&rd=MSTICAOF657&cd=&se=>

Sánchez Prado, Ignacio M. "Presentación." *El lenguaje de las emociones: Afecto y cultura en América Latina*. Ed. Mabel Moraña and Ignacio M. Sánchez Prado. Madrid: Iberoamericana, 2012. 11–16.

Sant'Anna, Affonso Romano de. *Música popular e moderna poesia brasileira*. Petrópolis: Vozes, 1977.

Santiago, Silviano. "A aula inaugural de Clarice Lispector: Cotidiano, labor e esperança." *O cosmopolitismo do pobre: Crítica literária e crítica cultural*. Belo Horizonte: Editora UFMG, 2004. 232–41.

Saramago, José. Preface to *Terra: Struggle of the Landless*. By Sebastião Salgado. Trans. Clifford Landers. London: Phaidon Press, 1997.

Sarduy, Pedro. "El cine, pibe, me interesa mucho." *La Gaceta de Cuba* 6.55 (February 1967): 5, 14.

Sarduy, Severo. *Barroco*. Buenos Aires: Editorial Sudamericana, 1974.

Sarduy, Severo. "El barroco y el neobarroco." *America Latina en su literatura*. Ed. César Fernández Moreno. Mexico City: Siglo XXI Editores, 1982. 167–84.

Sarduy, Severo. "Rumo a concretude." In *Signantia: Quasi Coelum / Signância Quase Céu*. By Haroldo de Campos. São Paulo: Perspectiva, 1979. 117–45.

Sarlo, Beatriz. *La batalla de las ideas (1943–1973)*. Buenos Aires: Emecé, 2007.

Sarlo, Beatriz. "Los dos ojos de *Contorno*." *Punto de Vista* 4.13 (November 1981): 3–8.

Sarlo, Beatriz. "¿Qué hacer con las masas?" *La batalla de las ideas (1943–1973)*. 2001. Buenos Aires: Emecé, 2007. 15–55.

Sarmiento, Domingo Faustino. *Facundo: Civilización y barbarie*. Ed. Roberto Yahni. Madrid: Cátedra, 1990.

Sartre, Jean-Paul. *The Reprieve*. Trans. Eric Sutton. 1945. New York: Bantam Books, 1968.

Sartre, Jean-Paul. *Search for a Method*. Trans. Hazel E. Barnes. New York: Vintage, 1968.

Sartre, Jean-Paul. *What Is Literature? And Other Essays*. Trans. Bernard Frechtman. Ed. Steven Ungar. 1947. Cambridge: Harvard UP, 1988.

Scheper-Hughes, Nancy. *Death without Weeping: The Violence of Everyday Life in Brazil*. Berkeley: U of California P, 1992.

Schüler, Donaldo. "Estelas e estrelas—uma incursão na poesia de Décio Pignatari." *Schulers*. Donaldo Schüler (1997). 3 October 2013. <http://schuler.com/donaldo/estelas.htm>

Schwartz, Jorge. "Brasil: Manifiestos." *Las vanguardias latinoamericanas: Textos programáticos y críticos*. Mexico City: Fondo de Cultura Económica, 2002. 144–86.

Schwartz, Jorge. "Um Brasil em Tom Menor: Pau-Brasil e Antropofagia." *Revista de Crítica Literaria Latinoamericana* 34.47 (1998): 53–65.

Schwartz, Jorge. *Vanguardia y cosmopolitismo en la década del veinte: Oliverio Girondo y Oswald de Andrade*. Rosario: Beatriz Viterbo Editora, 1993.

Schwarz, Roberto. "Culture and Politics in Brazil, 1964–1969." *Misplaced Ideas: Essays on Brazilian Culture*. Ed. John Gledson. London: Verso, 1992. 126–59.

Schwarz, Roberto. "Marco histórico." *Que horas são?* São Paulo: Companhia das Letras, 1987. 57–66.

Sebreli, Juan José. "Los 'martinfierristas': Su tiempo y el nuestro." *Contorno* 1 (November 1953): 1–2.

Sección especial: Poesía concreta. Special issue of *Ciberletras 17* (2007). Ed. Susana Haydu.

Sendrós, Paraná. *Fernando Birri*. Buenos Aires: Centro Editor de América Latina, 1994.

Shellhorse, Adam Joseph. "The Explosion of the Letter: The Crisis of the Poetic and Representation in João Cabral de Melo Neto's *Morte e Vida Severina*." *Luso-Brazilian Review* 50.1 (2013): 201–28.

Shellhorse, Adam Joseph. "*Formas de Fome*: Anti-Literature and the Politics of Representation in Haroldo de Campos's *Galáxias*." *CR: The New Centennial Review* 14.3 (Winter 2014): 219–54.

Shellhorse, Adam Joseph. "Latin American Literary Representational Regime." *The Encyclopedia of Postcolonial Studies*. Ed. Sangeeta Ray, Henry Schwarz, José Luis Villacañas Berlanga, Alberto Moreiras, and April Shemak. Vol. 2. Oxford: Wiley-Blackwell, 2016. 923–32.

Shellhorse, Adam Joseph. "Literature before Literature: Posthegemonic Mediation, the Body of Language and the Affect." *Política Común: A Journal of Thought* 6 (Fall 2014). 26 August 2016. <http://quod.lib.umich.edu/p/pc/12322227.0006.008/--literature-before-literature-posthegemonic-mediation?rgn=main;view=fulltext >

Shellhorse, Adam Joseph. "Radical Reinventions of Language: From the Avant-Garde to *Creacionismo*, *Ultraísmo*, Brazilian *Modernismo*, *Antropofagia*, and Surrealism." *The*

Cambridge Companion to Latin American Poetry. Ed. Stephen M. Hart. Cambridge: Cambridge University Press, forthcoming.

Shellhorse, Adam Joseph. "Subversions of the Sensible: The Poetics of Antropofagia in Brazilian Concrete Poetry." *Revista Hispánica Moderna* 68.2 (December 2015): 165–90.

Shtromberg, Elena. *Art Systems: Brazil and the 1970s.* Austin: U of Texas P, 2016.

Silva Brito, Mário de. "Fases da Poesia Modernista Brasileira." *Angulo e horizonte: De Oswald de Andrade à ficção-científica.* São Paulo: Livraria Martins Editora, 1969. 55–76.

Slater, Candace. "A Play of Voices: The Theater of Osman Lins." *Hispanic Review* 49.3 (Summer 1981): 285–95.

Soares, Marisa Balthasar. "O Retábulo de Santa Joana Carolina: O palco na palavra." *Osman Lins: O sopro na argila.* Ed. Hugo Almeida. São Paulo: Nankin Editorial, 2004. 169–77.

Solanes, Fernando, and Octavio Getino. "Towards a Third Cinema: Notes and Experiences for the Development of a Cinema of Liberation in the Third World." *New Latin American Cinema.* Ed. Michael T. Martin. Vol. 1. Detroit: Wayne State UP, 1997. 33–58.

Solt, Mary Ellen. "A World Look at Concrete Poetry." *Concrete Poetry: A World View.* Bloomington: Indiana UP, 1968. 7–66.

Somerlate Barbosa, Maria José. "Nivelamento em *Morte e Vida severina.*" *Hispania* 76.1 (March 1993): 30–37.

Sommer, Doris. *Foundational Fictions: The National Romances of Latin America.* Berkeley: U of California P, 1991.

Sommer, Doris. *Proceed with Caution, When Engaged with Minority Writings in the Americas.* Cambridge: Harvard UP, 1999.

Sorensen, Diana. *A Turbulent Decade Remembered: Scenes from the Latin American Sixties.* Stanford: Stanford UP, 2007.

Spatola, Adriano. *Toward Total Poetry.* Trans. Brendan W. Hennessey and Guy Bennett. 1979. Los Angeles: Otis Books, 2008.

Spinoza, Baruch. *Spinoza's Ethics and "On the Correction of the Understanding."* Trans. Andrew Boyle. New York: Dutton, Everyman's Library, 1979.

Spivak, Gayatri Chakravorty. *Death of a Discipline.* New York: Columbia UP, 2003.

Taylor, Joshua C. *Futurism.* New York: Museum of Modern Art, 1961.

Tealdi, Juan Carlos. *Borges y Viñas: Literatura e ideología.* Madrid: Editorial Orígenes, 1983.

Terán, Oscar. "Culture, Politics, and Intellectuals in the 1960s." *Listen, Here, Now! Argentine Art of the 1960s: Writings of the Avant-Garde.* Trans. R. Kelly Washbourne. New York: Museum of Modern Art, 2004. 262–75.

Terán, Oscar. *En busca de la ideología argentina.* Buenos Aires: Catalogos Editora, 1986. 195–253.

The Marrano Specter: Derrida and Hispanism. Ed. Erin Graff Zivin. Fordham UP, forthcoming.

The Thompson Chain Reference Bible. King James Version. Ed. Frank Charles Thompson. Indianapolis: B. B. Kirkbride Bible Co., 1964.

Tiré die. Second version. Dir. Fernando Birri, Hugo Abad, Blanca C. de Brasco, Edgardo Ates, Elena de Azcuénaga, César Caprio, Manuel Horacio Giménez, Rodolfo Neder, Juan Oliva, Carolos Pais, Ninfa Pajón, Edgardo Pallero, José M. Paolantonio, Jorge Planas, Viader y Enrique Urteaga, et al. Prod. Instituto de Cinematografia de la Universidad Nacional del Litoral, 1959/1960. The Collector's Item, 2007. DVD.

Unruh, Vicky. *Latin American Vanguards: The Art of Contentious Encounters.* Berkeley: U of California P, 1994.

Unruh, Vicky. *Performing Women and Modern Literary Culture in Latin America.* Austin: U of Texas P, 2006.

Unruh, Vicky, and Michael J. Lazzara. "Introduction: Telling Ruins." *Telling Ruins in Latin America.* Ed. Vicky Unruh and Michael J. Lazzara. New York: Palgrave Macmillan, 2009. 1–9.

Valles, Rafael. *Fotogramas de la memoria: Encuentros con José Martínez Suárez*. Buenos Aires: Rafael Valles, 2014.

Valverde, Estela. *David Viñas: En busca de una síntesis de la historia argentina*. Buenos Aires: Editorial Plus Ultra, 1989.

Van Delden, Maarten, and Yvon Grenier. *Gunshots at the Fiesta: Literature and Politics in Latin America*. Nashville: Vanderbilt UP, 2009.

Varin, Claire. *Clarice Lispector: Rencontres bresiliennes*. Quebec City: Éditions Trois, 1987.

Vieira, Else R. P. *The Landless Voices Web Archive*. 19 November 2014. <http://www .landless-voices.org/index.phtml?ng=e>

Vieira, Else R. P. "Music, Poetry and the Politization of the Landless Identity." Vieira and McGuirk xxviii–lxix.

Vieira, Else R. P. "Translating History and Creating and International Platform: Haroldo de Campos's 'o anjo esquerdo da história.'" ABRALIC International Congress, São Paulo. 13–17 July 2008.

Vieira, Else R. P. "Weaving Histories and Cultural Memories: The (Inter) National Materialisms of 'O Anjo Esquerdo da História." *Haroldo de Campos in Conversation*. Ed. Bernard McGuirk and Else R. P. Vieira. London: Zolius Press, 2009. 153–80.

Vieira, Else R. P., and Bernard M. McGuirk, eds. *Landless Voices in Song and Poetry: The Movimento dos Sem Terra of Brazil*. Nottingham: CCCP Press, 2007.

Vieira, Nelson H. "Clarice Lispector: A Jewish Impulse and a Prophecy of Difference." *Jewish Voices in Brazilian Literature: A Prophetic Discourse of Alterity*. Gainesville: U of Florida P, 1995. 100–150.

Viñas, David. *Argentina: Ejercito y Oligarquia; Cuadernos de la Revista Casa de las Américas* 2 (November 1967): 7–55.

Viñas, David. "Arlt y los comunistas." *Contorno* 2 (May 1954): 8.

Viñas, David. *Cosas concretas*. Buenos Aires: Editorial Tiempo Contemporaneo, 1969.

Viñas, David. *Dar la cara*. 1962. Buenos Aires: Centro Editor de América Latina, 1967.

Viñas, David. *De Sarmiento a Cortázar: Literatura argentina y realidad política*. Buenos Aires: Ediciones Siglo Veinte, 1971.

Viñas, David. "El escritor vanguardista." *De Sarmiento a Cortázar: Literatura argentina y realidad política*. Buenos Aires: Ediciones Siglo Veinte, 1971. 60–66.

Viñas, David. "Erdosain y el plano oblicuo." *Contorno* 2 (May 1954): 5–6.

Viñas, David. "Escribe David Viñas." *Gaceta Literaria* 17.1 (1959): 15.

Viñas, David. Interview with Pedro Sarduy. "El cine, pibe, me interesa mucho." *La Gaceta de Cuba* (Havana), 9.55 (1967): 5, 14.

Viñas, David. *Las malas costumbres: Cuentos*. Buenos Aires: Editorial Jamcana, 1963.

Viñas, David. *Literatura argentina y realidad política*. Buenos Aires: Jorge Alvarez Editor, 1964.

Viñas, David. *Los dueños de la tierra*. Barcelona: Biblioteca Letras del Exilio, 1985.

Viñas, David. "Nosotros y ellos: David Viñas habla sobre *Contorno*." Interview with Beatriz Sarlo and Carlos Altamirano. *Punto de Vista* 4.13 (November 1981): 9–12.

Viñas, David. "11 preguntas concretas a David Viñas." *El Grillo de Papel* 2 (1959): 24.

Viñas, David. "Pareceres y digresiones en torno a la nueva narrativa latinoamericana." *Más allá del Boom: Literatura y mercado*. Ed. Ángel Rama. Buenos Aires: Folios Ediciones, 1984. 13–49.

Viñas, David. "Roberto Arlt: Periodista." *Contorno* 2 (May 1954): 10–11.

Viñas, David. "Roberto Arlt: Una autobiografía." *Contorno* 2 (May 1954): 8–10.

Viñas, David. *Un Dios cotidiano*. Buenos Aires: Editorial Guillermo Kraft, 1957.

Viñas, David, and Héctor Olivera. "*El jefe* medio siglo después." *El jefe*. Buenos Aires: Emerald Video, 2008.

Viñas, David, Ismael Viñas, et al. *Contorno: Edición facsimilar*. Ed. David Viñas, Ismael Viñas, et al. Buenos Aires: Biblioteca Nacional, 2007.

Viñas, Ismael. *Análisis del Frondizismo: Claves de la política argentina*. Buenos Aires: Editorial Palestra, 1960.

Viñas, Ismael. "Orden y progreso." *Contorno* 9–10 (April 1959): 15–75.

Viñas, Ismael. "Una historia de *Contorno*." *Contorno: Edición facsimilar*. Ed. David Viñas, Ismael Viñas, et al. Buenos Aires: Biblioteca Nacional, 2007. III–IX.

Williams, Gareth. "Hear Say Yes in Piglia: *La ciudad ausente*, Posthegemony, and the 'Finnegans' of Historicity." *The Other Side of the Popular: Neoliberalism and Subalternity in Latin America*. Durham: Duke UP, 2002. 143–70.

Williams, Gareth. *The Other Side of the Popular: Neoliberalism and Subalternity in Latin America*. Durham: Duke UP, 2002.

Wolford, Wendy. *This Land Is Ours Now: Social Mobilization and the Meanings of Land in Brazil*. Durham: Duke UP, 2010.

Wright, Angus, and Wendy Wolford. *To Inherit the Earth: The Landless Movement and the Struggle for a New Brazil*. Oakland: Food First Books, 2003.

Beasley-Murray, Jon, 7, 104–5, 128, 200n5, 209n18

"beba coca cola" (Pignatari), 87, 88–89, 107

Benjamin, Walter, 189–91, 194–95

Bernini, Emilio, 50, 51–53

Bessa, Antônio Sérgio, 216n2, 217n13

Beverley, John, 5, 30–31, 39, 127, 133, 193, 200n4, 227n2

Bill, Max, 84

Birri, Fernando, 57, 60, 210n29; *Tire dié* by, 210nn29,30, 211n31

body, 46, 66–67, 69, 167, 201n6. *See also* Spinoza

body without organs, 27–28. *See also* Deleuze and Guattari

Boom. *See* Latin American Boom novels

Borges, Jorge Luis, 57, 72, 126

Bosteels, Bruno, 21, 200n4

Bourdieu, Pierre, 201n7

Brazil, 73, 96, 156; concrete poetry of, 13–14, 72, 74; culture of, 10, 29–30, 70, 79; dictatorship in, 14, 17–18; economy of, 126, 175–76, 218n2; history of, 79–83; literature of, 3–4, 115; military coup in, 76, 98–100; writers of, 6, 164–66, 220n19

Cabral de Melo Neto, João, 171, 178, 217n12

Campos, Augusto de, 71, 192; "América latina: contra-boom da poesia" by, 74–75, 75; "cidade" by, 107, 107–8; on concrete poetry, 38, 213n8, 215n22; "cubagramma" by, 9, 9–11; "mercado" by, 72, 93–95, 94; "OLHO POR OLHO" by, 88, 89–91; "sem um numero" by, 108, 109, 217n10; "TUDO ESTÁ DITO" by, 165, 166

Campos, Haroldo de, 123, 202n16, 217n11; on Andrade's cut-up technique, 73, 212n1; baroque effects in, 120–21; Benjamin's influence on, 194–95; on Brazil, 126, 175–76; on concrete poetry, 213n8, 218n1; criticisms of, 98, 192; "galactic" readings by, 217n8; *Galáxias* and, 14, 96–97, 100, 102–3, 116–17; Landless Workers Movement and, 175–77; on language, 118, 183, 217n9; on materiality, 183, 192–93; "nascemorre" by, 86, 86–87; on northeastern minstrels, 217nn12,13; "O anjo esquerdo da história" and, 15, 169–70, 172; participatory leap into politics, 97, 111; "Poesia e modernidade" by, 177–78; poetry of, 112, 119, 217n15; politics and, 105, 122, 194; "Servidão de passagem" by, 107; subaltern and, 108–9; use of language, 98, 106, 186–91. *See also Galáxias*; "O anjo esquerdo da história"

Candido, Antonio, 121, 212n2

cannibalism, 120, 122, 167; in Andrade's poetry, 71, 73–74, 79, 83, 93, 212n2; concrete poets and, 13, 72, 75–77, 83–94, 107; in "O anjo," 171–72; in "OLHO POR OLHO," 89–91

cantigas, 15, 137, 217n13

Cántigas of Alfonso the Learned, *138, 140*

capitalism, 76, 99

Castro, Fidel, 50, 89, 207n21, 208n16

Castro Rocha, João Cezar de, 213n3

censorship, in Brazil, 18, 76, 99–100

Center for Popular Culture, of National Student Union, 109

chance: in "O anjo esquerdo da história" 186; in reading of *Galáxias*, 98

Cheah, Pheng, 115, 202n14

"cidade" (A. Campos), 107, 107–8

cinema, 19, 208n13, 210n25; Viñas and, 13, 47–48

"circuladô de fulô," 111, 179

civilization *vs.* barbarism, 54, 65, 79, 214n9

Cixous, Hélène, 24, 31

concrete poets/poetry, 38, 72, 215n19; Andrade and, 72, 74–76, 78, 83–86, 93, 126, 212n2, 213n3; cannibalism and, 13, 72, 75–77, 83–94, 107; criticisms of, 77–78, 98, 123, 127–28, 192; effects of, 13–14, 120; evolution of, 119, 215n24; Haroldo de Campos on, 106–7, 213n8, 217n9, 218n1; manifesto statements by, 125–26; *paideuma* and, 72, 121; "participatory leap" into politics, 71, 74, 76–78, 87, 100; Pilot-Plan for, 219n7; politics and, 91, 93; subaltern and, 108–9

constituent power: and anti-literature, 164, 167; in *Galáxias*, 106; in "O anjo" 184, 186

constructivist writing, Lispector's, 18, 20–21

consumerism, 88–89, 93–95, 107–8

Contorno (journal), 46, 205nn3,4, 206n6, 210n27, 211n33

Cordeiro, Waldemar, 84

Cortázar, Julio, 124

Cosas concretas (Viñas), 64

Creole values, in Argentina, 48, 50, 53

Crespi, Maximiliano, 205n5

Criticism and Truth (Barthes), 202n16

Croce, Marcela, 205n5

"crônica" (Andrade), 79–83, 80

Cuba, 10–11, 91–93

"cubagramma" (A. Campos), 9, 10–11

Cuban Missile Crisis, 91–93

Cuban Revolution, 10, 52, 87, 200n8; *Dar la cara* and, 50, 56, 207n21; in "OLHO POR OLHO," 89–91

cultural studies, 30

culture, 8, 44, 149; Argentine, 46, 48, 53, 57, 208n13; invasion of North American, 130–31, 156; Latin American, 129–30; mass, 4, 50, 71; subversion of, 21, 110–11

Dar la cara (Viñas), 13, 45, 54, 207n10, 209n20, 212n37; body in, 66–67; civilization *vs.* barbarism in, 59, 65; film stills from, *59–60*, 65; film *vs.* novel, 60–63, 207nn21,22; film-within-film plot in, 53, 57, 62; history in, 55–56; as multimedial assemblage, 51–53; poster for, *49;* screenplay of, 47–48; social problems in, 52–53; social realism and, 57–58; time in, 51–52

death, in *A hora da estrela,* 39

Deleuze, Gilles, 10, 23, 51, 66–67, 120, 127, 157–58, 204n32, 209n18; influence of, 26, 210n25, 223n41; on perception, 167–68

dependency, Latin American, 129, 205n1

Derrida, Jacques, 114–16

Dialectic of Enlightenment (Adorno and Horkheimer), 105–6

dictatorship, in Brazil, 14, 17–18

Dove, Patrick, 8

Echevarría, Esteban, 54, 59–60

economy, Brazil's, 126, 175–76, 218n2

Eichelbaum, Edmundo, 208n12

El candidato (Ayala film), 47–48, *49*, 208n15

elites, 58, 129–30

elitism, 5–6, 31, 55

elsewheres. *See* Rabasa, José

El jefe (Ayala film), 47–48, *49*, 68, 208n12, 208n15

El juguete rabioso (Arlt), 57, 60–62

El matadero (Echevarría), 54, 59–60

Eloy Martínez, Tomás, 48

The Ends of Literature (Levinson), 5–6

"Estela ao Pensamento Bruto de Oswald de Andrade" (Pignatari and Nania), 85

"estela cubana" (Cuban stele, Pignatari), 91–93, *91*

Europe, 58; influence on Latin American, 57, 70, 129–30; influence on Lins, 159–60, 225n54

evolution of forms: in Brazilian concrete poetry 101, 219n7; in C. Fuentes's reading of Boom, 220n13; H. Campos's critique, 125

experimental writing, and anti-literature, 168, 194; in Deleuze, 78. *See also* form

existentialism, 44, 52

exploitation, 24–25, 139–41, 160

Facundo (Sarmiento), 58

Faulkner, William, 21, 50

Félix, Moacyr, 109

the feminine, writing, 12–13, 24–26

Fellini, Federico, 50

feminine economy, 24

Feracho, Lesley, 203n23

films. *See* cinema

Fitz, Earl E., 201nn5–6, 201n9

force of materiality, 114

form: and anti-literature, 7–8, 11, 23, 122, 166–67, 193–94; and the anti-poetic, 38; in Brazilian concrete poetry, 72, 217n11; and concretion, 84, 104, 119-120, 186, 188, 196, 217n9; in D. Viñas, 53, 66; in H. Campos, 183-184; and hierarchy, 5, 22, 64, 169; and intermediate space, 106, 113, 128; in "O anjo" 196-197; in O. Lins 135, 218n4; and the minoritarian, 7, 29, 67, 69, 133, 196; and multimedia, 7, 51, 55, 57, 71-72; and multitude, 141, 149, 152, 173, 186, 196; and nonverbal, 22, 73, 90, 95, 126, 166, 203n18; and regimes of signs 7-8, 45, 47, 72, 77, 164, 188, 197; and resistance, 118, 173; and social realism, 134; and time, 115-116; and violence, 157-158

Formação da literatura brasiliera (Candido), 121

forma de fome, 97, 112–13

formante in *Galáxias*, 99, 116,

Frizzi, Adria, 220n19, 220n21, 221n22, 223n46, 225n56

Frondizi, Arturo, 50–51, 56, 210n27

Fuentes, Carlos, 220n12

Galáxias (H. Campos), 14, 119, 180; Aguilar on, 100–102; Campos on, 100, 102–3, 116–18, 217n8; make up of, 98, 102; materiality of, 113–14; subversion in, 96–97, 110–11; use of language in, 103–4, 106, 216n2; writing of, 98, 120

generational issues: Argentina's lost generation, 51, 208n17; in Argentine cinema, 48–50; in *Dar la cara,* 52, 59–60

genres, anti-literature resisting, 14, 51, 102, 167–68, 170

Giunta, Andrea, 206n6

Graff Zivin, Erin, 199n2, 212n38

Grande Sertão: Veredas (Guimarães Rosa), 21–22

Greene, Roland, 111

Guattari, Félix, 23, 51, 66, 157–58, 168

Guerra sem testemunhas (Lins), 128, 132

Guimarães Rosa, João, 21–22, 123

Gullar, Ferreira, 98, 109–10

habitus, 201n7; *vs.* affect, 104–5

Hardt, Michael, 186

limit-texts, 97, 124–25, 149, 168–70

Lins, Osman, 14, 152, 161, 218n2, 221n24, 223n37; *Avalovara* by, 123, *124*, 125; background of, 128, 143; baroque poetics of, 15, 125, 139; concrete poetry and, 123, 128; fascination with medieval art forms, 159–60, 222n31; Frizzi on, 220n19, 220n21; influences on, 219n9, 219n10, 225n54; preoccupation with aperspectivism, 159–60; resisting North American cultural invasion, 130–31; use of ornamentation, 131, 141–42, 148–49, 221n23, 223n36, 225n56; using ornamentation to engage readers, 156, 158; voyage to Europe, 159–60; on writers, 132, 156, 158; writing style of, 221n22, 221n24, 226n62; on writing violence, 122, 157, 222n33. *See also* "Retábulo de Santa Joana Carolina"

Lispector, Clarice, 31, 53, 201n6, 203n18, 204n33; disdain for literature, 12, 17; fame based on *A hora da estrela*, 12, 19, 25; on language, 28, 30; language of life by, 18, 21, 38–39; as outsider to literary world, 20–21; on politics, 28–29; on vanguardism in Brazil, 29–30; on writing, 18, 38–39; writing style of, 42, 202n16

literary criticism, in Argentina, 46, 206n6

literary politics, 6–7, 45, 96, 101–2, 104, 112; context for, 128–29; new conception of, 168–69; of Viñas, 13, 68

literary subject, myth of, 66, 68

"Literatura e Justiça" (Lispector), 17

literature, 48, 93, 132, 194, 221n24; alienation from body, 46, 66–67; anti-literature *vs.*, 22–23, 166; Argentine, 46–47, 54, 58, 62; characteristics of, 12, 31, 161, 164; criticisms of, 17, 220n13; culture and, 8, 163; definitions of, 3–4, 163–64, 193; genre, 7, 168; as institution, 5–6, 22, 31, 74, 127, 132, 163, 193–94; limits of, 15, 19, 57, 72, 97, 169, 193; Lispector's disdain for, 12, 17; literature's outside, 20–21, 33, 55, 63, 110, 120, 164, 182; relevance of, 30–31, 57, 100; as state vehicle, 30–31, 53–55, 58–59, 168, 193; tasks of, 16, 22, 62, 68, 168; transformation of the discussion, 167; as untimely, 163–64

literary posthegemony, 7, 120, 200n5

Los dueños de la tierra (Viñas), 64

Macabéa, in *A hora da estrela,* 31, 39, 137, 203n18; depictions of, 203nn22,23; desires of, 33–35; subalternization of, 24–25; views of, 19–20

Maciel, Maria Esther, 170

Mahieux, Viviane, 199n1

Mallarmé, 219n10

Mansur, Gilberto, 159

March of 100,000 (Brazil), 18

Martínez Estrada, Ezequiel, 46

Martínez Suárez, José, 47, 52, 207n10, 207n22, 209n20, 211n35

marrano, 51, 66–69, 199n2, 212n38. *See also* Moreiras, Alberto; Graff Zivin, Erin

Marxism, 13, 27, 44-45, 205n5. *See also* social realism

Más allá del boom (Rama), 220n15

Masiello, Francine, 199n1, 206n6

Masotta, Oscar, 45

mass media, subversion of, 108

materiality, 102, 116, 192–93; in *Galáxias*, 14, 96–97, 113–14; of language, 96–97, 100, 183, 197

matter, and text, 114–16

media, 7–8, 19, 72–73, 108. *See also* multimedia

medium, anti-literature's, 10, 22, 167, 169. *See also* form

Mendes, Gilberto, 172

"mercado" (A. Campos), 72, 93–95, *94*

Meyer, 59

milieu, affective, 167–68; of mediation, 13, 64, 67; of sensation, 51, 104

military coup, in Brazil, 76, 98–100

military police, killing landless workers, 170, 172

minstrels: northeastern, 171, 217nn12,13; subaltern, 111–12, 179

mirror stage, 26–27

mística, of Landless Workers Movement, 171–72

modernism, in criticism of concrete poets, 77–78

modernity, 199n1

modernization, by Argentine elites, 55–56

Mondrian, Piet, 84

montage, 98, 137; by Andrade, *81,* 83–84; concrete poets', 91–93. *See also* multimedia

Moreiras, Alberto, 5, 21, 42, 134, 149, 212n38, 227n2

movies. *See* cinema

MST. *See* Landless Workers Movement (MST)

MST Funeral Vigil, Eldorado dos Carajás (Salgado), *173*

MST Occupation influence on *Gicometi Plantation* (Salgado), *174*

MST Occupation March (Salgado), *181*

multimedia, 11, 122; in concrete poetry, 38, 77; *Dar la cara* as, 45, 51–53; "O anjo esquerdo da história" as, 170, 184; in "OLHO POR OLHO," 89–91; in "Retábulo de Santa Joana Carolina," 150; in *Terra: Struggle of the Landless,* 173–75